P9-AOT-713

URBAN ADMINISTRATION:
MANAGEMENT, POLITICS, AND CHANGE

Kennikat Press

National University Publications

Interdisciplinary Urban Series

General Editor

Raymond A. Mohl

Florida Atlantic University

URBAN ADMINISTRATION

MANAGEMENT, POLITICS, AND CHANGE

Edited by

ALAN EDWARD BENT
RALPH A. ROSSUM

National University Publications
KENNIKAT PRESS // 1976
Port Washington, N. Y. // London
A DUNELLEN COMPANY BOOK

057571

© 1976 by the Dunellen Publishing Company, Inc. and
Kennikat Press Corp.

All rights reserved. No part of this book may be used or reproduced in any
manner whatsoever without written permission except in the case of brief
quotations embodied in critical articles and reviews.

Printed in the United States of America

Distributed in United States and Canada by
Kennikat Press, Port Washington, N. Y. 11050

Distributed in British Commonwealth (except Canada) by
Martin Robertson & Company Ltd., London

Library of Congress Cataloging in Publication Data

Main entry under title:

Urban administration.

    (National university publications)
    Includes bibliographical references.
    CONTENTS: Cantine, R. R. How practicing urban
administrators view themselves.—Miller, G. W. Manpower
in the public sector.—Bent, A. E. and Noblit, G. W.
Collective bargaining in local government. [etc.]
    1. Municipal government—United States—Addresses,
essays, lectures. I. Bent, Alan Edward. II. Rossum,
Ralph A., 1946-
JS356.U7 1976   352'.008'0973   76-17078

ISBN 0-8046-7106-0 (Hardcover)

ISBN 0-8046-7109-5 (Paperback)

CONTENTS

INTRODUCTION   3
   Challenges to Urban Administration   3
      Alan Edward Bent
      Ralph A. Rossum

PART ONE
URBAN ADMINISTRATION: MANAGEMENT PROCESSES

CHAPTER 1: THE URBAN ADMINISTRATOR   16
   How Practicing Urban Administrators View Themselves   19
      Robert R. Cantine

   Manpower in the Public Sector   31
      Glenn W. Miller

CHAPTER 2: URBAN ADMINISTRATION AND
           COLLECTIVE BARGAINING   40
   Collective Bargaining in Local Government: Effects of Urban Political
   Culture on Public Labor-Management Relations   46
      Alan Edward Bent and George W. Noblit

   The Implications for Public Administration   62
      Felix A. Nigro

CHAPTER 3: FINANCING URBAN GOVERNMENT   73
   The Beginnings of a Balanced Fiscal System   81
      Advisory Commission on Intergovernmental Relations

   Revenue Sharing in Theory and Practice   88
      Edward C. Banfield

CHAPTER 4: SERVICE DELIVERY AND
           URBAN ADMINISTRATION   100
   Dilemmas of Police Administration   105
      James Q. Wilson

057571

Problems of Judicial Administration: The Effect of Supreme Court
Decisions on Courts of Limited Jurisdiction   121
   Ralph A. Rossum

Education and Liberal Reform: An Interpretation   141
   David Silk

Planning for People, Not Buildings   152
   Herbert J. Gans

PART TWO:
URBAN ADMINISTRATION: POLITICS AND CHANGE

CHAPTER 5:   URBAN ADMINISTRATION:
               THE STATE-OF-THE-ART   175
The Political Economy of Public Organizations   181
   Gary L. Wamsley and Mayer N. Zald

Alienation and Bureaucracy: The Role of Participatory Administration   201
   Michael P. Smith

CHAPTER 6:   URBAN ADMINISTRATION:
               STRUCTURES FOR EFFICIENCY   212
Intergovernmental Relations and Contemporary Political Science:
Developing an Integrative Typology   217
   A. Lee Fritschler and Morley Segal

Metropolitan Reform in the U. S.: An Overview   245
   Joseph Zimmerman

Home Rule vs. Regionalism: The Experience of a Tri-State C. O. G.   267
   Alan Edward Bent

CHAPTER 7:   URBAN ADMINISTRATION AND
               CITIZEN SATISFACTION   281
Municipal Decentralization: An Overview   287
   Henry Schmandt

Street-Level Bueaucracy and the Analysis of Urban Reform   316
   Michael Lipsky

CHAPTER 8:   ADMINISTRATION OF THE URBAN NATION   330
Roles of the Urban Administrator in the 1970s: The Knowledge and
Skills Required to Perform These Roles   335
   Graham W. Watt, John K. Parker, and Robert R. Cantine

Administration of the Urban Nation   360
   Alan Edward Bent

LIST OF CONTRIBUTORS   382
AUTHOR INDEX   384
TITLE INDEX   385

URBAN ADMINISTRATION:
MANAGEMENT, POLITICS, AND CHANGE

ALAN EDWARD BENT and RALPH A. ROSSUM

INTRODUCTION

CHALLENGES TO URBAN ADMINISTRATION

It has become commonplace to speak of the urban crisis as the greatest domestic problem of America today. There is much evidence to support this point of view. Critical problems abound in the delivery of urban services. Thus, law enforcement officials have been unable to reduce appreciably the soaring rates of crime against persons and property. Schools have become little more than custodial institutions. Cities and towns develop or deteriorate, uncontrolled and unplanned. In many areas even simple tasks such as garbage removal are not being satisfactorily discharged.

A great deal of thought-provoking analysis has been conducted to explain the nature and extent of this crisis, and a good many proposals for reform have been advanced in an attempt to deal with these critical problem areas in a comprehensive and successful manner. A number of excellent volumes have been published which have brought together many of these more substantial contributions.[1] However, a good deal less has been written on the instruments through which such reform and change are intended to be effected, i.e., the administrative apparatus of our urban centers. What has been written — and much of it is significant — has never been brought together for those who would seriously consider this dimension of the urban crisis. This volume has been prepared with the intention of filling this gap in the literature. Through its introductory essays and selected articles, it explores the various managerial, functional, structural, and, above all, political problems inherent in urban administration. In so doing, they suggest that these problems not only limit the prospects for an alleviation of the present crisis but in fact intensify it.

The administrative apparatus of urban government does not operate in a "sanitized, technical world free from the swirls and uncertainties of

3

politics."[2] It is intimately tied to politics — the struggle over the authoritative allocation of social values and resources. Few students of public administration would deny this. Yet, as John Rehfuss in *Public Administration as Political Process* points out, the existing literature "rarely deals with these questions."[3] Many of the essays included in this volume have been selected because they do address these questions. They consider politics to be the driving force behind most administrative behavior. They share with Norton E. Long the belief that "[a] ttempts to solve administrative problems in isolation from the structure of power and purpose in the polity are bound to prove illusory."[4]

Power is the "lifeblood of administration."[5] This power, however, is not adequately supported by such "insufficient bases" as statutory authorization or budgetary allotments.[6] Rather, it rests "essentially on political support."[7] Francis Rourke has provided a useful model of how administrative agencies attempt to build, maintain, and increase political support. A summary of his model is in order, as it suggests limitations on what reasonably can be expected from urban administration. It depicts the administrative apparatus as often more concerned with amassing and preserving political power than with confronting the critical problems and programs before it.

Rourke's model focuses on two principal aspects of administrative power: its sources and its operation. There are two major sources of administrative power: mobilization of support and expertise. Support is mobilized from interest groups outside the government and from legislative and executive branches inside the government.[8] This amassed power largely accounts for whatever influence the administrative apparatus has on public policy. However, much of administrative power can be rather effectively neutralized by the presence of conflict within an agency over how this power is to operate.

Political struggle — and it is no less a political struggle because it takes place largely within the agency itself — tends to center around the question of who is to participate in decision making. The struggle involves three different sets of competing participants. First, there is a sharp difference in role and attitude between the political executives at the apex of the administrative hierarchy and the career administrators beneath them. Second, there is a wide divergence in outlook between the professionals "who employ the skills with which the organization serves the community"[9] and the administrators who tend to be concerned with efficiency and the maintenance of the organization itself. And third, there is a disparity of interest between the inside administrators and the outside experts who play advisory or consultative roles.[10] Conflict in an urban agency along any of these cleavages can dissipate its power, further politicize it, and thereby keep it from addressing those critical urban problems within its charge.

The problems that result from the manner in which politics and administration are intertwined are often intensified by policy makers who, in their zeal to provide easy and immediate solutions to the crises that beset the cities, overlook the fact that there are inherent limits on what large hierarchical organizations can accomplish. This is the essential "bureaucracy problem," as James Q. Wilson calls it.[11]

There has been a tendency among policy makers to believe that if a problem becomes a crisis, it must be solved, and "if it must be solved, it can be solved."[12] Alan Shank is representative of this point of view. He believes that "urban problems connected with education, employment, and housing" can be solved. "The essential ingredients for a massive, concerted, and energetic effort are creative leadership and a sense of urgency in reordering our national priorities."[13] Put simply, if a problem must be solved, it will be solved. It is only a matter of urgency and leadership — good intentions. Any concern for a clear and precise definition of the actual objectives to be accomplished is conspicuously absent. This is not strange. As Theodore J. Lowi points out, most policy makers are reluctant to engage in a precise definition of public policy. Caught in the grips of the "New Public Philosophy" — interest group liberalism — they prefer "policy without law," that is, broad delegation of power to administrative agencies which in turn decide upon policy through a bargaining process involving all interested groups.[14]

"Policy without law" has many attractions to policy makers. It does not demand a knowledge or understanding of the problem or crisis that would be sufficient to resolve it. It requires only a sense of urgency, the best of intentions, and a willingness to parcel out the "sovereignty" or policy-making powers of the state to those agencies and interest groups closest to and most affected by the problem.[15] Such "policy without law" does have its deficiencies, however. It leads to legislation utterly lacking in specificity. Such legislation in effect declares to administrative agencies: "We in the legislature don't know what the problems are; find them and deal with them." Given the relation between politics and administration and the efforts by administrative agencies to amass and preserve political power, it is not surprising that they have exercised this unrestrictive grant of power in a manner contrary to the intentions of those who gave it to them. It is not strange that failure to confront this "bureaucracy problem" with policies embodying clearly defined goals and standards should result in an increased frustration and cynicism, decline in governmental legitimacy, and an aggravation of the urban crisis itself.

A central political question that now challenges — and is likely to continue to challenge — public service in urban America relates to the issues of centralization and decentralization. There are a number of reasons for the move toward administrative and political centralization. To begin with, there are intense pressures for a national direction and solution to obdurate public problems, for the application of universal standards in policy determination, and for greater administrative efficiency and control. This trend toward centralized, national solutions is also aided by a general public concern with such issues as economic well-being, consumer rights, environmental protection and improvement, tax reform, and health insurance, all of which are matters that require an essentially holistic perspective. Likewise, the inability of local governments to deal with urban problems — often characterized by their area-wide dimensions and the spillover phenomenon — has required the transfer of policy decisions to a higher regional, state, or national level. Finally, technology and technological developments in the public service have also contributed to a strengthening of the forces of centralization.

As effective performance in managerial and decision-making roles calls for greater scientific and technical competence and for adopting a systems perspective, the responsibility and authority for design and performance of public programs tend to move to higher levels of government closer to the chief executive. The complex technology required for information and control functions and the use of temporary problem-solving groups which require sophisticated direction and coordination (and which are less accessible to local political forces) further centralization.[16]

There exist, at the same time, countervailing pressures for decentralization, an arrangement by which government functions are performed at a local level, thereby allowing the public served by these functions to exercise greater control over them. Revenue sharing is a good example of decentralization in operation. It is designed both to help finance state and local governments so that they may operate more effectively and to permit greater discretion by these lower levels of government over how the money is to be expended. Another case in point is the regionalization of urban areas. Although, from the vantage of local municipalities, the emergence of regional political processes designed to cope with metropolitan-wide problems is a centralizing trend, from the national perspective, the stimulation of growth of these authorities reflects an interest in decentralized policy making affecting issues of local interest. The interests in both efficiency as measured on a cost/per unit basis and effectiveness as measured by citizen satisfaction have energized devices providing for policy decisions closer to the grass-roots level. The same concerns have been raised in the delivery of public services, where efficiency measures are increasingly balanced against a concern for citizen satisfaction.

The tension between centralization and decentralization is not unique to this period of time. There have occurred in the United States historic trends that have either favored centralization or decentralization. In the present day, there exist cultural and political conditions that foster the current trend toward decentralization. Dwight Waldo depicts the cultural tension in terms of a struggle between two human potentials: the Apollonian and the Dionysian. The Apollonian man is characterized by such attributes as reason, rationalism, cognition, logic, and classicism; in contrast, the Dionysian man is marked by such qualities as faith, emotion, intuition, feeling, and passion.[17] Waldo believes that this is an age that has seen the Dionysian potential predominate over the Apollonian. In support of this contention he provides some examples of expressions of the current mood in society and their influence on contemporary social movements.

What's happening today is the revival of the arcane and occult including astrology and witchcraft; the widespread use of mind-blowing drugs; the popularity of (folk, acid, hard, etc.) rock; the establishment of more or less isolated and primitive communities; the exposition and practice of various forms of antinomianism; the fascination with Oriental religions and cults.[18]

These expressions of mood are linked to such social motifs as the emphasis on youth; the development of countercultures; the rejection of formality, conformity, and consensus as styles and goals; and a number of other attitudes that seek alternatives to the status quo. He concludes that "[a]ll these currents carry a mass of hostility toward *organization;* that is, the large, formal, complex organizations characteristic of the twentieth century, organizations in any way perceived as 'bureaucratic.'"[19] The animosity toward rationality and established order is thus concentrated against formal organizations, whose very essence is to achieve rationality and order, and this is what Waldo characterizes as the "Antiorganizational Revolution."[20] It follows that administrative trends toward efficiency through greater centralization are fundamentally at odds with contemporary cultural trends.

The animus against organizations carries over into the political sphere as well, underscoring the interlocking relationship of the culture and politics of society. Although charges against governmental centralization and the evils of modern organization — private and public — emanate chiefly from the left and counterculture critics, some of the indictments are shared across political lines. Waldo describes the way organization is perceived by its detractors:

Organization . . . is an evil in itself. It violates human dignity, denies and thwarts the innate human potential, and in its authoritarian and inequalitarian features, gives the lie to our democratic hopes. Working together with modern science and technology, it dulls moral sensitivity and degrades aesthetic sensibility; further abetted by the profit motive, organization creates a monstrous world of chrome and plastic, destroying much of nature and separating us from what remains. Organization separates and isolates. It squeezes the joy, the spontaneity, the creativity, the warmth, the very *humanness* from life. It is the root cause of the alienation that is the sickness of contemporary man.[21]

The attack on complex organizations takes in public organizations as well. Undoubtedly, all organizations – private or public – aspire to be rational. "We are associated, at least in intent, with order, lawful regularity, reasonableness, analysis, calculation, and science," Waldo writes about public administration and public administrators. "'To rationalize' is for us to specify objectives clearly and to arrange efficient means for their achievement. And to rationalize, for us, is *good*."[22] But, these efficiency-oriented principles have not excluded a value orientation in public administration that emphasizes democratic responsiveness and accountability. In public administration, democracy as a political principle is intrinsic to the administrative process itself.[23]

The long-honored tradition of political accountability in public administration takes the form of executive and legislative oversight over administrative practices and execution of policy. There is also an acknowledgment of the legitimate right of citizens to participate in the administrative process.

Thus, there is a long-established precedent, recognition, and tacit acceptance of the fact that labor, business associations, and regulated industries or industry-groups have a voice in manning key appointees to the departments, agencies and commissions which regulate, serve, or otherwise affect these interests. Likewise, professional or occupational groups participate in the development of licensing standards and regulations governing initial entrance into and subsequent practice of various specialized vocations. Participation also takes the time-honored form of committees representative of certain segments of the society – business, industry, agriculture, and, more recently, science – and serving in advisory-consultative capacities to the administrative departments and agencies. Such committees advise on policy and program development, provide technical knowledge beyond that available within the bureaucracy itself, serve as sounding boards for internally developed proposals, and provide feedback regarding the operation of particular programs and policies.[24]

However, the historic commitment of public administration to democratic principles has not prevented the accusations of nonresponsiveness. It is argued that access to government is limited to the well-financed and the well-organized, leaving the vast segment of society voiceless and powerless. Accordingly, there is pressure for increased citizen involvement. The proposals for citizen participation focus on the creation of a variety of decentralization arrangements which would provide for citizen oversight of the operations of administrative agencies. Examples of recommended instrumentalities that would allow for greater accountability of administrative processes include police review boards and formal complaint channels such as the office of ombudsman. Decentralization proposals also call for the creation of neighborhood city halls as a means of dividing municipal governments into grass-roots administrative units; local clientele control over functional programs — for example, direction by community action agencies of the poverty program or community control of public schools; and the removal of fiscal resources from central control — for example, revenue sharing with its block grants of funds and absence of attached strings specifying how the funds are to be spent.[25]

The contemporary disenchantment with administration and organization stemming from a widespread perception that there is a lack of opportunity for citizen participation coincides with a rising dissatisfaction of employees in the public sector. There is a growing sentiment that participation in the administrative process should also include worker participation in the management process. The theory of participative management holds that the effectiveness of an organization is increased by enlarging the participation of organizational members, even those at the lowest levels, in decisions that are related to their work. Moreover, participation in organizational decisions is felt to have motivational influences that lead to improved worker performance. Participation is also associated with improvement in the quality of organizational decisions because they are thus decentralized "to those points in the organization where the real expertise and best information are located."[26] Finally, participation is viewed as a means by which mature personalities can enlarge their capacities, realize their full potential, and, hence, achieve self-actualization. "From all this comes the general prescription that organizations benefit from increasing worker participation in organizational affairs, including certain management or administrative decisions."[27]

The self-assertion of public sector workers has been manifested by the rapid growth of public employee unionism. This phenomenon poses a challenge to traditional public service executive responsibility and authority and provides a new equation in the quest for economy and efficiency in public organizations. Undoubtedly, the character of public unions will vary as widely as their counterparts in the private sector. The unions of public employees whose values, goals, and behavior resemble militant craft unions will seek to participate in managerial decisions as well as to replace the merit principle with union seniority and union control over hiring, promotion, and dismissal. Large, militant unions will aid the movement toward centralization. "Just as organization for collective bargaining in the private sector has been a centralizing force increasing the power of top union leadership and its industrial counterpart, so union activity in the public service may lead to greater concentration of authority."[28] In view of the prevailing currents, the prospect for public administration is that traditional managerial power and authority will be faced with a double challenge: a rising unionism among public sector employees and a rising demand for citizen involvement in public decision making.

Fundamentally, the tendencies toward centralization and decentralization are a product of "the confrontation of the requisites of technological society with a growing demand for human community."[29] Stated another way, the tension has been created by the opposing requisites of technically determined centralizing tendencies versus democratically oriented decentralizing tendencies. The search for rational and orderly solutions to contemporary public issues has spawned a technological development in public administration, especially in the areas of computer science, automatic data processing, and systems analysis. The application of systems analysis is especially appropriate in attempts to come to grips with issues in American politics and the American environment that are interdependent in nature and perspective. Inevitably, the influence of computer technology and systems analysis techniques has provided imperatives for a centralized control over decision-making. At the same time, there exists a therapeutic need for involvement and participation in the administrative process and public decision-making by both the general public and the individual worker in public administration. The way in which these opposing tendencies are to be reconciled is not just a matter affecting institutional arrangements and the administrative process but is of major concern to the political system as a whole. Ultimately, the resolution of the tension must take a political form.

The forces of change in society can expect to influence public administration in the coming years. This will require adaptability and knowledge about changing trends and new developments on the part of public administrators. The pressure for greater citizen participation promises to further politicize the administrative process. Militant employee unionism may lead to a decline of the merit system and to a limitation of traditional management prerogatives. A growing emphasis on technological capabilities will place a greater importance on specialized administrative skills and on educating administrators for these capabilities. Education will probably become an ongoing experience if managers are to remain current with technical 'and organizational developments and changes. Finally, the increasing political nature of public administration cannot be stressed enough. The public administrator will be faced with a mounting political pressure as citizen intervention in the administrative process becomes institutionalized.

The future promises to be extraordinarily challenging to those who pursue careers in the public service over the next decade. In many respects, public administrators will have to be more adaptable, knowledgeable, patient, tenacious, and perceptive than ever before. Yet, they will have new tools of management, analysis, information, and control. Managing public programs will be even more demanding than it is today, but those challenges can be met if today's administrators take the lead in anticipating the future and preparing to meet it.[30]

To explore the challenges of urban administration, this volume has been divided into two major parts, Urban Administration: Management Processes; and Urban Administration: Politics and Change.

Part One, Urban Administration: Management Processes, is divided into four chapters. Chapter One introduces the urban administrator. It considers the character, roles played, and the challenges encountered by those who must determine (1) the procedural aspects of how the urban community should be governed, (2) the appropriate dimensions of governmental responsibility and response for the health, safety, and welfare of the community, and (3) how best to manage public resources to get the job done. The political nature of these decisions is obvious. The urban administrator is often required to identify community needs, plead for various causes, serve as a salesman for his ideas — in brief, become an active participant in determining how the issues will be processed through the political system. Yet, at the same time, he is responsible for the effective, efficient, and sensitive delivery of service. This relation between politics and administration and the limits it imposes on the prospects for urban reform is given close scrutiny.

The next two chapters explore the various personnel and fiscal resources available to the urban administrator. Since both the character and extent of these resources are frequently beyond his control, urban administrative problems arise. Chapter Two examines the new and increasingly significant problem of collective bargaining in the public sector. It considers in detail the effect that public employee unions now have, or may have, on traditional management authority and responsibility. The implications of the pressures for greater employee participation in decision making on management efficiency are examined.

Chapter Three takes up the problem of financing urban government and administration. Urban governments have been unable – or unwilling, as Edward C. Banfield would put it – to raise the revenues necessary for urban administration to deal effectively with the burgeoning cost of public services. They have come to rely increasingly on huge infusions of state and, especially, federal aid. However, as the federal government's role in raising revenues has increased, so has its role in spending them. After all, he who pays the piper calls the tune. The range of service delivery alternatives open to the urban administrator has therefore been restricted. The extent, if any, to which the emphasis on revenue sharing has changed this situation and the impact it has had on centralization-decentralization are explored.

Chapter Four reviews some of the various functional problems that confront urban administration as it attempts to deliver such vital urban services as police protection, criminal justice, education, housing, transportation, and planning. These functions concern the vital services that urban administrators provide their clients daily. The political nature of these service areas underscores the frustrations of resolving the urban crisis by rational, administrative means.

Part Two, "Politics and Change," is also divided into four chapters. Chapter Five explores the internal dynamics of public bureaucracy and its relationship with external agencies and the political process. It also reiterates the dilemma of the pressures for centralization to gain the advantage of technology and efficiency versus the pressures for decentralization for the sake of democratic responsiveness and accountability. Chapter Six explores structural attempts to obtain administrative efficiency. It deals with the inadequacies of many present-day governmental structures for coping with the functional problems that press upon them and shows the importance of metropolitan or consolidated administrative structures. However, it also focuses attention on the difficulties that accompany such movements toward metropolitan government and stresses the likelihood of failure for such reforms. The prospects for governmental reform in metropolitan areas, especially as it concerns structures that would merge the suburbs and the central city, have been made all the more remote as a result of the United States Supreme Court's ruling in *Milliken* v. *Bradley*, the Detroit busing case.[31] In this recent decision, a split Court held, five-to-four, that the Equal Protection Clause of the Fourteenth Amendment does not require multi-district, areawide busing of school children between suburbs and the central city for purposes of achieving racial balance. Since suburban citizens now do not have to face or fear the prospects that their children will be bused into the central city, the concern for the health and vitality of the city they might otherwise have been obliged to feel is not likely to arise. Principally, this chapter provides examples of structural efforts toward centralization to achieve a more efficient delivery of public services on an area-wide basis.

Chapter Seven examines the other side of the coin of efficiency in service delivery: the need to obtain citizen satisfaction. The selected essays explore more systematically and in greater depth the themes introduced at the onset in this essay, viz., the political nature of administration and the mounting pressure for citizen participation in the administrative process. They survey the source of existing political power as well as contemporary challenges to that power through such strategies as protest politics and community action programs. They depict the administrative apparatus as often more concerned with the preservation of its influence and hegemony than with the successful implementation of programs or even resolution of the urban crisis. They collectively suggest that the only way to restrict such administrative behavior is through the establishment of programs with clearly stated goals and specific standards of procedure, implementation, and delegation of authority.

With the various managerial, functional, structural, and political problems of urban administration explored, Chapter Eight turns to the future prospects for urban administration. It asks whether urban administration will be able to meet these many problems and challenges. In response, it conveys not only the confidence that many professional urban administrators and scholars have in education and national urban schemes but also the sober conviction of such men as James Q. Wilson that there are limits to what large hierarchical organizations can accomplish. In so doing, it reinforces the essential tension between administrative efficiency and citizen satisfaction and worker self-actualization. The volume closes with the suggestion that even when the root causes of the urban crisis have become fully ascertained, administrative resolution of this crisis will remain problematical.

Notes

1. See Robert A. Goldwin (ed.), *A Nation of Cities* (Chicago: Rand McNally & Co., 1968); Alan Shank (ed.), *Political Power and the Urban Crisis,* 2d ed. (Boston: Holbrook Press, 1973); Alan K. Campbell (ed.), *The States and The Urban Crisis* (Englewood Cliffs, N.J.: Prentice-Hall, 1970); and Stephen M. David and Paul E. Peterson (eds.), *Urban Politics and Public Policy: The City in Crisis* (New York: Praeger Publishers, 1973). See also Edward C. Banfield, *The Unheavenly City* (Boston: Little, Brown and Co., 1970); Theodore J. Lowi, *The End of Liberalism* (New York: W. W. Norton, 1969); Robert L. Bish and Vincent Ostrom, *Understanding Urban Government* (Washington, D.C.: American Enterprise Institute for Public Policy Research, 1973); and Robert L. Lineberry and Ira Sharkansky, *Urban Politics and Public Policy,* 2d ed. (New York: Harper & Row, Publishers, 1974).

2. John Rehfuss, *Public Administration as Political Process* (New York: Charles Scribner's Sons, 1973), vii.
3. *Ibid.*, vii. See also pp. 220–222.
4. Norton E. Long, "Power and Administration," *Public Administration Review*, Vol. 9 (Autumn 1949), p. 264.
5. *Ibid.*, p. 257.
6. *Ibid.*
7. Francis Rourke, *Bureaucracy, Politics, and Public Policy* (Boston: Little, Brown and Co., 1969), p. 1.
8. *Ibid.*, pp. 11–37.
9. *Ibid.*, p. 90.
10. *Ibid.*, pp. 90–103.
11. James Q. Wilson, "The Bureaucracy Problem," *The Public Interest*, No. 6 (Winter 1967), pp. 1–9.
12. *Ibid.*, p. 6.
13. Alan Shank (ed.), *Political Power and the Urban Crisis*, 2d ed. (Boston: Holbrook Press, 1973), p. xvi, Preface to the First Edition.
14. Theodore J. Lowi, *The End of Liberalism* (New York: W. W. Norton, 1969), pp. 126–127.
15. *Ibid.*, pp. 76, 82, 86.
16. Richard L. Chapman and Frederic N. Cleaveland, "The Changing Character of the Public Service and the Administrator of the 1980's," *Public Administration Review* (July/August 1973), p. 359.
17. Dwight Waldo, "Some Thoughts on Alternatives, Dilemmas, and Paradoxes in a Time of Turbulence," in Dwight Waldo (ed.), *Public Administration in a Time of Turbulence* (Scranton, Pa.: Chandler Publishing Co., 1971), p. 270.
18. *Ibid.*, p. 271.
19. *Ibid.*, p. 271; emphasis in the original.
20. *Ibid.*
21. *Ibid.*, p. 272; emphasis in the original.
22. *Ibid.*, emphasis in the original.
23. Marvin Meade, "Participative Administration – Emerging Reality of Wishful Thinking?" in Dwight Waldo (ed.), *op. cit.*, p. 175.
24. *Ibid.*, p. 179.
25. *Ibid.*, p. 180.
26. *Ibid.*, pp. 170–171.
27. *Ibid.*, p. 171.
28. Chapman and Cleaveland, *op. cit.*, p. 360.
29. Orion White, Jr., "Organization and Administration for New Technological and Social Imperatives," in Dwight Waldo (ed.), *op. cit.*, p. 152.
30. Chapman and Cleaveland, *op. cit.*, p. 364.
31. 418 U. S. 717 (1974).

PART ONE

URBAN ADMINISTRATION: MANAGEMENT PROCESSES

1

THE URBAN ADMINISTRATOR

The United States has unquestionably become an urban nation. In 1972, its 243 standard metropolitan statistical areas (SMSAs)[1] contained over 139 million people, or 68% of total population.[2] According to the 1970 census, the fifty largest SMSAs, ranging in population from 11.4 million in New York City to 629,000 in Syracuse, had a combined population of over 93 million, representing 46.5% of the nation's population. This has not always been the case. Until 1920, the United States was primarily rural in character; a majority of the population lived outside urban areas. However, from 1865 to 1920, the urban population of the nation quadrupled; 51.2% of the population was living in an urban setting in 1920. Since then, that figure has increased to nearly 70%.[3]

This growth of urban areas has stimulated the growth and underscored the importance of urban administration. As Robert R. Alford has written, this growth "has continually posed new problems for the local governments within those areas, problems that have been met by expanding staffs, establishing new departments, and hiring professional specialists to handle the technical tasks involved in traffic engineering, city planning, budgeting, and sheer administrative control."[4] However, this urban growth has also posed problems that cannot be solved simply through greater bureaucratization. These problems have arisen from changes that have taken place in the pattern of metropolitan growth.

Since the end of World War II in 1945, the outlying suburban areas of the SMSAs have grown at a much faster rate than the older central cities, which have declined relatively and, in many instances, absolutely, in population. Of the fifteen largest central cities in 1950, only Los Angeles and Houston have experienced any appreciable growth since then. Only

Houston has grown proportionately with the rest of its SMSA.

This relative and absolute decline in the population of central cities has been accompanied by other significant demographic shifts.[5] First, the middle class and prosperous working class have migrated from the cities to the suburbs in large numbers. Washington, D.C., is a case in point. During the decade of 1960-1970, it led the nation with a white net out-migration of 40% of the total white population. Second, the place of these groups has been taken by the latest group to move to the city — the blacks. Figures from the 1970 census show that almost 60% of the nation's blacks now live in the central cities of metropolitan areas. This shift in population has led to a situation where blacks now constitute or are approaching a majority in central cities and are resisting their potential loss of influence posed by the metropolitan government approach. Third, business and industry have also left the city in increasing numbers, thereby depriving the city of its primary source of revenue — taxable property.

Edward C. Banfield has argued in *The Unheavenly City* that these demographic changes in metropolitan growth are inexorable and inevitable.[6] He considers metropolitan growth, and the problems that attend it, to be the product of three imperatives. The first is demographical: the cities expand outward from core areas because increases in population cause intense competition for housing and industrial location. The second is technological: the development of transportation technology enables the more affluent to separate their place of work from their residence by traveling long distances over, for example, expressway systems. The third is economical: the unequal distribution of wealth and income permits the more affluent to afford new single-family suburban homes and the time and money to commute considerable distances to work while the less affluent must remain in the older central city housing vacated by the more affluent. These three imperatives of metropolitan growth place "stringent limits" on what can be accomplished. They place a premium on professional and dedicated urban administrators who are increasingly responsible for determining procedurally how these growing and changing urban communities should be governed, ascertaining the appropriate dimensions of governmental responsibility and response for the health, safety, and welfare of these communities, and managing public resources to get the job done. These imperatives also link administration all the more closely to politics. To carry out these responsibilities, the urban administrator must devote most of his time and talent to establishing and maintaining a sensitive information-gathering system of the world around him; setting and planning objectives; working to achieve consensus among his superiors, subordinates, and the community; promoting and selling those values and actions he believes to be in the public interest; arbitrating conflicts; promoting the fiscal integrity of his agency; and orchestrating the governmental machinery to accomplish the tasks at hand.

The essays in this chapter examine the problems that accompany these politically charged administrative efforts. Robert R. Cantine provides a most useful introduction with his "How Practicing Urban Administrators View Themselves." Reporting the results of a workshop on "Education For Urban Administration" sponsored by The American Academy of Political and Social Science, the Fels Institute Graduate Associates, the International City Management Association, and the National Academy of Public Administration, Cantine notes that urban administrators are acutely aware of the political dimension of their profession. Most feel that there are significant differences in substantive knowledge, skill requirements, outlook, processes, and context between urban administration and, for example, business administration. Cantine then goes on to discuss the kinds of activities that demand most of the time and talent of the urban administrator.

With the political nature of administration developed by Cantine, the importance of recruiting qualified and responsible professionals into the urban governmental structure becomes apparent. Glenn W. Miller, in "Manpower in the Public Sector," reviews the various problems that attend the recruitment and retention of high quality personnel in state and urban administration (for example, low salaries and wages and the negative image of governmental service). He argues that unless state and urban governments institute extended manpower planning, these problems will intensify.

Notes

1. With the exception of New England, a standard metropolitan statistical area is a county or group of contiguous counties that contains at least one city of 50,000 inhabitants or more or "twin cities" with a combined population of at least 50,000. In New England, SMSAs consist of towns and cities, rather than counties.
2. U.S., Bureau of Census, *County and City Data Book, 1972* (Washington, D.C.: United States Government Printing Office, 1973). The number of people residing in SMSAs had increased by 16.6% since 1960.
3. Charles R. Adrian and Charles Press, *Governing Urban America,* 4th ed. (New York: McGraw-Hill, 1972), pp. 17–19.
4. Robert R. Alford, "The Bureaucratization of Urban Government," in Daniel N. Gordon (ed.), *Social Change and Urban Politics: Readings* (Englewood Cliffs, N.J.: Prentice-Hall, 1973), p. 263.
5. Douglas N. Fox, "Some Aspects of Urban, Social, Economic, and Political Change Since 1945," in his *The New Urban Politics* (Pacific Palisades, Calif.: Goodyear Publishing Co., 1972), p. 4.
6. Edward C. Banfield, *The Unheavenly City* (Boston: Little Brown and Co., 1970), pp. 23–44.

ROBERT R. CANTINE

HOW PRACTICING URBAN ADMINISTRATORS
VIEW THEMSELVES

In June and August 1971 over seventy urban administrators of broad experience participated in workshops designed to elicit, and expose for discussion among colleagues, their views on who the urban administrator is, what kinds of activities demand most of his time and talent, the objectives of graduate professional education for urban administrators, and what knowledge and skills they require to perform effectively. The seventy practitioners had gone through rather extensive preparation for these workshops: each had completed a long questionnaire reflecting the questions described above, and had prepared a written statement of his own views on the emerging roles of urban administrators. The analysis which follows is focused on the exchange of ideas among these practitioners at the workshops.

WHO IS THE URBAN ADMINISTRATOR?

A very broad definition of the term "urban administrator" had been employed in selecting practitioners to participate in the survey-workshop-symposium series. In the workshops practitioners were asked to examine this expansive notion of the urban administrator. Can urban administrators be considered a relatively homogeneous group for which a common educational program could be developed? Is it true, as some would say, that "management is management is management — whether public, semi-

Reprinted by permission of the American Academy of Political and Social Science, from Frederic N. Cleaveland (ed.), *Education for Urban Administration* (1973), pp. 1-19.

public, or private"? If not, what differences are important to recognize? These practitioners found no easy answer to such questions. Two views were expressed regarding the similarity between public and private administrators. On the one hand, some contended that differences exist in objectives and "rules of the game" between public and business administrators, differences which influence considerably the knowledge and skill requirements, not to mention the variations in outlook and value commitments. These differences, they assert, work against the assumption that a common educational program can serve satisfactorily for a career in either sector. The remarks of a senior professional association official and those of a Model Cities executive illustrate this position:

I resist the notion that managerial competences are transferable; there is a big difference between the profit incentive and civic effort. They represent two basically different objectives . . . We as [urban public] administrators must have a good feel for social problems; we should be well versed in sociology and basic urban problems. We need that kind of exposure, where a private business executive may not need it that much.

In a 1971 study of private managers who went public, their biggest problem was what to do when someone says, "You can't do that, it's not politically feasible." They (private managers) tend to say "what do you mean — it's right, we've got the money, and we must do it." The public sector is different. You may waste half a million (by private standards) but you have to take the people's attitudes and feelings into account.

Other practitioners argued not only against a distinction in managerial skills, but also countered that to a certain extent, both public and private sector administrators are held accountable to the same objective standards, especially in terms of efficiency. This feeling was best illustrated by the following comments:

I find a lot of the same management techniques in training sessions of private business and our own profession. Theirs are of interest to me and vice versa. Management principles don't deal with profit, they deal with how to use your people.

There is a basic change in the concept the average constituent has towards the public agency — he considers it as a public business and expects the public business to be run as efficiently.

Despite these differences in viewpoint, there seemed to be agreement that certain analytical skills and "people-oriented" management skills would be of considerable importance to both types of managers. But beyond the similarities in knowledge and skill required to be an administrator in business or public service, differences exist in attitudes, objectives, value commitments, clients, sensitive relationships, and processes which clearly distinguish business and public administration. A common educational program would be beneficial to neither.

Discussion of the important differences among jobs within urban administration led to similar conclusions. Few of the practitioners would agree that a director of public health and a city manager should be products of the same curriculum. At the same time several practitioners recalled their experience in small municipalities where they had performed the functions of public works director, zoning administrator, recreation director, and so on. Some participants saw very practical differences in the amount of face-to-face contact with citizens experienced by the city manager in contrast to a regional federal official, or someone serving as a staff person in support of others. These differences in roles reflect important differences in knowledge and skill requirements. Hence to acknowledge such differences is to question the desirability of a common educational program for all types of positions which comprise the broad category of urban administrator. While practitioners agreed that the jobs of different types of urban administrators share many aspects in common, nevertheless they tended to reject the idea of a common educational program for all kinds of urban administrators. The following statements illustrate these views:

—At the local level there is a striking difference in the amount of face-to-face contact an urban administrator has with his public. It is not necessarily there at the state level, and seldom there at the federal level.

—There are different perspectives even in the public sector — a city versus a council of governments.

—The question is not whether to train someone to be a HUD administrator or a city manager; it's whether education is directed towards a policy analysis role or what we call "man-the-front-lines" role.

—The skill or technique of urban administration is transferable, whereas the substance (health, police, public works, and so on) is not.

In summary, these discussions among practitioners reflected a reluctance to support the notion that urban administrators are a homogeneous group who can be served by a common educational program. The workshop participants recognized that a spectrum of differences probably exists, differentiating between the positions of types of urban administrators. The educational background suitable for certain classes of positions might be common, for example, a senior official of an urban research organization, a city manager, and a senior official in a professional association. In addition, for all management positions — as opposed to strictly staff positions — a core curriculum focused on the development of management knowledge and skills would be clearly appropriate. There are, however, real differences in the substantive knowledge and skill required to perform effectively as a director of public works, a fire chief, a planning director, a school superintendent, or a city manager. These differences in requirements should be reflected in the options available through the educational program beyond the common knowledge and skills that every urban administrator ought to acquire.

CURRENT DEMANDS UPON THE TIME AND TALENT
OF URBAN ADMINISTRATORS

What is the urban administrator doing? What occupies most of his time and intellectual talent? How does he allocate his energy now? Will it be the same in the future? How is this behavior influenced by his expectations of what the job ought to be? By his environment? The dialogue among the seventy practitioners on these questions provides a fascinating glimpse into the varied and complex world of the urban administrator.

Information gathering and sensing problems or opportunities

Although not an entirely new or unknown activity, information gathering won high recognition from these practitioners as a primary demand on both their time and talent. This finding should be an important reminder to those planning educational programs. From the urban administrator's point of view this task of gathering intelligence about the environment in which he is working is basic to his performance, not to mention his survival. It is not the kind of information gathering carried out by sitting behind the desk and reading a book or two, or by studying the United States Census. It is the kind of information, often in the form of cues, which comes from being as close as possible to the center of communication flows between people whose actions an have an important impact on his work performance. As one practition r noted, "The manager needs a sensory system on the dynamics of a situation and where his city government fits in." It requires that the urban administrator work actively to establish and keep open his contacts within the community and with those in other governmental and private institutions. A very brief excerpt in the dialogue between a city manager, a senior executive in one of the nation's largest port authorities, and the senior official of a regional planning agency provides the best illustration of the meaning and significance of this activity:

057571

1st Participant: From my standpoint much of what takes my time is keeping up with what's going on outside.

Moderator: What do you mean by "keeping up"?

1st Participant: Being able to know what is going on so you can cope with it. The external side of the administrator's life is getting so complex that external events occur at considerable cost to the urban administrator's time just in keeping abreast of where he is.

2nd Participant: To keep up with what is going on becomes increasingly important because in most cities what is taking place in other levels of government and in nearby governments is important to you. Formerly this was not so much the case because what happened in the federal government years ago and in state government was not quite so important to you as an isolated urban administrator. Now you have to know a lot about federal aid programs, state aid programs, the politics and the policies and things that are going on in other areas around you, to say nothing of the developments within your own municipality. There are a number of events that take place within your municipality and I don't think you can do very much unless you have a good knowledge of all these programs. You have to have a background on which to build and insight into what these external and internal bits of information mean. I see that very much in the work that I do in the COG (Council of Governments). Here you have three levels of government that are very important and you have a tremendous number of things you have to know about each in order to read meaning into events.

Perhaps as significant as the notion of information gathering, is the practitioners' recognition of the continuing effort urban administrators make to utilize that information to cope with their environment. As J. Sterling Livingston reminds us, "Success in real life depends on how well a person is able to find and exploit the opportunities available to him, and, at the same time, discover and deal with potential serious problems before they become critical."[1] To the urban administrator this information gathering activity is his "wellspring" for finding the right things to do at the right time. In many instances the information is fragmentary, disguised, isolated, or indirect. It may come only in the form of an event occurring. In any case it is the administrator's skill at "reading meaning into events (information)" that permits him to identify and define problems and exploit opportunities.

Planning and setting objectives

Information gathering and the ability to use information in support of opportunities at hand presumes the existence of objectives about the future. Otherwise, there would be no basis on which an urban administrator could distinguish between useful and useless information.

Setting objectives and then considering alternative means to reach them is planning. To the seventy urban administrators planning represents an activity they struggle with continuously, but have perhaps less success with than other aspects of their jobs. The task of setting goals or objectives is a particularly difficult element of planning.

The act of setting a course for the future can occur at various levels in the organization, from an individual employee to the most comprehensive organization unit. It can be a conscious and structured activity or informal and instinctive. It can have a long- or short-time horizon. As might be expected, the more formal and systematic the effort of goal-setting becomes, the more difficult and time-consuming it seems to be. One administrator pointed out that "the greater part of weekly staff meetings for nine weeks, as well as an all-day meeting with twenty-two of his key staff, were devoted to the question of goals, not five years out but for the next year." The results appeared to be less than complete success considering the considerable time and talent invested.

The matter of "technique" is of course also involved. Different approaches reflect in part different styles of management. Some practitioners argued that goal-setting is easy: the urban administrator sets the goals and then either (a) he expects them to be accepted because of his position as organizational leader, or (b) he proceeds to persuade and gain the commitment of his subordinates and superiors to his goals. Other practitioners, typified by the earlier example, pursued the more complex but more participative "bottom-up" approach to goal-setting.

No matter how complex the urban administrator finds the task of setting goals and achieving commitment to them within his organization, he faces an even more complex task in working with the community. As one practitioner noted "Model Cities legislation asked that cities state in their Model Cities Plan what their strategies were for allocating resources and attacking city problems; cities had a terrible time complying with that [requirement]." In fact, several practitioners resisted the notion of trying to set community goals around specific values; instead they felt the administrator should try to achieve agreement on specific actions and in this way minimize the polarization of the community o er values.

Several practitioners focused on the urban administrator himself. Most saw him developing his own personal set of goals — for himself and the organization he serves. Whether he reveals these goals through the sum of his actions over time or lays them all out at on: time for examination, through some formal pronouncement, is a matter of individual style and the situation.

Is all this necessary? Is it a vital part of an urban administrator's performance? The answer seemed to be yes. Despite the time and effort involved, it is a necessary part of effective management. As one practitioner summed it up, "I don't know any other way, particularly where the range of activity is so vast and the number of people so great, that you can actually do the job without management by objectives and management by exception — and goal-setting is a prerequisite to this type of management."

Initiator of change

—The responsibility of a city manager is to persuade the community to move in a certain direction.

—The urban administrator today has a more active role to play in identifying programs needed by the community but not espoused by an articulate pressure group.

—I think the urban administrator has to be a sensor of the need for change. My life is devoted to being an architect of change. You try to change the governmental structure to meet the needs of the city.

These statements of three local government practitioners articulate the view of many urban administrators that their role is one of creating change, or at least adapting the organization to its changing environment.

Although the tendency is to associate such statements with the advocacy of certain social values and policies, the connection is not a necessary one. Indeed, the urban administrators seemed often to approach this issue in a pragmatic fashion, feeling that it was their role to initiate some change, perhaps one time slowing down the rate of change, and on another occasion taking action on a particular social need, depending on the community situation.

Orchestrating the governmental machinery

If the expressions of these practitioners generally reflect the situation in city hall and county courthouse, then the traditional neutrality associated with the British civil service certainly does not hold true for American local government. Indeed, the urban administrator is oftentimes caught in the middle between his subordinates and superiors on a variety of matters. The comments of a Council of Governments executive and city manager of a medium size city illustrate the pressure for an orchestrating role:

—Working with top and middle staff people and dealing with the elected bodies who are our superiors requires a balance of informal relationships and strategies.

—There is a gap between the idealism of my staff and the political realities, represented by my Board. The urban administrator must be a buffer between the staff and the policy setters; a translator, a smoother.

—I see several tasks which require a great deal of time — developing a team relation between the city manager and his assistants and integrating, that is, dovetailing demands and aspirations of his departments with those of the council and those of the public.

Clearly, the "city hall crowd" includes more than passive employees waiting to execute policy originated and decided by others. Indeed, judging from these practitioners, urban administrators continuously feel the pressure to support and be an advocate for the ideas of subordinates who, after all, may be only following the admonition of their bosses to show leadership and be articulate advocates.

As many urban administrators and politicians have found out, making the system work is much more difficult when city employees are disgruntled, feel ignored, have low morale, and are generally dissatisfied with the attention their ideas have received from the administrator or his superior. Several urban administrators at the workshops felt that this role as "buffer" or "orchestrator" is a significant and time-consuming task.

Salesman and consensus builder

General objectives can be set and new policies proposed, but the most universal and time-consuming role of the urban administrator remains the task of building consensus. Here it is that the administrator must invoke his skill in persuading others to accept a proposed action, or his ability to find an acceptable substitute agreeable to all parties. Perhaps among all his tasks, this is the responsibility for which his education and training have least equipped him. As one practitioner saw the situation, at some point in his career, "every student who becomes a city manager ought to sell shoes, automobiles, or something, whether or not for a living, in order to train in the technique of salesmanship. The two roles of salesman and arbitrator run throughout the function of the manager." Most other participants agreed with at least the last sentence of this assessment.

Arbitrator and manager of conflict

Perhaps a corollary of building consensus is the skill of conflict management. The administrator not only has to arbitrate conflict situations but oftentimes must also advise and educate parties to a conflict. One administrator most ably described the nature and intensity of this role in the following way:

We are always mediating strongly conflicting viewpoints on a particular item and I think that what we typically do is pull the threads off conflicting viewpoints and come up with what is practical, what is possible, what is achievable. There is always conflict within our organization. We are in the middle trying to come out with some kind of a feasible thing out of which there will come a meeting of the minds. And it is certainly true with the community groups vis-a-vis each other.

In a backhanded sort of way, this continuous engagement in the settling of conflicts is part and parcel of bringing about conditions which permit agreement to be achieved on other, perhaps more important, community issues. It involves skills which, again, few urban administrators have acquired through their formal education. By and large he has had to "pick himself up by his bootstraps," learning what he can by trial and error and picking up for his own use techniques he has observed being successfully employed by others. Tense confrontations are likely to remain a part of the urban scene for the indefinite future, and the urban administrator will be unable to avoid attempting to arbitrate or manage these conflict situations. As several practitioners pointed out, the urban administrator himself may at times be the creator of tension in the process of working to bring about change, or at least may use tension as an opportunity to move towards change.

Budget and financial management

—I would say that the greatest amount of time and talent is taken up with financial responsibilities. I think it is so because finance, perhaps even more than personnel, is involved in almost any type of activity. I don't mean just getting money but planning for it, using it, and controlling it.
—Younger men coming out of the university today don't have a good foundation in the theory and practice of public finance. Educators should be advised that regardless of problems facing the city administrator in the future, they must understand public finance.
—A constant is the budget problem — allocation of resources. It is a dependable task that won't change in the future.
—The most important task is being able to prepare a sound budget.

Responsibilities for budgetary and financial management continue to loom as time- and talent-demanding activities for the urban administrator. Many of the issues the urban administrator faces, both large and small, are "hassled out" through the budget process. This process provides the forum for a variety of analytical efforts aimed at determining the cost effectiveness of public services. In addition, the management complexity of budgeting and public finance has increased with greater dependence upon federal grants. Who knows how revenue sharing may escalate the importance of effective financial management in city halls.

Last, but probably foremost in importance, he has the heavy responsibility to protect the financial integrity of his community and its government. This requires a basic understanding of urban economics and public finance — as well as a keen insight into the taxpayers' willingness to forego further personal consumption for the benefits of increased public spending.

Getting the job done

—Just sheer active, organizational, driving management.

—The bulk of my time, perhaps fifty percent, is spent with department heads discussing and evaluating programs and policies.

—My time is divided into two parts: (1) keeping things rolling, carrying on what has gone before and improving on it, and (2) desperately struggling to carve out time to think creatively and move ahead.

—Managers tend to delegate anything and everything they can. They end up with a repository of things they haven't figured out how to delegate and these are the things they spend their time on.

—Three activities take most of my time: (1) "working" the government system which is becoming increasingly complex, and helping citizens to do the same. . . .

When all is said and done, all other activities add up to nothing unless time and talent are devoted to execution, to making sure things happen, or as one administrator put it, "to 'working' the system." This involves the traditional management activities of dividing work into tasks and assigning them, seeing that related tasks are coordinated, monitoring performance, and recruiting manpower. Equally important in these times of complexity, the task of getting the "job done" involves facilitating, expediting, and otherwise overcoming the encumbrances of traditional bureaucracy. Perhaps the present-day trend towards co-managers in many medium to large size cities is in reality simply a way to give more attention to "working the system." This is one area of activity where a strong and continuing payoff can reasonably be expected from a professional urban administrator.

WHAT'S IN THE FUTURE?

In some ways these practicing urban administrators seemed more certain and articulate about the demands of their job in the future than about their current activities. Perhaps it is a natural tendency to be less aware of those things one does instinctively than of the activities into which one has waded knee-deep and about which he is keenly sensitive concerning what may lie ahead under full immersion. The words of the practitioners themselves offer a good glimpse of what may be demanding much of their time and talent in the future:

—The urban administrator must maintain a stable base — a minimum level of organizational and community activity and service to hold the community together — giving the manager the opportunity to devote time and attention to responding to top priority problems of the future.

—The future will place a high priority on organizational maintenance — finding and holding people long enough to get the job done.

—We will be devoting more of our time to developing (educating, training) our people, those who work for us.

—Another aspect of this development will involve people in the community — keeping our eyes open for talent in the community.

—We are seeing more of the trend toward democratic styles of leadership in our organizations. The administrator of tomorrow has to be skillful in developing his people and including them in the decision-making process — it will be a group decision.

—He will have to pay more attention to the needs and sensitivities of elected officials. Now he doesn't understand their goals and pressures.

—Urban managers make decisions and know where they are going but they are extremely isolated from politics in many cities.

Citizens can't get into the system any more — there are no channels into the manager where they [citizens] can negate the influence and effect of elected officials. If we are to continue, the manager must become an astute politician. If citizens can't get to him, he must find a way to feel their wants.

These three themes of creating a stable situation from which to initiate and implement change, organizational maintenance, and developing political sensitivities seem to reflect important "lessons" of the 1960s and early 1970s. First, too much instability can make the management of change practically impossible. Second, to win from employees the personal commitments and positive attitudes essential to improved organizational performance will require something beyond the recognized formal authority of the urban administrator. Last, but not least, for the improved functioning of urban government there must be strong political leadership and strong administrative leadership. They are indispensably related, whether in the hands of one individual or two.

CONCLUSION

If these insights point in a single direction, it is that the urban administrator is a person of action. He is instinctively analyzing, developing strategy, searching for and seizing upon opportunities, and working the system to insure successful execution. A great part of this behavior is "real time" responding to situations, wants, and information as they emerge with little time for relaxed contemplation. Indeed, as many of the practitioners pointed out, one of the more critical problems for the urban administrator is effective use of his time. He can easily let it be consumed by the normal flow of demands made upon him. But if he chooses to take control of his time, the trade-offs in terms of how to invest energy and talent are complex, and a poor choice can have severe consequences.

These insights into the real world of urban administrators represent a challenge to the higher education community and to the individual educator. This picture of the urban administrator at work is not exhaustive. In fact, the image is imprecise in many ways, and it is certainly in flux, reflecting the countless variations which can and do occur from situation to situation and with the passage of time. The evidence may be sufficient, nevertheless, for the educator to begin reassessing the thrust of his curriculum and the effectiveness of his instructional techniques in equipping the potential urban administrator for this demanding career.

Note

1. *Harvard Business Review* (January-February, 1971).

GLENN W. MILLER

MANPOWER IN THE PUBLIC SECTOR

RISING NUMBERS OF PUBLIC EMPLOYEES

During the 1960s, the total number of civilians working for all levels of government increased about 45 percent; employment by the federal government grew more than 20 percent; state and local government by some 55 percent.[1] In 1970 almost one-sixth of all employed civilians worked for some level of government, a total of some 12½ million persons, compared with one out of ten or eleven in 1950, and one out of eight or nine in 1960.[2]

State and local governments seem likely to be major "growth industries" in the 1970s.[3] Yet here is where personnel policies have lagged most, wages and salaries have been least adequate, and employee unrest (especially at the local government level) has been far more pronounced.[4] Here also is where the taxpayer's resentment and resistance toward increasing costs of government is felt most directly and, in all likelihood, will continue with little or no abatement; though it seems clear that expenditures for labor on these levels of government must rise. The fact that state and local governments employ well over three-fourths of all government civilian employees (local government bodies over half) also supports centering attention on these echelons of government employment.

Any comments or evaluations made relating to such an enormous area of employment will not fit all situations in public employment. There are fifty state employers and in excess of 80,000 local government employing units — counties, townships, municipalities, school districts and

Reprinted by permission of the International Personnel Management Association, *Public Personnel Review*, XXX, No. 1 (January 1972), pp. 50-55.

other agencies.[5] This discussion deals only with state and local government employees other than in education.

RETENTION PROBLEMS SURVEYED

Manpower problems in the public sector are changing. The problem of recruitment and retention of manpower is much less knotty in 1971 than it was at the close of the 1960's,[6] due in part to the economic downturn of 1970 and early 1971. Organization of and collective bargaining by some public employees and improving public personnel practices also are contributing to improvement in the conditions under which public employees work. Yet state and, especially, local governments continue to face problems in recruitment and retention of many types of manpower.

What do personnel administrators in state and municipal governments believe are their more pressing current manpower and labor problems? Such information was sought in mid-1960 by writing to every state director of personnel and personnel officers of a random sample of fifty moderate sized or large cities. The inquiry was in the form of a letter raising broad questions and inviting comments or discussion. Roughly half of the letters produced responses. Recruitment and retention problems were reported as being less knotty, attributed to the loosened labor market and increasing efforts of public employers in recent years to improve personnel practices, wages and salaries, the image of public employment, and recruiting practices.

Despite an easing of recruitment problems, difficulty in recruitment of some types of manpower was reported quite frequently — highly trained personnel such as in medical services, statistical and computer work, and some types of engineering; stenographers seem to be in short supply almost everywhere. Some personnel officers still reported general recruiting difficulty with most kinds of labor. Relatively small rural area and southern cities reported fewer problems, along with those where general levels of unemployment are high.

WAGES AND SALARIES

Frequently, the observation was made that wages and salaries tended to lag behind those in the private sector. Where such a complaint was not voiced it was asserted that recent or soon-to-become-effective changes in rates of pay brought, or would bring, the city or state "in line," or nearly so, with other rates in the labor market. No one asserted general wage and salary leadership by the public employer. The one exception is, with statewide pay rates, states may pay relatively better for workers employed in the more remote rural areas. Setting a goal of being nearly as good as, or catching up with, other employers will continue the problem of attracting and retaining high quality manpower especially when the labor market is relatively tight.

TURNOVER

Turnover rates also suggest the problem government employers face. Many respondents only stated that their turnover rates were "acceptable." Those who gave estimates of their rate of turnover suggest figures clustering around 15 percent. One eastern state reported a 1969 turnover rate of about 30 percent. In late 1969, turnover rates in certain large cities were reported at 12, 15, 18, and 54 percent.[7] Yet only one respondent (a state personnel director) reported organized use of exit interviews.

High levels of turnover are obviously expensive, especially when it is among the more highly trained and competent. The fact that the personnel officers did not know why workers leave, the observations that turnover is "acceptable," and the report by only one employer of use of exit interviews suggest an acceptance of turnover that seems shortsighted and expensive, contributing to manpower problems.

Despite the absence of organized investigation of labor turnover, many respondents suggested reasons for separations, that younger women leave due to marriage, motherhood, or moving with their husbands and that young college graduates will work a few years for experience and move to other work. Implicit in many of the comments was the opinion that many of the voluntary separations were due to low wage and salary levels.[8]

IMAGE OF GOVERNMENT JOBS

The commonly held image of government service and the typical government employee detracts from recruiting success, especially at the more professional levels. Government jobs are looked upon as undemanding, hedged about by bureaucracy and red tape and requiring only minimally competent persons. This negative image of government work, coupled with traditionally lagging wage and salary levels, tends to limit the number of applicants and concentrate them among persons of limited capacities. Yet there is reason to believe, that, once on the job, public employment is not nearly as unattractive as the commonly held image.

Data drawn from about 1140 questionnaires returned to the writer by state and local government employees throws light on attitudes of employees that may affect recruitment and turnover. Persons to whom the questionnaires were mailed were non-supervisory, non-education workers, employed in five small to moderate sized cities in three midwestern states and in one state agency in each of the states; roughly 40 percent returned completed questionnaires.

A heavy majority reported general satisfaction with their jobs. In every one of the eight employing units surveyed, over 80 percent of the respondents rated their job as important, challenging and interesting; frequently 90 percent or more rated their job in that manner. Opinion on whether the job was "good" was not quite so favorable; from 70 to 87 percent of respondents in the reporting groups reported that they so considered the job. There is a backlog of satisfaction and good will toward their jobs that tends to hold many public workers on their jobs unless some conditions of work lag markedly behind the general level of employment practices in the labor market.

Each person was asked his or her opinion of how the job compared with jobs in the private sector and in other areas of government employment. From 20 to 25 percent of the respondents estimated their job to be not as good as those in the private sector. Roughly a third thought the job was about as good and some 40 percent estimated their jobs were better than in private employment. Breakdowns by sex, age, education, and type of job did not reveal marked differences. Much the same evaluation was expressed when the respondents evaluated their job in comparison to work at other levels of government; usually 20 percent or less rated their job not as good as other government jobs. However, in this rating there was a strong tendency to rate the job "about the same" as other government work, from 54 to 73 percent so reporting.

These evaluations suggest that those persons in the employ of state and local government generally are reasonably satisfied with their work. They do not evidence a strong desire to shift to other jobs. One other response supported the conclusion of general satisfaction: about 80 percent of all respondents stated that they intended to remain on their jobs.

"MOONLIGHTING"

A relatively large amount of secondary job holding, "moonlighting," was reported. From 14 to more than 50 percent of the respondents in the different groups surveyed reported income earned from a second job or self-employment.[9] This level of secondary job holding is markedly higher than the roughly 5 percent dual job holding reported by the Bureau of Labor Statistics in 1967 and in 1969.[10] Workers with a second job must give less effort to one of their jobs and/or to some of the family, cultural, or civic facets of a full life. To the extent that moonlighting detracts from the highest level of performance on the primary job, the practice contributes to manpower and efficiency problems in the public sector.[11]

GETTING HIGH-LEVEL PERSONNEL

Public administrators must not be reassured by the easing in recruitment problems that has occurred in many instances due to the presently loosened labor market. Such loosening of the labor market is not a long-term situation; state and local manpower needs will trend upward.

One area demanding attention is that of recruiting and retention of high-level manpower. Rather than reduce standards, state and local governments must improve on their wage and salary performance so that they meet the better personnel practices found in the private sector or in federal government; this should enable lower echelons of government to attract qualified personnel. The use of paraprofessional personnel should promote use of the highest capabilities of the professional to render strictly professional services.[12] The importance of the work and the opportunity to aid in rendering public services, aimed at solution of, or at least effectively combatting, major societal problems should be emphasized.

But selling the job to potential recruits, or persons on the job, must be supported by a number of major improvements. If we want competent, well-trained personnel and low turnover rates, the public must be willing to pay or improve on the going rates of wages and salaries, and other personnel practices must change — overtime payment is an example. Reimbursements by straight time or compensatory time is another indication of employment practices lagging behind the times; premium pay for overtime is hardly an innovative personnel practice today.

While at the federal and some state and some municipal levels, policies toward unions, negotiation and grievances are being reexamined and modernized, we have a long way to go. Most public employees believe that they need organizational representation on the job. Many public employers have failed to bring their employment practices into line with those imposed on the private sector and observed by federal and a considerable number of state governments. The wages and salaries, working conditions, grievance procedures, and the like that will result from wider recognition of and negotiation with employee organizations over a period of time will aid in the recruitment and retention of competent public employees.

LOOKING TO THE FUTURE

Finally, public employers must not become so deeply immersed in current problems that they forget that their problems may well intensify in the future. It is not enough to look at public manpower problems at the present. One state personnel director observed that "one significant problem is the general lack of planning to meet future manpower needs . . . there is an urgent need at the state level for a comprehensive, in-depth assessment of manpower needs in the foreseeable future, with provisions for updating and revising original estimates as additional data are accumulated."[13] Another commented in a similar vein ". . . the two greatest needs we face are to get into operation a manpower planning system which would be tied in with the budget process and to establish an on-going training program in management development."[14] In early 1970 in an examination of experience under the New Careers Program in a number of cities, a series of six "basic principles for the establishment of an effective city career opportunity program" were stated. Four of the six "basic principles" referred to the need for planning.[15] Still another observer commented recently, "Despite . . . the prediction that state and local governments will need 3.1 million new workers by 1975, 95 percent of all municipal governments in America . . . have no formal manpower plans."[16]

The level of state and local government employment seems very certain to continue to expand markedly. Recently, Irving Siegel and Harvey Belitsky expressed the opinion that "The most significant change that we expect is the emergence of government — federal, state, and local — as a dominant *employer of first resort* (not 'last resort') in meeting critical and social needs."[17] In the same vein they speak of ". . . the pursuit of comprehensive, non-crash programs to improve air and water supplies, to revive cities, to make adequate health care widely available . . ."[18]

NEED FOR PLANNING

The need for extended manpower planning rests on three foundation points. First, there is the likelihood that failure at the present time to plan and implement programs to obtain needed personnel may force the public employer to settle for poorly prepared or inexperienced personnel presently and in the future. (For example, in mid-1970, the personnel director of the state of Ohio was quoted as stating that graduates of two-year colleges and technical institutes would be considered qualified for jobs such as statistician, accountant, or information writer.[19]) Second, even as the labor market loosens, many government employers still find it difficult to recruit various types of trained manpower and general overall recruitment problems are frequently noted. Third, manpower problems in the public sector may well intensify, due to the need for workers in new areas where manpower is in short supply. The type and amount of manpower needed, when needed, and how it can be used most effectively as new or expanded functions are undertaken can be estimated and provided effectively only with careful advanced study and planning.

MINORITY GROUPS

One possible source of needed manpower for the public sector is minority groups and especially black Americans.[20] If one looks only at the percentage of Negroes employed by federal, state, or local government, it seems that the public employer has done well in employing minorities. The United States Civil Rights Commission reported in 1969 that slightly more than 25 percent of the total (noneducation) employment of state and local government in seven metropolitan areas — coast-to-coast and border-to-border — were from minorities.[21]

However, when the percentages of blacks hired in various types of work are examined, a pattern of failure to utilize black Americans in certain types of work and to concentrate them in less desirable types of work emerges. In the words of the Commission, "Not only do state and local governments consciously and overtly discriminate in hiring and promoting minority group members, but they do not foster programs to deal with discriminatory treatment on the job. . . . Rarely do state and local governments perceive the need for affirmative programs to recruit and upgrade minority group members for jobs in which they are inadequately represented."[22]

The Commission found Negroes noticeably low in employment in managerial and professional jobs and as uniformed personnel in fire and police work,[23] and most likely to hold managerial, professional, or white-collar jobs in health and welfare work. The lack of utilization was found not to rest realistically on lack of ability or capacity to be trained to meet job requirements.

FINANCING STATE AND LOCAL SERVICES

While the efficiency of the professional worker may be enhanced by job restructuring and the use of paraprofessionals, there are limits on this practice.[24] Most state and local governments are faced with the necessity of improving wages and salaries, overtime pay and other working conditions; and not too far in the future many more will be dealing collectively, whether they wish to do so or not, with organizations representing their employees. All of these developments promise to push up the cost of satisfactory quality manpower at the same time that the amount of manpower needed will be moving upward. The need is great for legislators who are willing to face realistically the problems of financing state and local services in a manner that does not necessitate "make-do" measures and apologies in lieu of personnel practices that will meet effectively the current and future manpower needs of state and local governments.

The public employer could recruit and retain a satisfied, well-motivated and stable labor force. Failure to do so testifies to the fact that, due to taxpayer resistance and lagging public personnel policies, wages and salaries, employee relations, and other conditions of work in the public sector compare unfavorably with conditions elsewhere in the labor market. Only by remedying this situation can the attitudes of public employees toward their jobs be improved.

Notes

1. *Monthly Labor Review,* Vol. 93, No. 7 (July, 1970), p. 6.
2. *Handbook of Labor Statistics,* U.S. Department of Labor (Washington, D.C.: U.S. Government Printing Office, 1968), p. 67.
3. *Manpower Report of the President,* March 1970, p. 302; see also *Occupational Outlook Handbook,* 1970–71 edn., pp. 811–826 (passim), both U.S. Department of Labor, 1970.
4. *Monthly Labor Review,* Vol. 92, No. 12 (December, 1969), pp. 29–34.
5. U.S. Bureau of the Census, *Census of Governments,* 1967, Vol. 1, Governmental Organization (Washington, D.C.: U.S. Government Printing Office, 1968), p. 26.
6. The Southwest Edition of the *Wall Street Journal* asserted on December 26, 1969, that a million jobs in public employment were vacant at the time.
7. Daniel Carbine, "Public Employers Feel Growing Pains," *Manpower,* Vol. 1, No. 10 (November, 1969), p. 15.
8. Not only do state and local wages and salaries tend to lag behind those paid at the private sector; in late 1969 federal pay exceeded that of all but six states. To deepen the problem, state wage and salary payments stood well above the pay of municipalities, counties, and other local governmental bodies. See *State Government News,* September 1970, and U.S. Bureau of the Census, *Public Employment in 1969,* pp. 13–18.

9. Secondary job holding was considerably higher among municipal employees (from 18 to 52 percent of city workers held second jobs) than among state employees (14 to 22 percent of whom reported secondary work). The figures for municipal workers were pulled up by firemen and policemen; from 18 to 80 percent of these workers reported second jobs.
10. *Monthly Labor Review,* Vol. 90, No. 10 (October, 1967), p. 17ff. and Vol. 93, No. 8 (August, 1970), p. 57ff.
11. To the extent that the second job is in the nature of a hobby or "happy work," it might contribute to a more contented and efficient worker. However, from three-fifths to two-thirds of the "moonlighters" surveyed in 1969 by the Bureau of Labor Statistics reported money-related (as contrasted to pleasure- or satisfaction-related) reasons for holding a second job. *Monthly Labor Review,* (August, 1970), *op. cit.*
12. Mark Haskell, *The New Careers Concept* (New York: Praeger Publishers, 1969), discusses job restructuring or redesign in New York, especially city hospitals.
13. Alan Drazek, Acting Director, Illinois Department of Personnel, personal letter.
14. John W. Jackson, Director, Minnesota Civil Service Department, personal letter.
15. Lawrence Williams, "City Jobs: Rich Potential For the Poor," *Manpower,* Vol. 2, No. 5 (May, 1970), p. 15.
16. Carbine, *op. cit.,* p. 87.
17. Irving Siegel and A. Harvey Belitsky, "The Changing Form and Status of Labor," *Journal of Economic Issues,* Vol. IV, No. 1 (March, 1970), p. 86.
18. *Ibid.,* p. 131.
19. Columbus, Ohio, *Citizen Journal,* August 21, 1970, p. 2.
20. Bennett Harrison, "Public Service Jobs for Urban Ghetto Residents," *National Civil Service League,* 1969.
21. United States Commission on Civil Rights, *For All The People . . . By All The People* (Washington, D.C.: U.S. Government Printing Office, 1969), p. XIII.
22. *Ibid.,* p. 131.
23. A special committee of the Human Resources Development Advisory Board reported very similar findings for city employees in Wichita, Kansas late in 1970. Report summarized in *Wichita Eagle and Beacon,* November 15, 1970.
24. Experience and problems under the New Careers Program are detailed in "National Assessment of the New Careers Program, July 1967-October 1969," U.S. Department of Labor, April 6, 1970.

2

URBAN ADMINISTRATION
AND COLLECTIVE BARGAINING

In labor relations circles, the 1960s have come to be known as "the decade of the public employee."[1] By 1971, more than 25 percent of all state and local governmental employees (2.7 million) were members of employee organizations.[2] In addition, well over 1 million federal employees belonged to employee organizations and better than 1,600,000 were represented in bargaining units. The American Federation of Government Employees (AFGE), a union of federal employees, reports that between 1960 and 1970, its membership rose from 70,300 to 324,900, a 362.2 percent increase. During that same decade, the membership in the American Federation of Teachers (AFT) climbed from 56,200 to 205,300, a jump of 265.3 percent, and the American Federation of State, County, and Municipal Employees (AFSCME) went from 210,000 members to 444,500, a rise of 111.7 percent.[3] These figures are in striking contrast to the 5 percent increase in membership experienced among private sector unions during the same time period.

The growth of public employee unions during the 1970s was also accompanied by a dramatic increase in the number of work stoppages or strikes. According to the Bureau of Labor Statistics, in 1958 there were only fifteen work stoppages involving 1,720 employees and the loss of 7,510 man-days. In contrast, in 1968 there were 251 strikes in the public sector, over a 16-fold increase. State and local government workers, totaling 200,120, participated in these strikes, with a resultant loss of more than 2.5 million man-days.[4] Since approximately 75 percent of all public employees are classified as white-collar workers and since, traditionally, this group has been the most resistant to unionization, this growth and increased activism of public employee organizations during the 1960s is especially significant, particularly for those who seek an understanding of the problems of urban administration and the constraints within which urban administrators must operate.

There are a number of factors that account for this increased unionization and activism among public employees. Gus Tyler of the International Ladies' Garment Workers Union (ILGWU) has explained one of them: during the 1960s, public employees finally became aware of "their collective presence and, hence, their power potential."[5] According to Tyler, American labor history has gone through three distinct stages in the twentieth century; each has been marked by the emergence of a new sector of the labor force that senses that its time has come. The first period, from 1900 to the mid-1930s, was dominated by the unionization of skilled craftsmen. The second, from the mid-'30s to the mid-'50s, was marked by the development of mass production industries and witnessed the addition of a "massive new tier" of semi- and unskilled workers to the labor movement. Finally, the third period, since the mid-'50s, has been characterized by the emergence of such service-providing industries as government, public utilities, trade, finance, and transportation, all of which employ many more white-collar than blue-collar workers. According to Tyler and his understanding of the dynamics of American labor history, the emergence of public employee unions in the 1960s was both logical and historically inevitable:

By that time the public employee was a large class in popular demand. Together with his conferees in the changed labor force — white-collar, service, professional, non-profit — the public employee was a major presence. He was in the same position as the mass production worker in the 1930s: numerous, needed, and neglected. In the '60s, the public employee repeated the history of the industrial employee thirty years before and of the craftsman sixty years before: having discovered his collective presence, he moved — like a teenager come of age — to express his collective power.[6]

Critics of the labor movement are likely to dismiss Tyler's understanding of the growth of public employee unions as mere union rhetoric; the real explanation for this growth, they contend, is to be found in the fact that labor (meaning the AFL-CIO and other unions) was acutely aware that its strength in private industry was on the wane and saw the public sector as a virtually untapped field for productive organizational efforts. However, this explanation oversimplifies the matter; it makes it appear that public employees are mere captives of labor. As Alan Edward Bent and George Noblit point out in "Collective Bargaining in Local Government: Effects of Urban Political Culture on Public Labor-Management Relations," public employees are not so much captives of as willing converts to unionism. Bent and Noblit enumerate four reasons that account for this conversion. First, public employees have come to embrace unionization for financial reasons. Public employees have traditionally earned less than their counterparts in the private sector. Unionization is seen as a way to bring equal treatment and compensation to the public realm. This impetus for unionization is reinforced by the effects of today's rampant inflation. Public employees believe that unions in private industry have been responsible for the negotiation of contracts for their members which have at least kept pace with inflation. They see unionization and collective bargaining in the public sphere as imperative if the government's reluctance to contribute to the inflationary spiral is to be overcome and if salaries and wages commensurate with those in the private sector are ever to be achieved.

Second, as governmental bureaucracy has grown, public employees find themselves increasingly unable to be heard by their employer unless they speak in a collective voice. Automation, which trivializes their work and diminishes their job security, certainly exacerbates these feelings. So does the " 'head-in-the-sand' attitude of many public employers," which distrusts the economic, political, and social objectives of unions and which, as Carl W. Stenberg observes, "has made the question of whether employee organizations will be recognized for the purpose of discussing grievances and conditions of work with management the second most frequent cause of strikes."[7]

Third, public employees, especially those who consider themselves to be professionals, see unionization and collective bargaining as providing them with an opportunity to participate in decisions concerning how and in what way their services are to be used.

Welfare workers protest about having to spend most of their time on clerical work; they see first-hand the inadequacies of the present welfare system, yet no one seems to listen to them. Nurses want better-administered hospitals; in their opinion, money is wasted that could be used to increase salaries and otherwise improve working conditions and services to patients. They claim that they are not treated with respect and that they are not allowed to participate in decisions where they could make a real contribution. Collective bargaining makes it possible to raise some of these issues at the bargaining table; if the matter is non-negotiable as far as management is concerned, the union may still be able to bring pressure on administrators and legislators to obtain the changes it wants.[8]

Finally, a change of attitude in government itself toward collective bargaining in the public sector has helped to promote the growth and activism of public employee unions. Until the early 1960s, public employers tended to seize every opportunity to resist the development of unionism in public employment. Their resistance was buttressed by the words of President Franklin D. Roosevelt, who, in a letter to Luther C. Steward, president of the National Federation of Employees, declared:

... The process of collective bargaining as usually understood, cannot be transplanted into the public service ... The very nature and purpose of government make it impossible for administrative officers to represent fully or bind the employer in mutual discussions with government employee organizations. . . .[9]

However, on January 17, 1962, President John F. Kennedy issued Executive Order 10988 on Employee-Management Cooperation in the Federal Service, and with the issuance of this order, resistance began to subside. The order stated that "the efficient administration of the Government and the well-being of the employees requires that orderly and constructive relationships be maintained between employee organizations and management officials." It required federal agencies to deal with employee organizations and to grant them official recognition for negotiation or consultation. Thus, it provided exclusive recognition and contract negotiation rights covering all employees in a bargaining unit for those organizations that had the support of the majority of the employees in the unit. For organizations with insufficient membership for exclusive recognition, it provided for two other forms of recognition (formal and informal) which essentially conferred upon them consultation rights. Executive Order 10988, of course, applied only to the federal government, but it had a spillover effect in state and local governments where it gave strong support to the principle of the right of public employees to organize. As a result, by 1971, twenty-five states had laws which required the public employer to bargain while eleven more authorized the employer to meet and confer or bargain.

The change in government attitude toward unionization since Executive Order 10988 is perhaps nowhere more evident than by the extent to which old arguments against collective bargaining in the public sphere have recently been abandoned. The fate of the "sovereignty argument" is typical. Although theoretically sound, its practical significance has been depreciated. Sovereignty may be defined as "the supreme, absolute, and uncontrollable power by which any independent state is governed."[10] It cannot be given to, taken by, or shared with anyone; if it is, the government is no longer sovereign. Yet, the "sovereignty argument" continues, the demand for collective bargaining by public employees represents an attempt to seize a portion of this sovereignty — it constitutes nothing less than a direct defiance of governmental authority. With the phenomenal growth of public employee unions, however, this argument and the problems it poses have been generally ignored. As Chester A. Newland observes:

> The right of employees to strike for their interests and the power of democratic government based on popular sovereignty to enforce its interests make up one [of the] most basic issues for resolution. The only simple answer to that is that society may be better off to live with the troublesome issue for a while than to adopt too simple a solution for it, since the matter goes to the basis of the society's authority concepts.[11]

Because the theoretical "sovereignty argument" is inconsistent with the practical reality of public employee unions, it is dismissed. If sovereignty is spoken of at all, it is a redefined pragmatic sovereignty which asserts either that (1) although government cannot be forced to bargain collectively, it serves its own best interests when it elects to do so, or (2) government employees as members of the public have a claim equal to that of government employers to the exercise of this sovereignty.[12]

The four reasons Bent and Noblit give in large part account for the growth and activism of public employee unions. However, not all units of government have experienced the same rate of growth or extent of activism. Using multiple correlations to measure the impact on municipal union agreements of the demographic character, political culture, and service orientation of a city, Bent and Noblit find that poor, heterogeneous, politicized cities with a "consumer welfare" orientation are more receptive to municipal employee union demands. However, while some cities are more receptive than others, no city has escaped altogether the effects of public employee unions. David T. Stanley, for example, has explored the ways in which urban administration has been influenced by them. He focuses on their impact on personnel systems, budget and finance activities, and the daily management of various substantive programs and concludes that union pressures have brought about changes that "mean that officials up and down the line are spending more time and using more of their staff on personnel matters and are more limited in their administrative discretion. Management officials are prodded, watched, resisted, and reasoned with by union stewards and agents. Thus management must administer more carefully and more responsibly."[13] Felix A. Nigro in "The Implications for Public Administration" enlarges upon Stanley's discussion and lists eight specific ways in which urban administration has been affected by collective bargaining in the public sector. In addition, he examines the relative influence different participants in the public policy-making process have before and after the introduction of collective bargaining and finds that collective bargaining, although the source of many problems for urban executives and administrators, is also the source of considerable power, certainly vis-à-vis the legislative branch. Finally, Nigro explores the effect of collective bargaining on the public interest and concludes that it is a mixed blessing. While collective bargaining has proved to be a salutory check on governmental arbitrariness and paternalism and has been an excellent antidote for the evils of bureaucracy, it has also encroached on the powers of the public and its legislative representatives and contributed to the financial crisis of state and local governments.

Notes

1. Felix A. Nigro and Lloyd G. Nigro, *Modern Public Administration,* 3d edn.; (New York: Harper and Row, 1973), p. 312.
2. *Ibid.* See also Carl W. Stenberg, "Labor Management Relations in State and Local Government: Progress and Prospects," *Public Administration Review,* Vol. XXXII, No. 2 (March/April 1972), p. 102.
3. Nigro and Nigro, *op. cit.,* p. 312.
4. Stenberg, *op. cit.,* p. 102.
5. Gus Tyler, "Why They Organize," *Public Administration Review,* Vol. XXXII, No. 2 (March/April 1972), p. 99.
6. *Ibid.,* p. 100.
7. Stenberg, *op. cit.,* p. 103.
8. Nigro and Nigro, *op. cit.,* p. 314-315.
9. Quoted in Sterling Spero and John M. Capozzola, *The Urban Community and Its Unionized Bureaucracies: Pressure Politics in Local Government Labor Relations* (New York: The Dunellen Publishing Company, 1973), p. 5.
10. Michael H. Moskow, J. Joseph Loewenberg, and Edward Clifford Koziara, *Collective Bargaining in Public Employment* (New York: Random House, 1970), pp. 16-17.
11. Chester A. Newland, "Collective Bargaining and Public Administration: Systems for Changing and Search for Reasonableness," in *Collective Bargaining and Public Administration* (Chicago: Public Personnel Association, 1971), p. 11.
12. Classical democratic theory contends that sovereignty is not vested in government but rather in the people. Public employees reject the notion that their employers are sovereign, for they are only "borrowing" their sovereignty from the people. As a part of the people, public employees claim a right to exercise their sovereignty, and they do so by collectively acting on behalf of their rights concerning working conditions. On this basis, they challenge the government's use of the "sovereignty argument."
13. David T. Stanley, "The Effects of Unions on Local Governments," *Proceedings of the Academy of Political Science,* XXX, No. 2 (1971), p. 43.

ALAN EDWARD BENT and GEORGE W. NOBLIT

COLLECTIVE BARGAINING IN LOCAL GOVERNMENT: EFFECTS OF URBAN POLITICAL CULTURE ON PUBLIC LABOR-MANAGEMENT RELATIONS

The increase in public employment at all levels of government is matched by the rising unionization of public employees. Since the 1960s the stagnation of the labor movement in the private sector has coincided with the flourishing of the movement among public employees — the fastest growing sector of unionization in America. "The 1960s have already earned the right to go down in labor relations history as the decade of the public employee" has been the pronouncement of one scholar in labor relations. "The rise of these unions is the most significant development in the industrial relations field in the last thirty years."[1] And this occurs at a time when the proportion of blue-collar and craft workers are diminishing and professional and sub-professional employees are growing in number. The spirit of unionization in public employment, and the attractiveness of union membership among the white-collar employees signals an emerging self-conscious proletarianism of a new class of workers. Even employee groups that normally eschew labor organization — teachers, social workers, nurses, engineers — now readily form and join unions.

The response of government — especially some state legislatures — to the emerging conditions in public labor relations has been a slow, almost grudging recognition of the union activities. However, a number of states have now followed the example of the federal government and have statutes authorizing or requiring collective bargaining in their municipalities. Some of the larger, more industrialized states have passed laws on labor relations that surpass those of the federal government. However, in general, government has had to play catch-up with the private sector

Reprinted by permission of the Institute of Governmental Studies and Research, Memphis State University, *Public Affairs Forum,* IV, No. 4 (February 1975).

in its knowledge about labor relations and in its availability of collective bargaining procedures. But, there now appears to be an acceptance of employee organizations on the part of government. Having failed to arrest the evolutionary progress of public employee unionization by claims of state "sovereignty" and government as a "model employer," and upholding of the merit principle as an antithesis to unions, governments at all levels of the federal system are learning to live within the framework of the new era in labor relations.

Organizing employees in the public sector was not an easy task. Approximately 75% of the public employees are classified as white-collar workers and, traditionally, this group has been the most resistant to unionization. Their bias against unionization has focused on the association of unions as "working-class" organizations; since white-collar employees like to perceive themselves as "professionals" they reject unionism as unsuited to their "class." Another problem that has faced unions in the public sector is that, in contrast to other workers, public employees have had a strong feeling of employment security as protected by civil service regulations and have, therefore, not felt the need for union protection. Union growth in the public sector was also impeded by restrictive governmental regulations. Until recent years, explicit legislation on all levels of government prohibited or made difficult public sector collective bargaining. In addition, governmental opposition also took more subtle forms such as intimidating white-collar workers by suggesting the position of trust and confidence that they enjoyed with management would be jeopardized by unionization.[2] Juris and Feuille conclude that the resistance to unionization in the public sector paralleled the attitudes found earlier in the private sector. "Employer resistance to public unionization has been phrased in many ways, but it reflects the same desires among public sector employers to avoid sharing managerial authority and to keep labor costs down that are historically found in the private sector."[3]

In addition to being hampered by employers another inhibiting factor to public unionization has been the existence of inter-union rivalry. Chamberlain and Cullen argue that it is in the unions' self interest to seek to define their membership as broadly as possible.[4] But, this has often led to jurisdictional disputes between unions attempting to organize and represent the same membership group. Vosloo defines union rivalries as generally drawn around one of two conflicts: the craft union versus the industrial union dichotomy or the affiliated versus the independent union split.[5] Both of these rivalries have played a part in the experience of unionization in the public sector. For example, such "industry-wide" public sector unions as the American Federation of State, County and Municipal Employees (AFSCME) and the American Federation of Government Employees (AFGE) have issued charters to any unaffiliated group within their broad boundaries that showed a desire to unionize. This practice has led to conflicts with such craft unions as the Building Service Employees International Union and the International Association of Machinists who have felt that they had a jurisdiction over some segments of the unaffiliated group.[6] Rivalries have also occurred between unions associated with the AFL-CIO and independent organizations which are often professional or employee associations. The independents claim that the tactics of the AFL-CIO are inappropriate for "professional" workers while affiliated unions portray the independents as mere dues-collecting agencies or worse, as being co-opted by management — "company-unions."[7]

Despite the obstacles in organizing, the public sector has seen a remarkable growth in unionization. This phenomenon can be attributed to four factors. First, inflation has eroded the buying power of public employees, as it has all workers; unionization is seen as a way of remedying this problem. Public employees believe that unions in the private sector have been able to negotiate economic gains for their constituents that at least keep pace with inflation. Without the advantage of collective bargaining they now feel that their salaries and wages will not grow as fast as those in the private sector because of the reluctance of legislatures to contribute to the inflationary spiral. The Twentieth Century Fund Task Force on Labor Disputes and Public Employment concludes: "It is in local government where what once may have been the advantage of being a public employee has been seriously eroded by rising living costs, greater economic gains by private employees, and in some occupations — policeman, fireman, and teacher, particularly — by increased job hazards. These conditions and the fact that unionism has become acceptable in American society and has demonstrated its effectiveness, have led public employees to organize."[8] Next, automation has made the work of public employees more menial. Blum writes that automation has had adverse effects on white collar workers: "Skills are reduced or disappear as their work becomes trivialized, trauma emerges as the goal of upward mobility within the organization becomes an illusion, and job security is diminished."[9] Third, while economic gains are still important, other issues such as working conditions and job security are also of great concern to public employees, many of whom see themselves as professionals. Unions, by negotiating for the manner in which public services would be provided in addition to bargaining for traditional economic benefits have broadened their appeal. This aspect of union activity has had particular impact on the organization of such professional groups as teachers who feel that questions pertaining to working conditions and the provision of their services are essential to their status as professionals.[10] Last, and certainly not least, is the increasing permissiveness of government towards collective bargaining in the public sector.[11] The changing attitude on the part of the public employer has undoubtedly given union organizing in the public sector its greatest impetus.

In terms of the collective bargaining process public and private sector unions bargain for similar things, with certain qualifications. Essentially, negotiation centers on two issues: the economic package and the scope of management authority. The economic package usually includes wages and salaries, fringe benefits, and working conditions. However, it is difficult to make a real assessment of the impact of unions on wages. There are problems in estimating what the wage would have been if unions were not present making any conclusions tentative.[12] Arguments have been put forth that unions have only a short-run impact in terms of increased wages and over time union and non-union wages become more equal.[13] But, it should also be considered that the very existence of unions may have the effect of forcing wages up in the non-unionized sectors. If nothing else, the very threat of unionization may influence employers to provide better economic packages than they would have under circumstances where there did not exist such pressures.

Public employee unions also bargain over traditional management prerogatives. Generally, this centers around union security provisions, hiring and rehiring, and grievance mechanisms.[14] The issue of negotiation over such items as promotion, selection and job classification has not been resolved with management adhering to the position that these are not negotiable items and unions making claims that they are within the scope of collective bargaining. Should these items become negotiable then this would have a serious impact on the merit principle that has ruled the public sector since the 19th century and has given management clear predominance in determinations concerned with these issues.

There is one area where the experience in the private and the public sectors differs markedly, and this applies to the scope of bargaining. While there has been some contention over the legitimacy of this issue in the private sector in the past, this has eroded over time. But, the scope of bargaining in the public sector has been controversial indeed. There is often an absence of specific legislation defining the legal grounds for bargaining. This leads to the peculiar situation where the scope of bargaining may not be something that government feels it can legitimately negotiate, yet lacks a definite basis on which to make this determination. Recently this has become a less contentious item as enabling legislation has been provided at all levels of government giving a legitimate basis for collective bargaining in the public sector. However, where legitimacy is still unclear, the practice has been one where a trade-off is obtained by broadening the scope of bargaining at the expense of other union demands, such as the economic advantages.

In the public sector the collective bargaining process is pursued on two levels. At the bargaining level the give-and-take of negotiations between management and labor follows a conventional format. But, the public sector has yet another level and that is where the public employee unions may circumvent the bargaining process by lobbying for gains directly to legislative bodies and to the general public. This presents public management with having to deal with organized employees in a traditional sense while at the same time realizing that the employees, through their unions, are a pressure group with uncommon capabilities. In the absence of statutory legislation directing a single source of representation for management, such as the City Personnel Director or some other official in the Executive branch, union representatives may try to obtain greater bargaining gains by attempting to bring political pressure to bear on bargaining outcomes. This "end-run" approach to collective bargaining where union representatives may reject a management position and attempt to bargain directly with a legislative body is construed as destructive of professionalized collective bargaining by management.[15]

Much of the research on public sector unionization has focused on the phenomena of growth, enabling legislation, and the problems and processes of collective bargaining. As a result, there is an absence of studies that seek to provide predictive models of environmental conditions that affect public sector collective bargaining. This kind of analysis would appear to be especially useful if environmental indicators significant to public labor-management relations could be developed for urban areas. Public employees unionization with its attendant collective bargaining is a new contingency that financially hard pressed local governments must now face. The short-run history of collective bargaining in local government has already introduced a number of measurable traits. By selecting certain indicators a pattern of commonalities may be discernable so that a collective bargaining experience can become predictable.

This study isolated the demographic character, political culture, and service orientation of a city and attempted to measure the impact of these variables on the ability of public sector unions to negotiate gains. Generally, it was expected that cities with a relatively homogeneous population in terms of income, race and education and a relatively noncompetitive political culture would not be as likely to accede to municipal employee union demands. Similarly, cities that are highly politicized and more heterogeneous demographically were expected to be more accommodating in view of the political realities of public sector collective bargaining. It was also anticipated that cities whose public policy is service-directed would be more likely to accept strong public sector unions. Finally, it was expected that of the three variables groups, political culture would be the most explanatory.

METHOD

The data for this investigation were obtained from 39 cities in the United States with populations of 250,000 or more, according to the 1970 census.[16] This sample represents 70 percent of all cities in the United States with similar populations. In 1972, the Bureau of Labor Statistics conducted a survey of municipal collective bargaining agreements in a number of cities and 39 of the cities returned usable data.[17] Data from this survey provided the measures of the dependent variable: strength of municipal union agreements. It is important to note that data were only available on cities that forwarded one or more agreements to the Bureau.

The first measure of strength is simply the number of agreements each city had with public employee unions. The number of agreements varied between one and thirty-two. This measure uncovers the dimension of collective bargaining activity within cities. However, it does not capture specific advantages that each union may have accrued in its collective bargaining agreements. We have already noted problems with assessing the relevance of wage packages. Fortunately, it is easier to evaluate the ability of unions to bargain over traditional managerial prerogatives. Accordingly, the study examined two dimensions of the test of union strength: the ability of the unions to negotiate for union security and for control over promotion — the latter consideration generally accepted as within manage-ment's prerogative. Union security was measured by the number of union security provisions. Union participation in promotion determinations was measured in terms of the number of promotion provisions that appeared in the union contracts. Each of these measures was also used as a proportion — the number of union security or promotion provisions relative to the number of contracts in a city. In this way, an assessment could be made of the relative strength of the agreements per city regardless of the actual number of contracts negotiated.

Our first independent variable measures, the demographic character-istics of a city, were abstracted from the *City-County Data Book* of 1972. Median education, median income, percent white-collar, and percent black citizens were all obtained from this source.

The measures of political culture were abstracted from a variety of sources. The reason for this was that political culture as defined in this paper includes government organization, and indicators of politicization as obtained from whether city governments were partisan or non-partisan and the degree of party competitiveness in the locality. Three basic forms of city government were used to evaluate government organization: mayor-council form, commission form, and council-manager form. Of the 39 cities studied none had a commission form of government organization and, thus, this form of government was subsequently treated as a dummy variable. The ("1") value was assigned for all cities having the highly politicized mayor-council form. A ("O") was assigned for those cities not having the highly politicized mayor-council — the "non-politicized" council-manager form cities. Political character was treated in a similar manner. A dummy variable was created using the dimension of "partisan" or "non-partisan" city government. The indicators of both government organization and political character of cities were abstracted from the 1970 *World Book Encyclopedia.*

The measures of political party competition and percent of population voting were again from the *City-County Data Book.* Election statistics were unavailable for the cities proper, but were available for most SMSA's and counties. SMSA data were used except for Boston and Seattle where election data from Suffolk and King counties, respectively, were substituted. Percent of the population voting was computed for the 1968 presidential election. The number of people voting was divided by the number of people eligible to vote within each SMSA or county. The denominator was based on the 1970 census data as reported in the source book. Thus, there may be some distortion in these figures.

Political party competition, normally measured by a party's margin of victory in an election, had to be somewhat modified. The 1968 presidential election had three contending parties: the Democratic, Republican and American Independent. So, another measure had to be devised. The measure of party competition for this investigation was obtained by subtracting the percent of vote of the leading party from 100. Thus, party competition increased as this measure increased.

The last independent variable, service orientation of a city, had two measures: the monthly payroll of a city and the city's per capita outlay. Both measures were obtained from the *City-County Data Book* of 1972.[18]

FINDINGS AND DISCUSSIONS

Municipal collective bargaining is distinctive inasmuch as it often involves, either directly or indirectly, three groups in the negotiations — management, labor and the public. Because public opinion may sometimes have a political effect on the outcome of collective bargaining in the public sector, it was expected that factors relating to the demographic character of a city's population would have a bearing on union strength in collective bargaining. However, our findings showed that while there were some interesting correlations between a city's demography and union strength in collective bargaining, these measures were the least significant in predicting union strength. In general, the findings supported expectations.

Increases in the educational level of the city's population coincided with a decrease in the strength of the union. This finding applied in all measures of union strength. This suggests that in the more "professionalized" cities unions are less likely to be able to negotiate contracts that are as advantageous as can be secured in cities with other demographic characteristics. A city's percentages of white-collar occupations and the income level of its citizens displayed a similar pattern of effect on the dependent variable measures. This was also consistent with our expectations. It is interesting to note that in the case of the number of promotion provisions in a contract, there was a slight negative correlation between this variable and income. However, the number of provisions relative to the number of contracts yielded a positive correlation with income. As the income level of a city increased so did the ability of the union to gain some inroads over traditional management prerogatives in the contracts it was able to negotiate.

The effect of a minority population in a city was relatively insignificant, but generally tended in the direction expected. As the size of the black population increased so did union strength, especially in terms of the promotion provision indicators. . . .While the characteristics of the city's population do influence the ability of the union to negotiate from strength in the area of the merit system of promotion, other measures of union strength — as affecting the number of contracts, the number of union security provisions, and the number of union security provisions relative to the number of contracts — are more influenced by other variables.

It was expected that the political culture of a city would have an important bearing on union strength in collective bargaining. This contention was supported by the logic that since contract negotiations in the public sector are highly political, the political culture would be the most significant of the three variable groups. In comparing the political culture-union strength zero order relationships and the demographic character-union strength relationships, it appears that, overall, political culture does seem to have a stronger effect. The pattern is not so clear, however, when comparing the effects of political culture and public policy output measured by a city's service commitment.

In terms of a city's governmental structure, subsumed in our consideration of political culture, mayor-council cities were more likely to have collective bargaining agreements that indicated some degree of union strength than were cities with less "politicized" government organization forms. However, there was an inconsistency in this pattern. Although mayor-council cities were more likely to have union security provisions, the pattern of union strength was not evident when union security provisions were measured relative to the number of contracts a city had negotiated. But, union strength was consistent under this type of governmental organization relative to the promotion provision indicators.

The partisan city is also more likely than is the non-partisan city to have agreements that indicate union strength. This bears out that the more politicized the city government the more likely it is to yield some management prerogatives to the unions. The more politicized a community, the more participation there is in the political process, and the more groups there are contending for power. Within this framework, power is continually contended and shared and for a government that means that it must achieve some accommodation with some of the groups in order to stay in office. In the continuous fluidity of this politically pluralist environment accommodation takes the form of reciprocal support; for a government it is to grant favors in some cases in exchange for support in others. It is here that an organized group such as a public employee union representing a large number of workers can advantage itself when bargaining with a government that cannot afford to alienate this important source of support or opposition.

The extent of a city's politicization continues to hold a positive correlation with union strength in collective bargaining. Looking at the more general political competitiveness of the city, it appears that as the citizens' participation in the political process increased, as represented by the percentage of the population voting, so did the city's incidence of yielding power to the union as manifested by collective bargaining provisions advantageous to the union. Interestingly, total consistency in this regard did not apply in the case of political party competition. Cities with a high degree of party competition did not have a large number of contracts nor did the contracts indicate union sharing in promotion determinations. Yet, union security provisions were obtainable in these cities. This indicates that cities with a high degree of party competition may have engaged in a trade-off in their bargaining with public employee unions: they may have granted union security provisions in exchange for maintaining management rights over promotions. This seems to display an effort for the co-existence of the merit system with collective bargaining. In this accommodation management guards some aspects of its prerogatives and unions achieve legitimacy and permanency through the union security provisions.

The last independent variable to be considered was a city's service orientation. It was expected that there would be a consistency in a city's perspective. This is to say, the more "consumer welfare-oriented" cities — cities committed to a public policy of maximizing services to its citizens — would be expending more public funds on services as well as on city employees. Unions, it was expected, would also profit from this orientation. The more "consumer welfare-oriented" the city, the more likely would it allow for public union strength. The consistency held up in the case of expenditure for city employees. Cities with a larger payroll per employee demonstrated a higher likelihood to have collective bargaining provisions that indicated union strength. However, this did not apply with the per capita outlay of funds indicator. While this indicator was related to the number of contracts, the number of union security provisions, and proportionate promotion provisions per number of contracts, it was not related to the proportion of union security provisions per number of contracts and number of promotion provisions. This indicated that cities with high per capita outlay were willing to trade some management prerogatives on a relatively high proportion of contracts for generally weak union security provisions relative to the number of contracts. A similar pattern, although not nearly as marked, was also evident when looking at the effect of city payroll on collective bargaining agreements. Thus, public unions in "consumer welfare-oriented" cities manifested strength in collective bargaining with the exception of the union security provisions. Curiously, this suggests a tenuous existence for public unions in "consumer welfare" cities in comparison with other cities.

The character of cities that have strong municipal employee unions begins to emerge. The cities that are less professional, less affluent with a high proportion of black residents are more likely to end up with municipal collective bargaining agreements indicating some degree of union strength. Also, overall, the more politicized the city, the stronger the public employee unions. "Consumer welfare" cities have more collective bargaining agreements but trade-off some degree of union strength for minimal union security provisions. In summary, heterogeneous, poor, politicized and "consumer welfare" cities are more likely to accommodate to municipal employee union demands.

There was a concern with which variable indicators explained the most variance in the four measures of union strength utilized in this study. As Table 1 shows, there was an explanation for more than 30 percent of the variance in only three of the dependent variable measures. The variable system used accounts for most of the variance in the number of contracts a city had, the number of promotion provisions present in these contracts and the proportion of promotion provisions per number of contracts. The independent variable measures explained little of the variance in the number of union security provisions per number of contracts. However, the use of 10 indicators was a high number for a multiple correlation technique. Thus, it would be expected that there are other significant dimensions to the problem at hand, not the least of which are union diligence at organizing, legislative regulations on bargaining, and the relative capability of the negotiators on the labor and management teams.

From the zero order correlations, it would seem that political culture and public policy output — service orientation — would account for more of the variance in municipal employee union strength than would

TABLE 1

Multiple correlations of all independent variable measures with measures of union strength

	R	R²
a) Number of contracts	.6205	.3850
b) Number of union security provisions	.3485	.1214
c) b/a	.3754	.1409
d) Number of promotion provisions	.5981	.3577
e) d/a	.5753	.3310

the demographic character of a city. The hypothesis was that political culture would explain more of the variance than either other variable group.

By looking at the effects of a city's population characteristics in Table 2 it can be seen that the four demographic indicators did not contribute much independent effect. While all the multiple correlation coefficients are appreciably higher than any of the zero order correlation coefficients, the amount of variance explained is negligible. Note that the promotion provision measures are the best explained of the dependent variable measures — a pattern consistent with the zero order correlations.

Similarly, little variance was explained by the political culture indicators as shown in Table 3. However, most of the multiple correlation coefficients were of similar size. That is, political culture was a more consistent predictor of strength in municipal bargaining agreements than was demographic character.

A city's service orientation, although having only half the number of

measures of the other two variable groups, seemed to be of similar importance to public employee union strength. Comparing the results in Table 4
with findings of the zero order, it appears that in the "consumer welfare-
oriented" cities the trade-off of allowing unions to participate in some
areas traditionally reserved for management — promotion determinations
— in exchange for little union security is not evident. In fact, the two
measures when combined showed that these cities had more contracts,
contracts with promotion provisions and, to a somewhat lesser extent,
contracts providing for union security. However, relative to the number of
contracts, there was less evidence of the coincidence of collective bargaining agreements providing for both union security and other union advan-

TABLE 2

Multiple correlations of city demographic characteristics with
measures of union strength.

	R	R²
a) Number of contracts	.2561	.0656
b) Number of union security provisions	.2182	.0476
c) b/a	.1919	.0368
d) Number of promotion provisions	.3686	.1359
e) d/a	.4466	.1995

TABLE 3

Multiple correlations of political culture measures with measures of union strength.

	R	R²
a) Number of contracts	.3437	.1181
b) Number of union security provisions	.1885	.0355
c) b/a	.3150	.0992
d) Number of promotion provisions	.3001	.0901
e) d/a	.3955	.1564

tages. Somewhat less variance is explained in the measures of union strength relative to the number of contracts.

To compare the relative importance of demographic character, political culture and public policy output, the size of R^2 for the three variable groups on each dependent variable measure was ordered. The ordering appears in Table 5. Note that service orientation and political culture are very close as indicated by the mean rank and this decidedly

TABLE 4

Multiple correlations of service orientation measures with measures of union strength.

	R	R^2
a) Number of contracts	.4816	.2319
b) Number of union security provisions	.2156	.0465
c) b/a	.1469	.0216
d) Number of promotion provisions	.4654	.2166
e) d/a	.2274	.6517

TABLE 5

Ranking according to amount of variance explained in union strength by each independent variable group

	Demographic character	Political culture	Service orientation
a) Number of contracts	3	2	1
b) Number of union security provisions	3	1	1
c) b/a	3	1	2
d) Number of promotion provisions	2	3	1
e) d/a	1	2	3
Mean rank =	2.4	1.8	1.6

explained more variance than did the city population characteristics. Interestingly, service orientation, the "best" predictor, explained the number of contracts, union security provisions and promotion provisions better than it showed union strength relative to the number of contracts. A city's degree of "consumer welfare-orientation" seemed to incur a large degree of collective bargaining activity, yet did not, as often, include provisions of union security thereby obscuring in this case, a valid assessment of the true nature of union strength.

CONCLUSION

Municipal collective bargaining is a complex phenomenon. It involves a negotiation process between representatives of labor and management that necessitates a great deal of sophistication and personal skill. Also important in the determination of collective bargaining is an appreciation of the environment in which the negotiations are carried out. This study attempted to explain some of the environmental factors that may influence public collective bargaining agreements. The data reveal that the most significant environmental indicators concern the city's political character and especially its public policy orientation in terms of a service commitment. But, it must not be overlooked that a number of other variables play a major role in municipal collective bargaining outcomes. The ability of the city or any other governmental organization to grant union demands in view of legislative and budgetary restrictions is an essential consideration. Relative skills and political support that each side can muster in the collective bargaining process undoubtedly has a bearing on the final outcome.

Other important factors include the timing of negotiations. Union demands for increased pay when out of synchronization with budgetary submissions and ratification places restrictions on management options. In a case such as this, management may grant union security provisions and other non-fiscal advantages to the union in exchange for a hiatus on pay raises. This trade-off may be made out of necessity in order to preserve industrial peace in the public sector. When one side's options are limited, the other side may gain bargaining advantages. On the other hand, an alternative to actual weakness is to put on a show of strength. Here bargaining may deteriorate into having one side acting arrogantly and irresponsibly − not out of strength but out of weakness. It is when power is evenly divided among negotiating "adversaries" that industrial peace is more likely to be kept. The history of collective bargaining in the private sector is instructive for its demonstration of trade-union responsibility accompanying the growth of trade union power.[19] The conflict that now engages public sector labor-management relations with the large number of strikes crippling vital services need not be an enduring phenomenon. It may simply be the manifestation of the growth-pains of unionism in the public sector. If a thorough understanding of collective bargaining in the public sector is to develop, there must be a concerted effort to synthesize the type of research utilized here with that of studies of the process of negotiation at close hand. At that point, the relative effects of the host of variables can be better assessed.

Notes

1. Jack Steiber, Director of the Michigan State University's School of Labor and Industrial Relations, quoted by David R. Jones in *The New York Times*, April 2, 1967.

2. Allan M. Carter and F. Ray Marshall, *Labor Economics: Wages, Employment and Trade Unionism* (Homewood, Ill.: Richard D. Irwin, Inc., 1967), p. 130.

3. Hervey A. Juris and Peter Feuille, *Police Unionism: Power and Impact in Public Sector Bargaining* (Lexington, Mass.: D.C. Heath and Co., 1973), p. 11.

4. Neil W. Chamberlain and Donald E. Cullen, *The Labor Sector* (New York: McGraw-Hill Book Company, 1971), p. 82.

5. Willem B. Vosloo, *Collective Bargaining in the United States' Federal Civil Service* (Chicago, Ill.: Public Personnel Administration, 1966), pp. 127–131.

6. Harry A. Donoian, "The AFGE and the AFSCME in Collective Bargaining for Public Employees," in *Collective Bargaining for Public Employees*, ed. by Herbert R.L. Marx, Jr. (New York: H.W. Wilson Company, 1969), pp. 24–25.

7. Leo Troy, "White-Collar Organization in the Federal Service," in *White Collar Workers*, ed. by Albert A. Blum, *et al.* (New York: Random House, 1971), pp. 186–187.

8. Twentieth Century Fund. Task Force on Labor Disputes and Public Employment, *Pickets at City Hall* (New York: The Twentieth Century Fund, 1970), p. 5.

9. Blum, *op. cit.*, p. 12.

10. Garbarino indicates that this is a very significant factor in organizing university faculty as well. See Joseph W. Garbarino, "Emergence of Collective Bargaining," in *Faculty Unions and Collective Bargaining*, edited by Edwin D. Duryea, Robert S. Fisk, and Associates (San Francisco: Jossey-Bass Publishers, 1973), pp. 7–9.

11. *Ibid.*, p. 4.

12. Belton M. Fleisher, *Labor Economics: Theory and Evidence* (Englewood Cliffs, N.J.: Prentice-Hall, Inc., 1970), p. 182.

13. Melvin Lurie, "Governmental Regulation and Union Power: A Case Study of the Boston Transit Industry," in the *Journal of Law and Economics* (October, 1960), p. 124.

14. W.D. Heisel and J.D. Hallibran, *Questions and Answers on Public Employee Negotiations* (Chicago, Ill.: Public Personnel Association, 1967), p. 29.

15. Sterling Spero and John M. Capozzola, *The Urban Community and its Unionized Bureaucracies: Pressure Politics in Local Government Labor Relations* (New York: Dunellen Publishing Co., 1973), pp. 130–134.

16. The cities included in the survey consist of: Akron, Atlanta, Baltimore, Boston, Buffalo, Chicago, Cincinnati, Cleveland, Columbus, Denver, Detroit, Fort Worth, Indianapolis, Jacksonville, Jersey City, Kansas City, Los Angeles, Louisville, Memphis, Milwaukee, Newark, New Orleans, New York, Oakland, Oklahoma City, Omaha, Philadelphia, Phoenix, Pittsburgh, Portland, Rochester, Sacramento, San Francisco, San Jose, Seattle, Tampa, Toledo, Tucson and Washington, D.C.

17. For a more complete summary of the Bureau's survey, see *Municipal Collective Bargaining Agreements in Large Cities,* Bureau of Labor Standards Bulletin 1759 (1972). The authors are indebted to the Bureau for providing the data for this part of the study and especially to Norman J. Samuels, Assistant Commissioner, Wages and Industrial Relations, for his assistance.

18. The authors recognize the weaknesses in many of the measures. However, they were the most available measures for this preliminary venture. For example, union security provisions are often limited by law. To get around this, agency shops, as opposed to union shops, were negotiated by unions. Thus the measures of union security had to take this into account. While some may be reluctant to grant the assumptions employed in this and other measures, the lack of earlier research in the area did not allow any clear guidelines to follow. Similarly, the assumption of an interval level of measurement was used to allow the use of more powerful statistics. Labovitz has argued for this. See: Sanford Labovitz, "The Assignment of Numbers to Rank Order Categories," *American Sociological Review* 135 (June, 1970), pp. 515–524. The authors are also aware of the criticisms and Labovitz's responses. See: Louis G. Vargo, Donald G. Schweitzer, Lawrence S. Mayer, and Sanford Labovitz, "Replies and Comments," *American Sociological Review* 36 (June, 1971), pp. 517 –522.

19. Harold L. Sheppard, "Approaches to Conflict in American Industrial Sociology," *British Journal of Sociology,* Vol. 5 (1959), pp. 324–340.

FELIX A. NIGRO

THE IMPLICATIONS FOR PUBLIC ADMINISTRATION

In this article, we will: (1) present in detail *eight* specific ways in which public administration has been affected [by collective negotiations in the Public Service]; (2) consider the resulting changes in the relative influence of different participants in the public policy-making process; (3) discuss the concern about the public interest; and (4) conclude with a final, evaluative balance sheet.

EIGHT SPECIFIC EFFECTS

First, bilateral determination of the conditions of work is now well-established for very large numbers of public employees. Fifty-eight percent of the federal work force is now represented by unions recognized as exclusive bargaining agents, which is ". . . far greater than the coverage in private employment."[1] Furthermore, contrary to a lingering misconception, 35% of all federal white-collar employees are so represented; indeed, there are now more white-collar than blue-collar workers so represented. Of the more than a million state and local government employees in New York, 900,000 are exercising their collective bargaining rights under legislation passed in 1967. In New York City, about 280,000 of the some 370,000 municipal workers are represented by the six major unions. Some education authorities consider that collective bargaining is now the "prevailing decision-making style" in the public school systems.[2]

The rapidly growing membership base justifies employee leaders'

Reprinted from the *Public Administration Review,* journal of the American Society for Public Administration, XXXII (March 1972), pp. 120–126.

optimism about winning representation rights for even higher percentages of the total work force. About one million federal employees are members of employee organizations, while, "membership in unions and employee associations currently totals about two million, or more than one-third of all non-instructional full-time employees of states, cities, counties, school districts and other local authorities, as compared with less than 30% organization of non-agricultural workers in the private sector."[3]

Second, public officials are increasingly being policed through binding grievance arbitration clauses in collective contracts. Four years ago such clauses were far less common, and management often resisted them tooth and nail. Executive Order 11616 continues the provision in Executive Order 11491 permitting union-negotiated grievance procedures with binding arbitration; and it also requires *all* new agreements to contain negotiated grievance procedures for resolving disputes over interpretation of contract terms.

The significance of binding grievance arbitration was clear in the recent school teacher strike in Newark, New Jersey. The strike became inevitable when the Newark school board announced it would not agree to a new contract containing the provision for binding arbitration. Teachers who grieve transfers can get them cancelled if the arbitrator agrees that management's action violates the contract or is otherwise unfair. Many teachers fear transfers to slum neighborhoods, and the whites are apprehensive that black-dominated school boards may transfer them out of their jobs. A compromise on this issue was reached as part of the final strike settlement in Newark.[4] While this was a dramatic confrontation, grievance arbitration is now curbing the discretion of numerous public officials in many routine and nonroutine matters, depending on the coverage of the contracts. The truth is that grievance arbitration, based on the principle of fairness guaranteed by final decision making by a neutral third party, is an important part of the "new public administration."

Third, unions are widening their participation in program policy making, whether or not they have this role in the contract. Many public officials are strongly opposed to contract provisions calling for joint management-union determination of program questions, such as class sizes, case loads, and number of police in patrol cars. While management should not, and legally cannot, abdicate its role in many program areas, it is obvious from recent developments, particularly in state and local government, that strong unions can influence and even determine certain program decisions even though denied such a role in the contract.

The instrument, both simple and blunt, is the "job action," threatened or actual. New York City is a good example; on repeated occasions, Mayor Lindsay and some of his department heads have insisted on their "management prerogatives" — but eventually made decisions which represent important concessions to union demands. Although it is thunderously proclaimed that management alone determines the budget, later it is quietly announced that the number of new positions requested for a particular department has been substantially increased. Management both decided — and listened to the unions!

According to one analysis, the "controversy over the establishment of an independent New York City Health and Hospitals Corporation to take over the city's decaying municipal hospital system remained insoluble until the union representing hospital workers gave its blessing — at a price in increased power for the union and its members that is not yet fully known."[5] Unions have always sought to influence decisions of this kind through lobbying and the political process, but now, despite antistrike laws, they have added the new wallop of the "job action."

Fourth, the unions have intensified their political activities. Success in collective bargaining, far from causing diminished political activity, has been accompanied by stepped-up political action to capitalize on the power of expanded union memberships and a record of success in contract settlements. Political activity coalitions are constantly forming, with doctrinal differences submerged in the interest of greater impact in lobbying and in rewarding or punishing elective officials at the polls. The alliance between the AFL-CIO-affiliated AFSCME and the NEA, with the latter's history of disdain for "labor," is a strange one, dubbed an "odd-couple" arrangement by the AFT (the NEA's big competitor), which claims that, although it also is AFL-CIO, it was not even consulted on the pact by AFSCME.

Fifth, collective bargaining settlements are substantially increasing the personal service budget and contributing to the financial crisis in government, particularly at the state and local level. While comprehensive research findings in this area are still in the preparation stage,[6] the relationship between contract settlements and soaring budgets is obvious in many places.

With large numbers of public employees, even moderate increases can raise the wage bill by hundreds of thousands of dollars. Wages, pensions, and other "fringes" accounted for 56% of New York City's $7.8 billion budget in one recent fiscal year, with rising labor costs accounting for half of the budget increase. This rise in the wage bill, in a period of declining revenues has naturally led to increased taxpayer interest in worker productivity, with management now in a better position to insist that the workers put out more. A beneficial result is that management is spurred to give greater attention to methods of evaluating program results and measuring worker productivity, whereas previously it tended to neglect these areas. At the same time, the unions, aware of the taxpayer discontent, know that they cannot expect the productivity question to be overlooked in contract negotiations.[7]

Sixth, the political environment of government makes collective bargaining different in important ways from bargaining in the private sector. While the role of "market discipline" in preventing excessive wage settlements has been exaggerated in the present era of giant companies and lessened competition, it is still true that consumers can elect to buy less expensive, nonunion-made products, or substitute products, of which many are available. The consumers of public (government) services have no such choice. Companies can move or go out of business; government agencies cannot.[8]

If this argument seems like theoretical economics not applicable today, evidence from the real world is clear, based upon the performance of principal "actors" in the political process — elective officials. When strikes in essential services are threatened or occur, chief executives and other politicians are very sensitive to the angry protests of the inconvenienced public which often hates the strikers, but the inconvenience more. The tendency is to make substantial, relatively quick concessions to the government unions. Walkouts are not very extended, and, as the private sector experience shows, it is the *long* strikes which are the hardest for the unions to win.

Private companies sometimes manage to operate during massive walkouts by using supervisors to provide at least limited service. In some governmental jurisdictions the supervisors have full collective bargaining rights (not permitted supervisors under Taft-Hartley), and they may walk out with the nonsupervisory employees or overlook slowdowns — which means they cannot be counted on to side with the top management during labor disputes.[9]

Public employee leaders like AFSCME President Jerry Wurf insist that many politicians are hostile and that the government unions do not have excessive power. This certainly is true in many parts of the country, particularly in the small towns and the rural areas. It is in the big cities with heavily unionized employees and a record of resort to strikes that the potential for excessive union power appears greatest. Those proposing solutions for public employee disputes sometimes fail to take into account these variations. New York City may be ripe for compulsory arbitration, but countless other jurisdictions do not need this last-ditch machinery.

The different environment in government does not justify denial of collective bargaining rights or even of a limited right to strike. To deny, however, the potential for undue union power in government under certain circumstances is simply to disregard the reality. The search for workable solutions in the public interest proceeds best when that reality is clearly understood and accepted.

Seventh, the decline in the power of civil service commissions, which are buffeted by forces besides the unions anyway, is continuing. The role of the commission, based on the civil service law, in recommending pay plans and revisions does not mean much when, as provided by another law, or on a de facto basis, pay and fringes are negotiated by management and union representatives. For various good reasons, the commissions, with rare exceptions, do not represent management at the bargaining table, and they usually are not in a position to influence the management stands greatly. Suffice it to say that a settlement desired by the chief executive and/or legislators will likely be concurred with by the commission, but it may not even be seriously asked for its opinion.

When collective bargaining agreements provide for final-step binding grievance arbitration, the civil service commission also loses its prestigious role as principal court of appeal for the aggrieved employee. Increasingly, important provisions of the civil service rules and regulations are negotiated along with economic benefits, which reduces the commission's policy-making role. It is not surprising that some labor relations experts, anxious to solidify management strength for dealing with the unions around the chief executive, are happy with the recommendation in the National Civil Service League's new Model Public Personnel Administration Law to abolish civil service commissions.

While the commissions decline, the position of many personnel directors is both clarified and strengthened. Frequently, they are either the chief spokesmen, or members, of the management's negotiating team, which makes it clear that they *are* part of management. The critical nature of labor relations, and their prominent role in it, give them an importance many have not had in the past. Their background for labor relations thus becomes a key consideration in their employment and training.

Eighth, the budgetary process is being affected in several ways. Negotiations and budgetary time tables should be synchronized; this is being attempted, but with not too much success since bargaining deadlocks often extend beyond budget submission and adoption dates. Somehow, chief executives and legislatures must make good estimates of the amounts needed in the budget to finance the labor contracts, so as to eliminate or reduce the need for supplementary appropriations, or for reductions-in-force or other cuts in already funded programs. Contrary to the long-expounded postulate of honesty in budgets, ways must be found to "hide" the estimated funds for the settlements in unsuspected parts of the estimates. The expectation is that the unions, if they knew the maximum amounts management would settle for, would ask for more.

RELATIVE ROLES IN THE POWER GAME

Collective bargaining in government is visibly altering the relative shares of different individuals and groups in the formulation and implementation of public policy. An agenda for research to identify these changes in selected jurisdictions is presented in Table 1. Based on this writer's analysis of kinds of changes which have occurred, a scheme of rankings is proposed for verification by researchers in different communities. The rankings show relative roles for different participants *before* and *after* the introduction of collective bargaining (CB). Since there are different phases of policy making influenced by labor relations, the rankings are separate for these phases, as defined in the footnotes in the table.

There is no precise agreement by the participants and observers as to these relative shares, even before CB, and, of course, the picture varies by place, depending upon the extent of unionization, strength of the labor movement in the area, and other factors. While civil service commissions have had important influence in recommending pay and fringe benefit plans, their greatest power has been in recommending and implementing the rules and regulations which cover all aspects of the technical personnel program. Although these rules and regulations usually require the approval of the chief executive and sometimes of the legislative body, such approval without major change is generally much easier to obtain than for recommendations in the economic benefit area. (If this assumption is wrong, its inaccuracy would be revealed by the projected research.) If the investigations in a particular community reveal that the unions have jumped in influence, not only in determinations on economic benefits but also in general personnel policy formulation, this would document one of the "impressions" in the table. Another "impression" to be tested is that the unions also have climbed up several notches in program policy implementation, but not quite as many in program policy formulation.

Undoubtedly, some of the rankings in the table of other participants such as department heads and the general public will look "wrong" to many readers; the idea, however, is to provide a usable guide for launching much-needed research in the volatile, emotion-laden area of labor relations. As to research methodology, interviewing and analysis of recorded decisions and of positions taken by the respective participants, and newspaper and other written accounts of the effective factors in the decisions

TABLE 1.
Public administration and collective bargaining: one impression of changed roles

Policies Governing Pay and Fringes		Other Personnel Policies[1]		Formulation of Program Policy[2]		Implementation of Program Policy[3]	
Before C B	After C B	Before C B	After C B	Before C B	After C B	Before C B	After C B
1. Legislature	1. Unions Chief executive	1. Legislature	1. Legislature	1. Legislature	1. Legislature	1. Chief executive	1. Chief executive
2. Chief executive	2. Legislature	2. Civil service commission	2. Unions Chief executive	2. Pressure groups (excluding unions)	2. Pressure groups (excluding unions)	2. Department heads (including budget director)	2. Department heads (including budget director)
3. Pressure groups (excluding unions)	3. Pressure groups (excluding unions)	3. Chief executive	3. Civil service commission	3. Chief executive	3. Chief executive	3. Pressure groups (excluding unions)	3. Pressure groups (including unions)
4. Unions	4. Budget director and department heads	4. Department heads	4. Department heads	4. Department heads	4. Unions	4. Legislature	4. Legislature
5. Civil service commission and budget director	5. Civil service commission	5. Pressure groups (excluding unions)	5. Pressure groups (excluding unions)	5. Unions	5. Department heads	5. Unions	5. General public
6. Department heads	6. General public	6. Unions	6. General public	6. General public	6. General public	6. General public	
7. General public		7. General public					

1. Recruitment, promotion, transfer, lay-off, reinstatement, service rating, training, disciplinary, and other personnel processes.
2. Determination of the content of legislation dealing with substantive programs of government.
3. Policies made in carrying out substantive program authorized by the legislature.

would be used. While the influence process is obscure in some aspects, there is plenty of information in the hearing and other records of civil service commissions, and in the briefs and published statements of unions and taxpayer and other groups. The collective contracts themselves will provide much of the data. Quite a few insightful public officials are available to contribute opinions to the "before" and "after" comparisons; the "before" is not so long ago.

THE PUBLIC INTEREST QUESTION

When, in the flush of their successes of the 1960s, some public employee leaders proclaimed the doctrine that collective contracts supersede provisions in existing laws and regulations, the "public interest" question came to the fore in an unprecedented way. If the price of bilateralism in determination of employment conditions was to be the shunting aside of the public and its legislative representatives in such decisions, then the net impact would be less democracy in the total political system.

Worries on this score have since lessened; as the result of court decisions, the resistance of appointed and elected officials, and a modification of the unions' own stand on this matter, the agreements generally are not wiping out laws and regulations.[10] It is now the *process* of collective bargaining in government which causes much of the concern about the public interest.

In an era of great pressures to reform existing institutions and make them "open," to some people the collective negotiations now taking place in government are unduly secretive. Too often the final "package," announced by management and union representatives after a long "blackout" period during which the press and the public are told very little, represents a very important commitment of community resources about which even legislators have had nothing to say.

Abe Raskin, the labor editor of the *New York Times,* knows that an essential element of private sector collective bargaining is closed negotiating sessions, but he and others believe that the public should be told in detail about management and union stands on proposals by mediators. Since the negotiations continue or resume after mediators intervene and make proposals, Raskin's position basically is that collective bargaining in government is different and requires divulgences to the public. "The people of New York are entitled to know what they are being asked to pay and what increased efficiency they can expect to get in return — before the deal is made, not after."[11]

Raskin may be wrong about making public mediators' recommendations, but his argument that the full costs, present and future, of settlements should be revealed to the public is unassailable. Management has sometimes been able to reduce the unions' demands for increased wages and other benefits by agreeing to liberal increases in pensions, to be funded, and therefore paid for, by the taxpayers at some future time.

Frank P. Zeidler, former mayor of Milwaukee, has suggested the possibility of public referenda on proposed contracts, just as on bond issues.[12] If the Rhode Island court interpretation is accepted, namely, that private arbitrators become public officials when they issue awards fixing government salaries, then it can be argued that there is clear justification for giving the public the opportunity to vote on arbitral awards and proposed settlements.

While collective bargaining in government has in recent years moved closer to the industrial model, there are many unresolved perplexing questions of how to modify that model to meet the special needs of government. The view is spreading that mediators, fact-finders, arbitrators, and the personnel of supposedly "neutral" labor relations agencies favor the "private" interests of the unions over those of the general public. The challenge is to create, in all necessary detail, a special kind of collective bargaining for government which will give sufficient protection to the public interest and thus allay these fears.

THE BALANCE SHEET

The tendency is either to be for the unions or against, but the picture is a mixed one, as is so often the case with complicated developments. Our conclusions are:

1. Collective bargaining has proved itself a salutary check on public employer arbitrariness and paternalism. No review group analyzing the experience under existing collective bargaining programs in government has recommended their termination. Whatever the shortcomings found, the desirability of collective bargaining has been upheld by such groups as proved in practice.
2. Collective bargaining is an excellent antidote for the evils of bureaucracy. The employee feels that he counts for something through the strength of his union: now management *must* listen. It is possible that the unions have done more to alleviate the much-discussed conflict between organization and individual needs than any other force or technique.
3. Curbs on excessive union power *are* needed, and, in some places, compulsory arbitration may be the answer.

4. The difficulties in financing contract settlements have made the need for tax reform very clear; indeed, union leaders with vision are pushing efforts for such reform. They have a common interest with local officials in ending the heavy reliance on property taxes which has caused the virtual bankruptcy of so many cities.

5. Legislatures must assert their role, else chief executives and the unions may relegate them to an increasingly minor role in labor relations. Since the collective bargaining process does contribute to executive power, this is another point at which the modern legislature should hold firm against encroachment on its powers.

6. Civic groups and individual citizens can get in the act by developing strong positions in advance on contract negotiations. At present, they are usually silent and inactive while public management and the unions busily negotiate in private. Surely there is a way for the public to be heard before it is too late; the trouble is that too few people have as yet figured out when and how to inject themselves effectively into the changed decision-making processes.

There is no inexorable force which will make collective bargaining turn out one way or another, nor are the developments so swift as to make it problematic that humans can shape the future picture. Dramatic as the unionism is, its significance has not yet been appreciated by enough of the public or, for that matter, of public management.

Notes

1. *Labor Management Relations in the Federal Service, Executive Order 11491 As Amended by Executive Order 11616 of August 26, 1971, Reports and Recommendations, United States Federal Labor Relations Council* (Washington, D.C.: The Council, 1971), p. 38.
2. See George R. La Noue and Marvin R. Pilo, "Teacher Unions and Educational Accountability," in Robert H. Connery and William V. Farr (eds.), *Unionization of Municipal Employees* (New York: The Academy of Political Science, Columbia University, 1971), p. 147.
3. Jack Stieber, "State, local unions pass industry and still going," *LMRS Newsletter*, Vol. 2, No. 7 (July 1971), p. 1.
4. See Fox Butterfield, "At Root of Newark Teacher Strike: Race and Power," *New York Times*, April 8, 1971.
5. John M. Leavens *et al*, "City Personnel: The Civil Service and Municipal Unions," in pamphlet published for Institute of Public Administration in New York by Sage Publications, p. 17.
6. The Brookings Institution will publish a monograph on this subject.

7. On educational productivity, see Myron Lieberman, "Professors Unite!" *Harper's Magazine*, Vol. 243, No. 1457 (October 1971), p. 69.

8. See Harry H. Wellington and Ralph K. Winter, Jr., "The Limits of Collective Bargaining in Public Employment," *The Yale Law Journal*, Vol. 78, No. 7 (June 1969); and John F. Burton, Jr., and Charles Krider, "The Role and Consequences of Strikes by Public Employees," and Wellington and Winter, "More on Strikes by Public Employees," *The Yale Law Journal*, Vol. 79, No. 3 (January 1970).

9. See Anthony C. Russo, "Management's View of the New York City Experience," in Connery and Farr, *op. cit.*, pp. 87-88.

10. See Felix A. Nigro, "Collective Bargaining and the Merit System," *ibid.*, pp. 55-67.

11. *New York Times*, editorial page, March 19, 1971.

12. Frank P. Zeidler, *New Roles for Public Officials in Labor Relations*, Public Employee Relations Library, No. 23 (Chicago: Public Personnel Association), p. 20.

3

FINANCING URBAN GOVERNMENT

Of the many problems urban administrators face, perhaps the most fundamental is the problem of financing urban government. As David Bernstein points out in "Financing the City Government," it "colors all the others."[1] In recent years expenditures for more and better public services have skyrocketed, as depicted in Table 1. Since 1966, educational expenses have risen over 80 percent, while police protection expenditures have jumped nearly 95 percent.[2] Public welfare costs have shot up 140 percent. Housing and urban renewal expenditures have increased over 80 percent as have health and hospital costs. In fiscal 1971-72, total general expenditures for all cities in the United States were $35.7 billion. This figure represents an 85 percent increase from fiscal 1966-67 when expenditures totalled $19.3 billion.

City revenues have simply not kept pace. In fiscal 1971-72, general city revenues came to 34.9 billion, an 80.1 percent increase from the $19.3 billion collected in fiscal 1966-67. Of that amount, however, city taxes accounted for only $17.1 billion or 49 percent of total general revenues. Intergovernmental revenues provided $11.4 billion or 32.7 percent. Cities have become increasingly dependent on federal, state, or intercity revenues for their financial support. David Bernstein has described their plight rather well: "The basic financial problem of the city government is that its present growth rate of expenditures is two or three times that of its revenues. The city [has] managed to finance its recently soaring costs [only] by huge infusions of state and federal aid."[3] The reasons for the inability of city revenues to keep pace with increasing expenditures must be explored. They place obvious constraints on what urban administration can hope to accomplish.

TABLE 1

Amount, Distribution and Percent Increase of Expenditures by Functional Programs in all Cities in the United States Fiscal 1966-67 ———— Fiscal 1971-72

Expenditure By Function	1966-67	%	1967-68	%	1968-69	%	1969-70	%	1970-71	%	1971-72	%	Total % increase
General expenditures	19,333	100	21,563	100	24,500	100	27,682	100	31,947	100	35,697	100	85.1
Education	3,194	16.57	3,405	15.8	3,978	16.2	4,548	16.4	5,242	16.4	5,827	16.3	82.4
Highways	2,025	10.52	2,142	9.9	2,288	9.3	2,499	9.0	2,664	8.3	2,768	7.7	36.7
Public welfare	1,265	6.56	1,739	8.1	2,145	8.8	2,215	8.0	2,688	8.4	3,031	8.5	139.6
Hospitals	1,084	5.37	1,219	5.6	1,289	5.3	1,464	5.3	1,780	5.6	2,089	5.8	101.4
Health	265	1.37	322	1.5	415	1.7	480	1.7	544	1.7	684	1.9	158.1
Police protection	2,046	10.61	2,261	10.5	2,604	10.6	2,994	10.8	3,471	10.9	3,942	11.0	92.7
Fire protection	1,302	6.75	1,400	6.5	1,565	6.4	1,762	6.3	1,996	6.2	2,208	6.2	69.6
Sewerage	1,118	5.8	1,188	5.5	1,263	5.1	1,458	5.3	1,767	5.5	1,964	5.5	75.7
Sanitation	793	4.1	863	4.0	948	3.9	1,095	3.9	1,243	3.9	1,334	3.7	68.2
Parks-Recreation	914	4.7	1,003	4.7	1,133	4.6	1,306	4.7	1,439	4.5	1,571	4.4	279.5
Housing-Urban Renewal	815	4.2	948	4.4	991	4.0	1,154	4.2	1,442	4.5	1,475	4.1	80.1
Airports	201	1.04	276	1.3	360	1.5	435	1.6	461	1.4	534	1.5	165.7
Water (Transport and Terminals)	61	.32	84	.4	104	.42	121	.44	157	.5	164	.46	168.9
Parking facility	130	.67	94	.43	125	.5	147	.53	145	.45	154	.43	18.5
Library	305	1.6	341	1.6	370	1.5	407	1.5	445	1.4	465	1.3	52.5
Financial Administration	333	1.7	361	1.7	408	1.7	457	1.7	515	1.6	565	1.6	69.7

Source: U. S. Bureau of Census, *City Government Finances in 1971-72* (Washington, D. C.: Government Printing Office, 1973) p. 5 and *City Government Finances in 1970-71* (Washington, D. C.: Government Printing Office, 1972) p. 5.

The most important source of city revenue is the property tax. In fiscal 1971-72, it accounted for $11 billion or 31.5 percent of all general revenues. Property tax revenues have shown an annual increase in terms of the absolute amounts collected. However, in terms of the percentage of total revenue, property taxes have declined while intergovernmental revenues have increased. Since the percentage of total revenue generated by sales and gross receipts taxes (9.1 percent in fiscal 1971-72) has remained relatively stable, the percentage of total revenue provided by taxes has declined — from 54.4 percent in fiscal 1966-67 to 49 percent in fiscal 1971-72. This has prompted many cities to become increasingly interested in developing new rate structures. Unfortunately, however, a number of factors limit their tax options. To begin with, cities are limited in their taxing schemes by what might be called horizontal competition.[4] As they strive to attract new business and increase their tax base, they are forced to keep their tax rates competitive with one another. Cities are also limited by multiple taxation, where the same tax base is taxed more than once, either by the same or different levels of government. A good example of multiple taxation is the property tax, where both state and local governments impose a tax rate on the same property base. Multiple taxation is not undesirable in itself, but it can lead to economic waste through duplication of governmental enforcement, and to inequity in the distribution of resources. Still another factor that limits cities and their tax policies is the tax rate itself. Should the tax be progressive, proportionate, or regressive? Regressive taxes — like the sales tax — are the most easily collected and for that reason are often preferred. But, most state and local taxes are already regressive. The cities must consider if they wish to add still another.

These factors, and others such as the enforcement of tax collection and the problem of tax shifting, have limited the revenue options of cities and have made them increasingly dependent on outside help — i.e., on intergovernmental revenues. Intergovernmental revenues now constitute the second most important source of revenue for urban governments. In fiscal 1970-71, they contributed $11.4 billion or 32.7 percent of total city revenues. State governmental transfers — typically in the form of tax sharing — accounted for the largest proportion of intergovernmental revenues, providing 25 percent of general revenues or $8.4 billion. Federal governmental transfers — principally through categorical grants-in-aid — totaled only $2.5 billion; however, this figure represented an increase of 21.5 percent since 1966. This dramatic increase in federal aid, and the increase in federal control this aid has allowed, has prompted a vigorous debate on how state and especially local governments are to be financed. This debate has centered on the question of revenue sharing.

On October 20, 1972, President Nixon signed into law the State and Local Fiscal Assistance Act of 1972, more commonly known as revenue sharing. This legislation was a key component of President Nixon's program for a New Federalism. It directs that a total of $30.2 billion be distributed to states and localities over a period of five years. Two-thirds of this amount is to go directly to local governments. Two formulas for determining the allocation of funds to the states and cities can be used: one is based on five factors — population, urbanization, per capita income, income tax collections, and general tax effort — and provides larger revenues to more urbanized states; the other is based on three factors — population, general tax effort, and per capita income — and favors less populous, rural states. These revenues may be used for "priority expenditures only" which include police and fire protection, environmental protection, public transportation, health, recreation, libraries, social services for the poor and aged, and financial administration. Revenue sharing funds cannot be used as matching funds for federal grants-in-aid; neither can they be used for welfare or education as both of these functions are already heavily supported with federal monies. Revenue sharing under this Act does not replace any existing grant-in-aid program. It does, however, provide states and communities with new unrestricted revenues. These key features are explored at greater length in "The Beginnings of a Balanced Fiscal System," by the Advisory Commission on Intergovernmental Relations.

Revenue sharing represents more than simply a new means for providing much needed revenues for states and localities. It represents a "dramatic alteration" in the pattern of federal-state-local relationships that have developed since the New Deal,[5] contributing a "true landmark in American federalism."[6] As President Nixon observed in his 1972 State of the Union Address, revenue sharing "can help reverse what has been the flow of power and resources toward Washington by sending power and resources back to the States, to the communities, and to the people."[7]

This devolution of political power has generated considerable controversy, however. Proponents of revenue sharing claim that this decentralization will result in more effective state and local decision making. Thus, President Nixon declared while signing the revenue sharing bill that "What America wants today at the state level, at the city level . . . is not bigger government but better government, and that is what this [revenue sharing] is all about."[8] It can improve government, revenue-sharing proponents argue, without increasing the size of government. This can be achieved in several ways. First, revenue sharing can make new revenues available to states and localities to be used in solving their problems. Second, it can enable state and local units of government to be more responsive to public needs, since decisions can now be made by local officials at the local level and not by federal grant officers in Washington. And third, it can allow state and local governmental units to concentrate on making and implementing decisions rather than on meeting administrative requirements established by Washington. The end result, proponents insist, is a federal system with dynamic and responsible units of government at all levels.

Critics of revenue sharing challenge these claims. They contend that revenue sharing and its decentralization of decision making is generally destructive, not supportive, of "better government." To begin with, they point out that the greater the scope of conflict over a decision, the more likely that the views of all segments of the community will be heard and taken into account and the more likely the decision ultimately reached will be in the public interest.[9] Revenue sharing restricts rather than expands the scope of decision making. As a result, the critics claim, it is likely to result in a reversal of many advances made by minority groups during the 1960s. As Michael Reagan contends:

[P]erhaps the major defect of the revenue sharing concept is that it moves us back to the level of separate state political cultures . . . as the context-setting environment in which public expenditure decisions will be made. In a number of states, the most obvious immediate impact of such a movement would be to return power to state-local officials for whom racial discrimination is still a wholly acceptable premise of public policy.[10]

Second, critics of revenue sharing argue that this decentralized decision-making process together with the lack of restrictions on the use of revenue sharing funds will result in the use of these funds for hardware-oriented items and not for essential but politically unpopular programs with limited clientele such as health and social services.[11] Third, critics also maintain that revenue sharing provides inadequate audit and control mechanisms and that, unlike categorical grants-in-aid, it fails to extend to local governments any technical or administrative skills. And, fourth, they fear that revenue sharing will encourage local irresponsibility by divorcing the onus of raising revenue from the propensity for spending it. These arguments convince the critics of revenue sharing that, far from "improving" local government, revenue sharing will corrupt it.

While controversy rages over the merits and demerits of revenue sharing, cities have had to make initial decisions about how these funds will be allocated. David A. Caputo and Richard L. Cole have investigated the impact these funds have had on the expenditure decisions of cities and on the procedures they use to reach these decisions.[12] They surveyed all cities with 1970 populations of 50,000 and over. Two hundred twelve of the 409 cities surveyed responded. Perhaps the most important finding of their survey is that cities have tended to concentrate allocation of revenue sharing funds in five expenditure categories: environmental protection, law enforcement, street and road repair, fire prevention, and parks and recreation. These categories account for over 50 percent of the total allocations. The demographical and political characteristics of a city influence revenue sharing decisions somewhat. Thus, cities with over 250,000 population are more likely to allocate revenue sharing funds for public safety and transportation, while smaller cities are more inclined to use these funds for tax relief. Geographically, cities in the South are more likely than others to use these funds for street and road repair. Suburbs generally allocate a greater percentage of their funds for parks and recreation than central cities. Mayor-city council cities with partisan ward elections tend to spend most of their funds for public safety and tax relief. However, despite these differences, the initial revenue sharing decisions of American cities are more approximately characterized by their similarities. As Caputo and Cole observe:

Regardless of demographic or political characteristics, most cities spent the largest proportion of their revenue sharing money in the areas of environmental protection, law enforcement, street and road repairs, fire prevention, and parks and recreation. Clearly, in all classifications of cities, social service areas received only a very small proportion of initial revenue sharing funds.[13]

This initial pattern of allocation of revenue sharing funds will only add to the controversy surrounding revenue sharing. The same can be said for Edward C. Banfield's "Revenue Sharing in Theory and Practice," where he contends that cities are not so much unable as unwilling to confront the financial problems that beset them. They would much rather use federal revenues than their own to support public services at high and rising levels. They could, however, if they had to. As Banfield notes in *The Unheavenly City,* rarely if ever does a mayor who declares that his city must have federal aid mean that without it his city will necessarily force some taxpayers into poverty. What such a mayor really means is that the citizens of his city hate to pay taxes and by crying poverty, perhaps he can shift the bill from them to someone else.[14] Banfield does not deny that cities should receive financial aid. However, he continues, that is not the question. The real question is, in what amount and on what principle of distribution should they be aided?

Revenue sharing will certainly aid in the financing of urban government. However, even with revenue sharing serious problems for urban administration remain. One such problem is posed in *San Antonio Inde-*

pendent School District v. *Rodriguez*[15] — does the Equal Protection Clause of the Fourteenth Amendment of the United States Constitution impose restrictions on local governments in terms of how they choose to finance their public services and at what level? *Rodriguez* involved an attack on the Texas system of financing public education, a system which relies heavily on local property taxes. The targets of the attack were the substantial interdistrict disparities in per-pupil expenditures which result primarily from the differences in taxable property values among the districts. The appellees in this class action suit were Mexican-American parents of children attending schools in the Edgewood Independent School District in San Antonio. They sued on behalf of children of poor families residing in districts having low property tax bases, claiming that these disparities favor the affluent and thereby constitute a denial of equal protection of the laws. The Supreme Court, in a decision written by Justice Lewis F. Powell, rejected appellee's contentions. As the Court noted:

This case represents far more than a challenge to the manner in which Texas provides for the education of its children. We have here nothing less than a direct attack on the way in which Texas has chosen to raise and disburse state and local tax revenues. We are asked to condemn the State's judgment in conferring on political subdivisions the power to tax local property to supply revenues for local interests. In so doing, appellees would have the Court intrude in an area in which it has traditionally deferred to state legislatures.[16]

The Court refused to "direct the States either to alter drastically the present system or to throw out the property tax altogether in favor of some other form of taxation." However, only five justices so refused. Four other justices would have used the Equal Protection Clause to restrict the means by which state and local governments finance their services. The issue remains very much unsettled and, as a consequence, persists as a problem that will attend the financing of urban government in the future.

Notes

1. David Bernstein, "Financing the City Government," *Proceedings of the Academy of Political Science,* Vol. XXIX, No. 4 (1969), pp. 75–89.
2. U.S. Bureau of the Census, *City Government Finances in 1971-1972* (Washington, D.C.: Government Printing Office, 1973). Table 1, Summary of City Government

Finances: 1971-72 and Prior Periods, p. 5. As this is being written statistics for the fiscal year 1970-72 are the most recent available. All of the statistics found in this discussion come from this source.

3. Bernstein, *op. cit.*, p. 75.
4. Urban Data Service, Stanley M. Wolfson, *Economic Characteristics and Trends in Municipal Finances* (Washington, D.C.: International City Management Association, Vol. 4, No. 11, November 1972), pp. 2-3. The following discussion relies heavily on this source.
5. Urban Data Service, David A. Caputo and Richard L. Cole, *General Revenue Sharing: Initial Decisions* (Washington, D.C.: International City Management Association, Vol. 5, No. 12, (December 1973), p. 1.
6. Thomas R. Dye, *Politics in States and Communities* (Englewood Cliffs, N.J.: Prentice-Hall, Inc., 1973), p. 60.
7. See *1972 Congressional Quarterly Almanac* (Washington, D.C.: Congressional Quarterly, 1072), p. 9-A for the full text of this message.
8. *Washington Post*, October 20, 1972.
9. See especially E. E. Schattschneider, *The Semi-Sovereign People* (New York: Holt, Rinehart, 1961).
10. Michael D. Reagan, *The New Federalism* (New York: Oxford University Press, 1972), pp. 126-127.
11. Caputo and Cole, *op. cit.*, p. 12 The following discussion relies heavily on this source.
12. *Ibid.*, pp. 1-16.
13. *Ibid.*, pp. 13-14.
14. Edward C. Banfield, *The Unheavenly City: The Nature and Future of Our Urban Crisis* (Boston: Little, Brown and Co., 1970), p. 9.
15. 411 U.S. 1 (1973).
16. 411 U.S. at 40.

THE BEGINNINGS OF A BALANCED FISCAL SYSTEM

In 1972, the nation's fiscal system began in a significant way to acquire the elements of balance and flexibility that this Commission has advocated for several years.

The most visible — and perhaps most far-reaching — step was the enactment of revenue sharing, which will transfer more than $30 billion in federal funds to state capitols, county courthouses, and city halls over the next five years with few "strings" attached as to how the money can be spent.

This landmark legislation was signed into law by President Nixon on October 20 in Independence Hall, Philadelphia. It implemented a recommendation adopted by the ACIR in 1967 to redress a general power imbalance that worked in favor of the federal government and against states and localities, hence against a strong decentralized form of government.

* * *

General revenue sharing became a reality more than three years after it was proposed by President Nixon, five years after it was recommended by this Commission and nearly a decade after the concept was put forth by economists Walter Heller and Joseph Pechman. The first "no strings" checks were mailed by the U.S. Treasury to state and local governments on December 6.

Reprinted from *Fourteenth Annual Report: Striking a Better Balance* (Washington, D.C.: U.S. Government Printing Office, 1973) pp. 4-9.

THE BATTLE FOR ENACTMENT

Despite its very considerable public exposure, revenue sharing did not have an easy road to passage. Hearings before the House Ways and Means Committee revealed divisions on the philosophy of revenue sharing, as well as on some very fundamental questions inherent in the program — including the basis for distributing federal money among and within states, the "no strings" provision and the permanent appropriation. These divisions were overcome, however, and the milestone State and Local Fiscal Assistance Act of 1972 cleared the Ways and Means Committee in late April. It was adopted by the full House on June 22.

As passed by the House, the legislation differed in several key respects from the administration bill and the 1967 recommendation of this Commission. Initial Senate debate was complicated by the fact that the Finance Committee regarded reform of the welfare system as its top legislative priority. When the emphasis was shifted to revenue sharing, debate tended to focus mainly on the issue of distributing federal money among the states, and a formula different from that of the House-passed version was adopted.

This difference in allocation formulas was a crucial issue facing the Conference Committee. It was resolved by using both methods to determine the distribution among states and applying that formula which yielded the largest total for a particular state. With the dual formula alternative, passage of the legislation was easily secured — by a vote of 281 to 86 in the House on October 12 and by a margin of 59 to 19 in the Senate on the following day. The measure was then signed by the President seven days later.

KEY FEATURES

In the most basic fiscal terms, revenue sharing is the distribution of federal revenues to state and local government officials.

For what?

One of the major features of revenue sharing is the wide latitude it gives to state and local government officials in spending decisions. It provides the flexibility to maximize the discretion of state and local officials in setting spending priorities with a minimum of federal regulations and red tape.

State officials are free to spend their revenue sharing allotments on virtually anything they choose. The only restriction on their spending authority — one that is also applicable to local governments — is that revenue sharing moneys *cannot* be used, either directly or indirectly, as the state or local share required to match other federal funds received for grant-in-aid programs.

Local governments, in addition to this specific prohibition, face a very general restriction in that revenue sharing money is to be spent only for "priority expenditures." Such priority expenditures are quite broadly defined, however, and encompass ordinary and necessary maintenance expenditures for (a) public safety — including law enforcement, fire protection and building code enforcement; (b) environmental protection —including sewage disposal, sanitation and pollution abatement; (c) public transportation — including transit systems and streets and roads; (d) health; (e) recreation; (f) libraries; (g) social services for the poor or aged; and (h) financial administration. Priority expenditures also include ordinary and necessary capital expenditures authorized by law.

How much?

Revenue sharing calls for a total of $30.1 billion to be turned over to state and local governments during a five-year period, one-third to state governments and two-thirds to localities. Annually, the sums are $5.3 billion (1972), $5.975 billion (1973), $6.125 billion (1974), $6.275 billion (1975), and $6.425 billion (1976).

In the first year's payments, the amount distributed to state governments generally ranged from 1.5 to 2.0 percent of state government expenditures — the extremes being 0.4 percent in Alaska and 2.8 percent in Mississippi. In per-capita terms, the average state government share was slightly under $9, with most states in the range between $7 and $12. The per-capita share for the first year varied, however, from $13.12 in Mississippi and $13.07 in West Virginia to $6.80 in Missouri and $6.49 in Ohio.

The total local government share for the first year averaged slightly more than $17 per capita. Among the one hundred largest cities, payments per capita generally ranged between $12 and $24, with Anaheim, California, receiving as little as $6.86 per capita and New Orleans as much as $27.93 per capita. Some of these variations may be adjusted in future applications of the distribution formulas.

The revenue sharing funds are drawn from a permanent five-year appropriation, placed in a trust fund, over which the Senate and House Appropriations Committees have no control.

Although the amounts involved are scheduled to grow year by year for the five-year period, the legislation does not provide a permanent source of funds to state and local officials. Yet, because the legislation covers a five-year period and is both an authorization and appropriation act, it does provide a high degree of certainty — an essential ingredient that will undoubtedly facilitate budgetary planning by state and local governments. To place this legislation under the authority of the Appropriations Committees — an effort that was made and probably will be renewed in the future — would not per se destroy the idea of revenue sharing. Nonetheless, the annual appropriation procedure might seriously erode the degree of certainty provided by the present legislation.

To whom?

Federal revenues are made available to all state governments and to nearly 38,000 general-purpose units of local government, regardless of their population size. In order to distribute the funds among these governments, the U.S. Treasury first determined how the total entitlement, the $5.3-billion total for 1972, would be allocated among the states.

The act calls for two methods of dividing the revenue sharing funds — a three-factor and a five-factor formula — with the formula yielding the higher state-local total to be applied. The two formulas use varying combinations of state population, urbanized population, relative personal income of state residents, state income taxes, and general state tax effort to distribute the funds.

After the amount to be allocated to each state area is computed, the state government receives one-third.

The remaining two-thirds, the local share, is distributed initially among county areas within the state on the basis of population, general tax effort, and relative income for each county area. The local area allocation is then further distributed among local units of government. County governments share in the local area allocation on the basis of their adjusted taxes (taxes other than for education and employer and employee contributions to social insurance or retirement funds) as a proportion of adjusted taxes for the county and other local governments in that county area. If the county area includes one or more township governments, the township share is calculated in the same manner as the county government's share. The remaining money allocated to the county area is then distributed among all other general units of local government on the basis of population, tax effort, and relative income.

These formulas for the division of funds among local governments are subject to certain safeguards. For example, no local government may receive more in revenue sharing money than half of its adjusted taxes plus intergovernmental aid. Moreover, in per-capita terms, no local government may receive less than 20 percent — or more than 145 percent — of the average per-capita distribution to local governments in the state. Those local governments, other than counties, that would be eligible for less than $200 and those that waive their entitlement get nothing. Their shares are added to the entitlement of their county government.

FEDERAL COLLECTION OF STATE INCOME TAXES

Seemingly destined to a position of relative obscurity, Title II of the State and Local Fiscal Assistance Act of 1972 provides for federal collection of state income taxes. This step toward tax coordination, recommended in 1965 by this Commission, constitutes yet another element in what is gradually emerging as a concern for developing an integrated fiscal system of federal, state, and local government taxation and expenditure programs.

The legislation requires that state income taxes closely conform to the federal tax base — and in practically all cases this will necessitate changes in state income tax laws if the federal collection process is to be activated. Moreover, these provisions do not go into effect until January 1, 1974, and then only if at least two states having in the aggregate 5 percent or more of the federal individual income tax returns filed during 1972 elect to seek federal collection of their income taxes.

SOCIAL SERVICE CEILING

Title III of the Conference compromise on revenue sharing placed a lid of $2.5 billion annually on federal contributions to the previously open-ended social service program. With the following exceptions — child care, family planning, and services to the mentally retarded, to drug addicts or alcoholics and to children under foster care — not more than 10 percent of the federal grant can be used to provide services for individuals who are not recipients of, or applicants for, welfare aid or assistance.

These federal funds are distributed among states on the basis of population. As a result of the ceiling, 23 states and the District of Columbia will receive less federal aid than they had estimated they would spend in fiscal 1973 under the open-ended program. Thus, some states and cities will have to curtail their spending plans for social services and all of the program agencies will have to account for use of the money in greater detail.

SOME LINGERING QUESTIONS

The State and Local Fiscal Assistance Act of 1972 is a major step forward in intergovernmental fiscal relations. It provides substantial federal revenues for the use of state and local officials with a high degree of certainty and with very few restrictions as to how the money may be used. Because of these features, state and local officials are strengthened in both revenue raising and decision-making. This legislation provides a very definite tilt in the balance of fiscal federalism — away from centralized bureaucratic policy making and toward a neater matching of needs and resources at the state and local levels.

Nonetheless, some unanswered questions remain — questions that are applicable both to the present and to the future of the revenue sharing program.

A precise matching of state and local needs with resources may, in fact, be the impossible dream of intergovernmental finance. While the ideal may be unattainable, the legislation makes a rough, but arbitrary stab at meshing the two. The act simply assumes a one-third state and two-thirds local division of fiscal and functional responsibilities, regardless of the existing division of these responsibilities between individual states and their local sectors.

Some imprecision also is likely to result from the fact that all states and general-purpose units of local government are eligible to share in the federal revenue. Since there is no population cutoff, funds will be allocated to all but the very smallest governmental units — funds that otherwise might have been available for other governmental units such as the core cities, where problems are more interrelated and expensive. The use of the 20 percent minimum and 145 percent maximum bounds (of the average per capita distribution for the state) for each local government indicates that the formula per se may not get the money where the biggest problems are.

Indeed, the provision of an alternative state plan further suggests the possibility that local needs and resources may not be fully meshed, but it provides a mechanism for resolution.

Consistent with the few-strings approach, revenue sharing provides no conditions regarding the modernization or consolidation of the existing governmental structure. Yet it must be recognized that revenue sharing is not a neutral instrument with regard to these objectives. Since all general units of local government are eligible to participate without regard to population size, the unwanted effect will be, at least to some extent, to freeze the existing governmental structure and to prop it up, without regard to its viability.

POTENTIAL PROBLEMS

More basic to the future of the revenue sharing program, however, are two potential difficulties.

The program as adopted gives very wide scope to the uses to which state and local governments may put the federal funds. The ability of state and local officials to solve their own problems will determine whether this trust becomes one of the great strengths of the program, or a future weakness.

Differences of opinion over priorities are bound to cause some controversy — particularly between those seeking program enhancement and officials who plan to use the funds to reduce property taxes. Critics of revenue sharing will undoubtedly search for frivolous expenditure programs and evidence of graft and corruption to make a mockery of the priority expenditure designation. Some "horror stories" will surely emerge and too many such instances would seriously erode the element of trust that revenue sharing presently embodies. However, state and local officials are bound to be on their guard against such possibilities and the glare of unwanted publicity may be a sufficient deterrent.

Yet revenue sharing shifts more than money and power to the state-local sector; it also shifts more responsibility. Failure to make progress, to get the job done, could ultimately lead to heightened disenchantment with government and federalism in general and the state and local sector in particular.

A second basic concern for the future of revenue sharing is its relationship to the categorical grant system. In the minds of most of its supporters, including this Commission, general revenue sharing was conceived as additive to — not a total substitute for — categorical and block grants. The myriad categorical grant programs obviously have their defects, but the solution to such problems rests in reforming and consolidating the categorical grants — not in merely replacing them with revenue sharing.

Revenue sharing has, in fact, come. The program means additional federal revenues for state-local use, along with increased state-local decision-making powers and heightened responsibilities for state and local government officials. The future of the program, and indeed of federalism itself, rests with the proponents of revenue sharing — who now become the major participants in making it work.

EDWARD C. BANFIELD

REVENUE SHARING IN THEORY AND PRACTICE

How one evaluates revenue sharing will depend upon what one takes the central issues to be. Oddly enough, what must appear to many people to be *the issue* — namely, how to keep the cities and states from going bankrupt — is not properly speaking an issue at all.

Mayor Lindsay has long tried to give the impression that catastrophe lies just ahead unless the federal government provides "massive" additional financial support. Recently other political leaders have been saying the same thing. "Countless cities across the nation," Mayor Gibson of Newark told the press recently, are "rapidly approaching bankruptcy." Governor Rockefeller, after having been informed of the administration's latest plans, remarked that the federal government must do even more to prevent the states and cities from "virtually falling to pieces." Meanwhile Governor Cahill of New Jersey was telling a joint session of his legislature that "the sovereign states of this nation can no longer supply the funds to meet urgent and necessary needs of our citizens, and institutions and our cities." A day or two later Senator Humphrey in a single sentence made two of the most outstanding rhetorical contributions. The cities, he said, are "mortally sick and getting sicker" and the states "are in a state of chronic fiscal crisis."

In fact, the revenue-sharing idea was, at its inception, the product of exactly such forebodings. Back in 1964, when Walter Heller and Joseph Pechman proposed it, many well-informed people expected that state and local governments would soon be in serious financial difficulties while at the same time the federal government would be enjoying a large and

Reprinted by permission of *The Public Interest*, No. 23 (Spring 1971), pp. 33–45, Copyright © by National Affairs, Inc., 1971.

rapidly growing surplus. The war in Vietnam was expected to end soon and, if federal income tax levels remained unchanged, the normal growth of the economy and the increase of population would yield large increases in revenue year after year. Thus, while the federal government fattened, the state and local governments would grow leaner and leaner. Because of rising birthrates and population movements, the demands made upon states and localities for all sorts of services, but especially schools, would increase much more rapidly than would their ability to raise revenue. Whereas the federal government depends largely upon the personal income tax, the yield of which increases automatically with incomes, state and local governments depend mainly upon sales and property taxes, which are inelastic. This being the outlook, it seemed sensible to make up the expected deficit of the state and local governments from the expected surplus of the federal government. Heller and Pechman proposed to do this by giving the states a claim on a fixed percentage of federal taxable income, subject to the requirement that a fair amount "pass through" the states directly to the cities. The idea quickly won wide acceptance. Both political parties adopted revenue-sharing planks, and in 1968 some 90 revenue-sharing bills were introduced in Congress.

What happened, however, was not what was expected. Federal expenditures rose unexpectedly (defense spending was cut, but increases in the numbers of persons eligible for social security together with higher payment levels and unexpectedly high costs for Medicaid took up the slack) and, because of the recession, tax collections fell off. Instead of a surplus the federal government faced a deficit. State and local governments meanwhile fared better than expected. Legislatures and electorates were surprisingly ready to approve new taxes and higher rates. In 1967, for example, the states increased their tax collections by 15%, and in 1968 they increased them by another 15%. Cities also found it possible to raise more revenue than they had expected. Between 1948 and 1969 state-local expenditures increased in real terms from 6.7% of Gross National Product to about 10%. For some time they have been the fastest growing sector of the economy. The credit rating of the cities has improved, not worsened. With respect to the fifty largest cities, only three (New York, Boston, and Baltimore) received lower ratings from Moody's Investment Service in 1971 than in 1940 and many (including Chicago, Los Angeles, and Cleveland) received higher ones.

Dangerous as even short-run predictions in these matters have proved to be, it therefore seems safe to say that no "fiscal crisis" looms for most states and cities. In 1975, according to an estimate cited in a recent article by Richard Musgrave and A. Mitchell Polinsky, state and local expenditures will reach $119 billion. Assuming that federal aid increases

at no more than the normal rate of recent years, this will leave a short-fall
of $17 billion. Eleven billion of this will be made up from normal borrow-
ing. The remaining deficit of $5 billion, Musgrave and Polinsky say,
"could be met by a 5% increase in tax rates at the state-local level, an
increase which seems well within the reach of state-local governments . . ."
As more and more state governments adopt income tax laws, their revenues will be less dependent upon the vagaries of legislatures and electorates. Moreover, thanks to the recent decline in the birthrate, the principal
item of state-local expense — schooling — will for at least a decade be
considerably less than had been expected.

INABILITY OR UNWILLINGNESS?

The "fiscal crisis" issue is spurious if defined as the inability (economic, organizational, legal or even political) of the states — and therefore
in a sense of the cities, which are their legal creatures — to support public
services at high and rising levels. It is real, however, if defined as their
unwillingness to support many of these services at what most reformers
deem minimum-adequate levels. Presumably what Governor Cahill meant
to tell the New Jersey legislature was something like this: "Any proposal
to raise state and local taxes to what everyone would consider satisfactory
levels would surely be voted down." The issue, then, has to do with using
federal revenue to raise the level of services above the level that, given
the realities of state and local politics, would otherwise exist. In other
words, it concerns the amount and kind of income redistribution that the
federal government should undertake.

That the federal government, and not state-local ones, should be
primarily responsible for any income redistribution has long been generally
accepted. In recent decades this principle has been used to justify giving
federal aid to states and localities in spectacularly increasing amounts.
As John M. DeGrove has pointed out, the increase was tenfold in the last
twenty years, fourfold in the last ten, and twofold in the last five. In 1970
federal aid to states and cities reached an all-time peak of over $24 billion.
The question therefore is not *whether* they should be aided but (a) by how
much and (b) on what principle of distribution.

In considering what is involved in this, it is necessary to distinguish
those state-local needs that are in some sense national from those that are
not. That millions of poor rural people have moved to the cities is not
something that the taxpayers of the cities should bear the entire financial
responsibility for; apart from fairness, there is another consideration —
presumably the nation as a whole will be injured if these millions do not

receive adequate school, health, police, and other services that only state and local governments can provide. This is one argument that may justify large additional federal support for the states even though they could — if they would — raise the necessary money themselves. Some state-local needs, however, are in no sense national. Most pollution control and much highway construction is in this category. Why, one may ask, should the people of New York be taxed to pay for cleaning up a river in Vermont? As Dick Netzer has remarked in his excellent *Economics and Urban Problems,* ideally such non-national needs should be met by the development of regional governmental agencies, interstate in some cases and metropolitan in others, that can collect taxes and distribute benefits with a view to whatever public is affected — and to that public only. Unfortunately, such jurisdictions do not exist and it is politically impossible to create them. There is, however, as Netzer points out, a substitute for them — namely, the state governments. So when mayors and governors demand *federal* aid for non-national purposes, they do not have a persuasive case. Not only is it unfair to shift the cost of essentially state-local benefits to the national public; it is also very wasteful, for when someone else is to pay the bill, the natural tendency is to be prodigal. (Since Uncle Sam is to pay, why not build the bridge or sewerage system twice as big and four times as costly as necessary?)

Still, there unquestionably do exist truly national needs which urgently require increases in federal aid. But aid to whom? Revenue sharing is not a self-evident proposition. In dealing with the redistribution problem, the Nixon administration itself has consistently put the emphasis on aiding individuals rather than governments. Shortly after taking office it exempted persons below the poverty line from paying federal income taxes. In its first two years its main effort was to bring into being the Family Assistance Plan, the effect of which would be to reduce those income inequalities that in large part constitute the "crisis of the cities."

Looking at revenue sharing from this standpoint, there is much to be said against it. Compared to the existing federal grant-in-aid programs, it would be much less redistributive.[1] The existing programs are redistributive because grants are generally awarded on the basis of some criteria of need. The shared revenue, on the other hand, would be distributed to states and cities on the basis of population and tax effort. This means that the wealthier states (in terms of per capita income) would benefit; the poorer states would not. Moreover, it is not likely that all of the money that went to the richer states would end up in the pockets of its neediest citizens. Such features of revenue sharing make for complications.

Under the present grant programs, for example, New Yorkers pay in taxes much more to the federal government than they get back in grants from it. In 1967, the per capita personal income tax paid from New York state to the federal government was $433 whereas the grants received in 1968 amounted to only $120 per capita. In North Dakota it was the other way around; there the per capita personal income tax payment was $177 and per capita grants were $357. On the basis of these figures, a New York politician (say Senator Javits) might decide that revenue sharing is a big improvement over the grant system. After all, under the administration's proposed plan, New York state, which accounts for 10.98% of the national income, would get 10.68% of the shared ('general') revenue, whereas under the present grant system it gets only (the figure is for 1968) 8.6%. On the other hand, an Arkansas politican might conclude that revenue sharing is a very bad idea. Arkansas, which accounts for .67% of the national income and gets (1968) 1.46% of the federal grants would, under revenue sharing, get only .86% of the $5 billion.

In the last decade or so, the movement of poor people from the country to the city has made income redistribution an intracity, or rather intrametropolitan area, problem, as well as an interstate one. Of the $17 billion granted in the fiscal year 1968, $10 billion went to metropolitan areas. Some of the largest grant programs — especially OEO, Model Cities, and Title I of the Elementary and Secondary Education Act of 1965 — put money mainly or entirely in so-called poverty areas. From the standpoint of the people who live in these areas, revenue sharing is subject to exactly the same objection that it is subject to in Arkansas: i.e., that it will give these areas less than they would get if the same amount were distributed under the existing grant programs. As Governor Sargent of Massachusetts has pointed out, the wealthy suburb of Newton would get $1,527,668 of the $5 billion that the administration proposes to share, whereas Fall River, a city that is really poor, would get only $827,760. One way to meet this objection, at least in part, would be to declare small cities, most of which are well-off suburbs ineligible to share in the fund. Two years ago, the Intergovernmental Relations Advisory Commission suggested limiting eligibility to cities of 50,000 or more but it has since been realized that this would leave more than 40% of all cities without an incentive to support the plan. The small suburbs are disproportionately Republican, of course, and this must also be taken into account by the Nixon administration.

That a state like Arkansas or a city like Fall River would rather have $5 billion distributed under the existing grant programs than under revenue sharing is quite irrelevant if, as some observers claim, Congress could not possibly be persuaded to increase the total of grants by any such sum. Those who think that the Administration must "come up with something new" if it is to have any chance of getting "massive" new money for the cities will presumably conclude that $5 billion in revenue sharing is preferable to, at best, a few hundred million more in grants.

Of course the choice need not be between revenue sharing and grants. There are indications that Congress might be willing to assume the costs of certain social programs, especially welfare. Insofar as the object is to redistribute income, it would certainly make more sense to allot the $5 billion to welfare than to revenue sharing. This has been the administration's position all along. Family assistance, not revenue sharing, was, and presumably still is, its first love.

A "NEW FEDERALISM"?

From the standpoint of the administration, the central issue is neither the alleged "fiscal crisis" nor the problem of income redistribution. Rather it is the direction in which the federal system is to develop. From his first statement on the subject (August 13, 1969), the President has emphasized the need to create what he calls a New Federalism. Revenue sharing, he said when he first proposed it, would "mark a turning point in federal-state relations, the beginning of the decentralization of governmental power, and the restoration of a rightful balance between state capitals and the national capital." By the end of the decade, he predicted, "the political landscape of America will be visibly altered, and state and cities will have a far greater share of power and responsibility for solving their own problems." In his recent State of the Union Message, he went even farther. He was proposing, he said, a New American Revolution.

. . . a peaceful revolution in which power will be turned back to the people — in which government at all levels will be refreshed, renewed, and made truly responsive. This can be a revolution as profound, as far reaching, as exciting, as that first revolution almost 200 years ago.

One of the things that caused the President to think along these lines was the rapid and continuing growth that has been — and still is — taking place in the number of federal grant-in-aid programs. As he pointed out in his 1969 message, this growth has been 'near explosive'; between 1962 and 1966, he said, the number of categorical grant programs increased from 160 to 349. There was no reason to think that the rate of increase would slow down, much less stop, of its own accord; but unless it *did* slow down, categorical programs would soon number in the thousands. Revenue sharing was one of the means by which the administration hoped to slow it down. Instead of creating more categorical programs, Congress would be asked to give the money to the states and cities "with no strings

attached." Along with revenue sharing, the President asked for authority
to order consolidations of categorical programs, provided that Congress
did not within 60 days disapprove his orders. He also proposed a Manpower Training Act which (among other things) would have permitted
the consolidation of about twenty more or less competing manpower
programs and would have given the governors of the states a good deal
of control over the consolidated program.

All of these measures had a common rationale — to simplify the
structure of federal aid to the states and cities in order to bring it under
control and reduce waste. With hundreds of grant programs, each with
its own laws and regulations, no central direction is possible. Cabinet
officers cannot keep track of — let alone exercise policy direction over
— the many and varied programs for which they are responsible. Governors cannot find out what federal money is coming into their states or
what is being done with it. The largest cities employ practitioners of the
new art of "grantsmanship," in some instances with great success; many
small cities, however, finding that they must apply to scores, or even
hundreds, of programs, each with its own special requirements and each
administered by a different bureaucracy, have more or less given up any
hope of getting much help. The system, if it can be called that, is as
wasteful as it is frustrating. A state or local government cannot trade a
project that is low on its priority list for one that is high. Perhaps it can
get $20 million for an expressway that it does not want but not $200,000
for a drug addiction project that it wants desperately. This involves a
double waste: first in what is taken (local authorities can rarely refuse
money that is "free") and second in the foregone benefits of desirable
projects for which grants are unavailable.

The proposals in the State of the Union Message represent elabora-
tions of those put forward in 1969. "General" revenue sharing differs
from the revenue sharing then proposed only in amount and in the percentage (now 48) to be "passed through" to the cities. "Special" revenue
sharing is (despite the confusing terminology) nothing but consolidation
of categorical programs on an all-at-once, comprehensive basis rather than
on a piecemeal one. As everybody presumably knows by now, a few
categorical programs would be eliminated and most of the others grouped
into six super-categories (urban community development, rural community development, education, manpower training, law enforcement, and
transportation) each under a cabinet officer. Under "special" revenue
sharing, grants-in-aid would be distributed among states and local governments on the basis of need as in the past, but the distribution would be
according to an agreed-upon formula (or rather formulae because each
super-category would have its own) rather than as the result of (among

other things) grantsmanship, endurance, "clout," and chicanery — criteria that cannot be excluded at present. Under the plans so far announced (in the nature of the case these are incomplete and somewhat tentative) some interests are bound to gain and others to lose. Mayor Hatcher of Gary, Indiana, for example, has complained that his city would lose about one-fourth of the $150 million a year that it now receives. To such complaints the administration has replied that it will hold in reserve a fund from which to make up any losses that local governments may suffer because of changes in distribution formulae.

ORGANIZED BENEFICIARIES

There is no doubt that state and local officials enthusiastically favor consolidating and simplifying the grant system and giving them (the officials) wide discretion in deciding the uses to which federal aid should be put. Congressmen, too, are well aware of the faults of the present system, and many have spoken out against it. Nevertheless, there is reason to think that proposals to change the system fundamentally will not prove acceptable now or later, no matter who proposes them or what their merits.

It must be remembered that every one of the categorical programs (the most recent estimate is 550) has its organized beneficiaries — not only those who receive grants but also those who are paid salaries for administering them. These beneficiaries have a much livelier interest in maintaining and enlarging their special benefits than the generality of taxpayers — unorganized, of course — has in curtailing them. If there happens to be a grant program for retraining teachers in secondary schools having high dropout rates, it is safe to say that there exists an organization that will exert itself vigorously to prevent the consolidation of that program with others. It is safe to say, too, that no organization exists to put in a good word for the consolidation of the teacher-retraining program with other manpower programs.

From the standpoint of organized interests, dealing with Congress and the Washington bureaucracies (a few key Congressmen and administrators are usually all that matter to any particular interest) is vastly easier and more likely to succeed than is dealing with the legislatures and governors of fifty states, not to mention the officials of countless cities, counties, and special districts. This consideration alone might well be decisive from the standpoint of organized labor, which knows just where to go and whom to see in Washington, even if the political complexions of the state and local governments were exactly the same as that of the national government. In fact, of course, they are not; some interests that are well received and can make themselves heard in Washington — organized labor, minority groups, the poor — would be ignored in certain state capitols and city halls.

Interest groups will not be the only, or probably the most important, defenders of the grant system, however. Congressmen — especially those on important committees — are fond of categorical programs for at least two reasons. One is that they constitute answers to the perennial question: What have you done for me lately? A narrowly defined category is ideal from this standpoint. It is custom-made to suit the requirements of some key group of constituents and the Congressman can plainly label it "from me to you." Revenue sharing, whether "general" or "special," altogether lacks this advantage. It gives benefits not to constituents directly but in wholesale lots to state and local politicians who will package them for retail distribution under their own labels, taking all of the credit.

Congressmen also like categorical programs because of the opportunities they afford to interfere in administration and thus to secure special treatment, or at least the appearance of it, for constituents among whom, as Jerome T. Murphy has shown in his case study of the politics of educational reform (*Harvard Educational Review,* February 1971) state and local as well as federal agencies sometimes figure prominently. These opportunities are plentiful because the Congressmen see to it that "ifs," "ands," and "buts" are written into the legislation in the right places, and because administrators are well aware that every year they must respond in public to whatever questions may be asked in appropriations and other hearings. Wanting to stay on the right side of those members of Congress with whom they must deal, administrators frequently ask them for "advice." Perhaps it is not too much to say that the categorical system constitutes a last line of defense against what many Congressmen regard as the usurpation of their function by the executive branch.

As this implies, the present coldness of Congress to President Nixon's revenue-sharing proposals is not to be explained solely or perhaps even mainly on the ground that he is Republican and Congress is Democratic. The crucial fact is that his proposals would involve a large-scale shift of power from Congress to the White House. *No* Congress would like that, although sooner or later one may feel compelled to accept it.

Revenue sharing would also shift power to governors and mayors. To hear some of them talk, one might think that they would like to have the federal government dismantled and the pieces turned over to them. In fact, most of them are likely to find excuses for not accepting powers that may be politically awkward — and what ones may not?

In his valuable book *The American System,* the late Morton Grodzins provides some evidence on this point. He tells at some length the story of the Joint Federal-State Action Committee, which President Eisenhower created in 1957 after a flight of oratory (". . . those who would be free must stand eternal watch against excessive concentration of power in government . . .") to designate federal functions that might be devolved to the states along with revenue to support them. The Committee was a very high level one; it included three members of the Cabinet, the Director of the Bureau of the Budget, and a dozen governors. After laboring for two years, it found only two programs that the federal government would give up and that the states would accept — vocational education and municipal waste treatment plants. As Grodzins explains, the difficulty was not so much that the federal agencies could not be persuaded to give up functions as that the governors would not accept them. They would not take the school lunch program, for example, because doing so would involve a fuss about parochial schools, and they would not take Old Age Assistance because they knew that the old people's lobby would not like having it transferred to the states. Modest as the Committee's two proposals were and strongly as President Eisenhower backed them, Congress turned them down.

Whether state and local governments would make good use of the federal funds if given them "with no strings attached" is much doubted by career civil servants in Washington and by what may be called the good government movement. State and city governments, it is frequently said, are in general grossly inefficient and in many instances corrupt as well. The charge is certainly plausible — one wonders whether New York City, for example, has the capacity to use wisely the large amounts that it would receive. The fact is, however, that no one really knows what the state and local governments are capable of. And even if their capacity should prove to be as little as the pessimists say it is, may it not even so be superior to that of the present system *as it will be in another decade or two?*

Administrators in Washington generally assume that the management capacity of state and local governments can be much improved by provision of special grants to strengthen the staffs of the chief executives and by teaching the techniques and advantages of comprehensive planning. The lessons of the last ten years give little support to this assumption, but the administration is nevertheless proposing a fund of $100 million for more such efforts. In my judgment the results are bound to be disappointing. It is the necessity of working out compromises among the numerous holders of bits and pieces of power on the state-local scene that is the main cause, not only of "inefficiency," but of corruption as well. Giving governors and mayors authority over the spending of federal funds would, by strengthening their political positions, reduce the amount of compromising that they must do and the amount of corruption that they must pretend not to see if they are to get anything done. In this way it would contribute more than anything else to increasing the coherence (to use the word that is favored among planners) of state-local programs. The $100 million in management assistance that the federal government proposes would probably work in the very opposite direction. In practice if not in theory, giving "technical assistance" usually means maintaining and extending the influence of the federal agencies.

THE PROSPECT BEFORE US

Insofar as there would be a real devolution of power to governors and mayors — and therefore, as the President said, to the people who elect them — the administration's proposals could bring the federal system closer to what the Founding Fathers intended it to be. In my opinion, this is a consummation devoutly to be desired. There is no denying, however, that the short-run effect of decentralization of power would be to take a great deal of pressure off those state and local regimes, of which there may be many, that have no disposition to provide essential public services on an equitable basis or at what reasonable people would regard as adequate levels. This is a powerful objection. It may, however, only be a temporary one. Within a very few years, the political arithmetic of every sizable city and every industrial state will be such as to give politicians strong incentives to take very full account of the needs and wishes of those elements of the electorate that have been, and in some places still are, neglected.

Still, given the political realities that I have mentioned — a public opinion that favors income redistribution but is divided as to how far it should go and how costs and benefits should be apportioned; tax boundary lines inappropriately drawn but not susceptible to being redrawn; hundreds of federal agencies having programs to protect; interest groups even more numerous and with more at stake in the status quo; interstate and intrametropolitan area differences of interest; Congressmen loath to see their powers diminished; governors and mayors equally loath to accept responsibilities that can be avoided — it is not to be expected that any quick or clear-cut settlement will be found for the issues that revenue sharing raises.

I expect that the federal government will continue to play a larger role in raising revenue for all sorts of purposes. As Julius Margolis has pointed out, the larger and more diverse the "package" of expenditure (or other) items that a government presents to its voters, the harder it is for the people to make their decisions on the basis of self-interest as opposed to ideology. This being the case, those who want to win acceptance for proposals that would not be accepted if self-interest were the criterion always try to include them in packages that are sufficiently large. That is, they prefer to have decisions made on a city-wide rather than a neighborhood basis, on a state-wide rather than a city-wide one, and on a national rather than a state one. It seems to me that the changing class character of the population reinforces this tendency. As we become more heavily upper-middle class, we are increasingly disposed to regard general principles (or ideology, as Margolis calls it), not self-interest, as the proper criterion.

If the federal government will have an ever-larger part in raising revenue, it is not likely to have an ever-smaller one in spending it. He who pays the piper calls the tune. To be sure, he may choose to permit, or even to require, others to do some calling when the number of tunes to be called is inconveniently large, and by so doing he may make everyone better off. The essential fact is, however, that the state governments can be what Governor Cahill called them — sovereign — only if they do what he says they cannot do — supply the funds to meet the urgent and necessary needs of their people. I myself am strongly in favor of the reforms that the President has proposed because I think they represent the largest improvement over the present situation that it is reasonable to hope for. I do not, however, share his expectation that these reforms will bring about "a historic and massive reversal of the flow of power in America." Indeed, in the event — unlikely, I am afraid — that his proposals are accepted and carried into effect, I would be very surprised if first Mississippi and then New York did not discover that they are ruled as much as ever by national public opinion, acting through national institutions — the Presidency, Congress, the Supreme Court — and that this opinion and these institutions, the White House most of all perhaps, will in the years ahead assert conceptions of the national interest more vigorously than ever.

Note

1. What is under discussion at this point is the so-called "general" revenue-sharing proposal: that is, the $5 billion, to start with, that would go to states and cities with "no strings attached." This is to be distinguished from "special" revenue sharing, which is the grant system much reorganized and with $1 billion in "new" money added to it.

4

SERVICE DELIVERY AND
URBAN ADMINISTRATION

Chapter One introduced the urban administrator and the political nature of the roles he is required to perform. He was depicted as having to identify community needs; plead actively on their behalf; serve as a high-powered analyst, salesman, and strategist; and act to protect and promote change in community values. As Chapters Two and Three have explored, these efforts are often complicated by personnel and financial problems. Along with all of these roles, however, the urban administrator remains the leader of his organization and is, therefore, responsible for effective, efficient, and sensitive delivery of service. This chapter examines some of the functional problems that confront the urban administrator as he attempts to deliver such vital urban services as police protection, criminal justice, housing, education, transportation, and planning. As Wallace Sayre and Herbert Kaufman have pointed out in their classic study of New York City government, these services provide or guarantee "the basic physical and biological requirements of urban life." They make the city "habitable, satisfying, and even reasonably comfortable" and thereby "help it hold together its prime source of greatness: its people."[1] The problems encountered by urban administrators in delivering these services underscore the frustrations of resolving the urban crisis by rational, administrative means.

Most of the problems examined in this chapter can be traced to an inadequate understanding of the functional dimensions of the particular services involved. Moreover, even when this understanding is achieved, these problems are often perpetuated and at times even exacerbated by a political, legal, and social environment resistant to change. Thus, James Q. Wilson contends in "Dilemmas of Police Administration" that policy-making for police departments is complicated by the fact that there is no public or official consensus as to the level or method of order maintenance desired and no strategy available by which to realize full law enforcement. It is this lack of understanding of "the nature of the police function" and not "the quality of the men recruited or the level at which authority is exercised" that makes for "difficulty in managing the police."

Wilson encourages the police to recognize clearly that order maintenance is their "central function — central both in the demands it makes on time and resources and in the opportunities it affords for making a difference in the lives of citizens." He suggests that reduction of crime can best be accomplished through the courts and correctional institutions. However, as Ralph A. Rossum argues in "Problems of Judicial Administration: The Effect of Supreme Court Decisions on Courts of Limited Jurisdiction," it is unrealistic to expect too much from the courts — especially those courts of limited jurisdiction where over 90% of all criminal prosecutions take place. As a result of various Supreme Court decisions in the realm of criminal procedure, these courts have had placed upon them increased demands which have complicated their procedure, generated inefficiency, stimulated the growth of a substantial if unwieldy judicial bureaucracy, and heightened the need for judicial reform and consolidation. Of course, the problems of judicial administration are not unique to urban areas. They are, however, so much exacerbated in metropolitan courts that they deserve to be treated in a volume addressed to the problems of urban administration.

Functional problems also accompany the efforts of urban administrators to provide decent and adequate housing for all urban Americans. As Daniel R. Mandelker and Roger Montgomery have noted: "[N]o other social issue cries out more for attention and amelioration, and no other comparable area of social concern can equal housing problems in complexity and in resistance to public intervention in the name of change and innovation."[2] One of the principal obstacles to the attainment of adequate housing is exclusionary local zoning regulation. For example, requirements for large lot sizes increase the amount of land used for housing and therefore its costs. Many suburban communities have enacted such local zoning laws requiring large lot sizes and have thereby made housing in those communities too costly for low or moderate income groups to afford. Large lot size — or low density zoning — is only one of many forms of exclusionary zoning controls that have been enacted in many parts of the country. Others include minimum-building-size requirements, single-family restrictions, restrictions on the number of bedrooms, prohibitions on mobile homes, and frontage (i.e., lot width) requirements.[3] As Daniel R. Mandelker points out in "A Rationale for the Zoning Process," these requirements constitute substantial obstacles when even marginal changes in land use patterns are attempted.[4] Since "[d]ecisions about marginal changes in land use should be easier to handle than more wide-sweeping proposals, such as new towns or massive urban reconstruction," Mandelker pessimistically concludes that housing is likely to remain a serious problem for the urban administrator.

By whatever standard employed, the largest economic enterprise in the United States, next to the Department of Defense, is the business of educating its urban population. In fiscal 1972, $48.7 billion were expended at the state, local, and national level for public schooling.[5] This high level of expenditures has been tolerated and even encouraged because it has been long believed that education is the key to the good life in the United States. As that leader of the public school movement, Horace Mann, wrote in the mid-nineteenth century, "Education . . . is the great equalizer of the condition of men . . ."[6] It provides all an equal opportunity based on merit, not wealth or position. However, much of this conventional understanding has recently been challenged by the sobering conclusions of such researchers as Christopher Jencks and his associates.[7] They found that (1) equality of schools (by whatever measure – teaching quality, money, facilities, programs, etc.) is far from reality; (2) regardless of these inequalities in schools, these factors are trivial in accounting for different pupil achievement when compared to family background and IQ; and (3) whatever minor effects schools may have on pupils, there is almost no correlation between education and later success measured by occupational status, income, and job satisfaction. David N. Silk reviews recent attempts to equalize opportunity in the United States through educational reform in "Education and Liberal Reform: An Interpretation." He argues that these attempts have failed to rectify inequality, because they have failed to affect "the causes of these inequalities, which are more often economic, political, and cultural in origin, than they are educational."

"That a few Americans orbit the globe in less time than it takes others to get to work illustrates the urban transportation problem."[8] The response of urban administration to this problem deserves close attention for a number of reasons. First, transportation facilities, whether roads or rails, are costly. The provision of a transportation network ranks next to education and police protection as a major item of urban public expenditure. Second, decisions about transportation are characterized by their permanence. The transportation network influences the location of housing, commerce, and industry and thereby has an impact upon the shape of the city that exists for generations. Third, transportation policy is clearly linked to America's energy and environmental problems. As John F. Kain has observed, the response of urban administration to the transportation problem has to date been "seriously deficient."[9] He blames these deficiencies on "existing institutional arrangements which badly fragment the responsibility for providing urban transportation services" and on urban administrators who (1) fail to consider feasible alternatives through premature imposition of constraints; (2) attempt through long range planning to optimize future rather than current or existing conditions and as a result give minimal attention to the problems of transition from current conditions to future "optimal" conditions; and (3) apply inappropriate and often inconsistent criteria in an attempt to meet pressing transportation needs. The need for urban administrators to remedy these deficiencies and to improve both the quantity and quality of urban transportation services constitutes still another major challenge for urban administration.

The final service of urban administration taken up in this chapter is that of planning — "the orderly and rational development of a community through anticipation and foresight, involving sequential problem-solving over time."[10] The need for planning has arisen out of a sense of failure of market forces and of private and public actions to provide adequately for the public interest. Yet, planning is itself not without serious functional problems which place rather stringent limits on this "orderly and rational development." Herbert J. Gans explores perhaps the most important of these problems in "Planning for People, Not Buildings." He argues that urban planning "has concerned itself primarily with buildings, and the physical environment, and only secondarily with the people who use that environment." This is so, he argues, for urban planners have planned principally for people of their own class culture, "for other middle and upper middle class professionals who want solid single family house neighborhoods and who use theaters, museums, civic centers, and other cultural facilities that cater to the upper middle class." As a result, however, urban planning has contributed less "to the solution of urban problems and the achievement of urban goals" than it might have, had its priorities been reversed.

Notes

1. Wallace S. Sayre and Herbert Kaufman, *Governing New York City: Politics in the Metropolis* (New York: W. W. Norton, Inc., 1965), pp. 34–35.
2. Daniel R. Mandelker and Roger Montgomery (eds.), *Housing in America: Problems and Perspectives* (Indianapolis, Indiana: The Bobbs-Merrill Company, Inc., 1973), viii.
3. *Ibid.*, Chapter 10, Land and Development, for a full discussion of the variety, use, and effectiveness of exclusionary land use controls.

4. Daniel R. Mandelker, "A Rationale for the Zoning Process," *Land Use Controls Quarterly,* IV (1970), pp. 1-7.

5. A total of $78.3 billion were spent for defense. Robert L. Lineberry and Ira Sharkansky, *Urban Politics and Public Policy* (2d ed.; New York: Harper and Row, 1974), p. 223.

6. Quoted in Arthur Mann, "A Historical Overview: The Lumpen-Proletariat, Education, and Compensatory Action," in Charles Daly (ed.), *The Quality of Inequality: Urban and Suburban Public Schools* (Chicago: University of Chicago Press, 1968), pp. 13-14.

7. Christopher Jencks, *et al., Inequality: A Reassessment of the Effects of Family and Schooling in America* (New York: Basic Books, 1972).

8. Lineberry and Sharkansky, *op. cit.,* p. 277. The following discussion relies heavily on this source.

9. John Kain, "How to Improve Urban Transportation at Practically No Cost," *Public Policy* XX, No. 3 (Summer, 1972), pp. 335-358.

10. Alan Edward Bent, *Escape From Anarchy* (Memphis, Tennessee: Memphis State University Press, 1972), p. 103.

JAMES Q. WILSON

DILEMMAS OF POLICE ADMINISTRATION

Policy making for the police is complicated by the fact that, at least in large cities, the police department is an organization with at least two objectives, one·of which produces conflict and the other of which cannot be attained.[1] The dilemmas facing police administrators arise out of their inability to obtain agreement on what constitutes satisfactory performance of the first objective, and their difficulty in finding a strategy which would permit the realization of the (agreed-upon) second objective.

OBJECTIVES

The first objective I call *order maintenance* — the handling of disputes, or behavior which threatens to produce disputes, among persons who disagree over what ought to be right or seemly conduct or over the assignment of blame for what is agreed to be wrong or unseemly conduct. A family quarrel, a noisy drunk, a tavern brawl, a street disturbance by teen-agers, the congregation on the sidewalk of idle young men (especially in eccentric clothes or displaying an unconventional demeanor) — all these are cases in which citizens disagree as to whether or how the police should intervene. If the police do intervene, one party or another is likely to feel harassed, outraged, or neglected. Though a law may have been broken, as with an assault inflicted by a husband on his wife, the police do not perceive their responsibilities as involving simply the comparing of a particular behavior to a clear legal standard and making an arrest if the

Reprinted from the *Public Administration Review*, journal of the American Society for Public Administration, XXVIII (September 1968), pp. 407–417.

standard has been violated. For one thing, the legal rule is, in many order-maintenance cases, ambiguous. A "breach of the peace" implies a prior definition of "peace" and this is a matter on which persons commonly disagree. For another thing, even when the legal standard is clear enough — as with an assault — the "victim" is often not innocent (indeed, he may have called for the police because he was losing a fight he started) and thus the question of *blame* may be to the participants more important than the question of "guilt" and they will expect the officer to take this into account. Finally, most order-maintenance situations do not result in an arrest — the parties involved wish the officer to "do something" that will "settle things," but they often do not wish to see that settlement entail an arrest. And in any case the infraction is likely to be a misdemeanor and thus, in many states, the officer cannot make a valid arrest unless the illegality was committed in his presence or unless the victim is willing to sign a complaint. As a result, the officer cannot expect a judge to dispose of the case; the former must devise a substantive solution for a disorderly event which the latter will never hear of.

The second objective is *law enforcement* — the application of legal sanctions, usually by means of an arrest, to persons who injure or deprive innocent victims. A burglary, purse snatch, mugging, robbery, or auto theft are usually crimes committed by strangers on persons who did not provoke the attack. Though there is, in these matters, a problem of finding the guilty party, once guilt is established there is no question of blame. For almost all such law-enforcement situations, the officer is expected to either make an arrest or act so as to prevent the violation from occurring in the first place. His task is the seemingly ministerial and technical act of either apprehending or deterring the criminal. The difficulty is that the officer lacks the means — the information, primarily — to apprehend or deter more than a very small fraction of all criminals. Leaving aside murder, rape, and aggravated assault — in which a high proportion of suspects are known or even related to their victims — few major crimes such as burglary and robbery that are of primary concern to the citizen are "cleared by arrest." In 1965 only 38 percent of all *known* robberies and 25 percent of all *known* burglaries were cleared by arrest, and even that figure is artificially high. The household victimization study done by the National Opinion Research Center for the President's Commission on Law Enforcement and Administration of Justice[2] showed that in 1965 there were over three times as many burglaries and 50 percent more robberies than were reported to and recorded by the police; thus, the adjusted clearance rates are only about 8 percent for burglary and 24 percent for robbery. But even those figures may be too high, for, as Skolnick points out, there are often strong organizational pressures leading detectives to induce arrested burglars and robbers to "cop out" to as many offenses as possible in order to boost the clearance rate.[3]

There is, of course, no way to measure the number of crimes prevented by police activity, but the number is not likely to be large. Crimes of passion that occur in private places (many, if not most, murders, rapes, and serious assaults are in this category) probably happen at a rate independent of the nature or intensity of police activity. Crimes of stealth, such as burglary and many forms of larceny, may in unknown ways be affected by police activity, but the effect is probably not great — no city, whatever its police strategy, has been able to show any dramatic reversal in the rising rates of reported thefts. There is some evidence that certain kinds of street crimes — muggings, purse snatches, holdups of taxi and bus drivers, and the like — can be reduced by very intensive police patrol, the use of officers disguised as cabbies or lady shoppers, the formation of citizen auxiliaries, and the like. But even with these crimes, which surely are the ones most disturbing to the average person, two problems exist. First, no one is confident that what appears to be a reduction is not in fact a displacement of crime (to other places or to other forms of crime), or that if a reduction genuinely occurs it will persist over time.[4] And second, the kinds of police activities apparently best adapted to suppressing street crime — intensive patrols, close surveillance of "suspicious" persons, frequent street stops of pedestrians and motorists, and so on — are precisely those most likely to place the police in conflict with important segments of the community — primarily with persons who because of their age, race, or social class are regarded (and, as far as the evidence goes, correctly regarded) as most likely to commit criminal acts. In short, in the one aspect of law enforcement where there may be opportunities for substantial deterrence, the police are obliged to act in a way which, like their actions in order-maintenance situations, is most likely to bring them into conflict with the citizen.

The dilemmas of police administration arise out of the difficulty confronting a chief who seeks policies which can guide his men in performing the order-maintenance function and a technique which will prove efficacious in serving the law-enforcement function. The conflict over how the police should behave in order-maintenance cases results from differing expectations as to the appropriate level of public or private order and differing judgments over what constitutes a just resolution of a given dispute. In a homogeneous community, where widely shared norms define both the meaning of order and the standards of justice (who is equal to whom and in what sense), the police role is comparatively simple. But where the community, usually because of differences of class or race, has no common normative framework, the police have no reliable guides to action and efforts to devise such guides will either be half-hearted or sources of important public controversy. The conflict that arises over the performance of the law-enforcement function, on the other hand, arises out of the lack of any technique by which crime can be reduced significantly and without incurring high costs in terms of other values — privacy, freedom, and so forth. The dispute about the law-enforcement function is, unlike the dispute over order maintenance, not over ends but over means.

CRITICISMS

Organizations to which society gives tasks that cannot be performed to the satisfaction of society suffer not only certain frustrations but some fundamental administrative problems as well. The criticisms directed at the police are well-known and often sound, but conditions giving rise to these criticisms are frequently not well understood by the critic. For example, police departments are frequently charged with hiring unqualified personnel, suppressing or manipulating crime reports, condoning the use of improper or illegal procedures, using patrol techniques that create tensions and irritation among the citizens, and either overreacting (using too much force too quickly) or underreacting (ignoring dangerous situations until it is too late) in the face of incipient disorder. All of these criticisms are true to some extent, though the extent of the deficiencies is often exaggerated. But let us concede for the moment that they are all true. Why are they true?

Explanations vary, but commonly they are some variation on the "bad men" theme. Unqualified, unintelligent, rude, brutal, intolerant, or insensitive men, so this theory goes, find their way (or are selectively recruited into) police work where they express their prejudices and crudeness under color of the law. Though a few of the commanding officers of the department may try to improve matters, on the whole they are ineffective. At best they invent paper palliatives — empty departmental directives, superficial community relations programs, one-sided internal disciplinary units — which do little more than offer a chance for issuing favorable, but misleading, publicity statements about the "new look." And at worst, the theory continues, such administrators exacerbate tensions by encouraging, in the name of efficiency or anticrime strategies, various tecnhiques, such as aggressive preventive patrol, that lead to the harassment of innocent citizens. The solution for these problems is, clearly, to hire· "better men" — college graduates, Negroes, men who can pass tests that weed out "authoritarian" personalities, and the like. And those on the force should attend universities, go through sensitivity training, and apply for grants to develop "meaningful" community relations programs.[5]

Some critics go even further. Not only do the police fail to do the right thing, they systematically do the wrong thing. Not only do the police fail to prevent crime, *the police actually cause crime.* Not only do the police fail to handle riots properly, *the police cause riots.* Presumably, things might improve if we had no police at all, but since even the strongest critics usually recognize the need for the police under some circumstances, they are willing to permit the police to function provided that they are under "community control" — controlled, that is, by the neighborhoods (especially Negro neighborhoods) where they operate. If police departments are at best a necessary evil, filled with inept or intolerant men exploiting the fact that they are necessary, then the solution to the problem of abuse is to put the police under the strictest and closest control of those whose activities they are supposed to regulate.

The view taken in this paper is quite different from at least the more extreme of these arguments. If all big-city police departments were filled tomorrow with Negro college graduates and placed under the control of the neighborhoods they are supposed to control, most of the problems that exist today would continue to exist and some in fact might get worse. The crime rate would not go down; indeed, owing to police timidity about making arrests among people who have a voice in their management, it might go up marginally. Police involvement in conflict and disorder would have no happier outcomes, because most disorders — family or neighbor quarrels — do not involve the community nor would the community necessarily have any better idea how to resolve them than do the police now. Perceived police abuse and harassment might decline in the neighborhood, but since each neighborhood would have its own police, the amount of abuse and harassment perceived by a person from one neighborhood entering a different neighborhood (say a Negro entering a white area, or vice versa) might increase. The conflict between neighborhood residents who want more police protection (small businessmen, home-owners, older people) and those who want less (teen-agers, transients, young men hanging on street corners) would remain and the police would tend, in the eyes of one group, to serve the standards of the other.

There would, of course, be some improvements. The police might have better information about the neighborhood if they were controlled by it and thus, in the event of large-scale disorders, be able to distinguish more accurately between solid citizens and troublemakers. They might also be more alert to the customs of the area and thus prepared to tolerate behavior (street-corner gatherings, loud noises) which the neighborhood tolerates, even though in other places such behavior might be regarded as breaches of the peace. And college-educated men might display more civility in routine encounters, handling incidents more impersonally and people more politely.

But it is difficult to say that such gains would be more than marginal. Some police departments (such as those on the West Coast) already have large numbers of men with some college training, but these departments (Oakland and Los Angeles, for example) are frequently criticized by Negroes for being "too tough," "too impersonal," "gung ho," and the like. (There may be no causal relation between police education and Negro criticism, but it is possible that while college men are more civil, they also have a stronger sense of duty.) It is not clear that departments with large numbers of Negroes patrolling Negro areas have experienced less community tension than departments with few Negroes, or that in any given encounter a Negro officer behaves much differently from a white one. This is not an argument against hiring Negro police officers; on the contrary, there are in my view compelling reasons for having as many as possible patrolling Negro areas. But their value would, in my opinion, be primarily symbolic (no less important for that!) and their presence would not make substantially easier the policy-making or administrative problems of the police. Nor are the consequences of different patrol and community relations policies clear. Some departments (San Francisco, Chicago) have made a major community relations effort, but they seem to fare no better than those (such as Philadelphia or Albany) with a "get tough" policy. Departments which use aggressive preventive patrol and have strict traffic enforcement policies (such as Los Angeles) produce criticism and experience disorders, but so do departments (such as Boston) which are less aggressive or strict. Though there are these differences in policy practices,[6] it is not clear how they affect the management of order, the enforcement of laws, or the maintenance of good community relations.

NATURE OF POLICE FUNCTION

The difficulty in managing the police arises, in my view, less from the quality of men recruited or the level at which authority is exercised and more from the nature of the police function. Mental hospitals provide a useful comparison to the police in this regard. Like the police, they are regarded as essential; like the police, they are routinely and repeatedly condemned for failures and inadequacies. The indictment of such institutions found, for example, in Ivan Belknap's book, has become commonplace.[7] The appalling conditions to be found in hospital wards, the apparent callousness and brutality of the staff, the denial of rights and privileges, the shortage of qualified psychiatric and medical staff, and (equally important) the inability of such professional staff as exists to control the practices of the hospital – all these circumstances have been described, and the accounts are no doubt in large measure correct. Repeated efforts at reform have been made. Budgets have been increased, hospitals have been reorganized, better-qualified personnel have been sought, staff services have been increased, and volumes of research have been published. And yet each decade sees essentially the same lamentable conditions exposed and the same indignation unleashed. With the failure of successive reform efforts, the prescriptions have become more radical. At first the need was thought to be for "better men" and "more money." Then the attack shifted to the professional staff itself – doctors and others were charged with "causing" mental illness, or at least retarding its elimination. The hospital was administration-centered; it should become patient-centered.[8]

In an incisive review of the literature on mental hospitals, Perrow concludes that the reason for the failure of reform has not been bad men or low budgets or improper organization or incompetent management (though all of those things may exist); the central problem is that we do not know how to cure mental illness. The problem is not one of ideology, but of technology. The hospitals are given a task they cannot perform, yet they must try to perform it, for the alternative (doing nothing) seems even worse.[9] The most important recent improvement in mental hospital care was the result of an advance in medical technology – the development of tranquilizer drugs. Changes in organization, leadership, and in the men recruited to hospital tasks have rarely produced significant or lasting results from the patient's point of view. To be sure, some hospitals manage to treat the inmates humanely – these are often small, heavily staffed hospitals with patients who can afford the high costs of such facilities. Bestial practices can be eliminated, but it costs a lot of money and requires large concentrations of scarce talent. But even in these circumstances, the improvement in the mental health of the patient does not seem to be much greater than whatever improvement occurs in less intensive (and less expensive) programs.[10]

The parallel with the police is striking. Abusive practices or indifference to citizen needs can be eliminated, but it typically requires a community that (like the intensive-treatment hospital) is small, expensive, and cooperative. In short, it requires a middle- or upper-middle class suburb. Some advocates of community control over the police argue that it is the close supervision of the police by the suburban community that accounts for the good relations between police and citizens to be found there; if one duplicates those political conditions in the central city –

if one, in short, "suburbanizes" the central-city neighborhoods — comparable improvements in police-citizen relations will occur. My research suggests that it is not the degree or kind of control that produces this effect in the suburbs, it is the class composition of the community. In a homogeneous, middle-class suburb there is relatively little public disorder; consequently the police rarely need intervene in situations of high conflict, and thus rarely need become parties to conflict. When the chief law-enforcement problem involves crimes of stealth (burglary and larceny) rather than street crimes (assaults, robberies, muggings), the police need not practice aggressive preventive patrol or otherwise keep persons on the streets under close surveillance; accordingly, it is rare for a suburban resident walking the streets at night to feel he is being "harassed." Finally, a socially homogeneous middle-class area provides the police with relatively unambiguous cues as to who should be regarded as a "suspicious person" and thus who should be made the object of police attention. Teen-agers hanging around a suburban ice-cream parlor late at night or a Negro in the back alley of an all-white residential community would be viewed suspiciously by the police and citizenry alike. Though this suspicion may be, in the particular case, unjust to the teen-agers or the Negro, acting on the basis of it does not bring the police into conflict with the community. (But though an affluent suburb may provide the conditions that reduce the likelihood of police-citizen conflict or of police abuses of their authority, it does not provide the conditions that make the management of such disorder as exists or the prevention of such crimes as occur any easier. In short, high-status communities permit the police to solve their ideological but not their technological problems.)

The policy implications of this argument are clear, though gloomy. Substantial and lasting improvements in police-community relations are not likely until and unless there is a substantial and lasting change in the class composition of the central city population — i.e., until the street-crime rate and the incidence of public disorder in the central cities becomes closer to that in the middle-class suburbs. Only then will it be possible to reduce substantially the police-community tension generated by practices like aggressive preventive patrol and the use of gross indicators such as race and apparent class as clues to criminal potential.

RACIAL COMPLICATION

Race complicates the issue, of course, and renders it more explosive. A black person is more likely to be regarded as lower class or otherwise suspicious than a white person, and thus a law-abiding and peaceful Negro is more likely to be treated as if he were potentially lawless and disorderly than an equivalent white person. Innocent Negroes so treated will naturally feel a deep sense of injustice. It is sometimes argued that this would not happen if police officers were not prejudiced. No doubt many officers are prejudiced (indeed, one study indicates that the vast majority are) and this prejudice may make matters worse.[11] But the crucial point is that large numbers of innocent Negroes would still be treated in (to them) unjust ways even if all policemen were entirely free of race prejudice so long as a disproportionate number of Negroes are lower class. Violent crime and disorder are predominantly (though not exclusively) lower-class phenomena;[12] Negroes are disproportionally (though far from exclusively) lower class; a black skin, therefore, will continue to be a statistically defensible (though individually unjust) cue that triggers an officer's suspicion. Among the consequences of this generalization will be continued police suspicion of blacks and continued Negro antagonism toward the police.

The point is perhaps more easily understood if we examine other cues to which police respond and other forms of prejudice which they may have. Young people commit a disproportionate share of many kinds of crime, especially crimes against property. Being young is therefore a statistically useful cue to an officer who is scanning a population in search of persons more likely than others to commit, or to have committed, a crime. In addition, it is quite possible that the police have "youth prejudice" — that is, they may impute to young people even more criminality than in fact they possess, just as officers having race prejudice impute to Negroes more criminality than in fact they display. But if all officers were cured of "youth prejudice," young people would still be singled out for special attention and suspicion. The difference, of course, is that young people outgrow their youth, while Negroes cannot outgrow their blackness.

The best evidence that race prejudice is not the crucial factor can be found in the behavior of Negro police officers. There has been no systematic study of such men, but my observations suggest that black policemen are as suspicious and tough in black neighborhoods as white officers. Indeed, in the long run Negroes have an advantage over youth. It may be possible to improve the class position of Negroes so that the crime rates found among them will be no higher (and perhaps even lower) than the rates found among whites. Then there will be no reason, other than prejudice, why an officer would treat a Negro differently from a white. By contrast, there is probably no way even in principle to reduce greatly the criminogenic properties of youth and therefore no way even in principle to make the police less suspicious of young people.

If the fundamental problem is one of class (admittedly greatly complicated by the problem of race), what can a police administrator do in the short run while he waits for society somehow to solve the class problem? If the point of view presented here is correct, not a great deal. But since even marginal gains are desirable when conditions are (or are widely thought to be) deplorable, it is worth considering palliatives, however slight may be their benefits.

First, the police should recognize clearly that order maintenance is their central function — central both in the demands it makes on time and resources and in the opportunities it affords for making a difference in the lives of the citizens. Hunting criminals both occupies less time (at least for the patrolmen) and provides fewer chances for decisive action. How well disputes are settled may depend crucially on how competent, knowledgeable, and sensitive the police are; how fast the crime rate mounts is much less dependent on the level and nature of police activity. (As will be argued below, other than by reducing the size of the lower class the best way society can affect the crime rate may be through the court and correctional systems rather than through the police.)

ORDER-MAINTENANCE FUNCTION

A police department that places order maintenance uppermost in its priorities will judge patrolmen less by their arrest records and more by their ability to keep the peace on their beat. This will require, in turn, that sergeants and other supervisory personnel concern themselves more with how the patrolmen function in family fights, teen-age disturbances, street corner brawls, and civil disorders, and less with how well they take reports at the scene of burglary or how many traffic tickets they issue during a tour of duty. Order maintenance also requires that the police have available a wider range of options for handling disorder than is afforded by the choice between making an arrest and doing nothing. Detoxification centers should be available as an alternative to jail for drunks. Family-service units should be formed which can immediately assist patrolmen handling domestic quarrels. Community-service officers should be available to provide information, answer complaints, and deal with neighborhood tensions and rumors.

Patrolmen who are given the order-maintenance function will obviously require a great deal of information about their beats — more than can be obtained by riding around in a patrol car or rotating frequently among several beats. Obtaining this knowledge will be made easier by the decentralization of the patrol function so that local commanders deal with local conditions subject to general policy guidelines from the police administrator. This decentralization need not always take the form of proliferating precinct station houses — these facilities, as traditionally used for mustering the watch, jailing prisoners, and keeping records, are expensive. Many of them, indeed, were built in a period when patrolmen, like firemen, slept in when they had night duty. Smaller, less elaborate, and more numerous "store front" police offices scattered throughout central-city neighborhoods might prove more effective and less expensive. Officers assigned to a particular neighborhood ought to remain in that area for long periods of time, rather than experience frequent rotation among neighborhoods. An even more radical experiment might be to assess the value of having patrolmen actually live in certain key areas. For example, some officers might be encouraged, on a volunteer basis, to live in public housing projects. To make such an assignment more attractive and to increase the pay of the officer, he could be given the apartment rent free or at a substantial discount.

Such decentralization of function requires the strengthening of the command system if it is not to produce inconsistent behavior, political intervention, and corruption. Supervisory officers, especially watch commanders, ought to have more authority to assign, direct, and evaluate their officers. Mechanical, fixed assignments and evaluation solely by written examinations decrease the possibility of inducing patrolmen to take seriously their order-maintenance function and lead them instead to emphasize following the safe routine, memorizing the penal code and departmental rule book, and "pushing paper" — filing reports, writing tickets, and so forth.

At the same time, if patrolmen are expected to devote themselves primarily to the most conflict-laden, unpleasant parts of their task, there must be rewards available that are commensurate with the burdens. At present, the major rewards open to the patrolman — promotion, higher pay, specialized duty — all take him out of the patrol force and place him in supervisory posts, criminal investigation, or headquarters staff units. If the patrol function is the most important and difficult job in the department, the best men ought to be rewarded for doing it well in ways that leave them *in* the patrol force and on the street. It should be possible to obtain substantial pay increases while remaining a patrolman, just as it is now possible to win higher salaries in the Federal Bureau of Investigation while remaining a special agent.

Getting good men to serve, not only in the police department, but in those police roles that are the most demanding, may produce only a marginal gain, but we are largely ignorant of how to achieve even that. Almost no systematic research has been done to define and measure those qualities characteristic of officers best able to keep the peace. Entrance examinations in many states and cities may not measure any relevant quality other than (perhaps) general literacy, familiarity with a police handbook, or some knowledge of current events.

POLICY STATEMENTS

If able men are found and assigned to neighborhood patrol forces under conditions that will facilitate their understanding of neighborhood conditions and personalities and if they are rewarded for successful performance of the peace-keeping function, what in concrete terms will these men actually do? How, in short, does one keep the peace? Some have argued that police departments ought to develop and issue policy statements that will give some guidance to officers who must necessarily exercise wide discretion with respect to matters where legal codes contain few applicable rules.[13] To the extent this is possible, of course it should be done, and it is not being done at all in many departments. But it would be a mistake to assume that policies can be found that will provide meaningful guides to action in most situations of real or potential disorder. The most feasible rules perhaps are those which tell the patrolman what *not* to do – don't use racial epithets, don't hit a man except in self-defense, don't grasp a man's arm or shoulder unless it is necessary to complete an arrest or prevent violence, and so forth. But relatively few rules can be devised that tell a patrolman what he *should* do with quarreling lovers, angry neighbors, or disputatious drunks. This is not because the police have had little experience with such matters (on the contrary!) or even because they do not know in a given case what to do (they may), but because so much depends on the particular circumstances of time, place, event, and personality. No psychiatrist would attempt to produce, much less use, a "how-to-do-it" manual for these cases, and he has the advantage of dealing with people at his leisure, over long periods of time, and in moments of relative calm. The best that can be done is to list "factors to be taken into account," but in the concrete case everything depends on *how* they are taken into account.

In the broadest terms, the patrolman in performing his order-maintenance function is neither a bureaucrat nor a professional, and thus neither increased bureaucratization nor increased professionalism will be of much value. He is not a bureaucrat in that he does not and cannot apply general rules to specific cases — there are no general rules, and thus his discretion is wide. (In performing his law-enforcement function, by contrast, he can act more nearly like a bureaucrat — the legal rules defining a crime are relatively unambiguous and the officer's discretion, especially if it is a serious crime, is narrow.) On the other hand, the patrolman is not a professional — there is no organized group of practitioners (as there is with doctors or physicists) who can impart to him by education certain information and equip him by apprenticeship with certain arts and skills that will make him competent to serve a "client" when the latter cannot be the sole judge of the quality of the service he receives. Nor do such external reference groups (professional societies) exist to certify that the patrolman is competent or to make him subject to a code of ethics and a sense of duty.

The patrolman is neither a bureaucrat nor a professional, but a member of a *craft*. As with most crafts, there is no generalized, written body of special knowledge; learning is by apprenticeship, but the apprenticeship takes place on the job rather than in an academy; the primary reference group from which the apprentice wins (or fails to win) respect are his colleagues on the job, not fellow members of his discipline wherever they may be; and the members, conscious of having a special skill or task, think of themselves as set apart from society and in need of restrictions on entry. But unlike other members of a craft — carpenters, for example, or journalists — the police work in an environment that is usually apprehensive and often hostile, and they produce no product (like a finished house or a well-written newspaper) the value of which is evident and easily judged.

An attempt to change a craft into a bureaucracy will be perceived by the members as a failure of confidence and a withdrawal of support and thus strongly resisted; efforts to change them into a profession will be seen as irrelevant and thus in great part ignored. Such gains as can be made in the way the police handle citizens are not likely to come primarily from either proliferating rules (i.e., bureaucratizing the police) or sending officers to colleges, special training programs, or human relations institutes (i.e., "professionalizing" the police). Instead, the most significant changes will be in organization and leadership in order to increase the officer's familiarity with and sensitivity to the neighborhood he patrols and rewarding him for doing what is judged (necessarily after the fact) to be the right thing rather than simply the "efficient" thing.

LAW-ENFORCEMENT FUNCTION

These recommendations leave out of account the law-enforcement function of the police. This has been deliberate, partly because the crook-catching, crime-stopping function is so often exaggerated. But obviously there is a law-enforcement function, and it is in any given case hard to separate from the order-maintenance function. Law enforcement ideally should be organized differently from order maintenance, however. It is, for example, more suitably managed through centralized command structures, the issuance of explicit rules, and the specialization of tasks (burglary details, homicide details, traffic-enforcement divisions, and so forth). Perhaps a police department should make the two functions even more separate than they are now. For example, there is some impressionistic evidence that such tactics worsen police-community relations.[14] Perhaps the roving patrol force should be composed of men different from those in the neighborhood patrol force, so that the tensions created by the former could be directed away from the role performed by the latter. Or perhaps intensive street patrol in a particular area could be done under the guidance of and on the basis of tactical intelligence furnished by neighborhood patrol officers who are best able to distinguish between innocent and suspicious behavior and between decent citizens and "bad actors."

But in crime prevention not too much should be expected of the police. I doubt that any deployment, any strategy, or any organizational principles will permit the police to make more than a slight or temporary reduction in the rate of most common crimes. As the police themselves are fond of saying, "we don't cause crime," and, as I would like to see them add, "we can't stop crime." They can and should make arrests and they can and should investigate suspicious circumstances. But I know of no police administrator who is optimistic that they can make more than marginal gains, however they behave. It would be well, therefore, not to "oversell" proposed improvements in police manpower, organization, training, equipment, or tactics. Already too many citizens share the rather dangerous view that if only we "unleashed" the police we could "stop crime" — dangerous because if we act on that assumption we are likely to produce only frustrated expectations and deeper passions.

Indeed, it might be well if we shifted the focus of our legitimate concern to the behavior of those institutions that dispose of criminals once arrested — the courts and the correctional and probation systems. For all offenses other than the most trivial, the vast majority of the persons processed by these institutions are repeaters. According to one estimate, 87.5 percent of all persons arrested for nontraffic offenses have been arrested before.[15] The average person arrested will be arrested 7.6 times in his lifetime.[16] The problem of recidivism is obviously of the greatest importance — if we fail to induce a person after his first arrest to avoid crime, there is a strong chance we will have to arrest him six or seven more times; how many more times we *should* arrest him for crimes we do not learn of is anyone's guess. In the simplest cost-effective terms, a dollar invested in the right correctional program is likely to have a higher marginal product than a dollar invested in the right police program.

But what is the "right program"? Do we have a correctional technology capable of significantly reducing the recidivism rate? I am not sure we do, or that we ever will, but I suspect that we have not tried very hard to find out. There have been some promising experiments with community-based, heavily staffed programs in California, Utah, and New Jersey, but there appears to be little organized effort to repeat these experiments elsewhere, or if they are repeated to evaluate them rigorously, or if they are evaluated to institutionalize what we learn from them.[17] In our preoccupation with the crime problem, we have come to identify it either as wholly a "social" problem (which can only be solved in three or four generations by programs which might — no one quite seems to be sure how — eliminate the lower classes) or as a "police" problem which can be solved only by taking the "handcuffs" off the police and "cracking down." I am certainly not opposed to ameliorating social problems or to increasing public support for the police, but I would like to see at least an equivalent amount of attention given to improving the way existing institutions now manage the offenders who have already shown by their actions that antipoverty programs are yet to have a therapeutic effect, and by their appearance in court that they have not managed to escape the police.

Notes

1. This article is in part adapted from material that will appear in my book-length study of the police, *Varieties of Police Behavior* (Cambridge: Harvard University Press, forthcoming).
2. Philip H. Ennis, *Criminal Victimization in the United States,* a report to the President's Commission on Law Enforcement and Administration of Justice (Washington, D.C.: U.S. Government Printing Office, 1967), p. 13.
3. See Jerome H. Skolnick, *Justice Without Trial* (New York: Wiley, 1966) pp. 167–181.
4. A "get-tough" policy by the police in Miami was reported to have led to a drop in street crimes, at least in one area of the city. (*New York Times,* February 19, 1968). When off-duty police officers began to work as taxi drivers in New York City, there was a drop in the number of robberies and assaults against cabbies (*New York Times,* February 20, 1968). After the stories appeared, however, it was reported that these street crimes had begun to show an increase, though they had not yet risen to the level they attained before the counter-measures were adopted. We know very little about how great a reduction in crime is the result of criminal perceptions of police intent and how much the result of the direct consequences of police actions, nor have we tried (except in a very few cases) to measure the persistence of such improvement as does occur.

5. Various proposals for changing police practices are reported in the President's Commission on Law Enforcement and Administration of Justice, *Task Force Report: The Police* (Washington, D.C.: U.S. Government Printing Office, 1967), p. xi, and the National Advisory Commission on Civil Disorders, *Report* (Washington, D.C.: U.S. Government Printing Office, 1968), chapter XI.

6. Differences in patrol styles or strategies are described and to some degree explained in Wilson, *op. cit.*, chapters IV–VII.

7. Ivan Belknap, *Human Problems of a State Mental Hospital* (New York: McGraw-Hill, 1956). It is striking to note the similarities between Belknap's description of mental hospital attendants and my description of patrolmen in large cities – see especially Belknap, pp. 115, 116, 138, 152, 154, and 170.

8. See the excellent analysis in Charles Perrow's "Hospitals: Technology, Structure, and Goals," in James G. March's (ed.) *Handbook of Organizations* (Chicago: Rand McNally, 1965), pp. 916–946, and the account of certain "elite" hospitals practicing "milieu therapy" in W. Caudill's *The Psychiatric Hospital as a Small Society* (Cambridge: Harvard University Press, 1958), R.N. Rapoport, *et al, Community as Doctor* (London: Tavistock, 1960) and A.H. Stanton and M.S. Schwartz's *The Mental Hospital* (New York: Basic Books, 1954.)

9. See Perrow, *op. cit.*, pp. 925, 926, 930, 934.

10. Rapoport, *et al., op cit.*, p. 208.

11. Donald J. Black and Albert J. Reiss, Jr., "Patterns in Police and Citizen Transactions," in *Studies of Crime and Law Enforcement in Major Metropolitan Areas*, a report to the President's Commission on Law Enforcement and Administration of Justice (Washington, D.C.: U.S. Government Printing Office, 1967), Vol. II, Section I, pp. 132–139. Observers working under the direction of Black and Reiss in Boston, Chicago, and Washington, D. C., Reported that 62 percent of all white officers and 28 percent of all Negro officers volunteered "highly prejudiced" or "prejudiced" comments about Negroes. There was, however, no clear relationship between attitude and behavior. "A recurring theme in the observer's reports was the great disparity between the verbalized attitudes of officers in the privacy of the patrol car, and the public conduct of officers in encounters with Negroes and members of other minority groups" (p. 138). After observing police behavior, Black and Reiss conclude that "policemen generally do not disproportionately behave aggressively or negatively toward Negroes," though they do "disproportionately behave amiably or positively toward white citizens" (p. 56).

12. A good summary of evidence on the disproportionately lower-class origin of assaultive crime in Marvin E. Wolfgang's *Crimes of Violence*, a report to the President's Commission on Law Enforcement and Administration of Justice (1967), pp. 166–169. Additional evidence based on direct observation can be found in Walter B. Miller's "Violent Crimes in City Gangs," *Annals*, Vol. 364 (March, 1966), pp. 96–112, and "Theft Behavior In Juvenile Gangs," in Malcolm W. Klein's *Juvenile Gangs in Context* (Englewood Cliffs, N.J.: Prentice-Hall, 1967), p. 34.

13. See President's Commission on Law Enforcement and Administration of Justice, *Task Force Report: The Police* (Washington, D.C.: U.S. Government Printing Office, 1967), pp. 21–27.

14. *Report* of the National Advisory Commission on Civil Disorders (1968), chapter 11.

15. Ronald Christensen, "Projected Percentage of U.S. Population With Criminal Arrest and Conviction Records," in President's Commission on Law Enforcement and Administration of Justice, *Task Force Report: Science and Technology* (Washington, D.C.: U.S. Government Printing Office, 1967), Appendix J, p. 220.

16. *Ibid.*, p. 227.

17. President's Commission on Law Enforcement and Administration of Justice, *Task Force Report: Corrections* (Washington, D.C.: U.S. Government Printing Office, 1967), chapter 4, especially pp. 38–39, 41–42.

RALPH A. ROSSUM

PROBLEMS OF JUDICIAL ADMINISTRATION:
THE EFFECT OF SUPREME COURT DECISIONS ON COURTS OF
LIMITED JURISDICTION

Chief Justice Warren Burger, in his 1968 address to the American Bar Association, generally known as the First State of the Judiciary Message, made reference to a famous speech delivered 62 years earlier by Dean Roscoe Pound to that same association. In 1906, Pound warned that the work of twentieth century courts could not be conducted through the use of nineteenth century methods and machinery. Chief Justice Burger, in commenting on how little Dean Pound's admonition has been heeded, declared:

. . . we are still trying to operate the courts with fundamentally the same basic methods, procedures, and machinery he [Pound] said were not good enough in 1906. In the supermarket age, we are like a merchant trying to operate a cracker barrel corner grocery store with the methods and equipment of 1900.[1]

Many factors — typically related to the uniqueness of the courts and the constraints and conflicts which their unusual role creates — help frustrate the attainment of better and more orderly judicial administration. Ernest Friesen has explored six of these.[2] First, courts depend almost totally upon political processes for their resources. The governmental system places responsibility for solving complex social problems on the courts without giving them the resources necessary for their effective resolution. Second, traditional adversary theory requires judges to assume passive roles, thereby placing responsibility for the administration of justice upon

Reprinted by permission of the *American Journal of Criminal Law*, Vol. 3, No. 1 (1974).

the performance, quality, availability, and attitudes of the American lawyer. Third, the practice of law tends to be highly individualistic. Attorneys are trained as soloists and are not prepared for membership in an organization. This professional independence — exhibited by attorneys and judges alike — prevents strong administration. Fourth, the jury system is a special constraint upon court management. The difficulties that attend the trying of a case with a cohesive team of jurors over any protracted period of time need no elaboration. Fifth, methods of selection and tenure of judges affect the performance of the judicial establishment. Efforts at reform, such as the Missouri Plan, often have made the judges less effective in court management and more dependent upon the good will of the lawyer. And finally, the statutory division of jurisdiction among courts (limited jurisdiction versus general jurisdiction) prohibits flexible administration. As Friesen notes:

Though there are clearly areas of the law and of justice which require more or less skill on the part of judges, the distribution of labor along traditional lines had not taken this into account. The critical legal problems of today are probably in the area of the relations of a tenant to his landlord, consumer credit, or juvenile behavior. The jurisdiction over these matters has traditionally been allocated to courts with lower-paid and lower-status judges.[3]

While each of these factors unquestionably limits the effectiveness of judicial administration, another factor must surely be considered: the impact on the lower courts of United States Supreme Court decisions. This study will explore this problem of judicial administration. It will focus on the effect of Supreme Court decisions upon courts of limited jurisdiction. These lower courts process minor criminal offenses, ordinance violations, and traffic infractions. Known by a variety of titles, including justice courts, district courts, city courts, police courts, magistrate courts, municipal courts, and county courts, their importance cannot be overemphasized. To begin with, there are an estimated 15,000 to 20,000 lower court judges; in contrast, there are only about 4,000 general jurisdiction judges. These lower courts handle over 90% of all criminal prosecutions in the nation.[4] Moreover, these courts are important qualitatively as well as quantitatively. They typically handle defendants with little or no criminal record. Offenders are often young, and their anti-social behavior has not progressed beyond misdemeanors. Consequently, intervention at this stage by these courts, may help prevent the development of long-term criminal careers. As the National Advisory Commission on Criminal Justice Standards and Goals points out:

The enormous crime-control potential of the lower courts is underscored by the fact that 80 percent of the major crimes of violence committed in the United States are committed by youths who have been convicted of a previous offense in a misdemeanor court.[5]

IMPACT STUDIES

The study of the impact of United States Supreme Court decisions has recently become an important field of research in public law. Empirical investigation of the Court's ability to implement the constitutional principles it enunciates, *i.e.*, to obtain compliance with its decisions, provides data useful in formulating generalizations about the Court as a political institution.[6] Decisions in the realm of criminal procedural protections have received special scrutiny.[7] Studies of this sort have typically sought to determine the success of certain court decisions, especially *Mapp v. Ohio*[8] and *Miranda v. Arizona*[9], in modifying either police behavior or courtroom procedure. These studies have generally concluded that there is "a rather wide gap between what the court says ought to be done and what in fact is actually done."[10] Thus Michael Ban, in his study of the impact of *Mapp v. Ohio,* points out that the effectiveness of the exclusionary rule was wholly dependent upon a number of Supreme Court assumptions:

The first and seemingly the safest of the Court's assumptions was that defense lawyers would move to suppress illegally obtained evidence and that they would do it with some skill. The Court also assumed that prosecuting attorneys would aid, or at least not actively impede, the judicial process. Next, the Court was assuming that lower court judges would grant valid motions to suppress and would, it was hoped, help to make the rules clear to police. And finally, the Court, by assuming that the actors in the local system of criminal justice would play their assigned roles, was assuming that in fact an adversary system of justice was operative at the lower court level, that the lower courts would be responsible to the Supreme Court.[11]

As Ban's research suggests, "such assumptions were unwarranted." Dallin Oaks' findings are somewhat at odds with Ban's, but this conflict hardly provides comfort for the Court. Analyzing the evidentiary grounds for arrest and subsequent disposition of misdemeanor narcotics cases in New York City before and after *Mapp,* Oaks concludes that the effect of *Mapp* has been to encourage "police perjury" designed to legalize an arrest and thereby avoid the effect of the exclusionary rule.[12] Studies on the effectiveness of *Miranda* — with its insistence on an accused's rights to silence and counsel during interrogation after arrest or detention — reinforce these assessments of the Court's limited power to secure compliance with its rulings. Neal Milner, for instance, argues that the "effectiveness of Supreme Court-imposed restraints on police behavior . . . is mitigated by the milieu in which the police officer operates, by the characteristics of the police decision-making process, and by the relationship police have with their reference groups."[13] Jonathan D. Casper reflects the general picture that can be drawn from studies of this sort:

The Court spoke in its *Miranda* opinion of redressing the balance between law enforcement officials and the suspect, of permitting him to make intelligent choices about how to proceed without coercion and with the advice of competent counsel should he so desire it. The studies on the impact of *Miranda* suggest that this goal has not been reached. The decision was no doubt a movement toward this goal, but the dynamics of the legal system — the gap between the "ought" of doctrine and the "is" of behavior — again demonstrate that the protection of civil liberties depends upon much more than the words of the Court.[14]

This chapter will pursue a generally unexplored, alternative approach to the study of Supreme Court decisions affecting the criminal procedural system. Rather than investigate the extent to which certain decisions have affected police behavior or courtroom proceedings, this study seeks to examine the consequences of various Supreme Court decisions in complicating the problems of judicial administration. It examines in detail the impact on courts of limited jurisdiction of four key Supreme Court decisions on criminal procedure: *Waller v. Florida*,[15] which held that a second trial by the state, following conviction under the municipal ordinance for the same offense, constitutes double jeopardy in violation of the fifth and fourteenth amendments of the United States Constitution; *William v. Illinois*,[16] which held that an indigent defendant cannot be imprisoned longer than the statutory maximum sentence for failure to pay a fine; *Tate v. Short*,[17] which held that a person cannot be made to serve out a fine for conviction of an offense otherwise not punishable by incarceration; and *Argersinger v. Hamlin*,[18] which expanded the principle of *Gideon v. Wainwright*[19] and extended the right to counsel to all indigent misdemeanants who face imprisonment as a punishment. On the basis of such an examination, this study concludes that the effect of compliance with these decisions on the lower courts has been the imposition of an increased set of demands on these courts which (1) complicates procedure, further overloads already crowded dockets, and generates inefficiency; (2) prompts the growth of a substantial judiciary bureaucracy to deal with these increased demands — e.g., full time city prosecutors and public defenders, probation officers, and increased court clerk staff; and (3) heightens the need for judicial reform and consolidation. In brief, this study emphasizes rather than minimizes the political power of the Supreme Court.

This study relies primarily on the experiences of the City Court of Memphis, Tennessee. The task of measuring outputs and performance of urban criminal courts is so difficult that any more ambitious undertaking would prove to be "overwhelming."[20] As James Eisenstein and Herbert Jacob observe:

Although the logical unit of analysis . . . is that of individual defendants, there are serious problems in discovering it. First, there are at least two major units of analysis used by court systems to report on their activities: the "case" and the "indictment" or "charges." Second, regardless of which is used, their content can vary along four important dimensions: (1) whether the actions of one or a number of individuals are being examined; (2) whether the charges arise from a single set of related events or from several incidents related only because the same people are charged in each; (3) whether a single offense or a series of offenses is formally charged; and (4) whether the disposition of the matter is linked to the disposition of matters involving other crimes or defendants. A "case," which can be thought of as a set of charges handled in a single proceeding can involve any combination of these four dimensions. In fact, combinations of these factors are found not only between jurisdictions but within the same jurisdiction.[21]

To minimize these measurement problems, the research in this study is limited principally to the City of Memphis and the State of Tennessee. They constitute an almost perfect setting. Tennessee's courts are archaic and cumbersome; their organization is complex and traditional; their jurisdictions are complicated and overlapping. Reform and consolidation are much needed. In such a system, the increased set of demands imposed by *Waller, Williams, Tate* and *Argersinger* has been all the more dramatically felt and is all the more immediately apparent.

THE JUDICIAL SYSTEM IN TENNESSEE

Henry Glick and Kenneth Vines have measured the extent of legal professionalism present in state court systems through the construction of a composite index based on five major factors: judicial selection, organization, administration, tenure, and salary.[22] On the basis of this index, Tennessee ranks 42nd among the states in terms of its degree of legal professionalism, tied with Georgia, Kansas, and Texas. Tennessee's judicial structure is "unusually and unnecessarily complicated."[23] Five different courts of limited jurisdiction comprise the base of the judicial pyramid: justice of the peace courts, general sessions courts, municipal courts, county courts of monthly sessions, and juvenile and domestic relations courts.[24] Above them stand three courts of first record or general jurisdiction: circuit courts, criminal courts, and chancery courts.[25] (Tennessee is one of the five remaining states in the United States which still use separate courts for chancery jurisdiction.) Next in the judicial hierarchy are the Court of Appeals, with jurisdiction to hear appeals from the circuit courts and the chancery courts, and the Court of Criminal Appeals, with jurisdiction to hear appeals from the criminal courts. Above these two appellate courts and at the apex of the judicial pyramid towers the Tennessee Supreme Court.

One of the more unsatisfactory consequences of this unduly complicated arrangement is the presence of "confusing, overlapping, and conflicting jurisdiction."[26] Presently before the 88th General Assembly of the Tennessee Legislature are proposals that would create uniform judicial circuits for circuit and chancery court jurisdictions and that would transfer all criminal jurisdiction to the circuit courts.[27] However, current legislative interest in judicial reorganization has thus far left unconsidered the complex problems facing the courts of limited jurisdiction — the courts that provide approximately 90% of the citizens with their first and only impression of this state's criminal justice system. Proposals to create a unified one-level trial court system with enough divisions to handle efficiently all types of claims have gone unattended; so have more moderate proposals to establish a state-wide court of limited jurisdiction, which would include all general sessions, municipal, probate, and juvenile courts and which would have exclusive jurisdiction over all state misdemeanors, city ordinance violations, probate matters, juvenile matters, civil jurisdiction up to $5,000, and equity jurisdiction up to $1,000.[28]

THE MEMPHIS CITY COURT

Within this system, marked by organizational disarray and legislative disinterest, operates the Municipal Court of the City of Memphis. Originally established in 1905 by a private act of the Tennessee legislature,[29] it was subsequently incorporated into the City Charter as follows:

There shall be a city court. Said court shall be a court of record and shall have original and exclusive jurisdiction of all violations of municipal ordinances, and shall also be clothed with the same powers and duties possessed by a justice of the peace, touching the arrest and preliminary trial, discharging, binding over, or punishing under the small offense law, of all persons charged with offenses against the state committed in the city.[30]

Its original powers were limited indeed. City court judges were empowered (1) to sit as "committing magistrates" — issuing warrants, holding preliminary hearings, and binding over cases to the grand jury; and (2) to impose fines on violators of city ordinances, but only in amounts up to $50.[31] At the time, however, these powers were regarded as sufficient. People thought of Memphis as a "big ole country town" — there was no need for its city court to have more authority. In fact, only in the last three or four years has a real appreciation arisen for the need for "changes, modifications, and improvements" in the city courts.[32]

A number of important "changes, modifications, and improvements" have taken place — most of them prompted by the excellent reform proposals of Bernie Weinman and Isadore Baer.[33] As a result, Memphis City Court may now set maximum penalties of 30 days imprisonment or $50 fine or both for violation of certain city ordinances, including the offenses of assault and battery, disorderly conduct, disturbing religious or other lawful assemblies, public drunkenness, indecent exposure, malicious mischief, shoplifting, carrying weapons, discharging firearms, reckless driving, and driving while intoxicated.[34] However, this power to imprison defendants has changed court procedures and performance less than its creation would suggest. Prior to this legislation, the court had routinely imprisoned violators of city ordinances, but only when they were unable to pay their fines.[35] Since the Supreme Court was contemporaneously declaring that such practices were unconstitutional violations of equal protection in *Williams v. Illinois*[36] and *Tate v. Short*,[37] this legislation has salvaged the court's power to imprison defendants. But it has not otherwise benefited the court, except to put some teeth in its probation program. With the threat of penal sanctions in the background, probation becomes a meaningful rehabilitative device.[38] If a defendant knows that violation of probation means nothing more than a $50 fine, he has very few incentives to follow the outlines set out in his probation program; however, 30 days in jail provides those needed incentives.

Besides these additions to its arsenal, the city court has experienced substantial changes in its structure and organization. The number of divisions of City Court has increased from three to five.[39] And public approval of a city ordinance by referendum provided the Court with the additional administrative machinery necessitated by its growth, both in size and jurisdiction. Included in the package was the establishment of a chief administrative judge with significant supervisory powers.[40]

Of all the changes that have taken place, perhaps the most significant has been the statutory authorization for the Memphis City Court to try state misdemeanor cases. The court received concurrent jurisdiction with the criminal courts and the general sessions courts to try state misdemeanors punishable by fines up to $1,000 and sentences of less than a year, provided a six-panel jury is used.[41] (When the jury is waived, the court's sentencing powers remain the same except that fines are limited to a maximum of $50.)[42] This change has proved significant in two respects: (1) it has increased the City Court's capacity to deter petty crime and (2) it has enabled City Court to process nearly 70% of all indictable offenses in Memphis, thereby freeing criminal court resources for the disposition of felony cases.[43] Both of these points deserve additional consideration.

City Court jurisdiction to try state misdemeanor cases has generally strengthened state sanctions in such cases — sanctions less frequently administered in any forum under the previous system. Before the City Court possessed this jurisdiction to try state misdemeanors, the inefficiency of the then existing court system encouraged the police to process minor illegalities as violations of city ordinances rather than as misdemeanors. For example, policemen making an arrest for assault had the choice of charging the defendant in city court with a city ordinance violation or of charging him with a state misdemeanor in general sessions court or criminal court. Given this choice of forums, they were typically reluctant to bring defendants to the state courts, which required police presence first at an arraignment, then at a special preliminary hearing, next, at the grand jury, and, finally, at the criminal court trial itself.[44] This burden of appearances encouraged the police to bring such cases to City Court where procedure was simpler. This posed a problem, however, in that city court could do no more than levy a $50 fine, often no deterrent at all. Chief Administrative Judge Weinman repeatedly heard defendants say, "If I had had another $50, I would have hit him again." However, empowering City Court with state misdemeanor jurisdiction has changed the situation. Although its procedures still remain simpler and although policemen still favor it over state court, the City Court now possesses power to impose jail terms of up to 11 months, 29 days — a force with which to be reckoned.

Jurisdiction to try state misdemeanor cases has also allowed city court to handle approximately 70% of all indictable offenses that occur in Memphis, thereby freeing the criminal courts for disposition of felony cases.[45] In 1973, the city court disposed of over 4,800 misdemeanor cases — up from 2,323 in 1972, the year in which the court first received this added jurisdiction.[46] In contrast, a total of 3,394 indictments were returned in the six divisions of criminal court: 2,688 felonies and 706 misdemeanors (including misdemeanor indictments returned in conjunction with felony indictments e.g., robbery with a deadly weapon and carrying a pistol). With city court hearing 85% of all misdemeanor charges, the criminal court has been freed to concentrate on felony cases. Table 1 shows the number of indictments returned by criminal court from 1965 to 1973. It demonstrates the dramatic impact on the criminal justice system of the new city court jurisdiction.

TABLE 1

Breakdown of Felony and Misdemeanor Indictments
From 1965 to 1973 in Criminal Court[47]

Year	Felonies	Misdemeanors
1965	1966	2238
1966	1904	1981
1967	1732	2220
1968	2120	2360
1969	2186	2590
1970	2328	2014
1971	2439	1456
1972	2411	594
1973	2688	706

This impact extends far beyond the mere number of cases that city court is able to hear. Government saves substantial time and money by processing misdemeanor cases in this manner. City court has reduced the time necessary to dispose of an average misdemeanor in Memphis from nine to twelve months from the date of arrest to thirty to ninety days, with the overwhelming majority disposed of within thirty to sixty days.[48] In terms of money, it has saved the system approximately $300,000 annually.[49]

PROBLEMS OF CITY COURT

Despite the benefits of city court misdemeanor jurisdiction vis-a-vis the criminal justice system as a whole, the effect on the Memphis City Court itself has been most deleterious. Memphis City Court has traditionally battled a set of difficult problems, and the increased responsibilities of state misdemeanor jurisdiction have only exacerbated them. These problems must be briefly explored, since they have typically been aggravated whenever new demands or responsibilities — such as the increased criminal procedural protections required by such Supreme Court decisions as *Waller, Williams, Tate,* and *Argersinger* — impose themselves on city court.

Perhaps the greatest problem faced by Memphis City Court and all other lower courts is that people regard them as the stepchild of the entire judicial system.[50] On the bottom rung of the judicial ladder, these courts do business considered ministerial, monotonous, and legally unchallenging. Influential forces for judicial reform, such as lawyer-legislators and bar association officers, seldom practice in these lower courts and, as a result, neither appreciate their problems nor have a personal stake in upgrading their operations. In Memphis, the Shelby County Bar Association is certainly a case in point. It has typically remained unconcerned with the criminal justice system until it feels that its own interests are being challenged, as for instance, when it mobilized to resist the use of public defenders by defendants out on bail.[51]

This neglect by those most able to scrutinize and aid the level of lower court performance extends even to the Tennessee Supreme Court.[52] The comments of Justice William H. D. Fones are typical. While admitting only a "layman's interest in or knowledge of courts of limited jurisdiction," he nevertheless believes that, with few exceptions, the members of their judiciary are "utterly lacking in judicial dignity, temperament, and legal sophistication." And, he continues, this is hardly surprising. Given the work they are required to perform and the relatively low salaries they receive, no really "self-respecting attorney" would seek such a position.[53]

Most of the other problems that afflict the city court stem from its ignominious status. For too long, the city administration has regarded it simply as a revenue producer. The attitude has been, "Let the cash registers ring with justice." This emphasis on revenue rather than on justice has significantly hampered city court. Since the city administration has stressed profits over quality, it has refused to provide a salary sufficient to attract uniformly good men to the bench.[54] Likewise, it has failed to adequately fund the court clerk's office. The clerks are overworked and underpaid.[55] Unhappy with their lot, they have organized a clerk's union, affiliated with Local 1733, American Federation of State, County, and Municipal Employees (AFL-CIO) — one of the few unions of court clerks in the nation.[56] This unionization has further decreased court efficiency, providing the staff a certain autonomy at the expense of the clerk of the court.[57]

This lack of supervisory control over the clerk's office has also aggravated still another problem of the city court — its archaic management and record-keeping systems. This problem is by no means limited to Memphis City Court. As Leonard Downie writes:

Although most court offices do have telephones, to step inside the local courthouse, in this age of space travel, trans-oceanic television, and computers, is to travel backward in time — if not to the Dark Ages, then certainly to an era generations ago. Modern improvements in management techniques, record-keeping, and communications are all but unheard of inside courthouse walls. Instead, U.S. courts continue to follow slavishly many of the same procedures as did courts in early rural America and the shires of England before that.[58]

At a time when computerized data processing could print out a daily calendar for each judge, provide additional information on the judges' case loads, determine how many cases each attorney has and when each case is scheduled for its next court hearing, aid in legal research, and enable court administrators to assess accurately the performance of each division, the Memphis City Court staff wastes much of its time and effort by keeping most records and preparing all dockets in longhand.[59] These "cracker barrel corner grocery store" methods, as Chief Justice Burger calls them, have produced both inefficiency and error.[60] As a case in point, over $4,000,000 in unpaid traffic tickets have accumulated.[61] These methods have proved totally inadequate in handling the tremendous volume of cases the city court hears.

The volume of Memphis City Court cases is simply staggering. In 1973, its four divisions heard over 200,000 charges.[62] Of that number an insignificant 201 were appealed *de novo* to circuit or criminal court, so the decisions it renders — for better or worse — must be regarded as final. Yet, the average docket for a morning or afternoon session contains from 200 to 300 charges. While the number of defendants or cases is often less than the total number of charges, the fact remains that the judges generally have less than one minute in which to dispose of each charge.[63] The result, of necessity, is "assembly line justice." Many of the charges presented do not raise issues that require consideration and can be resolved in this summary fashion. However, this "assembly line justice" also minimizes the likelihood that questions of substance will receive full or fair treatment, and it virtually precludes any meaningful correctional disposition.

To deal with these problems, the number of divisions of City Court has recently been expanded. A fourth division was added in 1972, and a fifth in late 1973. However, this expansion of the City Court has generated problems of its own. The five divisions of City Court, located on the Sixth Floor of the Memphis Central Police Station, are forced to share but three courtrooms. Completion of a proposed criminal justice center, which would ultimately relieve the situation, is at least five years off. The lack of court space has proved so intolerable that three judges have threatened to sue the city council and administration for two additional courtrooms.[64] Judge Churchill, aware of the city's overriding interest in the revenue the courts produce, has declared that he will impose no court costs on any defendant until adequate courtroom space is provided.

Expansion of the city court has also generated administrative problems. Although the court now has a chief administrative judge, he lacks any real power or sanctions. He can only do those things to which a majority of the judges have given their consent. As a result, this increase in the number of judges has simply decreased the likelihood of agreement among the judges and has further diminished administrative control. To help meet these problems, the Tennessee Law Enforcement Planning Commission (TLEPC) has proposed the establishment and funding of a court administrator for the Memphis City Court.[65] The Commission's intention is that the court administrator would oversee budgetary matters and dockets, encourage computerization of records and other administrative modernization methods, and work with the TLEPC. However, the program seems destined for frustration; without supporting legislation, the court administrator would be no better situated than the chief administrative judge to impose modern management and record-keeping systems on the independent judges and their unionized clerks.[66]

THE IMPACT OF *WALLER, WILLIAMS, TATE,* AND *ARGERSINGER*

The problem-ridden Memphis City Court has been described in detail. This detail is necessary in order to assess the effects, if any, of Supreme Court decisions such as *Waller, Williams, Tate,* and *Argersinger,* in the criminal procedural realm. The effects appear profound. These decisions by imposing an increased set of demands on City Court, have generated even greater inefficiency — complicating procedure, overloading dockets, prompting the growth of a substantial bureaucracy to deal with these increased demands, and intensifying the need for judicial reform and consolidation. Each of these decisions will be considered in turn.

Waller v. Florida,[67] which forbade prosecution under both state law and municipal ordinance for the same offense, has had a substantial impact. In Florida, Tennessee, and eighteen other states, a defendant was subject to both city and state charges for an offense violating both a local ordinance and a state statute, *e.g.,* driving while intoxicated. The Supreme Court had seemingly ended this practice in a previous case, *Benton v. Maryland,*[68] holding that "the double jeopardy prohibition of the Fifth Amendment represents a fundamental ideal in our constitutional heritage, and that it should apply to the States through the Fourteenth Amendment." But dual prosecution continued because these states did not actually regard it as constituting double jeopardy. Two differing understandings supported the states' continued practice, and both found expression in Tennessee Supreme Court opinions. One line of reasoning regarded a prosecution for violation of a city ordinance as "a civil, rather than a criminal, case; the fine or penalty being a debt."[69] This "civil action, in the nature of an action of debts, lies as the suit of the mayor and aldermen to recover penalties for violating town ordinances and bylaws, and the acts prohibited by the ordinances and bylaws may be such as are also criminal offenses against the State."[70] Whatever problems arose from considering a city prosecution as a civil action, double jeopardy — *i.e.,* two criminal actions for the same offense — surely was not one of them. The other rationale was based on "dual sovereignty" theory. "There are certain acts which constitute offenses against more than one sovereign and trial in the courts of one sovereign, of course, is not a bar to trial in the courts of other sovereign."[71] The U.S. Supreme Court rejected both of these understandings in *Waller.* It was particularly critical of the "dual sovereignty" theory, which it branded as an "anachronism." Relying heavily on the oral argument of Waller's attorney, the court found that

. . . the apt analogy to the relationship between municipal and state governments is to be found in the relationship between the government of a Territory and the Government of the United States. . . . [A] prosecution by a court of the United States is a bar to a subsequent prosecution by a territorial court, since both are arms of the same sovereign.[72]

As a result of *Waller,* the City of Memphis must now elect to press a city or a state charge. Since the city collects the fines assessed for city ordinance violations but not for state misdemeanors, it has an anxious preference to press municipal charges.[73] A competition of sorts has developed between the city and the state over which court — city or state — should try these charges. Since the city court can retain court costs from state misdemeanors, (which can run as high as $60 a case, approaching and at times exceeding the total of the maximum fines ($50) and maximum court costs ($5) imposed for a city charge) this competition has been kept within bounds. However, the police preference for the simpler procedures of City Court has weighted the competition in favor of City Court. As a consequence, its caseload has become increasingly more unmanageable while the state courts' dockets have dwindled and their courtrooms (held at such a premium in city court) have become idle.

William v. Illinois[74] and *Tate v. Short*[75] have similarly aggravated the problems of these courts. *Williams* raised the question of whether the state may extend an indigent's confinement beyond the maximum term specified by law for failure to pay a fine. Williams' attorney argued that such practice constituted a denial of equal protection because it imposed a heavier burden on the indigent than it did on the solvent offender. He argued that there were alternative ways of collecting fines without depriving the defendant of his liberty − *e.g.,* collection by installment arrangements, garnishment, or execution − and that the state should be required to exercise these alternatives.[76]

The State of Illinois contended that this practice was not unconstitutional because "the state's compelling interest in crime deterrence balances the disadvantages to the individual who cannot pay."[77] Moreover, since 48 other states had similar statutes, the result of requiring the alternatives suggested by petitioner would be "chaos." However, a unanimous Supreme Court, speaking through Chief Justice Burger, rejected these arguments. Aware that its holding would "place a further burden on states in administering criminal justice," the Court held the states may not "subject a certain class of convicted defendants to a period of imprisonment beyond the statutory maximum solely by reason of their indigency."[78]

Tate v. Short followed *Williams* in the next term. *Tate* considered whether a state can, consistent with the equal protection clause, "limit the punishment to payment of fines if one is able to pay it, yet convert the fine into a prison term for an indigent defendant without the means to pay his fine."[79] Attorneys for petitioner Tate argued no, insisting that a constitutionally permissible alternative was available: *i.e.,* the establishment of "an installment collection system." Attorneys for the state reminded the Court of all the problems that would attend such an alternative − for example, "how large are the installment payments to be?," "what will happen when people fall behind in their payments?"[80] They implored the Court not "to enter this Serbonian Bog." But "enter this Serbonian Bog" the Court did, and the Memphis City Court has felt the consequences. Because of *Williams,* and especially *Tate,* the city court can no longer fine an indigent defendant and then incarcerate him for a time sufficient to satisfy its fine at a rate of $5 per day. It must now give defendants time to pay or allow them to pay installments. These decisions have thus obliged the city court to become a virtual collection agency, increasing the burden on its bureaucratic apparatus and staff. Given its "neglected stepchild" status and its overworked, underpaid, and unionized clerk's office, collection of these fines has often been difficult. The court lacks the personnel to follow up on cases where people cannot pay, and presently, there are over $100,000 in uncollected fines.[81] This fact has concerned both the city, distressed at the loss of revenue, and the city court judges, fearful of the effect on their rulings and on public attitudes toward the judicial system.

Williams and *Tate* have also had another far-reaching effect. Before *Williams,* the jurisdiction of city court was limited to violations of city ordinances carrying fines not exceeding $50. It could incarcerate defendants only if they were unable to pay their fines. *Tate* deprived the court of this power and, at least with regard to indigent defendants, removed its only sanction. The Tennessee Legislature and the Memphis City Council responded by providing Memphis City Court with power to impose up to thirty days imprisonment for violation of certain city ordinances.[82] Exercise of this increased power gave greater stature to city court, and encouraged the state legislature to give it jurisdiction over state misdemeanors as well, thereby further enlarging its responsibilities and bureaucratic apparatus.[83]

Finally, *Argersinger v. Hamlin,* which provided the right to counsel for indigent misdemeanants, has also effected considerable change. The Supreme Court was aware of the impact this decision would have on the administration of justice.[84] But it was ultimately persuaded by the preponderance of evidence which showed the misdemeanor trial to be "characterized by insufficient and frequently irresponsible preparation on the part of the defense, the prosecution, and the court."[85] It cited a study of the American Civil Liberties Union which established that misdemeanants "represented by attorneys are five times as likely to emerge from police court with all charges dismissed as are defendants who face similar charges without counsel."[86] Its conclusion was irresistible: the problems associated with misdemeanor charges require the presence of counsel to insure a fair trial for the accused.

This right to counsel has prompted the growth of a full time staff of public defenders for the Memphis City Court.[87] But ironically, *Argersinger* has also stimulated the creation of a staff of full time city prosecutors for each courtroom. Prior to this decision, the police frequently had to serve the dual role of witness-complainant and prosecutor. But with defense counsel now likely, the police were at a disadvantage. They could be cross-examined by defense counsel but could not in turn cross-examine the defendant. On such occasions, the task of prosecuting the case typically fell where it most assuredly did not belong — on the judge. The need for city prosecutors became compelling. Thus, the city court judges and the Memphis Police Department legal advisor went before the City Council and, as needs to be done in Memphis, presented a "dollars and cents" argument.

They placed little emphasis on the prosecutor's importance in assuring a proper adversary proceeding. Instead, they stressed that if a prosecutor were to gain only one additional conviction a day, not because of more or better evidence, but simply through better presentation of the evidence available, the program would more than pay for itself. These revenue-related arguments proved persuasive, and the city court got full time city prosecutors.[88] Thus, *Argersinger* has helped increase not only the quality of city court justice but also the size of its legal bureaucracy as well.

THE NEED FOR JUDICIAL UNIFICATION

Waller, Williams, Tate and *Argersinger* have all placed increased demands on the Memphis City Court which have tended to complicate its procedures, stimulate the growth of a substantial if unwieldy bureaucracy, and exacerbate the need for judicial reform and reorganization. They have presented such severe problems for judicial administration that its chief administrative judge considers the only realistic solution to be the organization· of all courts in Tennessee into a unified judicial system financed by the state and administered through a statewide court administrator.[89] In his estimation, this unification is the only way to eliminate duplication and competition, end the use of city court for revenue-generating purposes, and insure adoption of modern management and record-keeping techniques. The National Advisory Commission on Criminal Justice Standards and Goals concurs. Its Standard 8.1 reads:

State courts should be organized into a unified judicial system financed by the State and administered through a statewide court administrator or administrative judge under the supervision of the chief justice of the State supreme court.

All trial courts should be unified into a single trial court with general criminal as well as civil jurisdiction. Criminal jurisdiction now in courts of limited jurisdiction should be placed in these unified trial courts of general jurisdiction, with the exception of certain traffic violations. The State supreme court should promulgate rules for the conduct of minor as well as major criminal prosecutions.

All judicial functions in the trial court should be performed by full-time judges. All judges should possess law degrees and be members of the bar.

A transcription of or other record of the pretrial court proceedings and the trial should be kept in all criminal cases.

The appeals procedure should be the same for all cases.

Pre-trial release services, probation service, and other rehabilitative services should be available in all prosecutions within the jurisdiction of the unified trial court.[90]

Serious obstacles stand in the way of such unification. Pressure to retain the status quo results from three factors: (1) a certain home town pride in having local courts; (2) the belief that these courts are "people's courts" where lawyers are not indispensable, and where trials take minutes, can be held shortly after a complaint is filed, and require little procedure or paperwork; and (3) the strong opinions of many judges that a redistribution of jurisdiction will somehow reduce the importance of the courts on which they sit.[91] The importance of this third source of resistance cannot be over-emphasized. The question of unification subjects the judges to cross-pressures. On the one hand, they stand to benefit considerably from the improved judicial administration. On the other hand, they are acutely aware of the status system in the judiciary. Most have become judges because of the status it affords them. Any reduction in their perceived status from unification may well reduce the number of lawyers willing to leave higher paying jobs to accept this heavy responsibility.[92] However, until these courts are restructured and unified, Supreme Court decisions that strongly affect the administration of justice will continue to aggravate the problems inherent in these "people's courts." The constraints and conflicts in judicial administration will only intensify.

Notes

1. Remarks of Warren E. Burger in an address to the American Bar Association, St. Louis, Missouri, August 10, 1968.

2. Ernest Friesen, "Constraints and Conflicts in Court Administration," *Public Administration Review*, 31, No. 2 (March/April, 1971), pp. 120-124. The subsequent discussion relies heavily upon this article.

3. *Ibid.*, p. 123.

4. *The Courts*, A Report of the National Advisory Commission on Criminal Justice Standards and Goals (Washington, D.C.: U.S. Government Printing Office, 1973), p. 161.

5. *Ibid.*

6. Theodore L. Becker and Malcolm M. Feeley (eds.), *The Impact of Supreme Court Decisions*, 2d ed., (New York: Oxford University Press, 1973); and Walter J. Murphy and Joseph Tanenhaus, *The Study of Public Law* (New York: Random House, 1972). See also Kenneth M. Dolbeare and Phillip E. Hammond, *The School Prayer Decisions: From Court Policy to Local Practice* (Chicago: University of Chicago Press, 1971); and Richard M. Johnson, "Compliance and Supreme Court Decision-Making," *Wisconsin Law School Review*, Vol. 1967 (Winter, 1967), pp. 170-185.

7. See Dallin H. Oaks, "Studying the Exclusionary Rule in Search and Seizure," *University of Chicago Law Review*, Vol. 37 (1970), pp. 665-753; Stuart S. Nagel, "Testing the Effects of Excluding Illegally Seized Evidence," *Wisconsin Law Review*, Vol. 1965 (Spring, 1965), pp. 283-310; and Michael J. Murphy, "The Problem of Compliance by Police Departments," *Texas Law Review*, Vol. 44 (1966), pp. 936-946.

8. 367 U.S. 643 (1961)

9. 384 U.S. 436 (1966)

10. Becker and Feeley, "Introduction," *The Impact of Supreme Court Decisions*, p.3.

11. Michael Ban, "Local Courts vs. The Supreme Court: The Impact of *Mapp v. Ohio*," paper delivered at the Annual Meeting of the American Political Science Association, New Orleans, 1973, p. 1.

12. Oaks, "Studying the Exclusionary Rule in Search and Seizure," *University of Chicago Law Review*, Vol. 37 (1970), pp. 665-753.

13. Neal Milner, "Supreme Court Effectiveness and the Police Organization," *Law and Contemporary Problems*, Vol. XXXVI, No. 4 (Autumn, 1971), p. 467.

14. Jonathan D. Casper, *The Politics of Civil Liberties* (New York: Harper & Row, 1972), pp. 265-266.

15. 397 U.S. 387 (1970).
16. 399 U.S. 235 (1970).
17. 401 U.S. 395 (1971).
18. 407 U.S. 25 (1972).
19. 372 U.S. 335 (1963).
20. James Eisenstein and Herbert Jacob, "Measuring Performance and Outputs of Criminal Courts," paper delivered at the Annual Meeting of the American Political Science Association, New Orleans, 1973, p. 9.
21. *Ibid.,* p. 3.
22. Henry Glick and Kenneth N. Vines, *State Court Systems* (Englewood Cliffs, N.J.: Prentice-Hall, 1973), pp. 11-12.
23. Lee Seifert Greene and Robert Sterling Avery, *Government in Tennessee* (Knoxville: University of Tennessee Press, 1962), p. 153.
24. Justice of the peace courts tend to exist only in isolated rural parts of the state. General sessions courts are often known as "small claims courts" since jurisdiction covers claims in amounts less than $300. Their jurisdiction also includes misdemeanors with fines of less than $50. Municipal courts have jurisdiction limited to violations of city ordinances carrying fines not exceeding $50. Their jurisdiction does not extend to cases arising under state law unless specifically provided for by the legislature. The county courts of monthly sessions are probate courts.
25. In Tennessee, there are 27 separate circuit courts. In 14 of these circuits, the courts handle both civil and criminal matters. However, in the remaining 13 circuits, where there are enough cases to warrant the existence of a separate court for criminal matters, criminal courts have been established separate from the circuit courts. See *Tennessee Code Annotated* (TCA), Sec. 16-207 to 16-236. There are also 17 distinct chancery circuits or "divisions" as they are called. The boundaries of these divisions may or may not coincide with the boundaries of the circuits. See TCA 16-237 to 16-255.
26. Greene and Avery, *Government in Tennessee,* p. 167.
27. See Senate Bill 182, 88th Tennessee General Assembly, March 7, 1973.
28. Institute of Judicial Administration, "The Judicial System in Tennessee," Report to the Tennessee Judicial Council, October, 1971.
29. Tennessee, *Private Acts,* Ch. 54, Secs. 36-39 (1905).
30. Memphis, Tennessee, *Charter and Related Laws,* Art. 35, Sec. 251 (1967).
31. Tennessee, *Constitution,* Art. VI, Sec. 14.
32. Bernie Weinman and Isadore B. Baer, "Municipal Courts in Tennessee: A New Era," *Memphis State University Law Review,* Vol. I No. 2 (Spring, 1971), pp. 311-320.
33. *Ibid.*
34. Tenn. *Public Acts,* Ch. 36 (1971).
35. Interview with David Vance, Clerk of Court, Memphis City Court, September 26, 1973.
36. Note 16 *supra.*
37. Note 17 *supra.*
38. Interview with Judge Bernie Weinman, Chief Administrative Judge, Memphis City Court, October 2, 1973.
39. Memphis, Tenn., Ordinance 1278, May 1, 1972.
40. Memphis, Tenn., *Charter and Related Laws,* art. 35, Sec. 251-265 (1967). His duties include presiding at *en banc* sessions of the court; appointing special judges; promulgating and publishing rules of the court; assigning cases to the divisions; supervising and controlling the clerk, his office, and the preparation of judicial statistics; preparing (with the advice of the other judges) the budget of the city court; requesting and convening conferences to consider the status of judicial business and to expedite and improve procedures in the administration of justice; carrying out the directives of a majority of the city court judges in all administrative matters; and carrying out such other duties as the city council by ordinances shall prescribe.

41. Tenn. *Private Acts*, ch. 288 (1972). See Tenn. *Public Acts*, ch. 62 (1971). The 1971 Public Act was identical to the 1972 Private Act in all respects but one; in Sec. 7 it diverted all fines and court costs into the municipal treasury. This provision aroused considerable controversy since many felt that the collected revenues should go to the state, not the city; and questions of the Act's constitutionality were raised. As a consequence, the 1971 Public Act was superseded by the 1972 Private Act, which distributed fines as provided by the law for general sessions courts.

42. Given the lack of jury-boxes in all but one courtroom, the lack of personnel to administer the jury-selection process, and the tremendous volume of cases heard (2,000 in 1972), a jury trial for a state misdemeanor charge has never been conducted in Memphis City Court.

43. Ronald W. Krelstein, "A Report of Case Dispositions In the City Courts," report presented to the Memphis City Court (January, 1974).

44. Interview with Judge Bernie Weinman, October 2, 1973.

45. Krelstein, *supra* note 43, at 2.

46. Because of the great number of guilty pleas, the conviction rate of misdemeanor cases tried in city court is approximately 88%. *Ibid.*, at 3.

47. Krelstein, "Addendum to Report on Case Dispositions," report filed with the Memphis City Court (January, 1974).

48. Krelstein, *supra* note 43, at 2.

49. *Ibid.*

50. Almost every individual of the Memphis City Court interviewed used this exact phrase: "City court is the stepchild of city government". See also National Advisory Commission on Criminal Justice Standards and Goals, *supra* note 4, at 161.

51. *Ibid.*

52. Tennessee, of course, is hardly unique in this respect. See *ibid.* See also L. Downie, Jr., *Justice Denied: The Case for Reform of the Courts* (Baltimore: Penguin Books, 1971), p. 159.

53. Interview with Justice William H. D. Fones, Tennessee Supreme Court, October 16, 1973.

54. The present salary for a city court judge is $19,000. It was increased from $9,500 to $16,000 in 1970. Memphis, Tenn., *Charter and Related Laws*, art. 35, sec. 254 (1967).

55. The beginning clerk starts at about $450 a month.

56. Interview with David Vance, Clerk of the Courts, Memphis City Court, September 26, 1973.

57. *Ibid.*

58. L. Downie, *supra* note 52, at 138-139.

59. See *Ibid* at 138-158. See also National Advisory Commission on Criminal Justice Standards and Goals, *supra* note 4, at ch. 11 for a discussion of some of the problems that attend computer assisted methods of management, and especially, legal research.

60. Memphis City Court has been reluctant to seek Law Enforcement Assistance Administration (LEAA) grants to help it overcome some of these problems for two reasons. First, the Court perceives LEAA as being generally unreceptive to the needs of courts and correctional agencies. Second, even if such grants were available, they involve so much "red tape", require so many progress reports, and impose so many administrative difficulties that the Memphis City Court – possessed of no grantsman and few administrative resources – would be unable to fulfill these administrative demands. However realistic the Memphis City Court's assessment may be of LEAA's posture toward the courts, LEAA funds have profoundly influenced the administration of justice. Through its grants, law enforcement agencies throughout the nation have been modernized and upgraded. They are now more efficient in their apprehension of offenders and have placed, thereby, even greater strains on the already overworked courts. Interviews with Lee Forbes, Metropolitan Criminal Justice Planning Commission, Memphis, Tennessee, October 15, 1973; Richard Borys, Director,

Memphis Pre-trial Release, October 12, 1973; and Judge Bernie Weinman, November 8, 1973.
61. Memphis *Commercial Appeal,* September 24, 1973.
62. Memphis *Commercial Appeal,* 13, April 8, 1974.
63. Interview with Judge Ray Churchill, December 4, 1973. For a discussion of the problems that attend legal research in terms of analyzing charges, cases, or defendants, see Eisenstein & Jacob, *supra* note 20. See also A. Blumberg, *Criminal Justice* (Chicago: Quadrangle Books, 1970), p. 8–12.
64. Memphis *Commercial Appeal,* 25, January 31, 1974.
65. Tennessee Law Enforcement Planning Commission, *The Five Year Comprehensive Plan for the Improvement of Law Enforcement in the State of Tennessee,* 1973, p. 423.
66. Interview with Chief Administrative Judge Bernie Weinman, November 8, 1973.
67. Waller, *supra* note 15.
68. 395 U.S. 784, 794 (1969).
69. *Nashville v. Baker,* 167 Tenn. 661, 73 S.W. 2d 169 (1934). See also *Kelly v. Conner,* 122 Tenn. 339, 123 S.W. 622 (1909).
70. *Bristol v. Burrow,* 73 Tenn. 128 (1880). See also *Meader v. Chattanooga,* 38 Tenn. 74 (1858). For another state taking much the same position see *Wisconsin ex rel. Keefe v. Schmiege,* 251 Wisc. 79, 28 N.W. 2d 345 (1947).
71. *Mullins v. Tennessee,* 380 S.W. 2d 201, 202 (1964). See also *O'Haver v. Montgomery,* 120 Tenn. 448, 111 S.W. 2d 449 (1908).
72. Waller, *supra* note 15, at 393.
73. Interview with Judge Bernie Weinman, November 8, 1973.
74. Williams, *supra* note 16.
75. Tate, *supra* note 17.
76. Williams, *supra* note 16.
77. *Ibid.*
78. *Ibid.* at 243.
79. Tate, *supra* note 17, at 400.
80. *Ibid.*
81. Interview with David Vance, Clerk of Court, September 26, 1973.
82. Tenn., *Public Acts,* Ch. 36 (1971).
83. Interview with Judge Bernie Weinman, October 2, 1973.
84. Mr. Bruce Rogow, Argersinger's attorney, was questioned intensely by the Court on this matter. Thus, Justice White wanted to know, "Does anyone have any facts at all on what kind of burden this would be on the judicial system or the attorneys of this country?" Chief Justice Burger was concerned about its effect on "isolated rural areas where there may not be public defender offices." On the same theme, Justice Rehnquist inquired if this right to counsel would not "necessarily require the abolition of 'justice courts' in a rural area?" See 10 CrL 4201 (1972).
85. 407 U.S. at 35.
86. *Ibid.,* at 36.
87. Actually, the public defenders are part of the staff of the Shelby County Public Defenders Office and are merely assigned to the City Court. The City, in turn, reimburses the County for the expenses it incurs.
88. Interview with Judge Bernie Weinman, September 18, 1973.
89. Statement to the Sub-Committee of the Judicial Council of Tennessee by Judge Bernie Weinman, 1972.
90. National Advisory Commission *Report on Courts, supra* note 4, at 164. See also *Five Year Plan, supra* note 65, p. 55; Memphis Delta Region Law Enforcement Planning Commission, *Memphis Delta Region Criminal Justice System: A Comprehensive Plan* (1971), sec. C.
91. See Friesen, *supra* note 2, at 124. See also National Advisory Commission, *Report on Courts, supra* note 4, at 160–163.
92. Friesen, *ibid.,* at 124. See also Herbert Jacob, *Urban Justice: Law and Order in American Cities* (Englewood Cliffs, N.J.: Prentice-Hall, 1973), p. 93.

DAVID SILK

EDUCATION AND LIBERAL REFORM: AN INTERPRETATION

From the middle of the nineteenth century, when the American public school system as we now know it was being fashioned, public leaders and makers of public policy have leaned heavily upon educational solutions to political and social problems. At first glance this seems appropriate for a democratic society where it is axiomatic that opportunity should be a function of merit which is often determined by educational credentials, rather than social position or wealth, but the most starry-eyed optimist knows that merit often has little to do with access to opportunity. Yet repeatedly educational panaceas have been tried and are still being tried. It is my view that they have failed to rectify the inequalities at which they were directed because they fail to affect the causes of these inequalities, which are more often economic, political and cultural in origin, than they are educational.

EDUCATIONAL REFORM DOES NOT EQUALIZE OPPORTUNITY

Lofty expectations of educational reform are typical and are evident throughout the nineteenth and twentieth centuries. In the middle of the 19th Century Horace Mann, in his Twelfth Annual Report as Secretary of the Massachusetts Board of Education wrote, "Education, then, beyond all other devices of human origin, is the great equalizer of the conditions of men in the balance-wheel of the social machinery."[1] But although Mann's eloquence went far toward the establishment of a more democratic system

---

Reprinted by permission of *The Goucher Quarterly* (Fall 1973), pp. 22–27.

of public education, it did little to disturb the causes of inequality in America in the 19th Century.

In the more recent past attempts to equalize opportunity in America through educational reform have had extremely modest results. The most high-powered of these recent assaults on inequality is the compensatory education movement of the 1960s. Based on the findings of psychologists, sociologists, social workers and educators working closely with children from the lower socio-economic classes, its rationale was that educational underachievement was the outcome of a form of cognitive deprivation arising out of cultural factors, what has come to be known as "cultural deprivation." If deprivation is the cause, then the antidote must be its negation, cultural enrichment.

The reasoning seemed sound and seemed to be based on substantial empirical study, so the war against underachievement was on, inspired by the faith that early childhood cultural enrichment could overcome the cultural deficit caused by lower-class childrearing practices and in general, the culture of poverty. President Johnson typified this faith when, as he signed the Elementary and Secondary Education Act of 1965 in the one-room Texas schoolhouse he himself attended, he stated:

> By this Act we bridge the gap between helplessness and hope for more than five million educationally deprived children. As a son of a tenant farmer, I know that education is the only valid passport from poverty. As a former teacher — and I hope a future one — I have great expectations of what this law will mean for our young people.[2]

And so to the new understanding of the causes of educational under-achievement was allied the promise of federal funding of compensatory education programs.

LINGUISTIC BOMBARDMENT AND PARENTAL INVOLVEMENT

Central to all of these programs of the 60s was an attack upon language and reading development, since so much research in America and in England had seemed to show that language conventions in the lower-class home were a poor preparation for the later development of the kinds of cognitive skills that become important in school. The typical compensatory program gave particular emphasis to linguistic skills. Head Start programs, for example, stressed a kind of linguistic bombardment of the child through the reading of stories by the teacher, the use of tape recorders to record children's speech and to have them listen to playbacks of their own voices, and much contact with objects of different size, shape and color on the assumption that any improvement of the ability to discriminate forms would facilitate the recognition of letters and in turn the learning of reading.

In addition to the emphasis upon language skills, most compensatory programs stressed parental involvement, beefed-up guidance facilities and personnel, and innovative reallocations of teacher resources such as team-teaching. In one well known program, the MES (More Effective Schools) Program in New York City, the per-pupil expenditure was doubled, from $450 to $900 in participating schools, and class size was reduced to a maximum of 20 pupils per teacher through increased staffing.[3]

COUNTERINDICATIONS IN COMPENSATORY EDUCATION

But not long after the initiation of the compensatory education movement, counterindications began to darken the horizon. Probably most well-known is the Coleman study, *Equality of Educational Opportunity,* conducted for the U.S. Office of Education. Its findings are fairly representative of similar studies of specific programs, though the scope of the Coleman study encompassed parameters examined on a national level and samples taken from over 4,000 elementary and secondary schools.

The findings of the Coleman Report provided little support for the assumptions to which compensatory education was moored. The general conclusion of the study was that school achievement is to only a small degree dependent upon manipulable inputs such as per-pupil expenditure and teacher-student ratios, whereas the factors that are significantly related to achievement are those that are not easily regulated, such as social class and other characteristics of the family and the academic orientation of student peers.

. . . the analysis showed what had already been well-known: the powerful relation of the child's own family background characteristics to his achievement, a relation stronger than that of any school factors.[4]

While additional spending can alleviate a problem of poor educational facilities or a problem of too few teachers, there is little that money spent on schools can do to alter the attitudes and beliefs about education which students bring to school from the home. A considerable crack had appeared in the foundation of compensatory education.

No less discouraging were some of the other conclusions of the Report, some of which challenged long-standing popular beliefs about education. For example, it seemed to show that the differences between minority and lower income group schools and white middle-class schools with regard to objective measures of school quality were nowhere near what had been believed to exist. While appreciable differences in school spending, staffing and facilities were found between schools in different geographical regions, such as between the North and the South or between urban and rural schools, within the same locale, differential spending and facilities were not so great as to provide an explanation of the differences in achievement between social classes and ethnic groups.

Though many have questioned the statistical validity and the experimental design of the Coleman Report, a recently published reanalysis of the data of the Report has upheld its general conclusions.[5] Moreover, similar studies of specific school districts further confirm the ineffectiveness of procedural changes in school policy toward remedying the effects of cultural factors on educational achievement. One such study conducted in the New York City schools concludes:

> We have recorded traditional variables that supposedly affect the quality of learning: class size, school expenditure, pupil-teacher ratio, condition of building, teacher experience, and the like. Yet there seems to be no direct relationship between these school measurements and performance. Schools that have exceptionally small class registers, staffed with experienced teachers, spend more money per pupil, and possess modern facilities do not reflect exceptional academic competence.[6]

Thus the conclusion about the effects of educational reform on inequality in America still seems to be that compensatory education has done little to right the skewness within the opportunity structure. Something must be fundamentally wrong with its assumptions.

THE MYTH OF THE DEPRIVED CHILD

Some of the most interesting work done in education in the last five years has been directed at these assumptions of compensatory education in an attempt to formulate alternative explanations. One of the most systematic and analytic studies to come out of this new skepticism is that of the psychologist Herbert Ginsburg. In his *The Myth of the Deprived Child*,[7] using Piagetian explanations of the principles of cognitive development in children, he argues that the entire cultural deprivation hypothesis upon which compensatory education is built is erroneous.

Ginsburg first attacks the validity of the I.Q. test, which is often used in the public schools as a basis for the practice of ability grouping. Since the I.Q. scores are considered to be a reliable predictor of academic success they are used as a basis for segregating students from one another within the same school according to their ability as determined by test scores. Typically the lines of this division are congruent with socio-economic distinctions, so that even in schools where children from the full range of social and economic backgrounds are bused into the school, in the classroom racial and social class segregation is evident.

Ginsburg argues that the nature of intelligence, especially where poor children are concerned, is obscured by the simplistic I.Q. tests. According to him the tests rest upon four "myths." First, they presuppose a unitary mental power, arbitrarily labelled "intelligence," whereas in fact mental abilities are varied and not always highly correlated with one another. The second myth is that the tests are a measure of basic intellectual differences between children. According to Ginsburg the tests merely highlight trivial differences in children's ability to perform rather prosaic skills while adumbrating more important similarities in the ways in which all children operate mentally. In the third myth the tests are taken as a measure of intellectual competence, whereas differences between poor and middle-class children's motivations to do well on the test may vitiate the results for poor children, who do not appreciate the significance of the test to begin with. Middle-class children on the other hand, are hot-housed from birth by their parents so that the entire reward system they are accustomed to is closely tied to the performance of cognitive skills. And finally the fourth myth is that the test measures innate ability, whereas intellectual skills are developing constantly.

Another major thrust of Ginsburg's attack is on the notion of the deficiency of the language of the lower-class. This argument is particularly lethal to compensatory education since it usually centers on a program of linguistic enrichment. Focusing on the work of the British sociologist Basil Bernstein, he contends that the language of the lower-class lacks neither subtlety, expressiveness, nor complexity. To the contrary, Ginsburg cites studies to show that when lower-class children are presented with a situation where a more formal and elaborate language code is called for they often have the requisite skills in their linguistic repertoire to complete the assigned tasks. That they choose ordinarily to use the "restricted" language conventions of the lower-class establishes only a difference of predilection rather than one of ability.

Ginsburg's complete argument cannot be given its due in limited space, but enough has been disclosed to suggest that it is a formidable attack upon the tenets of compensatory education — worthwhile fare for the interested reader. I myself had always found the cultural deprivation explanation of under-achievement offensive, as much for its doubtfulness, as for its arrogant implicit suggestion that most middle-class homes are culturally enriched, which I find preposterous.

Another recent explanation of educationally mediated inequality discounts the environmentalist assumptions of cultural deprivation and posits in their place a genetic account. The three names most closely associated with this view are Arthur Jensen, Richard Herrnstein, and most notoriously, William Shockley, the California engineering professor, who proposes the sterilization of persons of inferior intellect, with special consideration given the black race.

The genetic explanation is simply that inequality results from inherited differences between groups of particular racial and social class composition. In 1969, Jensen triggered a furor in the academic world by contending that compensatory education programs probably cannot boost the I.Q.'s of black children because the cause is more likely to be genetic than environmental. Seventy-five percent of I. Q. variations are inherited, he claimed. The remaining 25% may be environmentally caused, but this is minor compared to the genetic factor.[8]

THE SELF-FULFILLING PROPHESY

Still another explanation of the relationship between inequality and education employs the concept of the self-fulfilling prophesy. This is the view that the way in which a person perceives or experiences a situation will affect the outcomes of that situation in such a way that the original expectations of that person become converted into realities. Everyone has encountered this effect in the form of garden-variety prejudice. Once a category of people is labelled inferior (women, blacks, etc.) then others' expectations of them are diminished. Mitigated expectations affect the self-concept and the aspirations of the object person or group in such a way that they tend to live up to these expectations.

As an heuristic device applied to the schools, the hypothesis of the self-fulfilling prophesy has spawned some interesting studies. Rosenthal and Jacobson in a study conducted in a primarily lower and working class public school, chose 20% of the student population at random and described them to teachers as "spurters" who had been identified by a newly designed test. This group, the teachers were told, had latent abilities and could be expected to blossom soon. When tested at the end of the year the experimental group of "spurters" had gained as much as twelve I.Q. points.[9]

Though the validity of this study has been questioned it dramatizes what common sense should lead anyone who has taught children to conclude: teachers communicate their expectations to students. These expectations in turn profoundly and directly affect student performance. And the problem is compounded by the institutionalized school practices of tracking and ability grouping.

IS THERE A CONSCIOUS CONSPIRACY OF SCHOOLMEN AGAINST THE POOR?

And still another account of inequality construes it as the outcome of a conscious conspiracy on the part of schoolmen to reserve educationally mediated opportunity for their own children and other children of the "establishment" by denying it to the poor. A cogently argued account of this explanation is given by Lauter and Howe. Using the D.C. school system as an illustration, they argue that the practice of tracking is merely a gambit to insure that quality education will be denied minority group children and poor children in general, so that these same children will not later become competitors for admission to college and for the higher status and income positions that await the graduates of the "better" colleges and universities.[10] In addition there has always been a tendency for a bias to exist in the allocation of educational resources in the cities because of the under-representation of minority groups on urban school boards. However this tendency has been considerably reduced because of the growing political involvement of urban minority groups.

While I do not believe that the presence of tracking systems or the practice of ability-grouping establishes anything more than the need of coping with the problem of teaching groups of children representing an extremely broad range of interest, aptitudes and prior learning, nevertheless other evidence of deliberate partiality in the allocation of educational resources can easily be cited. For example, it is well-known by teachers that a transfer to a more desirable (more middle-class) school is viewed as a plum. Such plums are often reserved for those who are most compliant and denied those who are the most troublesome to the administration. Plainly the cumulative effect of this is for the schools in the poorer neighborhoods, where the teaching challenge is the most difficult, to become a repository for more than their share of the inexperienced, the disgruntled, and at times, the incompetents, though there remain many talented and effective teachers in these schools.

Another kind of evidence of deliberate biasing of resources is the practices of gerrymandering school districts wherein boundary lines are drawn (often with bizarre proportions) to conform to racial and ethnic housing patterns rather than proximity to schools. With such districts safely partitioned from the middle-class neighborhoods, it is possible to direct the best resources to the latter with impunity for middle-class children.

However, all three practices, tracking, transferring teachers as a reward or penalty, and gerrymandering of school districts, have been dramatically reduced in the past few years. The effects of this kind of reform combined with extensive busing have not yet been ascertained.

THE STRUCTURE OF OPPORTUNITY HAS CHANGED LITTLE

To this point I have sketched the kinds of educational reform that have been levelled at the problem of unequal opportunity in America. I have not discussed two additional attacks on inequality: busing, and recent court tests of the constitutionality of using local property taxes as a basis for the funding of the public schools. The battle over school busing is a matter of common knowledge by this time and so far, state supreme court decisions about funding the schools have not yet resulted in changes in practice.

At the present, after so many years of attempting to rectify economic injustice through educational reforms, the pattern of educational achievement remains approximately the same. Children from the middle and upper classes are, on the average, consistently at or above grade level in most school subjects as determined by standardized tests, while the children of the poor and of minority groups are just as consistently behind. And insofar as educational credentials are a necessary ingredient for success in America, the structure of opportunity has changed little.

The most recent confirmation of the inefficacy of educational reform toward equalizing opportunity is the Jencks study, *Inequality: A Reassessment of the Effect of Family and Schooling in America.* The general conclusion reached in this study is that there is no strong relationship between the things that schools do and one's level of educational attainment or personal income in later life.

Rate-of-return estimates do tell us that efforts to keep everyone in school longer make little economic sense. The average rate of return for post-secondary education is quite low. For the kinds of students who are not now in college, it is even lower. For working-class whites, blacks, and women, dropping out seems in many cases to be the most economically rational decision.[11]

Though Jencks does not argue against more and better education for everyone, he advises that if economic equality in America is to be brought about, then a less oblique approach than educational reform must be enlisted.

WHY ALIENATE STUDENTS?

With so much evidence stacked against the hope of equal opportunity via educational reform, there is little cause for optimism about the future, and the important question has become, "What have we learned from all of this?" It is with regard to this point that I would like to offer an interpretation.

As a high school teacher I was often deeply troubled by students from blue-collar families whose ability to do academic work was beyond question, but who were nonetheless doing poorly academically. In many cases, I had established a strong rapport with these students and they spoke to me frankly. Yet in no instance was I able to change the basic attitudes of any of these students toward school or toward the future. Those who had chosen futures as bulldozer operators or beauticians saw little cause for concern over school for it seemed to them to have little to do with their future needs.

I began to ask myself, what is the point of further alienating students by subjecting them involuntarily to an education that they perceive to be irrelevant? The more I agonized over the problem, the more convinced I became of the wrong-headedness of such a compulsory arrangement, for I believe that there is a fundamental incompatibility between education and compulsion. Skillful teachers can teach students who want to learn. What they cannot do is change the basic cultural orientations of students who are in school, not because they wish to be, but because they have to be, due to the compulsory education laws.

CAUSE OF UNDERACHIEVEMENT OFTEN
PSYCHOLOGICAL, NOT PEDAGOGICAL

A relationship exists between this problem and the failure of liberal educational reform to equalize opportunity, for in my view the major cause of the underachievement of poor and working class students is psychological and not pedagogical: many of these students have little desire to learn the things schools teach, and when curriculum content is presented in which they are interested, the disabilities often disappear. I have seen this so often that I believe that there can be little doubt of it. For example, I have seen students who were failing math, yet able to comprehend and employ subtle formulas governing the ignition-advance curve of their cars' engines; my wife has watched in utter amazement, black students of hers bounding through chapter after chapter of *Manchild in the Promised Land*, students who had been labelled failures in English because of a flat refusal to read the assigned work.

Yet it is through the agency of teachers operating in this inherently impossible compulsory situation, that society has expected equal opportunity to be brought about. And when the reforms fail to issue in the expected change, then the profession is criticized, when in fact, the reforms themselves have been badly misconceived.

EDUCATIONAL REFORM DIVERTS PUBLIC ATTENTION FROM CAUSES OF INEQUALITY

A more effective reform program would attack economic causes more directly. Unfair tax laws and discriminatory legislation and practices have more to do with inequality in America than does any weakness in our system of public education. This is so clear that it has often caused me to speculate as to the reasons why educational reform has been so heavily relied upon. My conjecture is that it has served as a diversionary tactic. Whether intentionally or not, educational reform has diverted public attention from the causes of inequality by offering them the promise of meaningful change without disrupting the economic status quo. The wealth of the country is still lopsided, i.e., a disproportionate amount of wealth and power is still in the hands of an embarrassingly small percentage, and past educational reforms have not disturbed this. And to make matters worse people from lower income groups have paid more heavily for those reforms than the middle-class and the wealthy for they are funded by public monies and persons with a lower income often pay a larger percentage of that income in taxes.

Thus I believe that we should have learned some significant lessons from past educational reforms. Foremost among those lessons is that one misconstrues the nature of education badly, if it is viewed as a panacea for social problems whose causes are economic and political in origin. Next in importance is the lesson that even insofar as education is capable of changing basic value orientations, it cannot even do this in an atmosphere of coercion or in a compulsory educational setting. In general, we have all been sold a bill of goods about the efficacy of education as a hedge against inequality.

A serious crisis of confidence exists today within education. Symptomatic of this malady is all the concern in professional journals and professional organizations about accountability and "behavioral" or "performance based" objectives. Many teachers I have talked to who have tried to cash in all their educational objectives in these crass terms know that it can only be done at the expense of trivializing their curriculum by concentrating on only the immediate and observable outcomes of instruction. I think that there can be little doubt that one important cause of this obsession with measurable outcomes is the false standard applied to education resulting from the unrealistic expectations made of educational reform. Presently education is being measured according to its ability to redress economic injustices. Schools whose students are below grade level are viewed as ineffective because these students' opportunity to compete will be curtailed, whereas opportunity seems in fact, to have little to do with academic performance for these students.

EDUCATOR ON RACK LONG ENOUGH

A reformulation of the criteria by which education is measured, if taken seriously, would result in massive changes in educational practices. The ability to rectify social and economic injustices is a poor way of measuring educational effectiveness. Moreover it is misleading in the way that it diverts public attention from the more immediate economic, political and social causes of inequality. The educator has been on the rack long enough. It is time now that we become aware that education is neither the cause nor the cure of the unequal distribution of wealth and power in America.

Notes

1. Charles Daly, ed., *The Quality of Inequality: Urban and Suburban Public Schools* (Chicago: The University of Chicago Press, 1968), pp. 13-14.
2. Sidney W. Tiedt, *The Role of the Federal Government in Education* (New York: Oxford University Press, 1966), p. 192.
3. Harry L. Miller and Roger W. Woock, *Social Foundations of Urban Education* (Hinsdale, Illinois: Dryden Press, 1970), p. 245.
4. James Coleman, "A Brief Summary of the Coleman Report," *Equal Educational Opportunity* (Cambridge, Mass.: Harvard University Press, 1969), p. 258.
5. Frederick Mosteller and Daniel Moynihan, eds., *On Equality of Educational Opportunity* (New York: Random House, 1972).
6. Institute for Community Studies, Queens College, New York 1971, *New York City School Fact Book,* in Arthur Jensen, *Genetics and Education,* (New York: Harper & Row, 1973), p. 63.
7. Herbert Ginsburg, *The Myth of the Deprived Child: Poor Children's Intellect and Education* (Englewood Cliffs: N.J.: Prentice-Hall, 1972).
8. Arthur Jensen, "How Much Can We Boost I.Q. and Scholastic Achievement?" *Harvard Education Review* (Winter, 1969).
9. Robert Rosenthal and Lenore Jacobson, *Pigmalion in the Classroom! Teacher Expectation and Pupil's Intellectual Development* (New York: Holt, Rinehart & Winston, Inc., 1968), p. 75.
10. Paul Lauter and Florence Howe, "How the School System is Rigged for Failure," *The New York Review,* June 18, 1970.
11. Christopher Jencks, *et al., Inequality: A Reassessment of the Effect of Family and Schooling in America* (New York: Basic Books, 1972), p. 224.

HERBERT J. GANS

PLANNING FOR PEOPLE, NOT BUILDINGS

The title of this paper is an oversimplifying catchphrase. Even so, it is
probably fair to say that city planning has concerned itself primarily with
buildings and the physical environment, and only secondarily with the
people who use that environment. As the title suggests, I believe these
priorities ought to be reversed; the aim of planning should be to help
people solve their problems and realize their goals.

THE PLANNER'S PHYSICAL BIAS

If the proverbial "Man from Mars" came face to face with city planners, he would surely be amazed. Here is a profession which sees itself as
planning for the community, but deals with only a portion of that community. In planning land uses, the location and design of buildings, streets,
other transportation facilities, utility lines and open spaces, the profession
sees mainly the natural and man-made physical artifacts of the city. It
aims to arrange and rearrange these artifacts to create an orderly — often
even static — efficient and attractive community. Even more strangely, it
tries to arrange these artifacts according to a theory of urban form which,
sometimes borrowing from the shapes of geometry, attempts to squeeze
the city into a star pattern or a series of fingers, as if the major purpose of
a city was to present a symmetrical and pleasing spectacle when seen from
an airplane.

By including only a limited portion of the community in his profes-

Reprinted from H. J. Gans, *Environment and Planning,* Vol. 1 (London: Pion, 1969),
pp. 33–46.

sional concerns, the planner ignores almost entirely the people who live in that community, and without whom there would be no buildings or land uses. He does not plan for them either as individuals or as members of groups. He pays no attention to the social structures, institutions, culture and subcultures, socioeconomic classes, age groups, and political blocs which are the fabric of society. He does not see that most people live most of their lives around the family, the job, their friends, the church, and a couple of clubs; he does not recognize that they have goals or aspirations, problems or worries; he sees them only as occupants of dwellings, offices, factories, and moving vehicles. Indeed, he does not even pay much attention to how they use these facilities. For the planner, people are little more than artifacts. They are expected to function within the housing, land uses, and other community arrangements which he provides, and are supposed to subordinate their personal and familial interests to the needs of the neighborhood, the community, and the community plan, and to share the planner's goals of order, efficiency, and beauty for their community.

THE HISTORICAL AND POLITICAL
SOURCES OF PHYSICAL PLANNING

Why has city planning taken this direction? Why has it not concerned itself with planning for the groups in which people live, and for the way in which they want to live? In America, the answer can be found in events in the nineteenth century and in more recent political alignments.

American city planning developed as a reform movement in the late nineteenth century, and grew out of earlier reform movements which had begun shortly after the middle of the century, particularly the model tenement, park and playground movements. These were organized by Protestant upper middle-class reformers and philanthropists who were disturbed by what was happening to the cities, which they and their class had once dominated politically and culturally, by the transformation from small predominantly middle-class towns to rapidly growing urban centers, and by the large numbers of non-Protestant poor European immigrants, who streamed into the cities and were forced to live in slums.

The reformers wanted to improve the terrible living conditions of these people. However, they also wanted to make the immigrants into middle-class Protestant Americans like themselves; people who would uphold the old sociopolitical order. Presumably the reformers could have developed anti-poverty programs, reorganizing the industrial economy so that unemployment and poorly paid employment would be eliminated.

They failed to do so, not because such programs had not yet been invented, but primarily because the reformers were politically quite conservative. They had no desire to change the economy or the social order, and were in fact fighting against the socialist movements which began to develop in the slums.

Partly because they were of a conservative nature, the reformers held what one might call *a facility-centered theory of social change*. They believed that if poor people were provided with a set of properly designed facilities, ranging from model tenements to better work places and parks and playgrounds, they would not only give up their slum abodes but also change themselves in the process. Thus, Frederick Olmsted, the great American park builder, thought that man could be truly healthy only in rural surroundings, and he proposed that large parks be built in the city as a substitute for these surroundings. The founders of the playground movement believed that if the poor could be provided with playgrounds and community centers, they would stop frequenting the taverns, cafes, brothels, and later the movie houses in which they spent their leisure time, and would desert the street corner gangs and clubs which they had created for social life.

This theory of social change was not entirely facility-centered. In fact, some of the reformers argued that the crucial ingredient was not the facility but the men and women who staffed it, and that if the poor came into contact with these well-intentioned middle-class people, they would soon give up their lower-class ways.

Today, we know that this theory was absurd. The immigrants were desperately poor people living in a strange land in which they were often discriminated against. Because they were poor, they suffered not only from economic problems but also from the social and individual pathologies which come with being poor; alcoholism, family breakdown, vice, and violence, for example. These pathologies were not deliberate as the reformers thought; they were by-products of a lower-class culture which enabled people to adapt to poverty, but which was (and still is) anathema to middle-class people because of its emphasis on sensual and material pleasures. What the immigrant poor needed was economic aid. To assume that they could be transformed into middle-class people simply by their joining settlement houses and other facilities was ludicrous. It was also wrong to assume that they would even come to such facilities, for the immigrants had their own social groups and had no reason to desert these for strange new facilities, staffed by strange and often condescending Yankees.

The reformers were not social scientists, however, and they had so little contact with the immigrant that they could not understand why he behaved as he did. Moreover, they were missionaries, and had the missionary's faith in their approach. To them it seemed that their theory worked; the few facilities which they were able to build were used by the immigrants, though rarely in the numbers that the reformers expected. What the reformers did not know was that the new amenities attracted an atypical minority — the upwardly mobile who were able and willing to become middle-class Americans.

By the early twentieth century, the reform movement had coalesced with business groups who were fighting the urban political machines, and the philanthropists were replaced by business leaders and their economic and political associates. The businessmen were mainly downtown retailers, large property owners, real estate agents, and builders. These groups were interested in creating an attractive downtown retail area that would bring in shoppers and office workers, in building middle-class residential areas to house them, and transportation facilities to move them around. They were particularly interested in making sure that the slums, usually located right next to the central business district, did not "infect" this district. They therefore wanted them contained or removed. As businessmen and property owners, they were, of course, concerned primarily with buildings and facilities, and they made common cause with the earlier reformers. However, seeing that the facility-by-facility approach did not achieve their aim of an orderly, efficient, and attractive downtown environment, they turned to zoning and then to comprehensive planning.

After the First World War, the business interests, supported by middle-class voters, had developed enough political strength to make planning and zoning into a municipal function, usually in the form of planning commissions — on whose boards they sat — which sometimes worked with, sometimes opposed, the political machines. Because the activities of the commission required a staff, a new profession was created, and because the work dealt with the improvement of buildings, neighborhoods, and facilities, it naturally attracted people trained in the manipulation of physical artifacts, that is, architects and engineers.

From about 1920 on, the new planners planned and zoned. They developed master plans which segregated land uses by a variety of criteria, most of them class-based, so that upper- and middle-class residences were separated from working- and lower-class residences, affluent shopping districts from poor ones, and industry, which employed mainly working and lower class people, from everything else. They planned for new transportation systems which would bring people into the central retail district, and in all areas, for all classes, they planned the parks, playgrounds, community centers, schools, and other facilities which the nineteenth century reformers had advocated. They also laid out new areas of the city for future growth, although, true to their reformer ancestors who wanted to stop the influx of immigrants, they were basically against growth itself and wanted to limit the size of the city. The new areas consisted of single-family houses in middle-class neighborhoods, having schools in the center, but including no housing or institutions for the poor. The planners assumed that if they planned for middle-class housing, poor people would somehow become middle class and so no new low-cost housing was envisaged. If the planners provided only middle-class facilities, people would use nothing else. Consequently, in an era when most Americans went to the movies at least once a week, the planners planned for cultural centers and museums, but did not bother to locate movie theaters.

For a long time, the formulators of comprehensive planning had no means to implement their proposals other than zoning or subdivision ordinances, the political power of their business and reform patrons, and moral appeals for good planning. In the late 1930s, however, the federal government created public housing projects, which, by clearing slums and replacing them with new housing, would enable the poor to live in good buildings and thus to stop behaving like poor people. A decade later, this escalated into slum clearance and urban renewal. It never occurred to the formulators of urban renewal that private enterprise could only rebuild for the affluent. The planners and housers were so convinced that slums "bred" the pathologies associated with poverty that they were sure that the behavior of the poor could be altered simply by tearing down homes, doing away with slum areas, and scattering the inhabitants all over the city.

When it became apparent that urban renewal did nothing but move slum dwellers into other slums, the planning profession embraced human renewal. It was hoped that through education, social casework and community organization, the poor could be helped and changed into middle-class people, while their homes were being renewed. With the coming of the Kennedy administration and the War on Poverty, some attempt was made to provide more low-income housing. In 1965 Congress approved the Model Cities legislation: a broad form of urban renewal which included provision for low-income housing, rent supplements, human renewal, and programs to deal with poverty, unemployment, and underemployment among the poor. Some of these innovations came from planners, and others from social scientists who entered planning after the Second World War. In a very real sense, however, the innovations came from the poor themselves. Slum dwellers had been saying for decades that they needed more jobs, higher incomes, and more low-cost housing, but it was not until they began to oppose urban renewal, and then to rebel and riot, that anyone began to listen to them. Even today, however, most planners continue to work on master plans, and to plan for the city orderly, efficient and beautiful.

THE AFFLUENT BENEFICIARIES OF PHYSICAL PLANNING

Although city planning has been concerned principally with improving the physical environment, it has also been planning for certain people, although only indirectly and implicitly. These people were the planner himself, his political supporters, and the upper middle-class citizen in general. Insofar as the planner was seeking to create the kind of city he himself liked, he was planning for himself and his professional peers. He formulated his plans so that they would gain the respect of his peers, just as architects often seem to design buildings so that they will be published in the architectural journals.

The planner was also working on behalf of his political supporters, the businessmen, and civic leaders who sat on planning commissions. The master plans emphasized a growing downtown retail area and many neighborhood shopping areas, and they often over-zoned for future business districts. The planner's ideal city was good for business and for property ownership.

Finally, the planner planned for people of his own class culture, for other middle- and upper middle-class professionals who wanted solid single-family house neighborhoods, and who used theaters, museums, civic centers, and other cultural facilities that cater to the upper middle class. This came out most clearly during urban renewal, when the planners justified slum clearance in order to bring the middle class back to the city. They favored this return because otherwise the poor might begin to dominate the city politically and culturally, and the cultural facilities which the planners liked would have to close down for lack of customers.

The planner did not realize he was planning for himself, his supporters, and people of his class, however; he thought that by focusing on what he felt were desirable types of housing, business and industry, he was planning for everybody. As a professional he thought he knew what was best for the community and for people. He thought he had the expertise that gave him the right to change the community, and to change people's lives according to the traditional dictates of the old reform movements. Because he was a descendant of a missionary reform cause he never questioned his aims or his activities.

Of course, the master planners were not really experts; their judgments were not based on expert knowledge or even on any kind of empirical analysis. Although they applied planning standards for housing, schools, libraries, and recreation facilities, for example, these standards were made up by housers, educators, librarians, and recreation officials who had the same missionary zeal — and a vested interest in building more of their own facilities. Thus the standards themselves were not based on expert knowledge or empirical analysis. Usually they measured the "best" facility in the country and translated these measurements into general planning standards for all communities. The planners did not notice that the best facilities were usually found in the most affluent communities, and that poorer communities could not afford them. Nor did they notice that all the standards together called for such large allocations of land and public expenditure that, if they were implemented, there would be little room or money left for anything else in the city.

In short, the standards and other tools used by planners in various community facilities often reflected the vested interests and cultural values and biases of the planner himself and of his allies. Sometimes the plans were even based on the fads and fashions of the era. For example, until about the Second World War, most planners shared the common middle-class belief that multifamily dwellings were undesirable. They thought that since poor people lived in them, and poor people exhibited high rates of individual and social pathology, apartments must be pathological. Consequently, planners wanted to put as many people as possible into single-family housing.

Today, planners generally favor just the reverse. With the development of post-Second World War suburbia, and the exodus of the lower middle class from the city, suburbs were no longer the ideal community they had been when they were exclusively upper middle class. Planners therefore decided that suburban single-family housing was undesirable, that it bred conformity, matriarchy, divorce, and a number of other pathologies which in England are described as the "New Town Blues." Now, the professional judgment was to build apartment housing, for apartments were identified with urbanity, and only by building on an urban scale could the city and the upper middle-class life style described as urbanity be brought to the new suburbs.

This brief history of planning is not intended to expose the city planner as a conspirator who intentionally allied himself with conservative political reformers, and then with businessmen and property owners, in order to enrich himself and his profession. Indeed, until recently, most planners were not aware of the political implications of their theory and their practice, and whatever they did, they usually did with the best intentions — which is, of course, part of the problem. Moreover, their plans have been by no means entirely undesirable. Even if they are often irrelevant to the city's problems, they have helped to create more orderly, efficient, and attractive communities, at least for the affluent. Their ideas and site plans for low density neighborhoods were borrowed by post-Second World War builders, resulting in better-designed suburbs for the newly affluent. Planners have also fought against the corruption of urban political machines, using planning principles to argue for facility, land use, and location decisions closer to the public interest than those made by politicians, whose first priority was often to enrich the political machine and its leaders. Even so, planning could have contributed more to the solution of urban problems and the achievement of urban goals had it not been saddled with the history from which only now is it freeing itself.

THE LACK OF EFFECTS OF PHYSICAL PLANNING

There is considerable evidence that the physical environment does not play as significant a role in people's lives as the planner believes. Although people reside, work, and play in buildings, their behavior is not determined by the buildings, but by the economic, cultural, and social relationships within them. Bad design can interfere with what goes on inside a building, of course, and good design can aid it, but design per se does not significantly shape human behavior.

A number of studies have now been carried out on the effects of what is, for people the most important part of the physical environment — their house. Wilner's study of slum dwellers who were moved to a new public housing project, Berger's study of factory workers who were moved out to suburbia, my own study of working and lower middle-class people who moved out to Levittown, and Willmott's study of the London slum dwellers who moved to Dagenham all indicate that lives are affected little by the change of community or by the change of housing. Wilner found no change in health, mental health, social life, or community participation. Berger and Willmott both found that the working class people they studied continued working class styles of life in their new surroundings, and I found that people's lives were not changed drastically either by the move from city to suburb, or even by the move from apartment to house.[1]

As reported in *The Levittowners,* research into changes in health, morale, boredom, loneliness, family life, social life, community participation and the like showed that generally about half the people reported no change, and those who reported change were changed in different ways. For example, among my sample of ex-city dwellers, 69 percent reported no change in the state of their marriage after coming to Levittown, 20 percent said it had improved and 11 percent said it had deteriorated. When changes were greater, for example in visiting neighbors and friends, which increased considerably, the cause of the change was not the community but people's goals; they had moved out to Levittown with the hope of improving their social life. The presence of young people with similar interests made the improvement possible, of course, but residents who did not want to do more socializing generally did not do so. Perhaps the most drastic change came for people who moved from apartments to houses, but here, too, the change was intended. People wanted to own a new house, and they believed, rightly so, that raising children was easier in a house than in an apartment. The greatest amount of *unintended* change, that is change other than that which people intended to make or which brought them to suburbia in the first place, was caused by the population mix, in other words, the kinds of people whom they met once they had arrived in the community. The primary effect on people is not created by the physical environment of the community, but by the social environment.

This conclusion is supported by the fact that the site plan and the provision of facilities had little impact on the Levittowners. This can be illustrated by an event which also tested the popularity of the classic neighborhood scheme. When the Levittown school board polled parents of a crowded neighborhood school on whether they wanted larger classes or preferred that their children be given transport to a less crowded school in another neighborhood, the data showed that the significant factor was neither the neighborhood nor even class size but the parents' attitude toward their child's teacher. Parents who liked the teacher opposed any change; those who disliked the teacher favored change, so that the child would get another teacher.

Moreover, for most people community facilities are relatively unimportant. The number of people who use such public facilities as playgrounds and libraries is always small. Although a few may be so attracted to the facility that their life is changed by it, the majority of people use a facility only rarely, and it becomes important to them only when it becomes part of their social environment. For example, teen-agers may shun a community center as individuals, but a gang or informal club may come in as a group and make it its headquarters. In fact, and ironically, unless a facility becomes part of the social environment it will be used on the whole only by the people excluded from that social environment, by marginal and socially isolated individuals. This is a worthy use, but it questions the planner's assumption about the importance of facilities in everybody's life.

Although research on the effects of the physical environment is still sparse, the data indicate so far that these effects are not as great as the planner believes. Unless neighbors are homogeneous, they do not choose their friends on the basis of physical closeness, and one site plan is about as good as another in its impact on social life. A site plan in which houses are bunched together so that people are forced to have visual contact will, of course, create more social contact than an open plan; it will create some friends, some enemies, and frenzied efforts to protect individual privacy. Similarly, overcrowding within a dwelling may have deleterious effects on the occupants, although one mental health study in New York found no correlation between mental illness and overcrowding.[2] Here, too, social and cultural variables play a major role. Middle-class individuals seem to need more privacy than working-class people, and I suspect that if the former had to live at the internal (or dwelling unit) density endured by many of New York's Negroes and Peurto Ricans, they would probably go crazy.

The lack of data on the effects of the physical environment on human beings has encouraged some planners to cite the ethological studies of rats and other animals, which show that they suffered intensely from overcrowding. These data cannot be applied to human beings in the city, however, because human beings do not live in as close and direct a relationship to land and space as do animals. It is possible, however, that if farmers were crowded in the same way as were the experimental rats, they might suffer in the same way, or else move off the land and go to the city.

What affects people, then, is not the raw physical environment, but the social and economic environment in which that physical environment is used. People's lives are not significantly affected by whether they live in cities or suburbs, in detached or multifamily dwellings, or with or without a certain amount of public open space. Webber puts it very well when he writes:

I contend that we have been searching for the wrong grail, that the values associated with the desired urban structure do not reside in the spatial structure *per se*. One pattern of settlement and its associated land use form is superior to another only as it better serves to accommodate ongoing social processes and to further the non-spatial ends of the political community.[3]

These social processes and nonspatial ends, people's lives and their life styles, are determined by their income, occupation, and education, by their age and sex, and to a lesser extent by their ethnic, religious, and political allegiances. These characteristics and allegiances are expressed in their behavior, their goals and their problems, and in the social, economic, and political environments in which they live. If the planner wants to affect people's lives, it is these environments for which he must plan.

HOW TO PLAN FOR PEOPLE

How then, does one go about planning for people? The first step, I would suggest, is to give up all traditional planning concepts related to the physical environment, and to begin at the beginning: to ask how people live, what they want, and what problems they have that need to be solved. Such questions would show quickly that people are not all the same; different age groups and classes have different life styles, goals, and problems. Once these groupings are identified, one can then develop plans that achieve their goals and solve their problems.

If one wanted to plan for lower middle-class Levittowners, for example, and began with their problems, it would emerge that the most urgent of these are financial and familial. Money shortages, husband-wife conflicts, parent-child conflicts, and illness are the greatest sources of worry. Planning to resolve financial problems would require intervention in the economy to give greater productivity and equality of income, so that income could be raised. Planning to resolve familiar conflict would involve a variety of programs. Some types of family conflict would be eliminated if the men could earn more; other types would be tackled by creating jobs for women, both to provide more money for the household and to give women an additional source of social usefulness. Parent-child conflict could be relieved to some extent by enabling women to get away from young children for part of the day, and to be with other adults. This would require day-care centers, and some counseling to relieve the guilt that many lower middle-class women feel about being away from their children. The generational conflict between parents and adolescents can be ameliorated by deliberate planning to increase the social and physical distance between the two age groups. By giving adolescents their own institutions where they can spend much of their after-school and after-work time, and where they can feel that their own culture is as valid as adult culture, many of the present conflicts could be minimized. Planning to reduce illness would, of course, require considerably more and cheaper medical care.

If one wanted to plan for the elimination of poverty, on the other hand, one would have to begin by identifying the different types of people who suffer from poverty. Older people, the majority of America's poor, simply need more social security and pension payments. Among young people, the primary need is for the elimination of unemployment, a higher minimum wage for the underpaid worker, job training programs, and general income redistribution. The most rapidly growing group of poor people in America, unmarried mothers, need income grants which are higher and less punitive than present social welfare payments, so that they can devote themselves to making sure that their children will grow up in a relatively stable home environment, can go to school, and can obtain the skills they need to get jobs and thus to escape from poverty.[4]

These examples are too few and too brief to serve even as outlines of plans, and are suggested only to show what planning for people means. This kind of planning would require the planner either to become a sociologist and psychologist or to work closely with behavioral scientists to observe what problems people are trying to solve and what goals they are seeking. This is not easy, for people cannot always identify their problems, and do not always know what they want. Interviews, observation, and planning *with* people rather than just *for* them can provide many of the answers. When these fail, the planner has two options. He can make inferences about problems and goals from people's behavior. In addition, the planner can provide for choice by offering people a *variety* of solutions and programs.

Planners have, of course, traditionally argued that if people only had more choice, they would choose what the planner thinks is best. In America, at least, planners often explain that people live in speculative builder suburbs like Levittown because they have not had enough choice; they have not been given a chance to live in a community designed on planning principles. Sometimes this is true, but equally often it is not. For example, one reason for the failure of the much-publicized planned new town of Reston is that people did not want what the planner thought they should want; they did not like the community-focus of the plan, in which public open space replaced private open space, and in which more attention was paid to community facilities than to the house. As a result, the houses were too small, and since most people buy a house, not a community, the development sold poorly.

Planning to solve people's problems and to help them achieve their goals does not, of course, rule out physical planning, but seeks to put such planning in its proper place. The social and economic environments to which planners ought to address themselves are located in houses, offices, community facilities, and communities, and in some, although not all, instances, plans for a social environment will require physical expression. However, the physical plan ought to express the goals of social environment planning; housing and other aspects of the physical environment ought to be planned in terms of what people want. Moreover, in the overall plan, it should be given the importance and priority that people assign to physical goals.

ON GIVING PEOPLE WHAT THEY WANT

The argument that the planner should give people what they want, not what he thinks himself is best for them, requires further discussion. I suggest that the planner gives people what they want on two grounds.

The first ground is practical; it is very difficult to change people unless they want to be changed; they are not likely to give up their habits, customs, or goals just because the planner asks them to do so. People can, of course, be forced to change, but this is neither democratic nor politically wise, for unless the change is in the public interest, and people agree that it is in the public interest, they will react politically and defeat the plan. The history of American planning is full of such defeats.

When people reject a planner's idea, it is rarely because they are stupid or evil but because they have different life styles and goals. For example, most Americans prefer private to public open space, not because they are anti-planning, but because they want to spend their spare time with family members and friends and do not want to have to share outdoor space with people they do not know or do not like.

Similarly, most Americans reject the planner's goal of urbanity because they do not practice or want the life style associated with urbanity. Whether they live in the city or the suburbs, people are intensely home-centered; they rarely go out even to the movies, and they do not often go to the theater, the museum, or other typically urban facilities. Most Americans do not enjoy walking, they do not like the city's congestion, and they do not much care for the heterogeneity of population they find in the city. They may want the excitement and vitality of the city when they go on vacation, but for their daily life they want the smallness of scale, the compatible neighbors, and what they call "the peaceful outdoor life" that they find in the single-family house areas of the outer city, and in suburbia.

Nor do most people accept the planner's ideal of the balanced community, in which people from diverse incomes and backgrounds are thrown together in order to mutually enrich their lives by their diversity. This ideal, which stems from the nineteenth century, when the reformers thought that if the poor were brought into close contact with middle-class people they would learn from "their betters," conflicts with the very basis of group formation, for most people want to have neighbors who are sufficiently like them in class and age to share the same interests; this is what creates much of the vital and positive social life of the suburbs. Nor do poor people particularly want to live next door to more affluent people, especially if they have young children. Poorer people do not want to be improved by "their betters," and they cannot afford to have their young-

sters come home demanding toys they have seen in affluent homes. The
ideal also ignores the fact that people do not want to lose prestige by living
near neighbors whom they consider to be of lower status. Indeed, the only
thing that can be said in favor of balance is that it provides a principle by
which to oppose the exclusion from a community of low income and
nonwhite people. Although no one should be excluded from any community on the basis of race, class or age, the planner's ideal of balance requires more tolerance of heterogeneity than even he can practice when he
chooses a place to live.

In almost all instances, the differences in goals between the planner
and the people for whom he plans are a function of class. Most planners
are upper middle class; most of the people they plan for are not. Although
there are a number of differences between working and lower middle-
class life styles, the two classes are united in their opposition to the urbane
upper middle-class style of involvement in "culture" and civic activity, and
they will reject plans which force them to live by that style.

Probably the biggest difference between the planner and the people
he plans for is in the priority given to aesthetics. Planners are trained in
aesthetics, and see the city from a perspective in which aesthetic goals
rank high; indeed, they often plan the city as if it were a work of art, not
a place in which people live. Most people give lower priority to beauty
than do the planners, and they pay little attention to the visual environment in their everyday life; this, too, is reserved for vacations. The planner
may complain that people are uncultured, but here again a basic difference
in life style is at work. The planner, true to upper middle-class culture, is
highly aware of objects; people who are not upper middle class are most
aware of other people; for them, the social environment is more important
than the aesthetic. Consequently, the planner is upset because he sees the
mass-produced houses of suburbia as objects, and as such they are all alike.
The suburbanites, however, see each house in terms of the people who live
in it, and, because every person or family is unique, it is as unimportant
that the house is mass-produced and much like the next, as it is that the
car is mass-produced and just like all the others.

Moreover, there are vast differences in standards of beauty between
the planner and the people he plans for. These differences again reflect
cultural distinctions between the upper middle class and the other classes.[5]
Although not all planners feel that Le Corbusier's buildings are attractive,
they tend to agree on aesthetic standards; many prefer simplicity to
ornateness, and functional design to design that seeks to hide a building's
function. Most of the people planned for, however, have quite different
standards of beauty. Simplicity, sparseness, and functionalism strike them
as cold and inhuman, and so many American home buyers prefer the

pseudo-Colonial elevations for their house, just as many English home buyers seem to prefer pseudo-cottages.

The second reason for believing that the planner should give people what they want is philosophical. I do not think the planner has the right, except in special circumstances to be described, to force people to change their behavior so that he can achieve his vision of the well-planned community. As I have tried to indicate, I believe that this vision is not based on expert knowledge but on the planner's own class culture, and I see no reason why people should be asked to give up their own culture for his.

I make this judgment for two reasons.

First, I do not believe that the planner has a monopoly of wisdom on goals and values, and I do not believe that his upper middle-class culture is the only desirable life style. There are many diverse ways of living in a heterogeneous urban-industrial society, and unless these can be proven to be harmful to those who practice them, or to other people, they should be treated as equally valid, at least within the present socio-economic system.

Second, life styles and their underlying goals and values do not develop in a vacuum; they are functions of the existential situations with which people must cope, and they are closely related to people's class position, particularly their educational level and income. Asking people to give up their life style for that of the planner is actually demanding that they change their behavior to that of a "higher" class without obtaining the socioeconomic prerequisites which that class enjoys. One could argue that, in the abstract, upper middle-class life styles are more desirable than lower middle- or working-class life styles, and I am willing to defend that position.[6] However, if planners want people to behave in upper middle-class ways, they must provide the funds and the education that will make them upper middle-class people. Until this is done people should be allowed to live in the way that accords with their level of income and education.

Only one exception might be made to this general rule. This is that the planner has the right to ask people to change if he can prove that a present behavior pattern or a community arrangement is dangerous either to the people concerned or to others. For example, if he can prove that parents who are unwilling to pay the taxes required for a good school system will make it impossible for their children to get a good job ten years hence, he has the right to ask them to change their behavior. Similarly, if he can prove that people living alongside a much traveled highway may get lung cancer from automobile exhaust fumes, the planner is entitled to ask them to move. He must, however, be able to present reasonable proof of the consequences he predicts, and he must demonstrate that these consequences will violate people's own values and interfere with the achievement of their own goals.

On the other hand, he cannot force people to accept changes because he thinks they are good by his own professional or personal values, or to give up a life style because he thinks it is bad. For example, he cannot demand that people stop moving to suburbia simply because the exodus conflicts with his goal of the urbane city. Nor can he argue that they stop moving to suburbia because he thinks it has pathological results for them, for he cannot prove that these results exist. Indeed, I think it is irresponsible to use pathology as an argument when there is no evidence. This is then merely a device for frightening people into changing their behavior.

It should be emphasized that in arguing to let people live as they choose, I am not proposing that the planner necessarily encourages them to live as they do now. As I noted before, he ought to provide them with choices, one of which is the present way of doing things. He should give them other choices as well, including even his own, but there must be a choice. If people are satisfied with the status quo, however, and resources are too scarce to provide many alternatives, the planner ought to limit himself to recommending experimental projects. He should then determine how people like them, and the results of these experiments could help him decide which choices ought to be offered on a wider basis.

PLANNING FOR THE ALLOCATION OF BENEFITS AMONG COMPETING POPULATIONS

My argument for a client-oriented or user-oriented approach is most relevant to planning for a relatively homogeneous population. It is only one consideration in planning for heterogeneous groups or communities. When the planner's client is the city, he must plan for a heterogeneous population, and in this process he is inevitably allocating scarce resources among sectors of the population, providing benefits to some and costs to others. For example, if he proposes a new set of highways, he is primarily benefiting the middle-class suburbanites who will be the main users of such a highway. If he proposes a low-income housing project in a middle-class neighborhood, he is benefiting the poor population and exacting status costs from the affluent.

Consequently, the planner must decide how to allocate resources among competing groups, and for which people to plan. This is probably the most difficult and perplexing question in planning, and only now is it beginning to be asked. In the past, the planner avoided the question altogether, for by focusing on buildings and land uses, he did not have to think about who would use them and benefit from them. Moreover, he saw himself as planning in the public interest and had few doubts about what that constituted; it was whatever he said it was, and coincided with his well-planned city.

Today, he can no longer feel so certain about the nature of this interest. The widespread political opposition to urban renewal, the ghetto rebellions, and the planner's rising influence in city government, which has brought him much closer to urban politics, are beginning to make him aware of the fact that his plans have benefit-cost consequences, that competing groups have different demands for what benefits and costs planning ought to award, and that there is no simple way of determining the public interest.

For example, urban renewal may do away with slums, but if it reduces the amount of low-cost housing and forces the poor to pay higher rents, where is the public interest? Advocates of urban renewal have suggested that, despite these costs to the poor, such programs are desirable because they bring the middle class back into the city, preserve the cultural facilities, and increase the tax rolls of the city. However, when there is no evidence that urban renewal does bring back the middle class, and when there is some evidence that the cultural facilities are only used by the affluent, and that many of these are suburbanites, and when developers of cleared areas can only be attracted by tax write-offs, where, then, is the public interest?

Similarly, the suburban exodus has made life considerably more pleasant for many middle- and working-class whites, but it has also increased residential racial segregation, and as industry has also moved to the suburbs, it has prevented Negroes from going where the jobs are. To what extent, then, is the suburban exodus in the public interest?

Moreover, it is often doubtful that there is a unique public interest, for in a heterogeneous community, there are few goals on which the entire community can agree, and still fewer goals which the community must pursue even if there is no consensus. Most residents in the community favor plans which will raise incomes for everybody, and economic plans to attract more industry are probably in the community interest — although attracting industry to already affluent cities may not be in the national public interest. Similarly, community survival is a goal which must be pursued even if not all residents desire it, and although, here too, the national public interest might demand the depopulation of communities no longer having a viable economic or social role.

How is this dilemma resolved? Once again, it is necessary to begin with goals, and by determining and understanding the goals of all the groups in the community, to identify those shared by all and those intrinsic to the community as a whole. But when the slim stock of such goals is exhausted, the planner must decide for which people to plan, and how resources are to be allocated between competing interests. These decisions are difficult to make, and there are no technical criteria for guidance. A partial solution to the dilemma is to look for allocations that will benefit as many groups as possible. For example, if the planner can demonstrate that a new highway will not only make commuting easier but will also attract industry, and create jobs for the unemployed, he can satisfy simultaneously the goals of two quite different sectors of the population. Similarly, if he can demonstrate that a system of family allowances, or another form of income grant to the poor, will not only help them escape from poverty but will also reduce the amount of pathology and antisocial behavior so as to improve the quality of city living and reduce the taxpayers' costs of fighting crime, he will in one program be satisfying the goals both of the poor and of the affluent taxpayer.

However, when benefit-cost studies indicate that a plan will aid one group more than another — and this is probably true of most plans — the planner must make a political decision and take a political stand. With respect to allocations for socioeconomic groups, for example, he can align himself with the poor and say that they need benefits more than the affluent; he can align himself with the working class — or the lower middle class — and say that they are most crucial to the community's economy, or he can align himself with the upper middle class because it pursues the goals and life styles which he himself favors. In the real world, only rarely can he choose between one or another group, however; usually he must decide who ought to get more of the economic pie and who ought to get less. He must also make other choices, for example between different age groups and ethnic or racial groups.

My own position is as follows. I believe that in America, private enterprise allocates resources primarily to the affluent, and that the government policies with which the planner is concerned ought to be *compensatory;* they ought to allocate as much as possible to the poor and deprived to reduce inequities in American society. This choice is partly a political position, for I believe strongly in an egalitarian society, but it is also partly a public interest position. I think that many if not most of the problems of American cities are caused, directly or indirectly, by the problems of the poor and nonwhite populations of the city, and that if poverty and segregation can be eliminated, even the so-called physical problems of the city will be ameliorated. Slums, after all, are primarily created by the inability of poor people to afford better housing and by the inability of Negroes to gain access to white neighborhoods, so that they become a captive market for slum landlords who can earn high profits without maintaining their buildings. The low quality of urban facilities, the city's tax problems, and many other urban problems are actually the result of urban poverty and segregation, and if the cities are to be saved, for the poor and the affluent alike, it is in the public interest to eliminate poverty and segregation. And once the presently poor can be incorporated into the affluent society, they will want the physically more orderly, efficient and attractive city for which city planners have been striving for all these years.[7]

THE ROLE OF THE PLANNER

In summary, I view the planner not as a reformer, nor as a professional who is free to impose his expertise and his values on the people for whom he plans. As a public official he ought rather to be their servant, helping them solve their problems and achieve their goals, except when these goals have antisocial and self-destructive consequences. In this process, the planner ought to propose a variety of programs to solve problems and achieve goals so that people have maximum choice; and in this variety, he ought to be free to include some programs that are based on his own goals. When it comes to planning for heterogeneous populations, however, and the public interest is difficult to determine, he has to take a political stand, and propose the allocation of resources so that the maximal benefits accrue to those people, interest groups and communities he feels are in greatest need of public benefits.

The prime function of the planner, however, is not to determine goals, for that is the duty of the elected official and of the electorate. The planner ought to concern himself principally with determining the best programs for achieving goals, and since most goals pertain to the improvement of the social and economic environments, he ought to devote himself to programs which will realize these goals. In this process he must also plan for the physical environment, but he ought to devote himself first to people, and only secondarily to buildings.

Notes

1. D. Wilner, *et al.*, *Housing Environment and Family Life* (Baltimore: Johns Hopkins University Press, 1962); B. Berger, *Working Class Suburb* (Berkeley, Calif.: University of California Press, 1960); H. J. Gans, *The Levittowners* (London: Allen Lane, The Penguin Press, 1967); and P. Willmott, *The Evolution of a Community* (London: Routledge & Kegan Paul, 1963).
2. T. Langner, Private communication of unpublished findings of the Manhattan Midtown Mental Health Study.
3. M. M. Webber, "Order in Diversity: Community Without Propinquity," in L. Wingo, Jr. (ed.), *Cities and Space: The Future Uses of Urban Form* (Baltimore: Johns Hopkins University Press, 1963), p. 52.
4. H. J. Gans, *People and Plans: Essays on Urban Problems and Solutions* (New York: Basic Books, 1968), ch. 5.
5. H. J. Gans, "Popular Culture in America," in H.S. Becker (ed.), *Social Problems: A Modern Approach* (New York: John Wiley, 1966), pp. 549–620.
6. *Ibid.*
7. The author recommends that for a more detailed statement of the argument given in the sections "The Planner's Physical Bias" and "The Historical and Political Sources of Physical Planning," the reader should consult H. J. Gans, *People and Plans: Essays on Urban Problems and Solutions,* ch. 5. In addition, a thoughtful analysis of the studies mentioned under the section "The Lack of Effects of Physical Planning" is to be found in a paper by P. Hall, "The Urban Culture and the Suburban Culture" presented at the Lions International Symposium, University of Puerto Rico, October 1967.

PART TWO

URBAN ADMINISTRATION: POLITICS AND CHANGE

5

URBAN ADMINISTRATION:
THE STATE-OF-THE-ART

The range of demands placed upon urban administration is extensive. Urban administrative agencies are expected to determine the appropriate dimensions of governmental responsibility and response in such widely diverse service areas as ecology, public order, land use, transportation, employment, economic development, housing, race relations, education, public health, and welfare. In addition, they are required to decide procedurally how the urban community should be governed as well as how managerially community resources should be appropriated so as best to get the job done.[1]

This diversity of demands and responsibilities has complicated efforts either to define or to describe the present state-of-the-art of urban administration. To the extent that a definition or a set of comments takes account of this diversity, it typically becomes so abstract that it provides no guidance and is rendered virtually meaningless. What Dwight Waldo has said regarding the problems that attend efforts to define public administration is equally applicable to urban administration:

The immediate effect of all one-sentence or one-paragraph definitions of public administration is mental paralysis rather than enlightenment and stimulation. This is because a serious definition of the term . . . inevitably contains several abstract words or phrases. In short compass these abstract words and phrases can be explained only by other abstract words and phrases, and in the process the reality and importance of "it" becomes fogged and lost.[2]

Efforts to escape this "mental paralysis" have for the most part met with limited success. Thus, even as prominent a student of public administration as Peter Woll is unable to describe administrative agencies with greater specificity and clarity than the following:

Administrative agencies are generally characterized by their size, the complexity of the decisions that they must make, specialization, and the combination of several governmental functions. Another characteristic of primary importance is the fact that no agency can exist without strong political support.[3]

This chapter begins by presenting one of the most promising efforts to date to provide a framework for the systematic study of public administration. Gary L. Wamsley and Mayer N. Zald, in "The Political Economy of Public Organizations," set forth a

framework with roots in organizational analysis that is simple but has enough heuristic power to make its application appealing to a wide range of students of public administration; that can pose questions for those areas still in need of exploration, and conceptually link them with those areas already well defined.

The authors believe that such an integrative framework can provide important explanations as to why individuals, groups, or organizations behave as they do in public administration; can explore how that behavior affects public policies; and can thereby help to underscore the political dimensions of public and urban administration.

The framework used by Wamsley and Zald is based on "the political economy approach." The phrase "political economy" refers to the interrelationship that exists between the structure of rule (politics) and a system for producing and exchanging goods and services (economics). The authors note that "just as nation-states vary in their political economies — their structure of rule authority, succession to high office, power and authority distribution, division of labor, incentive systems and modes of allocation of resources — so, too, do organizations." They regard political and economic variables as the major determinants of administrative structures and change and, consequently, see them as most important in defining or describing public administration.

The authors argue that the political economy can be divided analytically into external and internal aspects. Analysis of the external political economy of an organization focuses on its interaction with the environment. This interaction is characterized by external political exchanges entered into in order to secure legitimacy and basic "life-support." It is also marked by external economic exchanges engaged in to secure low-cost raw materials and the means of production and distribution.

Internally, Wamsley and Zald continue, analysis of public organizations can also be divided into polity and economy. Polity focuses on activities and behavior relating to the development and definition of agency mission, ethos, and priorities. It includes recruitment and socialization of the executive cadre as well as efforts to monitor the environment and the internal economy and harmonize the two. Internal economy centers on those phenomena and activities that relate to effective task accomplishment. It includes within its purview division of work and responsibilities, allocation of resources, and maintenance of an incentive system.

Wamsley and Zald's political economy approach provides a useful framework for examining the internal and external factors that determine what goals an urban administrative agency will set for itself and how it will seek to implement them. When read in conjunction with Michael P. Smith's "Alienation and Bureaucracy: The Role of Participatory Administration," it offers a rather comprehensive overview of the present state of urban administration.

Smith argues that the political economies of organizations are becoming increasingly dominated by a concern for technology. As Todd R. La Porte notes: "as a body of citizens and public officials, our nation has developed an enormous enthusiasm for the use of scientific technologies in the solution to public problems. We implicitly turn to the 'technological fix' as a solution to many social and economic problems."[4] Technology not only determines the way in which administrative organizations carry out their goals; increasingly it is also determining what these very goals should be. "We must adapt to technology," and "We must change our values and institutions so that we can better use technology" are the admonitions of the day. Yet, as Smith observes, this emphasis on technology can be terribly counter-productive. "Contemporary technological society places a heavy burden upon the individual to adapt to a large-scale, highly complex, and oftentimes impersonal bureaucratic environment. For a substantial number of members of modern mass societies this burden has become the source of pervasive feelings of anxiety and estrangement now fashionably termed 'alienation'."

Smith points out the tragic irony of bureaucratic alienation. Many of these bureaucratic institutions were originally intended to help men master their world: but now, for the most part, they constitute "obstacles to man's endless quest for self-expression, personal efficacy, and human fellowship." Smith explores the paradoxical factors in massive urban public service bureaucracies that contribute to this bureaucratic alienation. For him, the fundamental factor is the concern for efficiency.

Its [bureaucracy's] specialization of functions, while necessary when dealing with complex problems, tends to foster the fragmented or excessively specialized personality. Its hierarchical chain of command and multiple layers of supervision tend to produce dependency on the part of subordinates and unorganized clients. Bureaucracy's spirit of official impersonality and its routinized procedures, although designed to promote fairness in administration, also discourage warm interpersonal relationships. The form-filling approach, so necessary when processing large quantities of goods and services, often becomes counterproductive red tape which further contributes to a depersonalization of the environment. Corollary to the bureaucratic concern with techniques of rational efficiency is the treatment of employees and in some cases even clients as means to the realization of institutional ends.

In short, the entire internal and external political economy of an organization — what its goals are and how they are carried out, how it regards its employees and even its clients — is dramatically affected by a commitment to efficiency and its resulting alienation.

Smith turns to the urban school bureaucracy and the urban welfare bureaucracy for specific examples of the pathological consequences of alienation. In urban schools, administrative personnel are likely to be so committed to efficiency that they end up treating the school as an output factory and the child as a mere product. As a consequence, they are inclined to emphasize "quantitative indicators of subsystem expansion" over "qualitative concern for children." Similar pathologies exist in the urban welfare system. "In numerous welfare organizations the depersonalized problem solving orientation and the adjustment philosophy have combined to produce a kind of schizophrenic bureaucratic situation. The complex, hierarchical, norm-imposing regulations foster clientele dependency at the same time that the clients are demeaned by welfare agencies because they are dependent." As a result, Smith calls for decentralized and participatory administrative arrangements. Such participatory forms of administration constitute for him the cure for the pathologies of bureaucratic alienation. They are capable of "narrowing the gap between the planning and implementation of social services while also modifying the individual's anonymous and dependent environment when dealing with an organization; thereby giving him room to behave responsibly, intelligently, perhaps even creatively in his daily life."

Smith's call for greater decentralization and public participation in administration to overcome the alienative effects of an increasingly impersonal and technological world perhaps underestimates the extent to which technology has had an impact on the political economies of administrative organizations. As Todd R. La Porte argues, our nation's increasing reliance on the "technological fix" for solutions to our many social and economic problems has been responsible for three major consequences.[5]

First, it has "vastly increased our capacity to 'control' physical conditions." To a lesser extent, it has also increased our capacity to control
organizational and economic conditions. Second, it has prompted the
development of organizational systems, both in government and industry,
needed to activate technical potential increases and has, thereby, added
to "the overall complexity within and among economic, political, and
social institutions." Third, as a result of this increased complexity and
capacity to control, it has contributed to "a sense of increasing overall
uncertainty." "[I]ncreases in technical capacity and uncertainty of effects
tends to increase a sense of social, political, and psychological uncertainty
experienced by the public about the 'proper' ends of government."[6]
These three consequences have profound implications for the political
economy of urban administrative organizations, for they directly affect
not only the goals of organizations but also the manner in which they
carry them out. For example, they openly question the value of local
governments with their limited capacity to implement technical solutions
to problems of regional scope. As La Porte notes, the public is presented
with a dilemma:

We are forced to choose between either valuing technological solutions to
national and urban problems or maintaining quite deeply held social and
political values defining what many people mean by democracy. Let me
draw the choice more sharply. It is a choice between maintaining our value
of technology and changing our basic conceptions of social and political
values; or maintaining social-political values and reducing our enthusiasm
for technical solutions.[7]

This dilemma is a real one, but as La Porte points out, it can be
minimized, if not avoided altogether. For the most part, technology is
accepted "as a kind of force available to us on its terms." The general
perspective presents technology as offering the "one best way" and,
hence, obliging the public simply to adapt to it, changing its values and
institutions whenever necessary so that it can better use it. To escape from
this dilemma, La Porte argues that the public must alter its perspective on
technology. "Whether or not we become captive of an apparently deter-
ministic technology depends upon our understanding of technical processes and our philosophical wits. It is time to alter our perspective of
technology and turn it more directly to shaping a future based on a clear
declaration of desirable future values."[8]
La Porte declares that the public must become aware that technology can be used to serve political and social values as well as economic
and security needs. A question arises at this juncture, however: what
political and social values should technology be used to serve? As La Porte

rightly points out, this question is "very close to the realm of political and social philosophy." Nonetheless, it is a question which urban administrators must face; it is but another challenge to urban administration.

Notes

1. See Watt, Parker, and Cantine, Chapter 8.
2. Dwight Waldo, *The Study of Public Administration* (Garden City, New York: Doubleday, 1955), p. 2.
3. Peter Woll, ed., *Public Administration and Public Policy* (New York: Harper & Row, 1966), p. 13.
4. Todd R. La Porte,"The Context of Technology Assessments: A Changing Perspective for Public Organization," *Public Administration Review,* XXXI (January/February, 1971), p. 63.
5. *Ibid.,* p. 64.
6. *Ibid.,* p. 65.
7. *Ibid.,* p. 66.
8. *Ibid.,* pp. 69–70.

GARY L. WAMSLEY and MAYER N. ZALD

THE POLITICAL ECONOMY OF PUBLIC ORGANIZATIONS

The search for a theory of public administration often takes on aspects of a quest for the Holy Grail or a hunt for the mythical unicorn. Public administration theory has meant variously: a search for "scientific principles"; broad ruminations on what phenomena are included within "the field"; and general orientations of students of the subject, both professional and academic.[1]

Seldom has theory referred to systematic, empirically based explanations of a phenomenon; a system of related and proven propositions that answer the question "Why?" Though this article cannot begin to present such a theory, hopefully, it does more than issue another pious call for one. It is intended to set forth a framework with roots in organizational analysis that is simple but has enough heuristic power to make its application appealing to a wide range of students of public administration; that can pose questions for those areas still in need of exploration, and conceptually link them with those areas already well defined. A framework that can perform such an integrative role would represent a major step toward explanations of why individuals, groups, or organizations behave as they do in that part of the political system we have analytically abstracted and labeled public administration; and it would tell us something about how that behavior affects public policy. If we can better answer the "why" questions, we can also answer better the "how to do it," or the "what should be done" questions that have been so important to the field in the past.

Needless to say, we feel no such framework currently exists. A con-

Reprinted from the *Public Administration Review*, journal of the American Society for Public Administration, XXXIII (January/February 1973), pp. 62-73.

sensus approach to theory building is needed that can integrate knowledge not only within the field, but from different disciplines; one that focuses on the study of *public* rather than general administration, and therefore has organic links to political science and policy analysis, as well as to organizational sociology.

THE PRIOR QUESTION: IS THERE "PUBLIC" ADMINISTRATION?

After decades of debate, public administration theory is still mired down in debate over whether a meaningful distinction can be made between public and private administration. While granting that to understand the political system, it is necessary to understand public agencies, some argue that for those interested in administration-*qua*-administration, the distinction is counter-productive since it obscures important similarities. Others contend that even if the aim is to understand the political system, it is still possible to assume all administration is the same, and merely "plug in" variables and concepts borrowed from the study of private management.

Our position is that public organizations have distinctive characteristics which make it useful to study them in a separable but interrelated discipline. If we seek to understand public agencies and treat some aspect of them as dependent variables, we find that they are subject to a different set of constraints and pressures than private ones. Specific variables take on different weights in the public sector. If one treats public policies and the agencies that shape and execute them as *independent variables* affecting political effectiveness and legitimacy, he will need an understanding of public organizations quite different from that necessary to understand the effectiveness and legitimacy of private organizations.

A government is a system of rule, distinctive from nongovernmental institutions in that: (1) it ultimately rests upon coercion and a monopoly of force, and (2) if legitimate, it symbolically speaks for the society as a whole, or purports to do so. From these fundamental features flow definitions of membership, rights, expectations, and obligations in relation to the state and its agencies. Citizens and ruling elites both feel they have different "rights" and "expectations" with regard to the FBI than they have with General Motors.

The public organization is more dependent upon funds influenced by political processes or agents. The recipient of services is usually not the immediate funder[2]; and the taxpayer finds it hard to discern linkage between his taxes and any benefits accruing from organizational output. The price-utility relationship is lost, and political considerations not found in the marketplace result. When, for example, the British National Health Service decided to charge for prescriptions, the issue was raised in the House of Commons.

Public administration is also distinctive in the crucial role played by public organizations in shaping and executing public policy, of visibly rewarding and depriving the name of society. Some organizations and their processes contribute to certain policy outcomes, and others facilitate different outcomes. Current concern over policy analysis calls for a theory of public rather than general administration; a theory that can be focused on the consequence of organizational structure and process for policy development and implementation. The abilities, problems, and limits of agencies in developing and carrying out policies are part of the process by which allegiances and regime support are shaped and effected.

These distinctive aspects of public organizations — symbolic significance, differences in funding, perceptions of "ownership" or rights and privileges, and resulting resource constraints — and the relationship of public organizations to public policy point to a potential unity and intellectual coherence in the field of public administration that will be useful for both analytical and normative purposes.

THE POLITICAL ECONOMY APPROACH

Granted that the phenomenon called public administration evokes some relatively distinctive concerns, can the previous approaches to the subject which have come from a variety of sources and disciplines be unified and integrated? Elsewhere we have reviewed and criticized such approaches.[3] The political economy approach draws strongly upon the literature of "organizational analysis" or "complex organizations" (as contrasted with scientific management, bureaucratic analysis, or human relations approaches).

Organizational analysis has been most useful to us because it treats organizations as social systems — dynamic, adapting, and internally differentiated — eschews the search for a "one best" model of organization, and has been non-normative, or at least accompanied prescriptions for effectiveness, with contingency statements.[4]

Since it is a structural-functional approach, organizational analysis has tended to treat the full range of social system processes — recruitment and socialization, authority and control patterns, conflict and tension resolution, role conflict, goal adaptation, management processes, technology of task accomplishment, and adaptation to environment — as ongoing processes of an integrated social system. This breadth of approach, however, is also one of its limitations. Analysts alternately claim the greatest heuristic and analytic leverage lies in goals, communications, raw materials and technology, socialization, etc. There has been little agreement about what are the most important variables accounting for structure and change. The political economy framework, however, tries to overcome this weakness by focusing attention on precisely such key variables.

The phrase "political economy" has a long history and several different meanings. It once meant that relationship of government to the economy which promoted a competitive marketplace and thus produced efficient allocation of resources and production. Modern welfare economics uses the phrase in a normative sense to refer to the quest for that policy alternative benefiting most people at least cost. The late 1960's saw the development of a variety of techniques for analyzing policy options. We use the phrase descriptively as the interrelationship between structure of rule (polity) and a system for producing and exchanging goods and services (economy).

We suggest that just as nation-states vary in their political economies – their structure of rule authority, succession to high office, power and authority distribution, division of labor, incentive systems and modes of allocation of resources – so, too, do organizations. And political-economic variables are the major determinants of structure and change.

Throughout this article the term "political" will refer to matters of legitimacy and distribution of power as they affect the propriety of an agency's existence, its functional niche (in society, political system or policy sub-system),[5] its collective institutional goals, the goals of the dominant elite faction (if they vary from institutionalized goals), major parameters of economy, and in some instances the means of task accomplishment (if the task is vague enough to raise value questions or if values change sufficiently to bring established means into question).[6]

"Economic" refers to the arrangement of the division of labor and allocation of resources for task accomplishment and maximization of efficiency; and the combination of factors affecting the cost of producing and delivering a given level of services or output.[7] If goals are well-established and means routinized, an organization becomes largely an administered device, an economy.

An organization's political economy can be analytically divided into internal and external aspects.[8] Analysis of the external political economy focuses on the interaction of the organization and its environment.

EXTERNAL POLITICAL ENVIRONMENT:
STRUCTURE AND INTERACTION

Traditional and neo-classical writings in public administration have tended to treat both external political and economic factors as given, beyond the scope of public administration theory. For us they are central concerns in efforts to develop dynamic analyses because so many of the pressures for change occur in the external environment.

Public organizations exist in an immediate environment of users and suppliers, of interested and disinterested "others." Together, the organization and its relevant others make up a policy subsystem; an arena of individuals, groups, and organizations affected by and interested in influencing a policy for which the organization has prime responsibility and concern. These relevant others include a variety of actors in and out of government: interest groups, competing public organizations, legislative committees, control agencies. They may be competitive, hostile, overseeing, etc.; regardless, a policy subsystem shapes the conditions of existence for an agency.

An external political structure represents the distribution of sentiment and power resources among an agency's relevant others, i.e., opposition or support to the agency, its goals and programs. The distribution of sentiment and power is a reflection of: the dramaturgy or emotive element in the public organization's operations; its perceived expertise; the degree to which its impact is felt; the breadth (number of groups and individuals affected or interested) of its relevant others; the intensity of their interest; the resources they can bring to bear in exerting influence, and their ability and willingness to use resources.[9]

Sentiment distribution alone offers only a partial description of an agency's political environment. The power resources of actors, their willingness or ability to use them, and their skill in building coalitions also represent an important part of the equation. Some actors have intense interest but are relatively powerless, e.g., prisoners *vis-à-vis* the U.S. Bureau of Prisons; others have power resources but fail to use them because of political costs or internal conflicts over which action to take. Thus, sentiment patterns are weighted by the power resources and capabilities of relevant others.

Nor do public organizations merely accept the existing sentiment and power distribution; they also manipulate it with varying degrees of success. Administrators try to routinize the controversial by obtaining an equilibrium of interests, by benignly institutionalizing their environments.[10] The task is never complete, for the equilibrium can be upset by administrative error, changes in influence patterns and technology, or the suddenly negative attention of a latently powerful actor, e.g., the U.S. Tea Tasting Board's "discovery" and proposed abolition in 1970, or the CIA in the aftermath of the Bay of Pigs fiasco.

External political structures tend toward rigidity. Change does not come easily in a public organization or its policy subsystem either by dint of its manipulation *or* impingements of the environment. Goals and procedures may be frozen by conditional patterns of support and hostility. A press for change mobilizes opposition. The incentive system of public organizations seldom works for change. A change agent must generate issues, mobilize a coalition of forces, and gain the support of key proximal others in a policy subsystem. Though difficult, change does occur through interaction and political exchange. Political exchanges result from conscious efforts of: (1) external actors to affect a public organization's niche and related goals; or (2) an agency to manipulate its relevant others in order to alter its legitimacy and the order of magnitude of resources, and thus its overall goals and direction. The effects can thus alter niche, the general functional goals related to it, internal political patterns, processes of task accomplishment (if they involve legitimacy), and even survival.

When we think of the external political interactions of an organization and its environment, most of us think of the obvious, such as the Nixon Administration's efforts to subtly shift the goals of the Civil Rights Division of Justice and the Office of Civil Rights for HEW from zealous pursuit of desegregation in the South to a diverse nationwide approach of lower intensity, less inimicable to the growth of Republicanism in the South.[11] But this is the obvious. The more subtle and on-going source of interactions are the efforts by the executive cadres of organizations to alter their own domain or that of their neighbors, and thus alleviate uncertainty. Domain may include claims on future functional-level goals and the requisite resources to achieve them as well as those presently held.[12] In this on-going political interaction over niche or domain, agencies vary along several dimensions in their sensitivity to political impingements and capacity to manipulate.

Goals, Ambiguity and Clarity

Where goals are clearly defined and subject to surveillance, an agency like the Social Security Administration may be left little room for choice or maneuver in goals, program objectives, and perhaps even means of task accomplishment. But if goals are ambiguous or multiple, an organization's elite may press for one definition or another and, within the bounds of political feasibility, allocate resources internally in pursuit of this choice (correctional institutions: treatment or custody).

Surveillance

Some agencies effectively avoid scrutiny by superiors and other external actors. The CIA with its budget hidden in other departments' appropriations, is the most notable example. But ambiguity of goals, hidden missions, or simply overwhelming complexity of programs and accounting information also hinder effective surveillance and diminish sensitivity.

Centrality of Values

If a public organization is perceived to fulfill a central value of the political culture, its autonomy is enhanced as long as it does not drastically alter niche goals. If the agency loses effectiveness, surveillance increases and autonomy declines. A state fire marshal's office charged with ensuring fire safety in schools, institutions, and public buildings may hardly be reviewed until a tragic fire occurs.

Personnel and Funding Allocation

Not all agencies are equally subject to influence by external and superior actors in the matter of funds and personnel. Special, strategically placed allies like a chairman of an appropriations subcommittee can help or hurt them in terms of financial support. Or those operating on users fees, trust funds, or special funds may enjoy greater freedom from surveillance by superiors than those operating from general funds, though they are subject to special scrutiny from the clientele from which the revenues derive.

Public organizations have a relative lack of control over executive appointments. Central budget and personnel offices often have "position control" over personnel. But the nature and extent of this control varies. Some terms of appointment are long, and in the case of many boards they are staggered. Other agencies at the state level are headed by elected officials, which gives them a strong base of autonomy.

The Structure of Support and an Established Feed-Back Loop

Autonomy increases if an organization offers a well-received product to efficacious clientele who are able to influence key, proximal others. They, in turn, enlarge the organization's share of resources and legitimacy. This requires the right balance of numbers, geographic dispersion, and of efficacy. Sometimes this means the establishment of advisory committees, propaganda aimed at relevant others, news media, and mass public, or even the actual organization of interest groups by the agency.

Political interactions and exchanges take place between an agency and relevant others at its boundary. Transactions involve such outputs as strategically timed withholding or providing of products or services, "leaks" to news media, providing of information to allies; and such inputs as interest group demands, demands of a chief executive, influence of an appropriation subcommittee chairman. Inputs or outputs are political rather than economic if they are of sufficient magnitude to alter niche, overall goals and direction, the order of magnitude of resources, or major economic parameters.

ECONOMIC ENVIRONMENTS AND EXCHANGES

An examination of a public organization's economic environment requires an analysis of costs and behavior necessary in obtaining factors of production and exchange of output at organizational boundaries. It means emphasizing what in the private sector would be called "industry structure," markets, and the elasticity of supply and demand. Special attention must be given to the degree of "industry concentration," the relationships among competitors, distinctive aspects of technology, supply of raw materials and labor, and "markets" or factors affecting the distribution network for outputs.

The industry structure of public organizations is generally ignored on the assumption that they have monopolistic or oligopolistic status. But many have competitors among other agencies and in the private sector as well. In addition, the supply and prices of the factors of production for public organizations are directly affected by events in the economy at large.

However, many phenomena which might be treated as economic in the private sector must be treated as political-economic in the public sector. Demands are aggregated, filtered, and channeled through the budget process and an agency's policy subsystem, as questions about the legitimacy of spending public funds for certain purposes are raised and as its resource needs are thrown into competition with others. The process is pronounced in the United States with its strong separation of executive and legislative functions and its weak party system, but is also found elsewhere.

The lack of market controls for a public organization and the corresponding lack of efficiency incentives have led to elaborate accounting and budgeting controls in an effort to simulate market functions. Contract clearance, position control, independent audits, control of category transfers, competitive bidding, apportionments, cost-benefit analysis, and performance budgeting are devices for controlling cost and registering preferences. Often these are purely instrumental and economic in nature, but the analyst must be aware of their political ramifications as well.[13]

The cost curves of producing and delivering a public organization's product vary considerably and can become political in nature. The steep costs of putting in a new weapons system for deterrence or damage limitation may trigger a national debate over national priorities, the risks of attacks, etc. In contrast, political crises over school costs are slower to develop because they rise incrementally rather than in "lumps" that might mobilize opposition.

What, then, is treated as strictly an external economic exchange for a public organization? Economic exchanges are neither intended to nor do they actually affect niche, functional goals, order of magnitude of resources, or major economic parameters; rather they are designed merely to implement established goals and tasks, and are seen as legitimate by both the dominant coalition of an organization, its opposition, and by relevant others. Government agencies, for example, bargain over price and quality of certain elements of production, but do so without conscious effort to manipulate their environment politically.

Often economic considerations are ignored in the literature of public administration because of a failure to conceptualize public organizations as obtaining raw materials from an economic environment and processing or converting them into products offered to consumers.[14] Even public organizations which we assume have highly charged political environments have established some niche and carry on some "production" that no longer raises questions of legitimacy. For example, the Joint Chiefs of Staff produce "products" like advice to the Joint Staff, translation of policy into strategic orders, decisions on weapon systems and force level priorities that we normally fail to recognize as products. Many of the JCS's products resemble those of a private consulting firm. They are produced by collating information and beliefs (the raw materials) through "technologies" of debate, compromise, defined disagreement, suppression of the source of raw materials, delay in processing, ambiguous decisions, agreement not to disagree, and technical loyalty to the Administration but covert disloyalty. Some products like decisions on weapon systems have definite political effects, but many of them, like advice to the Joint Staff, no longer raise questions of legitimacy and are most meaningfully seen as economic[15] because they are relatively routine. If public organizations are viewed as procurers and processors of raw materials, and offerers of products at their boundaries, then their external economic exchange (and internal economic structures) become more readily apparent.

General economic and manpower pictures can also affect a public organization. Full employment and inflationary economy make it more difficult for public organizations to recruit personnel because of their lower status and lag in pay scales. The costs of public organizations are closely tied to labor rates because they produce services rather than manufactured goods, and it is difficult for them to substitute machines for labor. As wages rise, public costs spiral. Workloads also respond to economic and manpower outlooks. Some workloads rise as the economy declines, e.g., welfare and unemployment insurance agencies; while that of others, like Selective Service, declines as unemployed men volunteer and lower draft calls result.

Broad and diffuse changes in demand are also economic and are so perceived by agencies, e.g., the increase in camping that has vastly changed the National Park Service. Similarly, technological changes are usually perceived as economic, though they may drastically alter an agency and its exchanges with its environment — Internal Revenue Service and computers; the Army and helicopters.

Public organizations seek to manipulate their economic as well as political environments. Competitive bidding and mass central purchasing are obvious examples; but cost-plus-fixed-fee contracts, grants, loans, and leasing out of capital assets are all methods used to overcome hesitancy of contractors and suppliers.

Public agencies exist in a web of political and economic exchange structures that shape long-run functions and directions of change, as well as short-run interactions and concerns. Changes in societal values and the values of relevant others can alter an agency's functional goals and legitimacy, while cost factors and the pattern of "industry structure" affect its ability to accomplish task. Public administration must be able to analyze agencies' environments in order to predict change, and an understanding of public policy and changes in it calls for a political economy analysis of the organizations that are prime actors and relevant others in a policy subsystem.

INTERNAL POLITICAL STRUCTURE AND PROCESS

The internal policy refers to the structure of authority and power and the dominant values, goals, and ethos institutionalized in that structure. The executive cadres of agencies may have their range of domain options more limited by statute and oversight than is true of private organizations. But because statues are vague and extraordinarily complex, and because oversight is imperfect, there remains room for interpretation that marks the political function. Executive cadres also come to identify with the agency, its ethos and goals, and its long-range survival, growth, and status in a way that is more than merely utilitarian. Because public organizations are involved in pursuing commonwealth values, cadres are likely to see their agencies as embodying high purpose. This infusion of an instrumental structure with values that give it purpose other than task accomplishment (maintenance, survival, aggrandizement) provides another fundamental basis for political functions.[16]

Four major political functions of the executive cadre can be identified: (1) developing and defining agency mission, ethos, and priorities; (2) developing boundary-spanning units and positions to sense and adapt to environmental pressures and changes; (3) insuring recruitment and socialization of agency elite to maintain coherence and pursuit of goals; (4) overseeing the internal economy, harmonizing it with shifts in niche or goal proprieties.

The four polity functions are initiated and carried out by executive cadres to insure survival, growth, and adaptation. Sometimes they are less than successful: goal consensus among cadre is seldom perfect; adequate boundary-spanning units are often not established; elites are improperly socialized; and internal economies are sometimes poorly monitored. To some extent the manner in which cadres perform these functions is dependent upon the shape of the internal political structure as it varies along several dimensions: (1) constitutions, (2) degree of goal consensus, (3) unity of authority, (4) patterns of subunit power, demand aggregation-articulation, and conflict resolution, and (5) patterns of leadership succession and cadre maintenance.

Constitutions

The constitution (written or unwritten) of any social group consists of the basic norms involving the ends and means of power — conceptions of legitimate purposes and of legitimate ways of wielding authority in pursuit of them.[17] They determine the types of incentive exchanges existing or possible for an organization, i.e., time, energy, and commitment it can expect from different members and what rewards they expect. If norms of exchange are weak or non-binding, an organization's polity tends to be fragile. For example, if its exchange system is solidly utilitarian, it will find it difficult to survive a crisis requiring near total commitment of its cadre, unless utilitarian rewards can be made extraordinarily high.

Constitutional norms also indicate the range of discretion and decision responsibilities for organizational elite and mass. For example, the keystone of Selective Service's constitution historically was "local board autonomy." This established roles in hierarchical interaction over cases. Quiet but intense daily struggles occurred in operationalizing the norms, but always within constitutional parameters. Such norms also set parameters for the relationships between an organization and its relevant others. To whom is it responsible or responsive, and under what conditions? Is the Corps of Engineers more responsive to presidential policy guidelines on ecology or congressional demands for pork barrel projects?[18]

Constitutions specify the political foci of collective actions, i.e., the matters within or without its area of concern — domain, clientele groups. Often they prevent adoption of a new assigned function because of inability to give the proper attention.

Goal Consensus

Few public organizations have total cadre unity over purpose and general direction; moreover, they are often vulnerable to divisiveness from external political influences. But usually there is a prevailing coalition (perhaps supported by outside actors) with its own *Weltanschauung*. Factionalism crises arise from sources like empire building by units, ambiguity of statutory mandate, influences of external actors, lack of cadre homogeneity, operations that must span wide areas, and tasks that are complex, vague, or diverse.[19]

Unity of Authority

Some organizations have goal consensus but a splintered authority structure; not all have a singular head and a unitary chain of command. Most obviously, boards and commissions are structures fostering factionalism, coalition patterns, and pursuit of multiple goals. Other organizations represent a conglomeration of functions thrown together by fate and congressional whimsy. A federated authority pattern often results.

Patterns of Sub-Unit Power, Demand
Aggregation-Articulation, and Conflict Resolution

Because they are usually responsible for different goals or phases of task accomplishment, sub-units develop differing interests, and their power capabilities differ because of: their essentiality to accomplishment of overall goals, or epitomization of organizational mission; their access to and influence over information and communications (internal and external); or the support they marshal from the general public or powerful in-contact others.

Internal polities differ in the way demands of sub-units, lower-level membership, or elite factions are patterned. Many of the demands themselves are of an instrumental or economic nature, but the particular *patterns* followed are a reflection of internal polity, for they shape direction, goals, and functional niche. The patterns determine responsiveness to change, vulnerability to pressures, indeed survival capacity. Patterns are shaped by sub-group identity and cohesion, perceived grievances, and the costs and benefits of expressing them. Some public organizations are unionized and face strike threats, others have elaborate employee associations that lobby, a few have lower-level members that are so dispersed and fractionated in their interests that scarcely any demand pattern emerges, and in still others the costs of expressing demands or grievances are so great as to militate against pattern emergence. The inability of an organization to handle demands and resolve conflict at lower levels vitally affects its direction and existence.[20]

Leadership Succession, Cadre Recruitment, and Socialization

The formal structure of the executive cadre, appointment power and criteria for dismissal, promotion, and transfer are often set for an agency by external political forces. Still, some discretion remains. What appears to be the external imposition of a procurator is often an established pattern that also reflects internal forces. Appointments of political executives must satisfy expectations of organizational elite as well as those of relevant others (unless outside powers are trying to bring about drastic change). Succession patterns may take several forms: a "crown prince" system with an anointed successor; a "stand-off" or consensus successor wearily agreed upon by intensely conflicting factions; a "new majority" and clandestine coups; or a discontented sovereign outside the organization may send a procurator.

Public organizations do not merely tap into civil service pools for cadre. Cadre recruitment and socialization follows definite patterns in each organization. The State Department cadre is drawn heavily from "prestige" universities and socialized into a "gentlemen's club," while the Department of Agriculture draws upon land-grant colleges, and the military intensely socialize in academies. Organizations find ways of being selective about cadre either in recruitment or socialization.[21]

Public administration has not yet begun to provide the concepts and schemas for analyzing the rich variations in internal polities of organizations — the widely varying ways in which the authority relating to overall goals and directions of an agency is organized.

Internal Economy

At the heart of every organization is a "sub-organization whose 'problems' are focused upon effective performance of the technical function." The main concern of persons filling the cluster of roles in the internal economy are: the "exigencies imposed by the nature of the technical task";[22] problems growing out of the nature of the raw materials to be processed; the division of work and responsibilities so that the cooperation required for task accomplishment is forthcoming; and allocating resources and maintaining an incentive system to efficiently accomplish tasks. Public organizations, like private, must coordinate behavior and allocate resources in order to produce an output which satisfies relevant others.

It is the internal economy in which the broader technological aspects of the organization are concentrated, where instrumental and efficiency norms take precedence over legitimacy. In this realm, role incumbents are likely to see problems of overall direction and survival as "someone else's business."

Buffering and Nourishing the Technological Core

Organizational polities seek to protect and insulate the technological core from external contingencies that would disrupt task accomplishment. They do so because they are established to accomplish tasks, and efficiency concerns are thrust upon them by scarcity, goal achievement drives, budget constraints, or output evaluations. Efficiency efforts can bring about major changes, a possibility that links internal economy to both internal and external political concerns. The quest for efficiency leads to efforts to buffer out disruptions of constant and routine affairs by smoothing input and output flows, or by forecasting fluctuations and scheduling adjustments.

Buffering can be done in some organizations by "stockpiling," preventive maintenance, or an extension of organizational jurisdiction and operations to encompass crucial contingencies. An example of the latter is public organizations like narcotic rehabilitation centers which seek to change people. Often they seek to induct the raw material so as to better monitor it, control it, or cope with contingencies.

One means of nourishing the internal economy is to expand clientele. An agency that applies standard techniques to large populations may have considerable slack resulting from putting in new technology or equipment, e.g., automation of a records system is done with machinery designed for existing load *plus* future growth. The resulting slack may be a temptation to enemies or an embarrassment to the organization that motivates client expansion. Sometimes slack is handled by diversification of functions to avoid charges of waste.

Not all agencies can protect their technological core. To the extent they cannot, they lose economies of scale, lose advantages of specialization, incur high coordination costs, and run risks of collecting bad accounting information.

Task Structures

Structure within the internal economy refers to the patterned interaction of sub-units and roles in accomplishment of organizational tasks. Classical public administration theorists like Gulick and Urwick sought to discuss how work should be organized (purpose, process, clientele, or area). Neo-classicists like Simon convincingly showed that their predecessors had no firm answers, but their work was more directed at "how" to organize to obtain "correct" decisions than it was at explaining "why" task structures follow the patterns they do.

To the extent that norms of efficient task accomplishment prevail, (a matter to be settled empirically in each case) the basic dimensions of hierarchy and coordination in an agency's internal economy are laid down primarily by raw materials, technologies, and task dimensions.[23]

Within the basic dimensions, however, task structure is further elaborated by: (1) the variety of "products" offered by the organization (the Department of Commerce offers everything from commercial statistics to weather forecasts); (2) the scope of operations necessary to deliver a product (in order to develop the Tennessee River and its tributaries, TVA must do everything from build dams to produce fertilizer); (3) the degree of geographic dispersion (TVA and the Corps of Engineers have similar scopes of operations and products to deliver, but the Corps is much more geographically dispersed); and (4) by the particular nature of role interdependencies requiring role clustering at different hierarchical levels in order to reduce coordination costs.

The internal economy is thus an arrangement of authority and power, but on the level of instrumentality and efficiency rather than on the level of legitimacy and survival — the economic aspects of authority rather than the political. One affects the other and the two power structures may be one and the same, with role incumbents merely acting out different facets of their multidimensional roles. But they *do* make the distinction and it is observable in their behavior. Nor it is a distinction confined to certain types of political systems. Both parliamentary and revolutionary regimes, for example, may recognize the distinction between political and technical functions, e.g., the Red Army.

Resource Allocation and Incentive Systems

Budgets and accounting systems are means of allocating resources within the internal economy. They are vital mechanisms for maintaining the level of activity and types of cooperation necessary for efficient task accomplishment.[24] Accounting systems record variable data which communicate trends in efficiency, effectiveness, inter-unit comparison, etc., to organization elite concerned with internal economy.[25] For example, a new division assigned a crucial function for the first time may incur unexpectedly heavy costs, indicating a need for change in task structure or drastic upward revision of appropriation requests. Resource allocation needs to be looked at as a key part of internal economy: a compounded function of traditional rules, intergroup bargains, mechanics for deciding economy conflicts, and elite perception of new areas for opportunity.

Within the internal economy, incentives are allocated to motivate performance. They may be symbolic, monetary, or nonmonetary (status, interpersonal), and vary not only in the "needs" they fulfill but in their delivery rate, tangibility, divisibility, and pervasiveness. Organizations have different stocks of incentives to draw on: the Peace Corps uses psychic incentives; the Post Office, monetary and security; and Selective Service uses symbolic and psychic incentives. A major organizational change often entails a change in the incentive system.

In the rush to study "politics" of bureaucracy, political scientists have left analysis of internal economy to business administration, organization analysts studying the private sector, or Bureaus of Public Administration (viewed by universities as community service agencies). But the subject requires more serious attention in broader perspectives. Alterations in internal economy can be a major source of change, setting off an internal polity struggle or fundamentally altering an organization's relation to its environment.

IS THE APPROACH USEFUL?

The political economy approach can only become a true paradigm for empirical theory building if it can (1) help unify the fractionated fields that are related to public administration, (2) contribute to traditional and emerging concerns of scholars in those fields, and (3) at the same time merge the strengths and move beyond the weaknesses of each. In conclusion, let us briefly indicate how our framework might contribute to these goals.

Each of the traditional concerns of public administration dealt with a key aspect of organizational political economies, but in a piecemeal and normative fashion and without conscious conceptual distinction between political and economic matters. Scientific management was, and a substantial part of the field today remains, concerned with structuring the task environment for efficiency — a matter of internal economy. Students of budgeting from the Taft Commission of 1912 to the PPBS of today have placed most of their emphasis on budgeting as a surrogate market mechanism. Only recently have the political aspects of the subject been acknowledged or effort made to sort out whether "reforms" are having political or economic effects. Similarly, personnel administration has gone through one trend after another from the great civil service reform to the more recent "decentralization" moves. Always students of public administration played more of a participant role than one of analytical observer, and seldom did they differentiate between political and economic matters. What has been most lacking is a focus upon an empirical entity — the public organization as a key actor in a policy subsystem.

Even if the American students of public administration become less reform-minded and interventionist, this seems unlikely to hold for persons studying "developing administrative systems." Many of these persons are taking up these concerns with fresh zeal. But it would be unfortunate if the same pitfalls experienced by the field in America were to be repeated. To avoid past mistakes these subjects must be approached in a broader and less normative way. The concerns of "interventionist-practitioners" are spotlighted by our framework as internal economy matters. An effort by them to apply the framework objectively can result in dividends. Their work will be better informed of the interaction between political and economic variables, and assuming the framework aids theory development, and advances toward answers to "why" questions, there will also be better answers to the "how to" questions. The unintended consequences of the many reforms or counter-reforms, and the political-economic costs and benefits that ensue would be made clearer.[26]

The framework could also be useful in a new concern bordering the field of public administration — policy analysis. Recent efforts have focused on systemic inputs; but this focus has left the field considerably short of explaining why certain policies take the particular patterns they do. This "input" approach of Dye and others has tended to show high correlations between economic development variables and policy outputs in certain areas; but low correlations between the outputs and so-called political variables.[27] The results are provocative but explain little, for the research has defined politics too narrowly (voter participation, party competition, degree of malapportionment). The entire realm of interplay in policy making between public organizations and their relevant others has remained untapped. Policy is made at the nexus of politics (particularly micro-politics) and economics. Economic development merely provides the resource backdrop for such policy making. A more thorough analysis must penetrate the organizational and policy context in which policy is made, and the political economy framework could prove useful.

The framework may also make a contribution in political analysis of regimes. Such analysis has sought to find out who is behind certain policy and government action. The answer in more cases than has heretofore been acknowledged is not necessarily a power elite, voters, or a consensual outcome of plural elite struggle, but an organization and its particular political economy needs; or an individual actor playing a role defined by his organizational membership, his organization's processes, or its place in a policy subsystem. Policy then, is as much, or more a product of the political economy of conversion structures within the interstices of the system's "black box" – as it is of pressures or inputs from outside.

Analysis has seen actions of government as a chess game with pieces moved by "outside forces," i.e., "the people," "the power elite," or a squabbling team of plural elites. But perhaps we need to think of them moving as a result of "internal forces," as though each piece has a set of wheels, internal motor, sensory devices, miniature computer and guidance system. That is to say, it may be moved by outside forces or players, but it also moves in response to its own environment reading and its own internal dynamics. Imagine also that each piece's ability to "read" environment responsively, and its repertory of responses, are limited and conditioned by political and economic factors.[28]

To carry things further, picture all of the above conditions plus the fact that as observers we can see only one game board, but that each piece is playing in several other unseen games; and further that the game boards overlap in a variety of ways. Accordingly, the visible self-directed piece, unbeknownst to us, is moving in several games at once, playing out strategies dictated by differing locations on each game board. A particular organizational move may be a function of simultaneous calculations in several different games.[29] The visible move may or may not be a conscious, coordinated synthesis of the different game strategies. Thus, public organizations are not merely important actors in a policy process; often their goals, myths, processes, procedures, or domain consciousness in effect "make" policy.

Utilization of the political economy framework could be not only a serious step toward developing a systematic empirical theory of public administration, but could also contribute to the development of important areas of study in both political science and sociology. It would be a useful enterprise, however, if it contributed to any one of these goals.

Notes

1. Martin Landau, "Sociology and the Study of Formal Organization," in CAG Special Series No. 8, Washington, D.C., 1966. His description of a preparadigmatic field should be uncomfortably familiar to students of public administration. See p. 38.

2. Some public organizations such as the Post Office are funded by customers, but there are still differential costs and benefits, and rates are subject to political constraints.

3. Wamsley and Zald, *The Political Economy of Public Organizations: A Critique and Approach to the Study of Public Administration*, forthcoming. Previous work on our framework can be found in Mayer N. Zald, *Organizational Change: The Political Economy of the YMCA* (Chicago: University of Chicago Press, 1970), and in his essay "Political Economy: A Framework for Comparative Analysis," in Mayer N. Zald, ed., *Power in Organizations* (Nashville: Vanderbilt University Press, 1970), pp. 221-261.

4. Prominent among the contributors to the literature of organization analysis are the works of Philip Selznick and his students upon whom we draw heavily. Representative of other "strands" are the works of Alvin Gouldner and Peter Blau and their students.

5. The concept of niche is borrowed from studies of biotic communities in which each organism has a niche in an interdependent and symbiotic relationship. Similar and used interchangeably is the concept of "domain." See Sol Levine and Paul White, "Exchange as a Conceptual Framework for the Study of Interorganizational Relationships," *Administrative Science Quarterly*, Vol. V (March 1957), pp. 444-463.

6. Even tasks performed by lower functionaries can become political if values within and without the organization are affected by the discretion they wield. Performance of a vague task may define values, or a long-established pattern of task accomplishment may run afoul of changed environmental values.

7. More than a few economists will be unhappy with our definition. Modern analytic economics tend to focus on maximization and resource allocation. Our definition includes them, but focuses on the structure of the economy, the extent and limits of differentiation and coordination.

8. If our framework focused solely on *internal* political economy the phrase "political-administration" or "political-managerial" might suffice, but it is also important to describe the structure of the *external* economic environment.

9. Rourke, *Bureaucracy, Politics and Public Policy* (Boston: Little, Brown, 1969), chapters 2, 3, and 4.

10. For example, see Gary L. Wamsley, *Selective Service and a Changing America* (Columbus, Ohio: Chas. E. Merrill, 1969), ch. 7.

11. See L. E. Panetta and P. Gall, *Bring Us Together: The Nixon Team and Civil Rights Retreat* (New York: Lippincott, 1971).

12. Levine and White, *op. cit.*

13. Aaron Wildavsky, "The Political Economy of Efficiency, Cost Benefit Analysis, Systems Analysis, and Program Budgeting," *Public Administration Review*, Vol. XXVI (1966). For examples of accounting becoming "political," see Thomas J. Anton, *The Politics of State Expenditure in Illinois* (Urbana: University of Illinois Press, 1966), pp. 46-47, 69-70, 203-204.

14. See Charles Perrow, "A Framework for the Comparative Analysis of Organizations," *American Sociological Review*, Vol. XXVI (1961).

15. The JCS operate in a highly competitive milieu. Their legitimacy depends on an occasional product acceptance. They not only act as a "consulting firm" but a "coalition of normally competing firms." Each member (except the chairman) plays a role as representative of his service as well as a collegial role. Example based on analysis as of early 1960's.

16. Selznick, *Leadership in Administration* (New York: Harper & Row, 1957).

17. In public organizations, constitutional analysis begins with statutes, promulgated regulations, and various memoranda. Also revealing are: documents describing the organization to outsiders or new members; histories written by members; or situations in which there has been a violation of a constitutional norm, conflict, or withdrawal of resources.

18. Arthur Maas, *Muddy Waters: The Army Engineers and the Nation's Rivers* (Cambridge: Harvard University Press, 1951), p. 63.

19. See Anthony Downs, *Inside Bureaucracy* (Boston: Little, Brown, 1967), pp. 224-226.

20. Public administration theory lacks a typology of conflict resolving mechanisms within agencies paralleling knowledge of those in the society and legislative arenas. A good beginning, though not applied directly to public organizations, is found in James D. Thompson, "Organizational Management of Conflict," *Administrative Science Quarterly*. Vol. 4, No. 4 (1960), pp. 389-402.

21. See Harold Seidman, *Politics, Position and Power* (New York: Oxford University Press, 1970), pp. 113-114.

22. James D. Thompson, *Organizations in Action* (New York: McGraw-Hill, 1967), p. 10. This section draws on Thompson and Charles Perrow, *op. cit.*

23. For a discussion of the types of technologies see Thompson, *op. cit.*

24. They may also be used in polity struggles to reward and punish and bring about change. Here we single out their economic importance.

25. They also transmit information that may be used politically to cadre factions and other actors in the policy subsystem.

26. But caution is needed in applying organizational analysis to societies with quasi-organizations or in which organizations are "fronts" for other social groups. See Fred W. Riggs, "Organization Theory and International Development" (Bloomington, Ind.: Carnegie Seminar on Political and Administration Development, 1969).

27. Thomas R. Dye, *Politics, Economics and Public-Policy Outcome in the American States* (Chicago: Rand-McNally, 1966).

28. Graham T. Allison, "Conceptual Models and the Cuban Missile Crisis," *American Political Science Review*, Vol. LXII (September 1969), pp. 689-718;

29. Norton E. Long, "Local Community as an Ecology of Games," *American Journal of Sociology*, Vol. 64, pp. 251-261.

MICHAEL P. SMITH

ALIENATION AND BUREAUCRACY:
THE ROLE OF PARTICIPATORY ADMINISTRATION

Contemporary technological society places a heavy burden upon the individual to adapt to a large-scale, highly complex, and oftentimes impersonal bureaucratic environment. For a substantial number of the members of modern mass societies this burden has become the source of pervasive feelings of anxiety and estrangement now fashionably termed "alienation."

The tragic irony of the modern era is that some of the institutions originally designed to help men master their world have instead created obstacles to man's endless quest for self-expression, personal efficacy, and human fellowship. These three values form the basis of what people have traditionally sought from their social and political institutions — an opportunity for creative development, a means to control their environment, and a sense of community. Yet the more deliberately men have sought to maximize these values through human organization, the more elusive they have become.

This essay will explore the paradoxical factors which contribute to man's growing sense of bureaucratic alienation within the context of the massive urban public service bureaucracies. The chosen focus is particularly well suited to illustrate the roots of modern man's sense of estrangement from the bureaucratic life. Close students of aggression and violence have shown that the sheer size and growing anonymity of urban life help to produce generalized feelings of powerlessness in the face of large-scale institutions.[1] This diminished sense of personal efficacy, in turn, may result in estrangement from such institutions as well as from the larger

Reprinted from the *Public Administration Review*, journal of the American Society for Public Administration, XXXI (November/December 1971), pp. 658–664.

society. Moreover, unlike factories and corporations, the professed goal of urban public service bureaucracies is helping people rather than selling products. Alienation is likely to become particularly acute among the workers or unorganized clients of such bureaucracies when persons rather than things are the goals likely to be displaced by impersonal, routinized practices, by excessive specialization of functions, or by prolonged clientele dependency.

THE ALIENATED SELF

Although man's search for creativity and self-mastery within community is as old as human history, his daily encounter with large-scale organizations is a uniquely modern phenomenon. The classical Greek *telos* when applied to the individual entailed a sense of wholeness — a striving to fulfill one's creative potential in and through the larger society. Hence, Aristotle saw effective participation in the life of the community as essential to the fulfilled personality. But as nation-states emerged, as societies grew more complex, and as industrialization and urbanization increased, the humanist's optimism diminished as he saw man's chances for community and self-fulfillment threatened.

Thus the early Marx, writing just after the dawn of the industrial age, spoke of and to the self-alienated worker for whom work had become a matter of compulsion; a mere instrument for satisfying other needs during his leisure time. Specialization, routinization, and the cult of production (i.e., the worship of things) had conspired to alienate Marxian man from himself, from his work, and from his fellows. The early industrial man was a shrunken man and, ironically, the large-scale organizations initially designed to provide for his needs also highlighted his feelings of impotence and estrangement. In the words of the young Marx: "The more the worker expends himself on his work the more powerful becomes the world of *objects* which he creates in face of himself, the poorer he becomes in his *inner* life and the less he belongs to himself.[2]

John Stuart Mill was another 19th-century philosopher concerned about the intangible consequences for the individual of large-scale organizational society. Mill perceived bureaucracy as a regularized ordering of human life which, if left unchecked, could diminish both creative thinking and self-direction. His central argument was that self-expressive faculties like "perception, judgment, discriminative feeling, mental activity, and even moral preference are exercised only in making a *choice*," and hence can be improved only by being used.[3] Accordingly, Mill feared that routinized, hierarchical decision making might eventually replace concrete discernment, individual spontaneity, and personal moral choice.

Twentieth-century technological society also has its humanistic critics, in revolt against what they perceive as the abstractness and impersonality of modern bureaucratic life. Modern existentialist philosophers speak out against the tendency of organizational societies to judge people in terms of their adaptability, rather than their integrity; their productivity rather than their character. They fear that a cult of efficiency within the bureaucratic climate will force man to identify his entire personality with his formal activities and the products of his labor. In the view of such writers as Martin Buber and Gabriel Marcel, large organizations transcend the concrete fellowship and understanding which is possible within small, intimate groups. Thus it is less likely that integrity and fraternity can be nurtured in large urban bureaucracies. Rather, in the technocratic era the existentialists fear lest the administrator objectify his work relationships, treating subordinates and clients as mere "inputs" to be manipulated in the solution of larger abstract problems rather than as whole persons with developing personalities.[4] Since deeply personal "I-Thou" relationships are required before the individual can experience completeness and fulfillment, the bureaucratic situation becomes in their view dehumanizing both for the administrator and the individual consumer of bureaucratic services. Excessive specialization of functions leads to the fragmentation of man.

PUBLIC PROBLEM-SOLVING AND ALIENATION

Today it is becoming increasingly clear that the process of alienation from the bureaucratic life is more than merely the pet fantasy of ancient philosophers and contemporary poets. Many segments of American society[5] already seem to be in revolt against what perhaps might best be termed the cyclical paradox of highly developed mass societies.

In any advanced society, when an abstract social or economic problem is identified, bureaucratic machinery is mobilized to solve the problem, to cope with or control the situation. Yet as the bureaucracy's resources are mobilized, so are its potentially harmful tendencies. Its specialization of functions, while necessary when dealing with complex problems, tends to foster the fragmented or excessively specialized personality. Its hierarchical chain of command and multiple layers of supervision tend to produce dependency on the part of subordinates and unorganized clients. Bureaucracy's spirit of official impersonality and its routinized procedures, although designed to promote fairness in administration, also discourage warm interpersonal relationships. The form-filling approach, so necessary when processing large quantities of goods and services, often becomes counterproductive red tape which further contributes to a depersonalization of the environment. Corollary to the bureaucratic concern with techniques of rational efficiency is the treatment of employees and in some cases even clients as means to the realization of institutional ends. Ironically, the impersonality and even greater complexity introduced into the problem by the administrative apparatus has in some cases led to a decrease in the individual's sense of efficacy and control, regardless of whether or not the organization is marginally coping with its problems.

The Urban School Bureaucracy

Consider, as a major case in point, the increasingly differentiated urban public school bureaucracies. In the urban schools several potential pathologies conspire to deny the individual student an open and creative educational environment. The foremost pathology is a matter of underlying operating philosophy — the commitment to efficiency — i.e., the tendency to regard the school as an output factory and the child as a mere product. Some educational professionals devote more of their time and energy to nuts and bolts maintenance functions, such as acquiring larger budgets, higher salaries, costlier buildings, and more equipment, than they devote to the children. This orientation has several unintended consequences.

Goal displacement is the first major byproduct of the "output factory" mentality. Some of the urban public schools are so highly organized and excessively professionalized that in a very real sense they have lost sight of their primary purpose. Such schools are in constant danger of responding to professionally defined needs and entrenched institutional biases rather than to individualized student needs.[6] For these schools system maintenance has displaced creative teaching. Quantitative indicators of subsystem expansion have replaced qualitative concern for children.

Appropriately enough, it is this same kind of bureaucratic displacement of goals which, in some measure, accounts for the ever more vocal demands for public school decentralization and community control. For example, in *110 Livingston Street*, David Rogers explains the failure to desegregate the New York City public schools partially in terms of individual racism, but also partially in terms of the bottlenecks created by the headquarters staff bureaucracy. Integration, like all innovations, was perceived as a threat to the regular pattern of administrative behavior; an unwelcome inconvenience; a challenge to habitual routines.[7] Failing to achieve integration, the Black community has turned in frustration to demands for community control.

In many urban school systems excessive bureaucratization also has resulted in the routinization of teaching practices, which, in turn, has added to the deindividualization of the learning process. Even those teachers and principals who are person-oriented rather than task-oriented can be constrained by the weight of procedural strictures and paper work emanating from the central headquarters staff. In the St. Louis public school system, for example, teachers at the elementary level are required to organize their entire work week according to a printed form.[8] Such behavior leaves little room for spontaneity or that leap of imagination we call creativity.

The bureaucratic reward system further encourages conformity rather than innovation. Public school personnel practices, featuring detailed promotion procedures and a relatively rigid seniority system, pose a clear threat to individualized teaching. The successful completion of standardized advancement examinations is often required to move from one step on the ladder to the next. In addition to encouraging cautious conformity to the conventional wisdom embodied in standardized examinations, this type of reward system also may discourage the teacher from developing important talents which otherwise might be regarded as criteria for advancement, e.g., a stimulating classroom environment, attention to the relevance of the curriculum to the individual student, etc.

Finally, as a result of the production mentality and the climate of protectionism, public participation in the life of the school often has been kept at a minimum. In theory, educational professionals argue that parental involvement in their child's education is likely to improve student motivation and achievment. Yet, in practice, schoolmen tend to relegate parental involvement in school affairs to essentially trivial matters, since effective community participation in the educational process (i.e., influence respecting staffing, budgeting, or curriculum) would run counter to the pathologies mentioned above.

Interestingly enough, some recent research suggests that increased community participation may be related to bureaucratic as well as student motivation and achievement. In a recent study of six large urban school districts (Detroit, Philadelphia, New York, St. Louis, Chicago, and Baltimore), Marilyn Gittell and T. Edward Hollander found that innovation in the districts (defined in terms of program innovations, administrative reorganizations, and the magnitude of federal aid for new programs) was strongly related to administrative decentralization and high levels of public participation.[9]

Despite findings such as these, urban school bureaucracies still tend to resist efforts in the direction of greater community involvement. In consequence, because of the cumulative effect of its overorganization, the prevailing system has lost many of the supposed merits of centralization ("efficiency," effectiveness, etc.) while simultaneously failing to maximize any of the values usually associated with decentralization and public participation (e.g., flexibility, innovativeness, increased individual efficacy, greater citizen control).

Welfare Colonialism

The public school bureaucracy clearly is not the only large-scale public institution which contributes to the depersonalized urban bureaucratic environment. Urban welfare bureaucracies often suffer from similar pathologies. In the welfare bureau the cult of efficiency reappears in the form of a patronizing rehabilitation orientation which encourages welfare bureaucrats to treat recipients as impersonal, abstract problems – as objects – cases to be adjusted; or rolls to be reduced. This attitude is reflected in the fact that 78% of the urban social workers responding to a recent survey undertaken for the National Advisory Commission on Civil Disorders believed that a major part of their responsibility was to "teach the poor how to live."[10]

Large caseloads, demeaning clientele investigations, and an incredible panoply of formal rules further contribute to the dependent, impersonal nature of the situation. Rules and regulations governing recipient behavior are so elaborate and so custodial as to control nearly every important aspect of a person's daily life.[11] The human consequences of this kind of situation are not to be taken lightly. The impact of the maze of formalized rules and procedures on the people affected by social services has been well stated by Harry Levinson:

Social services . . . have become progressively more institutionalized. These and similar organized efforts have taken the place of the more personal services and charitable acts characteristic of a previous era, "more personal" meaning that people believed there was more affection and concern in the noninstitutional services. The change therefore represents a perceived loss of certain sources of love – "Nobody really cares."[12]

In numerous welfare organizations the depersonalized problem solving orientation and the adjustment philosophy have combined to produce a kind of schizophrenic bureaucratic situation. The complex, hierarchical, norm-imposing regulations foster clientele dependency at the same time that the clients are demeaned by welfare agencies because they are dependent. The poor are blamed for failing to assume a self-reliant posture, although the situation, by fostering dependency, works to prevent independent, self-expressive behavior. The result is a built-in conservatism. Adjustment therapy implies that something is fundamentally wrong with the individual rather than the environment. The basic philosophy of social work produces in many urban welfare bureaucracies a trained incapacity to look for faults in the social and institutional setting within which individuals live. These agencies have fallen victim to a kind of Shavian self-fulfilling prophecy. They have helped to turn the poor into bootblacks while using their bootblack status as evidence of inferiority.

In many of our metropolitan centers, the paradoxical bureaucratic situation just described has prompted an intensification of demands for more participation, more democracy, whether in the form of decentralized decision making, community control, or participatory planning. The outpouring is by no means surprising. Such demands focus on the psychological deprivations of alienated lower-level bureaucrats and unorganized clientele groups — their felt need for individual self-expression, for a sense of community, and for control over their immediate environment. Hence, the popularity of local city halls, the ombudsman concept, and the welfare rights movement, all of which can be interpreted as efforts to hold large bureaucracies accountable to the people they were designed to serve.

It seems we have returned full circle to the philosophy of Aristotle. Effective participation in the life of community institutions is once again believed to be essential to the realization of the good life, fully lived.

Why is participation seen by so many as so important? Much can be said in support of the instrumental values of participatory administrative arrangements both for the individual and the organization. For example, participatory planning arrangements which involve unorganized clientele groups in making decisions about goals, practices, and policies are likely to act as a healthy check on the careerist dimension of professionalism by introducing another perspective into the planning process and by focusing attention on the human consequences of some decisions heretofore regarded as strictly technical.[13]

Public participation, coupled with decentralized administrative arrangements which involve lower-level administrators more directly in the planning process, can also become an effective vehicle for improving the communication process essential to all successful planning. More frequent consultation means more feedback. Feedback provides vital information to higher-level administrators on the felt needs of both staff and clientele groups and on the effectiveness of the bureaucracy in dealing with them.

Moreover, to the extent that the people immediately affected by social services become mutually involved with professionals in the definition of policies, it is likely that each group will increase its commitment to implementing the results of the joint effort. As Victor Thompson has said in commenting on the problem of excessive central planning: "There is nothing impelling about a plan on paper unless it represents the results of one's own analysis and decision."[14]

It also should be noted that, beginning with the classic Western Electric experiments, numerous studies have shown that reducing the decision-making point to the lowest possible level in a large-scale bureaucracy tends to be associated with higher levels of individual effort by subordinates and more innovative practices. Conversely, rigid hierarchy and close supervision tend to work against both of these values.[15]

Carrying the argument to another level, an expansion of the arena within which bureaucratic decisions are made may have other, purely individual consequences. For the lower-level bureaucrat or social service recipient, participation in decision making means more opportunity to exercise personal judgment. This, in turn, encourages (although it does not guarantee) the development of intellectual and emotional independence. In contrast, the man who never exercises personal judgment can hardly reach the level of responsibility we call adulthood.

Moreover, mutual involvement in matters of common concern may work against anonymity and isolation. But a truly mutual relationship is possible only through the kind of respect which occurs in situations of relative equality. Participatory planning, by encouraging the exercise of independent judgment by all parties concerned, seeks to equalize a heretofore unequal bureaucratic-clientele relationship. In so doing, fraternity is given the chance to overcome paternalism.

In sum, a viable argument can be advanced in support of participatory forms of administration as mechanisms for narrowing the gap between the planning and implementation of social services while also modifying the individual's anonymous and dependent environment when dealing with an organization; thereby giving him room to behave responsibly, intelligently, perhaps even creatively in his daily life.

Some promising efforts have recently been initiated to democratize large-scale social service bureaucracies by involving representative clientele groups more directly and extensively in decision making. Large size, remoteness, and impersonality have begun to come under direct attack. For instance, the Connecticut State Department of Community Affairs has developed guidelines which provide urban neighborhood residents access to the agency and a voice in its planning and decision making through such mechanisms as town meetings, neighborhood branch offices, and a neighborhood advocate hired by the agency to act as a kind of ombudsman.[16]

Similarly, the South End Tenants Council, an association formed to fight slumlords, has begun to command the attention of the sometimes impervious Boston Redevelopment Authority. The Council has obtained a major voice in planning the rehabilitation of properties in a six-block central-city neighborhood. According to a "memorandum of understanding" accepted by all parties in May 1969, the approval of the Tenants Council is required at each stage of operation including "all plans involving rent schedules, architectural plans, financing, rehousing and relocation."[17]

Orien White, Jr.'s recent study of the Wesley Agency, a church-related social service agency operating in a low-income area of San Antonio, Texas, is another case in point. The operating philosophy of the agency stresses a "client as peer" approach.[18]

Despite these hopeful signs, a cautionary note is in order at this point. Those who agree with this essay's general thesis concerning administration and alienation must be wary of taking heart in the mere adoption of participatory planning proposals without examining the way in which such devices are implemented, and their human consequences.

At least two possible dangers are readily foreseeable. The first is the possibility that public agencies will adopt token or purely symbolic public representation schemes to be used as a public relations device or to co-opt possible community opposition.

Next there is the perplexing problem of the young professional's role in participatory planning. Many studies have shown that participative management within a bureaucracy clearly lessens the anxieties of the bureaucrat and increases his personal sense of efficacy. But this increased sense of personal importance can cut two ways. On the one hand, if the lower-level bureaucrat feels secure in his position, he may be less inclined to fear innovations such as the client as peer approach. In contrast, full confidence in his professionalism may produce resistance to the inclusion of new, nonprofessional perspectives in agency planning. Participatory schemes which encompass the low-level bureaucrat but fail to include representative clientele groups in any meaningful way may actually create a greater obstacle to individual growth than strict hierarchy. A bureaucratic organization thereby freed from the normal internal anxieties and tensions may come to constitute a most pervasive form of institutionalized power over individual clientele preferences in its sphere of competence. The atmosphere of mutual trust necessary for effective participatory planning is most likely to develop when shared power rather than total bureaucratic control or total community control is the prevailing norm.

In summing up, it has been argued that large-scale bureaucracy and alienation are intertwined. As a result of the efficiency orientation, unorganized bureaucratic clients and lower-level employees are sometimes treated as mere objects to be administered. The routinized, impersonal, custodial administrative situation can stifle the creativity and sense of efficacy of both the administrator and the recipient of social services.

Nevertheless, there is some room for hope. Much of the recent effort in the direction of participatory forms of administration suggest that those concerned with social service bureaucracies have given at least some thought to the philosophy of John Stuart Mill when he wrote: "A state which dwarfs its men in order that they may be more docile instruments in its hands, even for *beneficial* purposes — will find that with small men no great thing can really be accomplished."[19]

Notes

1. For example, psychologist Philip G. Zimbardo, after conducting laboratory experiments on anonymity and aggression and a field study of vandalism and violence, concluded that city life contributes to the development of a "deindividuation" process, manifest in highly emotional, intensive behavior and a reduction in individual response to social norms. Three of the key causative factors isolated by Zimbardo were the growing anonymity of city life, the sheer size of the city, and the bigness of its institutions. See *New York Times,* April 20, 1969, p. 49.

2. Karl Marx, "Alienated Labor," *Economic and Philosophical Manuscripts,* first manuscript, XXII, T. B. Bottomore (trans.), in Erich Fromm, *Marx's Concept of Man* (New York: Frederick Ungar, 1961), pp. 95-96, 98.

3. John Stuart Mill, *On Liberty* (Indianapolis: Library of Liberal Arts, 1956), p. 71. Interestingly, Mill couches his antibureaucratic argument in terms of a conflict between reformist bureaucracy and individual spontaneity: "But the evil is that individual spontaneity is hardly recognized by the common modes of thinking as having any intrinsic worth . . . what is more, spontaneity forms no part of the ideal of moral and social reformers, but is rather looked on with jealousy, as a troublesome and perhaps rebellious obstruction to the general acceptance of what these reformers, in their own judgment, think would be best for mankind," p. 69.

4. See Gabriel Màrcel, *Man Against Mass Society* (Chicago: Henry Regnery, 1952); *Being and Having* (Westminster: Dacre Press, 1949); and Martin Buber, *I and Thou* (New York: Charles Scribners, 1958). See also Michael P. Smith, "Self-Fulfillment in a Bureaucratic Society: A Commentary on the Thought of Gabriel Màrcel," *Public Administration Review,* Vol. XXIX (January/February 1969), pp. 25-32.

5. For example, the roots of the postwar, middle-class suburban movement have been traced to a widespread desire to escape the complex bureaucratic life in the city; to regain a sense of personal efficacy; to rekindle the friendship ties lost by the breakup of family life. Similarly, the student perception of a remote, indifferent educational bureaucracy is said to be one of the primary stimuli to campus unrest. On the latter point see, for example, Allen H. Barton, "The Columbia Crisis: Campus, Vietnam and the Ghetto," *Public Opinion Quarterly,* Vol. XXXII (Fall 1968), p. 333.

6. This argument has been advanced so often by critics of the urban school bureaucracy that it is necessary to caution against its uncritical acceptance as valid for all urban school systems. Two recent comprehensive case studies by critics of the urban schools are: David Rogers, *110 Livingston Street: Politics and Bureaucracy in the New York School System* (New York: Random House, 1968): and Marilyn Gittell

and T. Edward Hollander, *Six Urban School Districts: A Comparative Study of Institutional Response* (New York: Frederick A. Praeger, 1968). For a recent review essay which is critical of Gittell and Hollander's methodology and data interpretation but nonetheless concurs in their conclusion that innovation in matters of curriculum and administration is associated with administrative decentralization and high levels of public participation, see Bruce C. Eckland, "Public Participation, Innovation, and School Bureaucracies," *Public Administration Review*, Vol. XXIX (March/April, 1969), pp. 218-225.

7. Rogers, *op cit., passim.*
8. Patricia J. Doyle, "St. Louis: City with the Blues," *Saturday Review* (February 15, 1969), p. 93.
9. Gittell and Hollander, *op. cit.,* p. 52.
10. David Boesel, *et al.,* "White Institutions and Black Rage," *Trans-Action* (March 1969), p. 28. This patronizing approach, which I have termed the rehabilitation orientation, has been designated "sociotherapy" by S. M. Miller and Martin Rein; see their "Participation, Poverty, and Administration," *Public Administration Review,* Vol. XXIX (January/February 1969), p. 16.
11. See Paul Jacobs, *Prelude to Riot* (New York: Random House, 1966), pp. 70-88, 287. Jacobs also indicates that welfare caseworker job frustration leads to a high turnover rate, which creates still another obstacle to an individualized approach to welfare administration.
12. Harry Levinson, "Reciprocation: The Relationship Between Man and Organization," *Administrative Science Quarterly,* Vol. X (March 1965), p. 372.
13. See Miller and Rein, *op. cit.,* p. 23, who argue that professionalism in the urban public services has resulted in attempts to "depoliticize" decisions such as urban renewal, which are clearly political in impact.
14. Victor Thompson, "Administrative Objectives for Development Administration, *Administrative Science Quarterly,* Vol. IX (June 1964), p. 102; see also Thompson's discussion of the organizational importance of feedback from groups importantly affected by planning, pp. 103-106.
15. See, for example, Robert T. Golembiewski, "Organization as a Moral Problem," *Public Administration Review,* Vol. XXII (Spring 1962), pp. 55-56; and Chris Argyris, *Personality and Organization* (New York: Harper and Row, 1957).
16. Community Development Action Plan, Guideline No. 1, "Inter-Personal Communication and Citizen Participation" (Hartford, Conn.: State Department of Community Affairs, 1968).
17. "Memorandum of Understanding," Boston Redevelopment Authority and South End Tenants Council, mimeo. (Boston, 1969).
18. Orion White, Jr., "The Dialectical Organization: An Alternative to Bureaucracy," *Public Administration Review,* Vol. XXIX (January/February 1969), pp. 32-42.
19. Mill, *op cit.,* p. 141 (emphasis added).

6

URBAN ADMINISTRATION:
STRUCTURES FOR EFFICIENCY

Urban administration is responsible for the effective, efficient, and sensitive delivery of vital urban services. In the United States, urban administration is directly affected by both intergovernmental relations and the structures of government in metropolitan areas. Thus, in the context of intergovernmental relations, what an urban administrator can do is often limited (intentionally or otherwise) by state or national officials. Likewise, in the metropolitan context, urban administration is frequently restricted by metropolitan fragmentation. This chapter emphasizes these limitations on urban administration and the restrictions they place on administrative efficiency in the resolution of the urban crisis.

A. Lee Fritschler and Morley Segal explore the effect that intergovernmental relations has had on local government and administration in "Intergovernmental Relations and Contemporary Political Science: Developing an Integrative Typology." They point out that "[f]rom the local point of view, government officials devote most of their time operating in an intergovernmental system." In fact, perhaps the maintenance of dead end streets is the only function controlled by strictly local interests. They note that "it is probable that the impact of political and administrative factors in the intergovernmental system, which are largely *outside* of the local system, have as great an impact on local policy as those factors determined by events occurring *inside* a jurisdiction's political boundaries." In so doing, they highlight the need to place the problems of urban administration in the broader context of the governmental system.

Fritschler and Segal emphasize how intergovernmental relations pervade every aspect of urban administration and its problems. Yet, as long as the American federal system remains, so will the restraints it places on urban administration. Thus, most students of the urban crisis have focused their attention on the micro or metropolitan level and have diagnosed fragmentation of authority and overlapping jurisdictions among numerous units of local government to be perhaps the most serious and urgent problem of urban administration. There is much evidence to support this diagnosis. The 1972 Census of Governments enumerates 78,269 separate governmental units in the United States, including 3,044 counties, 18,517 municipalities, 16,991 townships, 15,781 school districts, and 23,885 other special districts.[1] Of the 78,269 separate local governmental units, 18,151 are located in 153 Standard Metropolitan Statistical Areas (S.M.S.A.s) having populations in excess of 200,000. As the Committee for Economic Development (C.E.D.) emphasized in *Modernizing Local Government:*

1. Very few of the [se] local units [of government] are large enough — in population, area or taxable resources—to apply modern methods in solving current and future problems. . . . Even the largest cities find major problems insoluble because of the limits on geographic areas, their taxable resources, or their legal powers.

2. Overlapping layers of local government — municipalities and townships within counties, and independent school districts within them — are a source of weakness. . . . This [overlapping] impairs overall local freedom to deal with vital public affairs; the whole becomes less than the sum of its parts.

3. Popular control over government is ineffective and sporadic, and public interest in local politics is not high. . . . Confusion from the many-layered system, profusion of elective offices without policy significance, and increasing mobility of the population all contribute to disinterest.

4. Policy-making mechanisms in many units are notably weak. The national government, [however] has strong executive leadership, supported by competent staff in formulating plans that are then subject to review and modification by a representative legislative body. . . .

5. Antiquated administrative organizations hamper most local governments. Lack of a single executive either elective or appointive is a common fault. Functional fragmentation obscures lines of authority. . . . The quality of administration suffers accordingly.[2]

These figures and findings have led many analysts to propose consolidation of all smaller jurisdictions into a single overall unit of government for each urban region or metropolitan area. Such a consolidated unit would be of "sufficient size and authority to plan, administer, and provide for financial support to areawide problems."[3] And, they argue, such an arrangement would fix political responsibility, making it possible for citizens to hold officials accountable for their actions.

A serious problem confronts those policy analysts who favor consolidation, however. Put simply, voter response to consolidation proposals has been distinctly negative. As Vincent L. Marando and Carl Reggie Whitley observe: "[W]hen given the opportunity, voters generally reject this form of local governmental reorganization."[4] Thus, since 1945, only seven city-county consolidation referenda have been approved in areas over 100,000 population: Hampton-Elizabeth City-County, Virginia; Columbus-Muscogee County, Georgia; Virginia Beach-Princess Anne County, Virginia; Lexington-Fayette County, Kentucky; Baton Rouge-East Baton Rouge Parish, Louisiana; Nashville-Davidson County, Tennessee; and Jacksonville-Duvall County, Florida.[5] Voters have not been persuaded that consolidation will provide them with these benefits. Nor do they favor constitutional arrangements under which only a few policy making officials are elected and a single chief executive controls a highly integrated command structure. As Marando and Whitley report, the larger the number of separately-elected administrative officials (sheriff, tax assessor, and the like) in the consolidation charter, the greater the voter support.[6] This voter response has prompted the Advisory Commission on Intergovernmental Relations to arrive at the following generalization: "Political feasibility and acceptability have varied inversely with effectiveness; that is, what has been most politically feasible or acceptable has been least effective in dealing with general areawide problems and what has been most effective has been least politically feasible or acceptable."[7] Obviously, some approach other than outright consolidation is needed. In "Metropolitan Reform in the U.S.: An Overview," Joseph F. Zimmerman reviews the alternatives to consolidation. He categorizes these approaches as Semiconsolidationist, Statist, and Ecumenical. Semiconsolidationists propose a two-tier approach, with a consolidated upper tier performing areawide functions and a lower tier of small local units dealing with community or neighborhood problems within the larger consolidated unit. Statists argue that only state governments have the requisite authority and resources to order organizational devices appropriate for metropolitan problem-solving. Metropolitan ecumenicists believe that areawide problems can be met by interlocal cooperation without altering the existing governmental framework.

The ecumenical approach has proved to be the most popular — at least insofar as growth is concerned. There has been a dramatic increase in the number of voluntary associations of local elected officials, loosely known as Councils of Governments (COGs) — from 9 in 1965 to over 300 in 1971.' However, even COGs — a timid first step toward metropolitan government as they are — have had their problems. As Professor

Zimmerman notes, "Any organization built upon cooperation between local governments with widely differing socio-economic makeups and aspirations is predestined to experience serious difficulty in attempting to develop a program, based upon conjoint action, to solve major problems." Alan E. Bent, in "Home Rule Versus Regionalism: The Experience of a Tri-State COG," explores this difficulty, relying on the experiences of the Mississippi-Arkansas-Tennessee Council of Governments (MATCOG). Bent emphasizes how imperative the support and cooperation of the central city is to the success of such metropolitan ecumenism.

However, even if all those obstacles to effective metropolitan unification can some day be overcome, consolidation may still remain highly problematical. To begin with, two relationships are inherent in the thinking of the consolidationists: (1) increasing the size of urban government through consolidation will be associated with improved output of public services, increased efficiency, increased official responsibility, and increased citizen-satisfaction. (2) Reducing the number of jurisdictions in an urban area will also be associated with increased output, efficiency, responsibility, and satisfaction. A critical question arises: do these relationships obtain in the operation of urban government? If they do, then the more consolidation the better. However, if the reverse holds, then the smaller the units and the more duplication the better. There may also be intermediate possibilities. As Robert L. Bish and Vincent Ostrom point out, "an increase in size for some functions might yield improvements to some magnitude and yield net disadvantages beyond that magnitude. In other circumstances a decrease in size might yield improvements to some magnitude but yield net disadvantages if reduced to a still smaller size."[8] These intermediate possibilities have only very recently come under scrutiny. The work of Elinor Ostrom, Roger V. Parks, and Gordon P. Whitaker, "Do We Really Want to Consolidate Urban Police Forces? A Reappraisal of Some Old Assertions," explores these questions.[9] Their research suggests that neither total consolidation nor total decentralization is likely to lead to more efficient police services in metropolitan areas. Rather, "[c]onscious use of overlapping jurisdictions of varying sizes may be necessary to combine the advantages of both small and large scale."[10] However, even when a proper mix of large-scale metropolitanwide components and small-scale locally controlled components is achieved which can provide for the most efficient delivery of police services, problems will remain, for the findings of Ostrom and her associates challenge the importance of efficiency altogether. They conclude that effectiveness as measured by citizen satisfaction, not mere efficiency as measured on a cost/per unit basis, is the true criterion for evaluating service delivery by urban administration. In so doing, they provide a valuable reminder that consolidation, whatever its merits, will never be a panacea for all the problems that confront urban administration.

Notes

1. U.S. Bureau of the Census, *Census of Governments, 1972: Governmental Organization,* Vol. 1 (Washington, D. C.: U.S. Government Printing Office, 1973), pp. 1 and 10. In the 1967 *Census of Governments,* there were 81,299 separate governmental units, including 3,049 counties, 18,048 municipalities, 17,105 townships, 21,782 school districts, and 21,264 other special districts. At that time, 17,856 of the 81,248 separate local government units were located in the 148 SMSA's having populations in excess of 200,000.

2. Committee for Economic Development, *Modernizing Local Government* (New York, 1966), pp. 11–12.

3. *Ibid.,* p. 44.

4. Vincent L. Marando and Carl Reggie Whitley, "City-County Consolidation: An Overview of Voter Response," *Urban Affairs Quarterly,* Vol. 8 (December, 1972), p. 182.

5. Advisory Commission of Intergovernmental Relations, *Regional Decision Making: New Strategies for Substate Districts,* Vol I: *Substate Regionalism and the Federal System* (Washington, D. C.: U.S. Government Printing Office, 1973), p. 12.

6. Marando and Whitley, p. 191.

7. *Substate Regionalism and the Federal System,* p. 11.

8. Robert L. Bish and Vincent Ostrom, *Understanding Urban Government: Metropolitan Reform Reconsidered* (Washington, D. C.: American Enterprise Institute for Public Policy Research, 1973), p. 10.

9. Elinor Ostrom, Roger B. Parks, and Gordon P. Whitaker, "Do We Really Want to Consolidate Urban Police Forces?" *Public Administration Review,* XXXIII, No. 5 (September/October, 1973), 423–432.

10. *Ibid.,* p. 430.

A. LEE FRITSCHLER and MORLEY SEGAL

INTERGOVERNMENTAL RELATIONS AND CONTEMPORARY POLITICAL SCIENCE: DEVELOPING AN INTEGRATIVE TYPOLOGY

Advanced methodological and analytical techniques have been applied by now to most of the subfields of political science. Even Professor Herson's lost world of municipal government[1] has been reclaimed by the application of modern methodologies to the politics of state and local government.[2] One subfield which has not received the professional attention it deserves is intergovernmental relations.[3] In the growing intensity of professional interest in teaching and research involving state and local affairs, intergovernmental relations remains largely untouched — a kind of methodological Cinderella after midnight.[4] A recent survey by the Advisory Commission on Intergovernmental Relations indicated that intergovernmental relations also receives second rate treatment at best in today's college and university classrooms. Many more institutions favor intermediate and advanced courses in state and local government than courses related to intergovernmental problems.[5]

This lack of attention is unfortunate not only for intergovernmental relations itself, but also for the state-local and American government subfields of political science. As Professor Grodzins very accurately pointed out in his American government text, intergovernmental relations pervades every aspect of the system's political life.[6] It is difficult, even misleading, to think, write or talk about government and politics in the United States today without taking into consideration the politics of modern federalism. From the local point of view, government officials devote most of their time operating in an intergovernmental system. Citizens' groups also find their actions deeply touched by the machina-

Reprinted from *Publius*, Vol. 1, No. 2 (Winter 1972), pp. 95-122.

tions of political life great distances from their communities. Maintenance of a dead end street seems to be the only function controlled by strictly local interests.

From the national point of view, grants-in-aid to state and local governments are about 23% of the national domestic budget.[7] National inputs into domestic programs nearly always have to be through state and local governments. As these governments find it increasingly necessary to rely on the national government for funds, stimuli, and the political and administrative mechanisms needed to develop responses to twentieth century problems, both the importance and the complexity of the intergovernmental system are bound to grow.

For those who operate in the intergovernmental system there is an understood and at least partially accepted set of rules which guide their actions. These rules and the modes of operation established by them (including attempts to circumvent or even change them) affect local decision-making and policy outputs in important ways. In fact, it is probable that the impact of political and administrative factors in the intergovernmental system, which are largely *outside* of the local system, have as great an impact on local policy as those factors determined by events occurring *inside* a jurisdiction's political boundaries. During the past decade several useful studies have explored (some with the benefit of sophisticated empirical techniques) the relationship between a variety of socio-economic and political variables and such things as form of government, local reformism, community power and policy output.[8] Few of these studies have incorporated variables which are primarily affected by events outside of local jurisdictions or in the intergovernmental system.[9] To better understand local policy output differences and such things as local power configurations it would seem necessary to know more than the effects of locally generated inputs. One has to gain understanding of how the intergovernmental system works and how its impacts on local politics might be included in the calculus of output determinations.

This article examines some of the work done on intergovernmental relations, explores the possibilities of building intergovernmental considerations into contemporary political research and develops a typology to facilitate the use of intergovernmental factors in such research on a systematic basis.

Before discussing the typology in detail it is instructive to survey the growth of intergovernmental relations as a subfield and also to examine the arguments which led the authors to develop this typology.

INTERGOVERNMENTAL RELATIONS
AS A SUBFIELD OF POLITICAL SCIENCE

The substantive importance of intergovernmental relations has nurtured a continuing interest in the field, but with notable exceptions the debate is still largely ideological and philosophical. The remains of "dual federalism" were laid to rest in the 1950's. More recently the debate has centered upon the classification of "cooperative" and "creative" federalism with the Nixon version of "national localism" raising familiar questions about the nature of political and administrative relationships within the intergovernmental system.[10]

One pattern which emerges in the academic development of sub-fields in political science is that scholars first use legal abstractions to artifically develop a focus for study. Then they become immersed in the complexities of the political process. Finally, behavioral variables are developed as a focus for continued study.[11] This process of artificial isolation is necessary; indeed, most schemes of analysis require some degree of artificial isolation and simplification. The old legal ideas of dual federalism and state sovereignty fulfilled a useful purpose by removing one aspect of intergovernmental relations from the complex swirl of American politics so they then could be studied. Morton Grodzins pointed out that as appealing and simplistic as this legalistic analysis might be, it was dangerously misleading. The very notion of two independent spheres of sovereignty directed attention and nostalgia to bygone days which never existed and simultaneously prevented analysis of the real political process.[12]

The myth of dual federalism prevailed for a long time both in the public forum and in academe. It prevailed in public life because of the self-serving nature of states rights ideology and the practical self interest of its proponents. It prevailed in academic studies of intergovernmental relations for another reason — the provision of intellectual clarity where otherwise there would be only a chaotic jumble of relationships. More than most other fields, intergovernmental relations needs an analytical structure for clarity. While intergovernmental relations are a pervasive part of the entire field of American government, they are at the same time an elusive, almost ephemeral, phenomenon. These relations are sometimes highly visible (Governor Wallace in the schoolhouse door), but most often they are virtually indistinguishable from the overall political process.

Intergovernmental relations tend to fade into the general political process. In other subfields scholars attempting to develop more sophisticated methods can anchor their studies in concrete actors or institutions.[13]

The subfield of intergovernmental relations differs in that the focus of the field is upon a relationship. For this reason, the idea of sovereignty was borrowed from the study of nation states where it was a useful term, and transformed into dual sovereignty in intergovernmental relations where it led to the study of narrow legalisms. This application was misleading because, unlike nation states, the units of study in intergovernmental relations gain their identity within the field almost solely in terms of their relations with each other; furthermore, this identity shifts and changes depending upon the levels of government and the situation involved. The states are important in intergovernmental relations not because they are legal entities but rather by the manner in which they relate to other units of the system. The legal fiction of dual federalism froze states so that they could be studied as the fountainhead of both local and national power.

Grodzins demolished the handy myth of dual federalism, pointing out the relational nature of the identity of the units in intergovernmental relations. States are both the source and recipient of national and local power. National and local governments also occupy constantly shifting relational identities. Grodzins realistically immersed intergovernmental relations in the mainstream of almost every level of government, and this immense scope of shared functions was described under the all encompassing rubric of "cooperation."

Grodzins and his students applied the concept of cooperation in a number of valuable studies. Cohen and Grodzins in a pioneering policy output study attempted to measure the consistency of the economic impact of national and state-local governments.[14] Students of Grodzins and others have:[15]

1. identified the political and administrative techniques by which national and state-local governments influence grant-in-aid programs (Levine), and local communities influence both grant-in-aid and direct national programs (St. Angelo).
2. identified processes and attitude areas in which national and state-local officials have developed patterns of cooperation through budget channels (Carey and Vermuelen), and through common professional goals and attitudes (Weidner), and perceptions of cooperation and conflict (Carroll).
3. identified areas of conflict regarding federal programs as occurring within rather than between governments (Weidner), and described conflict as more of a characteristic of interpersonal relationships than intergovernmental policy differences (Carroll).

The initial premise as well as the general conclusion of the above studies is that intergovernmental relations are characterized by friendliness and cooperation and that conflict, when it does occur, occurs not between governments but within governments or between branches of the same level of government.[16] Although Grodzins granted early recognition to the existence of possible benefits from intergovernmental conflict (termed "squeak points"),[17] his later work and that of his students stressed the pervasiveness of cooperation, not conflict.

The weakness of the cooperation-conflict dichotomy is not its falsity but its generality. The dichotomy obscures a number of types of relationships in the intergovernmental system — types which cannot be described as purely cooperative or purely conflicting. David Walker recently alluded to the inadequacies of our professional conceptualizations of intergovernmental relationships. "If the marble cake theory is true, why is there so much conflict and hostility in the system? If the layer cake theory is true, how can we explain the many collaborative interactions that take place? . . . We have reached the point at which we must look at the interactions vertically and horizontally and then must develop a new theory from that perspective."[18] The sharing hypothesis is open to such criticism because in order to demolish the myth of dual federalism and perpetual intergovernmental warfare, Grodzins and others were forced to overstate the pervasiveness of cooperation and ignore distinctions which emerge only from a closer examination of both vertical and horizontal interactions. Before the effects of events in the intergovernmental system can be included in the calculus of local policy determination, refinements have to be made in the precision with which one differentiates between types of relationships in that system.

A TYPOLOGY OF INTERGOVERNMENTAL RELATIONSHIPS

The typology developed in this article provides the framework for systematic analysis of both vertical and horizontal variations in intergovernmental relations. This typology should be viewed as a first step toward employing the techniques now utilized in other subfields of the discipline. The next important steps include: operationalizing the variables, testing their interrelationships, and developing experimental models for each of the types. The typology itself defines most of the conceivable political relationships within the intergovernmental system in a four-fold scheme of interaction. Hopefully it also enhances the possibility of analysis in empirical terms. It contains four basic types of relationships. The four types are:

1. Joint policymaking
2. Mutual accommodation
3. Innovative conflict
4. Disintegrative conflict

Two of the types are variations on the cooperation-sharing scheme: "routine policymaking" and "mutual accommodation." The first emphasizes pre-imposed and generally accepted procedures, the second, slightly less cooperative, is characterized by low-keyed bargaining and harmonious compromise. The third type, "innovative conflict", starts with conflict and ends with cooperation, and the fourth, "disintegrative conflict," is the type which includes those instances of severe intergovernmental disagreements stressed in the dual sovereignty literature.

The types are described by variations in five procedurally oriented factors pertinent to the policy process in each type. These variables help to identify the ways in which the four types differ from each other:

1. Differing political styles and attitudes of the participating governments. (Identified on typology as: "Attitudes of Actors")
2. Specific units of government and political actors involved in different types of intergovernmental relations. ("Actors and Levels of Decisionmaking")
3. Differing scope of the various sections and subsections of the political system involved in the relationships. ("Scope of Participation")
4. Boundaries and extent of imposed rationality in bargaining. ("Nature of Bargaining")
5. Variations in administrative guidelines from well understood and flexible to inflexible. ("Nature of Administrative Guidelines")

Thus in summary, each of the four relationships in the typology can be analyzed and described in terms of the listed variables.

Attitude of Actors

One way of identifying variations between the types of intergovernmental relationships is to classify differences in the attitudes of the participants or actors in intergovernmental decisionmaking. Attempts were made in two national questionnaire surveys to determine how well such terms as "cooperative," "friendly," "competitive," "hostile," etc., described the attitudes of local officials toward federal agency officials. These surveys also asked local officials to describe the extent of flexibility of federal agencies in adapting their program and procedures to fit local circumstances.[19]

These surveys indicate that "cooperation" is the most generally accepted term by local officials in describing their relationship with the federal government. However the studies also confirm that when questioned about specific aspects of these relationships significant points of stress and strain appear. When asked to generalize about their relationship with the federal government three out of four Federal Aid Coordinators selected the choice of words, "cordial and friendly." Yet, when chief

A TYPOLOGY OF INTERGOVERNMENTAL POLITICAL RELATIONSHIPS

Type of Political Relationships	Attitudes of Actors	Actors and Levels of Decision-making	Scope of Participation	Nature of Bargaining	Nature of Administrative Guidelines
Joint Policy-making	Cordial and friendly	Bureaus	Functional hierarchies	Routine	Understood and accepted by all parties
Mutual Accommodation	Competitive	Bureaus, special interest groups, congressional subcommittees, aid coordinators	Subsystems	Negotiated bargaining	Flexible
Innovative Conflict	Manipulative-defensive	Department heads, special interest groups, congressional subcommittees and non-committee members, aid coordinators, White House staff	Subsystems with "outside" interventions	Non-negotiated bargaining followed by negotiated bargaining	Less flexible
Disintegrative Conflict	Hostile	Department heads, special interest groups, congressional committees and delegations, local political actors, courts	Macro (System-wide)	Non-negotiated bargaining	Inflexible

administrators in cities over 10,000 were asked which government, federal or state, was most helpful in solving their problems, a sizable minority, 27%, responded that *neither* government was helpful. When this response is broken down into city type the "neither" response moves up to 34% for for suburban cities. (Table 1)

TABLE 1

Level of government most helpful in dealing with city problems
(Perception of chief administrative officers)

Classification	Number of cities reporting	Federal govt. %	State govt. %	Neither %	No opinion %
Total, all cities	802	38	21	27	14
Population group					
Over 50,000	171	54	14	21	12
10,000 to 50,000	631	34	23	29	14
Geographic region					
Northeast	174	23	32	29	16
North Central	239	43	18	27	12
South	205	48	15	23	15
West	184	37	19	30	14
City type					
Central	131	62	13	14	12
Suburban	376	28	23	34	15
Independent	295	41	21	24	13

Source: "Federal, State, Local Relationships," *op. cit.*, p. 12.

A more precise indication of varying attitudes within the federal system was found when City Administrators and Federal Liaison Officers were questioned about the flexibility of federal agencies. Three out of four Chief Administrative Officers responded that Federal Agencies are either only occasionally (46%) or seldom or never (29%) flexible in adjusting their programs to meet local needs. The response of the local Federal Aid Coordinators to this same question was broken down in terms of functional programs thus indicating that attitudes vary considerably from program to program. The older departments with well established client groups are viewed as most often inflexible e.g., Agriculture 35%, Public Housing 30%.

Those cited as least inflexible tend to be either the newer programs or the older but smaller and more limited ones e.g., Juvenile Delinquency

11% inflexible, Metropolitan Development 13%. (Table 2) Attitudes also varied between city and county aid coordinators. Relationships between city officials and Federal Model City administrators were mostly "cordial and friendly." Only 13% of city aid coordinators characterized Model Cities as inflexible. Yet, when county aid coordinators were asked the same question, 39% of them rated Model Cities administrators as inflexible.

Attitudes in intergovernmental relations thus range over the variations described in the typology. The survey responses indicate that they are most likely to be cordial and friendly between officials serving nearly identical client bases, such as the Department of Agriculture bureaucracy and closely related county officials. Here one finds a clear cut case of joint policymaking. However, in the relationship described as mutual accommodation the number of actors increases and while all parties accept the general parameters of the system, there are important differences concerning how an intergovernmental program should be run and how financial technicalities should be handled. These differences, while apparently just technical or administrative, can have a real impact on the outcome of a program. In the mutual accommodation relationship the attitude of the participants thus changes from friendly and cooperative to competitive. When one of the actors attempts to manipulate the rules or structure of a situation to his own advantage the relationship changes again to that of innovative conflict, and the attitude of the participants likewise changes from competition within a framework to defensive manipulation of the framework itself. In innovative conflict there continues to be some hope for constructive change, but when one or both sides become wedded to a non-negotiable position the relationship changes to one of disintegrative conflict and the attitudes change to that of clear hostility.

Actors and Levels of Decisionmaking

E. E. Schattschneider notes that ". . . the outcome of all conflict is determined by the *scope* of its contagion. The number of people involved in any conflict determines what happens; every change in the number of participants, every increase or reduction in the number of participants affects the result."[20] Increasing the number of actors and changing or raising the level at which a decision is made is a useful tactic for both local and federal officials as they deal with one another. The potential number of actors in any decision situation is very large. This is true even at the stage when a decision is made on whether or not to apply for a grant and which one to apply for. Private groups and individuals are increasingly serving as stimuli for grant applications. According to the survey data, private consulting firms are the most frequent outside stimulant according to 64%

of the cities responding. (Table 3) Chambers of Commerce and local businessmen were also cited as important stimulants to grant applications. Once a grant has been made there are additional opportunities to alter the character of the intergovernmental relationships by increasing the number of actors and the level at which decisions are reached within a city. City officials have choices as to whom they contact in the federal establishment while a program is being administered. For example, in the relatively neutral matter of information-giving, i.e., information concerning applications and assistance in completing grant application documents, cities seem to remain within the appropriate functional hierarchy. The survey shows that city officials usually first contact the federal regional office of the department involved. (Table 4) However, when difficulties arise — such as expediting grant application approvals or suggesting amendments to administrative guidelines — cities move toward and contact actors at the partisan political level. Table 4 shows that when difficulties in the grant process arise the source cities' first contacts tend to be congressmen, state officials, national associations, and for the larger cities, their own Washington offices.[21]

The federal aid coordinators are likely to play an important role in changing the number of participants and the level at which decisions are made in intergovernmental politics. Most cities seem to justify the hiring of a coordinator in terms of their usefulness in bringing more grants into a city.[22] More and more the coordinators are involving themselves in general policymaking roles within city government.[23] Although the position of aid coordinator was practically unheard of before 1966, coordinators are already beginning to have some impact on the way decisions are made. Table 5 shows that coordinators are spending about 20% of their time advising local officials. These advisory activities have added a new political actor representing the intergovernmental dimension to local decision-making. About 15% of the coordinator's time is spent acting as a political broker, bringing community groups into the decisionmaking process. Table 6 expands on the brokerage roles of the coordinators indicating the extent of the "coordinating" work they do not only for government agencies, but for organizations outside of the official hierarchy.

Scope of Participation

When the number of actors and level or levels at which a particular set of decisions are made is isolated for examination, the investigator has a focus for the scope of participation. Each of the four categories of intergovernmental relations in the typology involves a relatively precise and identifiable part of the larger political system. In the relatively routine category of joint policymaking the actors are mostly bureaucrats and the level of decisionmaking is generally limited to the operating bureau itself. This would typify the idea of functional hierarchies.

In the mutual adjustment category, interest groups, congressional sub-committees and perhaps aid coordinators become involved in the negotiation and bargaining. Mutual adjustment would involve some disagreement among participants involving how programs should be run, how financial technicalities should be handled, but these differences are worked out through well understood channels with give and take on both sides. The inclusion of non-bureaucratic, but functionally related actors such as interest groups or congressional committees enlarges the scope from that of a functional hierarchy to that of a political subsystem. Many intergovernmental problems can be resolved within such subsystems, but occasionally outside intervention is necessary. This intervention comes from higher departmental or White House staff, or members of the relevant committees. This intervention is directed toward restructuring the subsystem in which the mutual adjustment is taking place. In such cases the relationship would change to the category of "innovative conflict." Here the actors attempt to manipulate the system so as to create enough innovation space in which to act. E. Lester Levine describes the situation in which state agencies play other agencies and governmental levels against each other in order to free themselves to act.[24]

This conflict can be productive in that it leads to appropriate social change. The typology provides the opportunity to study the consequences and even the values of conflict in intergovernmental decisionmaking. Instead of dismissing conflict as an unfortunate deviation from the "cooperation and sharing" syndrome, it becomes possible to apply the theories of Lewis Coser and others to intergovernmental politics.[25] Most applicable to the intergovernmental system are those cases in which conflict produces new alliances or even new solutions to old problems.

Conflict can of course be destructive as well as constructive. The typology provides for this with the category "disintegrative conflict." It too can be defined partly in terms of numbers of actors and levels of decisionmaking. When "disintegrative conflict" occurs it is likely to be systemwide including the courts, cabinet members and the chief political representatives of local and state governments.

The next variable in the typology — "nature of bargaining" — is related to the other variables, described above, and flows from them. Cause and effect relationships would ultimately have to be tested to refine the typology.

TABLE 2

Percentage of Aid Coordinators Perceiving Federal Agencies as "Seldom or Never Flexible"

Federal Agencies	Total, all cities		Over 250,000		50,000–250,000		Under 50,000		Metro		Nonmetro		All counties		All states	
	No.*	% of total**	No.	%	No.	%	No.	%	No.	%	No.	%	No.	%	No.	%
Housing and Urban Development	84	13	14	0	41	17	29	14	68	15	16	7	20	20	17	24
Urban Renewal Administration	115	17	17	12	54	15	44	23	92	19	23	13	23	35	18	22
Public Housing Authority	93	30	16	25	41	31	35	31	74	30	19	32	20	15	18	17
Model Cities Administration	62	21	16	13	29	17	17	35	55	22	7	14	18	39	22	18
Metropolitan Development	108	12	16	0	57	7	35	26	90	11	18	17	27	19	13	15
Health, Education and Welfare	33	15	9	0	15	25	9	22	29	14	4	25	7	0	14	7
Public Health Service	65	15	12	25	32	16	21	10	50	16	15	13	25	4	18	11
Office of Education	50	20	11	9	26	23	13	23	42	19	8	25	22	18	18	22
Juvenile delinquency	53	11	10	30	26	6	17	6	44	14	9	0	23	17	18	17
Agriculture (FHA)	40	35	5	40	20	30	15	40	30	33	10	40	23	3	16	13

TABLE 2 (cont)

Justice (LEAA)	117	21	17	47	55	9	45	27	95	21	22	23	37	5	18	6
Urban Mass Transportation Administration	80	20	17	29	31	7	22	36	66	17	14	36	27	15	15	7
Highway & Safety	89	19	16	31	46	11	27	26	72	21	17	12	32	3	19	9
Labor—Manpower Administration	66	23	15	7	31	26	20	30	57	25	9	11	22	23	19	11
Office of Economic Opportunity	73	16	15	7	35	17	23	22	60	15	13	23	25	16	18	6
Commerce—EDA	70	26	17	41	30	20	23	22	55	27	15	20	25	12	21	33
Interior—Water Pollution Control Administration	91	20	15	40	40	13	36	19	66	21	25	16	30	13	20	15

Source: "Local Intergovernmental Coordinator," *op. cit.,* pp. 22 and 23.

*Number of coordinators responding to question.

**Percentage of coordinators describing agency as "seldom or never flexible."

TABLE 3
Private Groups Serving for Grant Applications in Governments

	No. of gov'ts reporting	Chamber of Commerce		Local business		National firms		Trade associations		Consultants	
	(A)	No.	% of (A)	No.	% of (A)	No.	% of (A)	No.	% of (A)	No.	% of (A)
Total, all cities	108	61	56	38	35	3	3	9	8	69	64
Population group											
Over 250,000	17	8	47	8	47	2	12	1	6	11	65
50,000–250,000	46	25	54	18	39	1	2	7	15	28	61
Under 50,000	45	8	18	12	27	0	0	1	2	30	67
Geographic region											
Northeast	19	12	63	6	32	1	5	1	5	11	58
North Central	34	21	62	10	29	1	3	3	9	23	68
South	34	18	43	9	26	1	3	3	9	25	74
West	21	10	48	13	62	0	0	2	10	10	48
City type											
Metropolitan	82	43	52	32	39	3	4	8	10	52	63
Non-metropolitan	26	18	69	6	23	0	0	1	4	17	65
Form of government											
Mayor-council	43	25	58	13	30	3	7	5	12	29	67
Council-manager	59	32	54	23	39	0	0	3	5	36	61
Other	6	4	67	2	33	0	0	1	17	4	67

Source: "Local Intergovernmental Coordinators," *op. cit.,* p. 19.

TABLE 4
Source First Contacted About Grant-in-Aid Problems*

	Regional offices of fed. depts.		Dep't. hdqtrs. in D. C.		Nat'l assn.**		Congressmen or their staffs		Senators or their staffs		Total Congress***		Offices of U.S. Pres. or V. Pres.		Your own Wash. D. C. office		Governor's office		State Sen. or Rep.	
Total no. of cities reporting	Rank	%	Rank	%	Rank	%	Rank	%	Rank	%	Rank	%	Rank	%	Rank	%	Rank	%	Rank	%
Application for grants — 876	1	85	4	5	4	5	2	12	3	7	2	20	–	–	6	1	5	3	5	3
Administrative difficulties with grant in progress — 841	1	64	4	17	7	1	2	33	3	22	2	55	7	1	7	1	6	2	5	3
Completing applications — 861	1	94	2	3	4	1	2	3	1	3	2	6	–	–	–	–	3	2	4	1
Expediting application approval — 844	3	35	4	11	7	1	1	60	2	43	1	100	7	1	–	–	6	5	5	6
Suggesting amendments or reinterpreting guidelines — 784	1	51	4	15	5	6	2	40	3	28	1	67	7	2	–	–	6	3	6	3

*Percentages are based upon total number of cities citing each office as first source of contact for each problem. Rank based upon percentage. Percentage total more than 100 because many cities indicated more than one first source.

**Such as NLC-USCM, NACO, etc.

***These to-date represent a combination of previous two columns. Ranking represents position of total Congress while previous two columns represent rank of House and Senate independently.

Source: Segal and Fritschler, "Emerging Patterns of Intergovernmental Relations," op. cit., pp. 26 and 27.

TABLE 5

Median Percent of Time Spent by Coordinators and Their Staffs on Certain Activities

Classification	Writing grant applications		Coordinating Fed. Grant program		Advising local officials		Administering grant programs		Consulting community groups		Other activities	
	Coordinator	Staff	Coordinator	Staff	Coordinator	Staff	Coordinator	Staff	Coordinator	Staff	Coordinator	Staff
Total, all cities	16%	29%	25%	15%	20%	14%	20%	25%	15%	10%	15%	5%
Population group												
Over 250,000	10	28	40	15	20	18	15	20	10	10	15	*
50,000–250,000	17	25	20	14	15	10	25	23	14	12	15	10
Under 50,000	18	30	40	20	16	14	15	25	15	14	20	25
Geographic region												
Northeast	20	30	27	19	25	10	10	23	20	14	20	10
North Central	19	28	21	8	16	11	20	30	13	13	12	5
South	11	25	25	19	20	20	25	17	13	10	20	15
West	17	34	23	15	16	10	20	33	16	10	20	30
City type												
Metropolitan	15	27	25	15	20	15	20	20	15	10	20	22
Non-metropolitan	18	30	18	25	15	12	17	25	12	6	14	5
Form of government												
Mayor-council	10	30	30	15	18	17	14	25	14	10	17	10
Council-manager	18	25	22	20	14	13	25	23	15	10	17	23
Other	16	30	20	10	20	10	20	23	11	10	15	5
All counties	14	16	28	20	20	12	20	40	15	10	20	18
All states	5	5	15	25	20	10	5	15	10	20	10	15

*Data not available.

Source: "Local Intergovernmental Coordinators," op. cit., p. 13.

TABLE 6

Public and Private Agencies for Which City and County Coordinators Perform a Coordinating Function

Classification	No. of gov'ts reporting	City/County administrative agencies		Private agencies funded by the Federal Government*		Private agencies not funded by the Federal Government		Other	
	(A)	No.	% of (A)	No.	% of (A)	No.	% of (A)	No.	% of (A)
Total, all cities	59	47	92	32	20	21	13	16	10
Population group									
Over 250,000	23	22	96	7	30	2	9	2	9
50,000–250,000	73	69	95	17	23	16	22	9	12
Under 50,000	63	56	89	8	13	3		5	8
Geographic region									
Northeast	22	20	91	5	23	4	18	4	18
North Central	45	44	98	10	22	8	18	2	4
South	53	49	92	12	23	8	15	3	6
West	39	34	87	5	13	1	3	7	18
City type									
Metropolitan	25	17	94	28	22	18	14	12	10
Non-metropolitan	34	30	88	4	12	3	9	4	12
Form of government									
Mayor-council	57	54	95	16	28	11	19	5	9
Council-manager	92	84	91	13	14	8	9	9	10
Other	10	9	90	3	30	2	20	2	20
All Counties	55	53	96	14	26	7	13	4	7

*Private agencies funded by the Federal Government such as CAA, EDP, CDA, etc.
Source: "Local Intergovernmental Coordinations," *op. cit.,* p. 17.

Nature of Bargaining

Most descriptions of bargaining in the intergovernmental system have centered upon routine relationships in which the guidelines under which decisionmaking occurs may be complex but they are understood and for the most part accepted by all parties concerned. The cordial and friendly relationships described in the survey of aid coordinators and the relationships described in previous studies (Carroll, Wiedner, *et al.*) involve such routine bargaining. Beyond the routine areas of bargaining, Lewis Froman's categorization of congressional bargaining offers helpful guidelines in delineating the stages of negotiation which also occur in intergovernmental relations:[26]

Non-negotiated Bargaining	Negotiated Bargaining
1. Unilateral action	3. Simple logrolling
2. Anticipated reaction	4. Time logrolling
	5. Compromise
	6. Side-payments

It is likely that all four of Froman's types of negotiated bargaining occur in the category "mutual accommodation." The involvement of aid coordinators in a city's policymaking is an indication of the necessity for cities to make adjustments in their own legislation, budgets and personnel practices in order to receive and administer grants — an obvious form of bargained compromise.

Not all non-negotiated bargaining takes place between local and federal officials. Responses from aid coordinators concerning the relative difficulty in coordinating different types of programs is an indication that a range of bargaining techniques are needed to coordinate grant programs. (Table 7) The most difficult programs from the coordinators' perspectives are those which have built independent power bases such as poverty and education programs. These are the programs which drew the highest percentage of "very difficult to coordinate" responses from the local aid officials.

In such programs the department head or program director can use his contacts with outside groups — state legislators, local activists, congressional or federal agency personnel — to build support. A pattern of non-negotiable positions followed by negotiation probably occurs — and this could be worked into the typology in the "innovative conflict" category.

The negotiations between state and national governments over the provisions of the Law Enforcement Assistance Act is a good example of the non-negotiated followed by negotiated bargaining phenomenon. In this case the federal government refused to consider state plans for the program until a number of conditions, such as special pass-through provisions to the cities, were included. Negotiations proceeded after these provisions had been met.[27]

In "joint policymaking" the range in which change can take place is narrow. There are few risks and few opportunities to gain more than a prearranged formula provides. This type of bargaining can best be described as routine. In the "mutual adjustment" relationship some true bargaining involving compromise, side payments, log rolling, etc. does take place, but neither side takes a unilateral non-negotiable position. In "innovative conflict" the actors do adhere to non-negotiable positions, but the stance of non-negotiation serves to establish the boundaries in which negotiation then takes place.

If the particular stance of non-negotiation is unacceptable to the other parties who then in turn adopt their own position of non-negotiation the entire character of the relationship changes to that of "disintegrated conflict." In this relationship there is little likelihood that a new alternative acceptable to all parties will emerge. In "disintegrative conflict," in order for one party to win the other must lose. Such relationships have rarely occurred in American intergovernmental relations, but the long deadlocks and occasional violence involved in school desegregation demonstrates that the possibility is present.

Pure non-negotiated bargaining represents an apparent breakdown in intergovernmental policymaking or at least a temporary stalemate. When a governor stands in the schoolhouse door or when other forms of unilateral actions occur and bargaining ceases, the system appears to stop working. By the time matters have gone this far the scope of participation is system-wide involving all levels and types of actors including perhaps the President himself and eventually the courts.

Nature of Administrative Guidelines

This variable is included as an indication of the ways in which the typology can be expanded and sharpened for use as an analytical tool. Program guidelines differ from program to program in ways which can be defined to fit the four types of intergovernmental relations discussed in this article. One can speculate that guidelines in many cases are well understood and accepted by all of the actors in the intergovernmental system. This situation reinforces all of the other variables (i.e., those under the headings Attitude of Actors, etc.) in the category "joint policymaking." Guidelines vary in their flexibility just as regional officers do as perceived by the aid coordinators. (See Table 2) It would be useful to develop

TABLE 7

The Degree of Difficulty in Coordinating on an Interdepartmental Basis Local Programs Financed Through Federal Grant-in-Aid by Functional Areas

	Total, all cities		Over 250,000		50,000-250,000		Under 50,000		City-type				All counties	
									Metro		Nonmetro			
	No.	% of total	No.	% of total	No.	% of total	No.	% of total	No.	% of total	No.	% of total	No.	% of total
Education—total	64	—	12	—	33	—	19	—	53	—	11	—	27	—
Very difficult	8	13	1	8	4	12	3	16	7	13	1	9	2	7
Difficult	19	30	3	25	8	24	8	42	12	23	7	64	8	30
Not difficult	37	56	8	67	21	64	8	42	34	64	3	27	17	63
Transportation—total	88	—	18	—	49	—	21	—	76	—	12	—	28	—
Very difficult	12	14	5	28	5	10	2	10	10	13	2	17	1	4
Difficult	16	18	2	11	10	20	4	19	14	18	2	17	5	18
Not difficult	60	68	11	61	34	69	15	71	52	68	8	67	22	79
Health—total	73	—	14	—	38	—	21	—	62	—	11	—	33	—
Very difficult	6	8	1	7	4	11	1	5	5	8	1	9	3	9
Difficult	6	8	1	7	4	11	1	5	5	8	1	9	3	9
Not difficult	46	63	10	71	23	61	13	62	42	68	4	36	27	82
Urban renewal—total	112	—	19	—	51	—	42	—	93	—	19	—	22	—
Very difficult	10	9	2	11	3	5	5	12	8	9	2	11	5	23
Difficult	29	26	5	26	15	29	9	21	25	27	4	21	7	32
Not difficult	73	65	12	63	33	65	28	67	60	65	13	68	10	46
Housing—total	116	—	19	—	53	—	44	—	94	—	22	—	38	—
Very difficult	10	9	4	21	6	6	3	7	8	9	2	9	5	15
Difficult	29	25	5	26	15	28	9	20	26	28	3	14	6	18
Not difficult	77	66	10	53	35	66	32	73	60	64	17	77	27	67
Planning—total	112	—	20	—	52	—	40	—	94	—	18	—	36	—
Very difficult	11	10	1	5	5	10	5	13	9	10	2	11	4	11
Difficult	20	18	7	35	6	12	7	18	18	19	2	11	4	11
Not difficult	81	72	12	60	41	79	28	69	67	71	14	78	28	78
Poverty—total	37	—	7	—	12	—	12	—	29	—	8	—	16	—
Very difficult	10	27	1	14	6	33	3	25	7	24	3	38	4	25
Difficult	12	32	3	43	6	33	3	25	11	38	1	13	6	38
Not difficult	15	41	3	43	6	33	6	50	11	38	4	50	6	38

TABLE 7 cont.

Law Enforcement Police—														
total	30	—	20	—	59	—	51	—	05	—	25	—	35	—
Very difficult	14	11	2	10	5	8	7	14	10	10	4	16	2	6
Difficult	24	18	8	40	10	17	6	12	23	22	1	4	11	31
Not difficult	92	71	10	50	44	75	38	75	72	67	20	80	22	63
Fire—total	82	—	15	—	36	—	31	—	64	—	18	—	23	—
Very difficult	4	5	1	7	2	6	1	3	3	5	1	6	2	9
Difficult	9	11	1	7	3	8	5	16	6	9	3	17	3	13
Not difficult	69	84	13	87	31	25	81	55	86	14	78	18	76	
Street Maintenance—total	93	—	15	—	43	—	35	—	74	—	19	—	30	—
Very difficult	5	5	3	20	1	2	1	3	4	5	1	5	10	0
Difficult	13	14	1	7	6	14	6	17	8	11	5	26	5	17
Not difficult	75	81	11	73	36	84	28	80	62	84	13	68	25	83
Sanitation—total	98	—	17	—	47	—	34	—	81	—	17	—	31	—
Very difficult	5	5	1	6	2	4	2	6	4	5	1	6	1	3
Difficult	15	15	4	24	7	15	4	12	13	16	2	12	6	19
Not difficult	78	80	12	71	38	81	28	82	64	79	14	82	24	77
Sewage—total	16	—	18	—	52	—	46	—	93	—	23	—	35	—
Very difficult	6	5	1	6	2	4	3	7	4	4	2	9	2	6
Difficult	20	17	4	22	8	15	8	17	17	18	3	13	8	23
Not difficult	90	78	13	72	42	81	35	76	72	77	18	78	25	71
Welfare—total	63	—	11	—	33	—	19	—	52	—	11	—	32	—
Very difficult	5	8	1	9	4	12	0	0	5	10	0	0	3	9
Difficult	20	32	5	45	9	27	6	32	17	33	3	27	5	16
Not difficult	38	60	5	45	20	61	13	68	30	58	8	73	24	75
Environmental Control—total	93	—	17	—	48	—	28	—	78	—	15	—	32	—
Very difficult	9	10	2	12	5	10	2	7	8	10	1	7	1	3
Difficult	19	20	4	24	7	15	8	29	15	19	4	27	7	22
Not difficult	65	70	11	65	36	75	18	64	55	71	10	67	24	75

Source: "Local Intergovernmental Coordinators."

relatively precise definitions of flexibility and inflexibility for inclusion in the descriptions of the other categories of relationships included in the typology.

CONCLUSIONS

As an academic field, intergovernmental relations has not had a framework which could be used to link findings in other fields to its principal concern, the relationships between governments. The typology presented in this paper is a step toward applying to intergovernmental relations recent advances in such fields as state and local government. Jacob and Lipsky's assessment of studies in state and local government offer a useful research outline for the intergovernmental field.[28]

Their outline categorizes recent advancements in state and local government under four headings: Policy Analysis, Synoptic Indicators of the Political Process, Community Power Studies, and Classification Schemes of Political Phenomena.

Policy Analysis

Policy analysis research is currently limited by the absence of intergovernmental factors which impact on local policy processes and outcomes. Federal and state spending in addition to the rules and guidelines which accompany those expenditures have important, although largely unexplored effects on public policy at the local level. Some areas for research in intergovernmental relations which would contribute to studies in policy analysis include:

1. State and local policy in direct and/or anticipated response to federal grants.
2. State, county, and regional policies concerning decisions to apply or match funds and change structure or procedures.
3. Variations in federal decisions to grant or refuse to grant funds.
4. Variations in congressional and administrative guidelines and the processes used to change those guidelines.
5. Variations in enforcement of the guidelines.

The types of relationships within each of these probably varies widely. For example, the relationship involved in the federal decision whether or not to make a grant could be a relationship similar to mutual accommodation or even innovative conflict. The type of relationship involved in the issuing of grants has important implications for the whole federal system. If one set of governments is involved in an essentially routine operation, then its involvement may be superfluous; but if the involvement yields compromise, as in mutual accommodation, or innovation, as in innovative conflict, then our complex federal system may be working better than we imagine. In any event, the correlation between policy and the type of relationship which produces the policy is a promising area of investigation.

Synoptic Indicators of the Political Process

Grant-in-aid decisions are substantively as important as decisions of state and local legislative bodies, but they have not been studied as such. As the typology of this article is operationalized, techniques of analyzing key areas of legislative decisionmaking can be applied to intergovernmental relations. Following are some key areas of decisionmaking which have recently received attention in the study of state and local government, accompanied by the referent terms from the typology of intergovernmental relations.

1. Role perceptions and role systems of decision makers, both in individual levels of the bureaucracy and between several levels. (Attitude of Actors)
2. Behavior in collegial groups, including federal bureaucratic groups, interagency committees, and regional groupings and state-local groups. (Attitude of Actors and Nature of Bargaining)
3. Social origin and recruitment studies of grant-in-aid decision makers at all levels. (Attitude of Actors and Levels of Decisionmaking)
4. Content analysis of grant-in-aid documents, both applications and responses. (Nature of Bargaining and Attitude of Actors)
5. Interest group involvement in the grant-in-aid process. (Scope of Participation)

Community Power Studies

Analysis of community power structures, while certainly a major contribution of the past twenty years, is limited by the inability of scholars to link such research questions involving power to the larger political community. Studies of the grant-in-aid community would provide such a link and would also represent a new application of the community power idea to functional hierarchies, intergovernmental and interagency groups.

Schemes of Classification

The typology itself is one scheme of classification. There are other possibilities, however.

1. Demographic patterns. Do choices involving applications for grants, grant awards, and grant administration suggest any classification by city location, size, or type in terms of success in receiving grants?
2. Political functions of grants. Is there any pattern of political variables such as support, innovation, role perception, or professionalization, which seem to result from receipt of grants-in-aid?

The typology described in this article could also be used to facilitate research in public policy areas associated with grants-in-aid and the intergovernmental system in general. Questions concerning the effects of revenue sharing on domestic political processes and the processes of social change are an example. A series of questions concerning administrative reorganization on all levels of government also arises. One might be: are traditional departments suitable structures for running programs mixed in nature and tied to the intergovernmental system?[29]

A great deal more must be done to bring the subfield of intergovernmental relations into the mainstream of political research. Although the typology presented in this article needs more testing and verification before it can be used systematically in this research, it represents a starting point in a research program which should be rich with possibilities.

Notes

1. Lawrence J.R. Herson, "The Lost World of Municipal Government," *American Political Science Review,* Vol. 51 (June, 1957), pp. 330–345.
2. Jacob and Lipsky have examined the application of four significant developments in political science approaches and methodologies to the field of state and local government. The developments are discussed under the following headings:
   a. Policy output studies.
   b. Internal decision making studies.
   c. Community power structure.
   d. Classificatory schemes of various aspects of political behavior.
See: Herbert Jacob and Michael Lipsky, "Outputs, Structure and Power: An Assessment of Changes in the Study of State and Local Politics," *Journal of Politics,* Vol. 30 (May, 1968), pp. 510–538.
3. One prominent exception is the work of Daniel J. Elazar, especially his efforts to explain some of the variations in intergovernmental policymaking through a politico-

cultural typology. See: Daniel J. Elazar, *American Federalism: A View from the States* (New York: Thomas Y. Crowell Company, 1966), esp. chapter 5. A recent survey cited Elazar's book as the most frequently used text in undergraduate inter-governmental relations courses. Carl Stenberg and David B. Walker, "Federalism and the Academic Community: A Brief Survey," *PS*, Vol. 2 (Spring, 1969), pp. 155–167.

4. Alan Campbell of Syracuse University lamented the absence of empirical research on contemporary federalism before a congressional committee in 1967:

. . . I would like to point out that the academic community has begun, only recently, the serious research necessary to a full understanding of the nature of contemporary federalism. For a great variety of reasons political scientists, econo-mists, and sociologists, over the past 30 years, have concentrated their research ef-forts on the National Government and international affairs. There has been some work done on the legal and constitutional relationships among the levels of govern-ment and there has been some research on the fiscal side, but this has not produced a body of cumulative knowledge from which empirically based generalizations may be drawn. This lack of any solid body of empirical research findings means that the doctrines which dominate this field are still those which emerged from the reform movement of the early 20th Century. . . . The unfortunate result is that in many instances arguments concerning the character of contemporary American Federalism revolve around slogans rather than interpretations of factual data.

See: U.S. Congress, Senate Committee on Governmental Operations, Subcommittee on Intergovernmental Relations, *Creative Federalism*, Part 2-B., 90th Cong., 1st Sess., 1967, pp. 846–7.

5. Stenberg and Walker, *op. cit.*

6. Morton Grodzins, *The American System: A New View of Government in the United States*, Daniel J. Elazar, ed. (Chicago: Rand, McNally, 1966).

7. Among the most unreliable statistics in government today are those concerned with federal grants-in-aid. Total amounts per jurisdiction below the state level are not tabulated by the government, for example. The best measures of magnitude of grants-in-aid are probably these: approximately 16 percent of total federal revenues collected are returned through grants (FY 1968) and there are between 550 and 600 separate programs. Practically all federal agencies are responsible for the administra-tion of one grant program or another. *Congressional Quarterly* carries a good semi-annual summary of the available data. See for example: *Congressional Quarterly Guide to Current American Government* (Washington, D.C.: Congressional Quarterly Service, Spring, 1970).

8. For representative selection of those works which examine local policy output in terms of strictly local inputs see: Jacob and Lipsky, *op. cit.;* Robert R. Alford and Harry M. Scoble, "Political and Socioeconomic Characteristics of American Cities," *Municipal Yearbook* (Washington, D.C.: International City Management Association, 1965); Robert R. Alford, *Bureaucracy and Participation* (Chicago: Rand McNally, 1969); Raymond E. Wolfinger and John Osgood Field, "Political Ethos and the Structure of City Government," *American Political Science Review*, Vol. 60 (June, 1966); Robert L. Crain, Elihu Katz, and Donald B. Rosenthal, *The Politics of Com-munity Conflict* (Indianapolis: Bobbs-Merrill Company, Inc., 1969); Robert L. Line-berry and Edmund P. Fowler, "Reformism and Public Policies in American Cities," *American Political Science Review*, Vol. 61 (September, 1967). The literature dealing with the states is even more voluminous but here also state policy determinants are seldom thought to include inputs from intergovernmental or non-state sources. See for example: Thomas R. Dye, *Politics, Economics and the Public: Policy Outcomes in the American States* (Chicago: Rand McNally, 1966) and Ira Sharkansky, ed., *Policy Analysis in Political Science* (Chicago: Markham Publishing Company, 1970).

9. A group of notable exceptions to this is the work done by Morton Grodzins,

Daniel J. Elazar and others in intergovernmental relations. Elazar writes: "The casual civics student knows that local governments are creatures of the state and that the states are linked in union under a federal government whose influence is widespread and whose hand is felt in the local community in many ways." *Cities of the Prairie* (New York: Basic Books, Inc., 1970), p. 367. See also: Daniel J. Elazar, *American Federalism: A View from the States* (New York: Thomas Y. Crowell Company, 1966). An interesting article by Woo Sik Kee, "Central City Expenditures and Metropolitan Areas," *The National Tax Journal,* Vol. 18 (December, 1965), contains a discussion of the impact of state and federal funds on local policy determination. One of the few community power studies to discuss the impact of decisions made at other levels of government on local power is Robert Presthus, *Men at the Top* (New York: Oxford University Press, 1964). Presthus writes: "In effect, the initiation and control of local decisions was to a considerable extent shared with external sources of power. ... the dependence of both communities [Riverview and Edgewood] upon external sources of governments was a major condition of decision-making in almost all of the [functional] areas analyzed." (p. 238).

10.   For the latest example of the continuing philosophical debate see: Publius (William Safire), "New Federalist No. 1," Cato (Tom Huston), "Federalism: Old and New, or The Pretensions of New Publius Exposed," mimeographed n.d., available for inspection at the Library of the Advisory Commission on Intergovernmental Relations, Washington, D.C.

11.   This three-step process was suggested by Glendon Schubert's description of judicial studies: traditional, conventional, and behavioral. The authors agree with Professor Schubert that in practice the three approaches form a continuum. While they developed roughly on a chronological basis, all three are significant in their distinctive contributions to the field. There is a continuing need in intergovernmental relations as in judicial studies for the application of all three approaches. See: Glendon Schubert, *Judicial Policy Making* (Glenview: Scott, Foresman and Co., 1965) and Glendon Schubert, "Academic Ideology and the Study of Adjudication," *American Political Science Review,* Vol. 61 (March, 1967), pp. 106–129.

12.   For a concise summary of leading American theories of federalism see the introductory chapter in Daniel J. Elazar, *The American Partnership* (Chicago: University of Chicago Press, 1962).

13.   A good example of the successful use of a concrete actor as the basis for more abstract analysis is the use of state legislators as the basis for the development of role systems. See: John C. Wahlke, Heinz Eulau, William Buchanan, and LeRoy C. Ferguson, *The Legislative System: Explorations in Legislative Behavior* (New York: John Wiley and Sons, Inc., 1962).

14.   Jacob Cohen and Morton Grodzins, "How Much Economic Sharing in American Federalism?," *American Political Science Review,* Vol. 57 (March, 1963), pp. 5–23.

15.   A number of works by Grodzins' students, some previously unpublished, have been brought together with commentary in Daniel J. Elazar, *et al,* eds., *Cooperation and Conflict: Readings in American Federalism* (Itasca, Illinois: F. E. Peacock, Inc. 1969). All of the articles referred to in the text and below appear in this volume:

> E. Lester Levine, "Federal Grants-in-Aid: Administration and Politics," pp. 177–182.

> Douglas St. Angelo, "Formal and Routine Local Control of National Programs," pp. 442–452; and "'The Broker Role' of Local Political Parties and Federal Administration," pp. 543–552.

> William D. Carey and Abram M. Vermeulen, "Intergovernmental Cooperation Through Budget Channels," pp. 260–267.

> Edward W. Weidner, "Decision-Making in a Federal System," pp. 278–292.

> R. Bruce Carroll, "Intergovernmental Administrative Relations," pp. 292–318.

16.   Grodzins' notion of "sharing" pervades his work and that of his students who participated in the University of Chicago's Federalism Workshop. The most succinct statement of the sharing idea can be found in Morton Grodzins, "The Federal Sys-

tem," The President's Commission on National Goals, *Goals for Americans* (Englewood Cliffs, New Jersey: Prentice Hall, Inc., 1960).

17. Morton Grodzins, *The American System, op cit.*, p. 277.

18. David B. Walker, "Response: Relevant Research Required," *Public Administration Review*, Vol. 30, No. 3 (May/June, 1970), p. 269.

19. These surveys are referred to frequently in this section. The first survey was done by the authors and Professor Douglas Harman of American University during the fall of 1969. A detailed questionnaire was distributed to the chief executive officers of all cities over 10,000 population. The total response rate was 45 percent (938 cities out of 2,072). The rate by population group was as follows:

Population Group	Number	Percent
Over 500,000	15	56
250,000 to 500,000	23	85
100,000 to 250,000	57	59
50,000 to 100,000	112	48
25,000 to 50,000	230	48
10,000 to 25,000	501	41

A full report of the survey including all tables may be found in "Federal, State, Local Relationships," *Urban Data Service* (Washington, D.C.: International City Management Association, December, 1969). Further analysis of this survey data may be found in Segal and Fritschler, "Emerging Patterns of Intergovernmental Relations," *Municipal Yearbook* 1970, Vol. 37 (Washington: International City Management Association, 1970). The second survey questionnaire was mailed to all state, county and city federal aid coordinators (part-time and full-time). The response rate was as follows:

	Surveyed	Responded	Percent
States	49	26	53
Counties	246	58	24
Cities	309	164	53

For a full report of the survey see: A. Lee Fritschler and John D. Norton, "Local Intergovernmental Coordinators," *Urban Data Service* (Washington, D.C.: International City Management Association, August, 1970).

20. E.E. Schattschneider, *The Semi-Sovereign People* (New York: Holt, Rinehart and Winston, 1960), p. 2.

21. By 1970, approximately 14 states and 26 local governments had offices in Washington, D.C.

22. There appears to be some justification in that belief. Cities with aid coordinators receive, on the average, $45.27 per capita in federal grants each year while all cities, on the average, receive $17.42 per capita, yearly. See: "Local Intergovernmental Coordinators," *Urban Data Service, op. cit.*, Table 1, p. 4.

23. One coordinator expressed the view that he and his colleagues are involved in much more than money raising at one of the national meetings of aid coordinators. See: National League of Cities/U.S. Conference of Mayors, Proceedings of the Intergovernmental Federal Aid Coordinators Second National Conference, San Diego, California, November 30, 1969 (Washington, D.C.: National League of Cities/U.S. Conference of Mayors, 1969).

24. E. Lester Levine, "Federal Grants-in-Aid: Administration and Politics," in Elazar, *et al*, eds., *op. cit.*, pp. 177-182.

25. Lewis Coser, *The Functions of Social Conflict* (New York: The Free Press, 1956). Theodore Lowi has explored the impact of majority and minority status on

political party innovation. He concluded that a markedly weaker but not totally hopeless minority party is most likely to innovate. This approach could be modified to explore the impact of competition for grants-in-aid on innovation in city government. See: Theodore Lowi, "Toward Functionalism in Political Science: The Case of Innovation in Party Systems," *American Political Science Review*, Vol. 57 (September, 1963), pp. 570–583.

26. Lewis A. Froman, Jr., *The Congressional Process* (Boston: Little, Brown and Company, 1967), pp. 22–27.

27. B. Douglas Harman, "The Bloc Grant: Readings from a First Experiment" *Public Administration Review*, Vol. 30 (March/April, 1970), p. 145.

28. Herbert Jacob and Michael Lipsky, *op. cit.*

29. For further discussion of policy oriented research needs see: W. E. Hulcher, "Another Viewpoint," *Public Administration Review*, Vol. 30, No. 3 (May/June, 1970), pp. 271 and 272.

JOSEPH ZIMMERMAN

METROPOLITAN REFORM IN THE U. S.: AN OVERVIEW

The metropolitan problem, variously defined, has been accorded recognition since the early part of the 20th century, and numerous proposals have been advanced for a restructuring of the system of local government to solve the problem. With relatively few exceptions, reorganization proposals have been rejected by voters who apparently have been influenced more by arguments promising to keep the tax rate low and the government close to the people and free of corruption than by arguments stressing the correction of service inadequacies and the economical and efficient provision of services.

Interest in the structural reform of the local government system appeared to reach its peak in the 1950s. Frank C. Moore wrote in 1958 "that more surveys have been initiated in the last five years than in the previous thirty."[1] Seventy-nine of the 112 surveys initiated between 1923 and 1957 were launched between 1948 and 1957, compared to one or two per year from 1923 to 1948.[2]

The number and nature of surveys underwent a significant change in the 1960s, primarily as the result of requirements in various federal grant-in-aid programs. A sharp rise in transportation and comprehensive land-use studies occurred. The number of transportation studies rose from 15 in 1960 to 118 in 1966, 154 in 1967, and 198 in 1968.[3] Comprehensive land-use studies increased from 15 in 1960 to 48 in 1966 and 73 in 1967, but decreased to 71 in 1968. Studies concerned with governmental organization declined from 40 in 1960 to 34 in 1966 and 29 in 1967. Thirty-six

Reprinted from the *Public Administration Review*, journal of the American Society for Public Administration, Vol. 30, (September/October 1970) pp. 531–543.

such studies were launched in 1968. Although the results of a comprehensive canvass of metropolitan studies are not currently available, it appears that there has been a vast upsurge since 1968 in the number of governmental organization studies, particularly in the South.

THE CONSOLIDATIONISTS

Nineteenth century metropolitan reorganization took the form of city-county consolidation without referenda in Boston, Philadelphia, New Orleans, and New York City. In addition, entire towns were consolidated by legislative edict with the central city; Charlestown, Dorchester, and Roxbury were consolidated with Boston. And annexation also commonly was used by the central city to keep pace with urbanization.[4]

The leading consolidation advocate in recent years has been the Committee for Economic Development (CED), composed of 200 prominent businessmen and educators, which maintains there is a great need for a revolutionary restructuring of what is labelled an anachronistic system of local government. In 1966 CED urged an 80 per cent reduction in the number of units to no more than 16,000, with increased reliance being placed upon reconstituted county governments everywhere except in New England, where the proposal was advanced that towns should be consolidated or closely federated to form metropolitan governments.[5] Interestingly, CED in February 1970 recommended "as an ultimate solution a governmental system at two levels."[6]

The National Commission on Urban Problems (Douglas Commission) in 1968 accepted the CED's basic consolidation recommendation. The Commission was convinced that the solution of housing and other problems was seriously impeded by a multiplicity of local governments, many of which have restrictive codes designed to discourage low-income persons from migrating to these communities. A major recommended solution was the use of federal revenue sharing as a catalyst to encourage local governments with a population under 50,000 to consolidate.[7] Units with a population of less than 50,000 would be ineligible to share in the revenue, and units with a population between 50,000 and 100,000 would share in the revenue based on the percentage by which their populations exceed 50,000. No action has been taken by Congress on this proposal, and it is improbable that any action will be taken until the federal budgetary situation improves substantially and inflationary pressures are sharply curtailed.

When we speak of consolidation we may refer either to the consolidation of functions which occurs when a function is shifted to a higher level of government — this is labelled centralization by some — or to a consolidation of units of government. The creation of a metropolitan federation also may be referred to as a type of consolidation in view of the fact certain functions are taken away from municipalities and assigned to the newly created upper-tier unit.

City-county consolidation may be complete or partial. In a complete consolidation, a new government is formed by the amalgamation of the county and municipal governments. Partial consolidation may involve the merger of most county functions with the cities to form a new consolidated government, but the county continues to exist for the performance of a few functions required by the state constitution. A second form of partial consolidation involves the merger of several but not all municipalities with the county.

TWENTIETH-CENTURY CONSOLIDATIONS

Prior to 1947 there was relatively little 20th-century interest in city-county consolidation. The Hawaiian Territorial Legislature did merge the City and County of Honolulu in 1907 without a referendum, but only three proposals for consolidation in other areas reached the ballot and each of the proposals was defeated.

Louisiana voters in 1946 approved a constitutional amendment permitting a home rule charter to be drafted for the Baton Rouge area. Voters in 1947 approved a charter providing for the partial consolidation of the City of Baton Rouge and East Baton Rouge Parish effective in 1949. The city, parish, and two small municipal governments were continued and a city-parish council was created. It is composed of the seven-member city council and two members from the remainder of the parish.

After rejecting a consolidation charter in 1958, voters approved a similar charter in 1962 creating the Metropolitan Government of Nashville and Davidson County. The charter created an urban services district and a general services district, and authorized a separate tax rate for each district based upon services provided. Six small cities were exempted from the consolidation, but may disincorporate and join the urban services district when it is expanded to their area.

The next major partial consolidation occurred in the Jacksonville area as the result of a 1967 referendum when a charter consolidating the City of Jacksonville and Duval County was approved. The voters of three small cities and a town voted to retain their separate corporate status. Patterned largely upon the Nashville model, the new city has a general and an urban services district.

A minor consolidation — Carson City and Ormsby County, Nevada

— received voter approval in 1969. A more major consolidation occurred in the Indianapolis area on January 1, 1970, as the result of the passage of an act by the Indiana Legislature consolidating the city and Marion County.[8] This consolidation is particularly noteworthy in that it is the first one in the northern United States, as well as the first one implemented without a popular referendum since 1898 when New York City was formed by a five-county consolidation.

UNIGOV, the popular name for the new government, is a misnomer in that the existing 58 units of government in the county are only partially consolidated. Two small cities and a town are excluded from the consolidation, as are 16 townships, school corporations, Marion County Health and Hospital Corporation, and Indianapolis Airport Authority. The latter two units are subject to budget review by the city-county council.

The elective county constitutional officers are continued, and there is no change in the County Welfare Board, County Assessors, and County Tax Adjustment Board. Police and fire protection services remain unchanged as the office of sheriff continues and a police special service district was created within the old city. Furthermore, a fire special service district was created within the old city and volunteer firemen continue to serve the remaining area.

After a ten-month study in 1969, the Charlottesville, Virginia, City Council and the Albemarle County Board of Supervisors prepared a charter consolidating the city, county, Town of Scottsville, and Crozet Sanitary District.[9] The charter on March 3, 1970, met with voter disapprobation by negative margins of two to one in the city and four to one in the county. As a result of the charter defeat, the city has decided to initiate annexation proceedings.

A proposed consolidation of the City of Roanoke, Roanoke County, and the Town of Vinton in Virginia was rejected by voters in November 1969. Approval required a concurrent majority in the city, county, and town; city voters approved the proposal but it was rejected by county voters.

CONSOLIDATION STUDIES UNDERWAY

In 1969 the North Carolina Legislature created an 18-member Charlotte-Mecklenburg Charter Commission charged with the duty of creating a single government charter for the county and presenting it to the voters no sooner than December 1, 1970.[10] The charter must contain a provision allowing Cornelius, Davidson, Huntersville, Matthews, and Pineville voters to decide whether they want to merge their governments with the city and county.

The South Carolina General Assembly, in January 1969, created a 25-member commission to prepare a charter consolidating the governments in Charleston County. In November the commission released the first six articles of a proposed charter consolidating all governments into a new City of Charleston.

A 15-member council would govern the new city, with 12 members elected by single-member districts and three members elected at-large. The chief executive would be a mayor elected for a four-year term, but limited to two consecutive terms. He would possess the veto power and would be authorized to appoint department heads with approval of the council. Two service districts would be established – an urban services district and a general services district. A separate tax rate would be established for each district and the council would be authorized to extend the urban services district whenever the consolidated government is able to provide the necessary services.

Local governments in the Atlanta area have been under pressure from the Georgia Legislature to reorganize. In 1969 the House of Representatives voted 89 to 61 to consolidate Atlanta and Fulton County without a referendum, but the bill lacked the constitutionally required majority of the entire house. Although the 1970 Legislature did not pass a bill consolidating the city and county, a bill was enacted authorizing the creation of a commission to study the proposed consolidation of Macon and Bibb County.

The Institute of Public Administration prepared for Atlanta and Fulton County a report which recommends the consolidation of the two governments.[11] The proposed merger would be a partial one, as the report indicates there is no need to include the smaller municipalities in the merger, but recommends that enabling legislation should provide these units with the option of joining the amalgamated government at any time by means of a referendum.

Consolidation of governments is complicated by the fact that 8.0 per cent of Atlanta's population and 6.3 per cent of its land area are in DeKalb County. Since the Institute's polls reveal that only 32 per cent of DeKalb County voters favor merging the county with the consolidated government, the Institute came to the conclusion that it is politically infeasible to include the county in the merger.

Recognizing the need for a governmental mechanism to handle problems transcending Fulton County, the report recommends the creation of a limited-purpose regional council to be responsible for water supply, aviation, sewage and solid waste disposal, recreation, and a few other functions. The suggestion was advanced that the proposed council might incorporate the functions of the Metropolitan Atlanta Council of Local Governments, Atlanta Region Metropolitan Planning Commission, and the Metropolitan Atlanta Rapid Transit Authority.

Although the precise structure of the proposed government would be determined by a charter commission, the report recommends a mayor-council plan with 10 councilmen elected by districts and seven elected at-large with a requirement that each of the seven live in a different area.

A 10-member Metropolitan Charter Commission for Chattanooga and Hamilton County, Tennessee, was elected on September 18, 1969, to prepare a charter for submission to the voters. The state constitution stipulates that approval of a charter is contingent upon a concurrent majority of votes in the city and the remainder of the county.

A Local Government Consolidation Study Committee was appointed in Chatham County, Georgia, in 1969 by the elected officials of the county, City of Savannah, four small cities, and the county legislative delegation. In January 1970 consulting firms were invited to submit proposals for the preparation of a report "on the feasibility of consolidation and the alternative forms of consolidation of governments and/or services."

The Hillsborough County Home Rule Charter Commission has prepared a charter providing for the consolidation of the City of Tampa and Hillsborough County. Currently, the county legislative delegation is considering the charter, subject to amendment, for introduction as a local bill. If approved by the legislature, the proposed charter will be placed on the November 3, 1970, ballot for voter action.

The proposed charter provides for city-county consolidation and the consolidation into the new government of all "boards, districts, authorities, agencies and councils other than the public school system, the Junior College System, the Tampa Port Authority, the Hillsborough County Aviation Authority, [and] the Tampa-Hillsborough Expressway Authority."

The municipalities of Plant City and Temple Terrace would be allowed to continue their separate corporate existence, but their ordinances, with the exception of zoning, could not conflict with the ordinances of the consolidated government.

The unified government would be governed by a 21-member council. Twenty members would be elected by districts and the chairman — the vice-mayor — would be elected at-large. A popularly elected mayor would be the chief executive officer and his appointments would be subject to council confirmation. The charter also provides for the initiative, referendum, and recall.

Earlier, the Hillsborough County Local Government Study Commission issued a report in 1964, and the voters on June 27, 1967, rejected a charter creating a unified government of Tampa and Hillsborough County.

In a related action, the Escambia County Legislative Delegation is drafting for introduction in the legislature the final version of a bill providing for the consolidation of the City of Pensacola, Town of Flomaton, and Escambia County.

In Niagara County, New York, the Local Governments Improvement Commission — LOGIC — released in January 1970 the first draft of a charter creating a consolidated government by the amalgamation of three cities, 12 towns, five villages, and the county.

In January 1970 a 14-member task force, appointed by the Louisville, Kentucky, Area Chamber of Commerce, proposed that the city be enlarged to include all unincorporated areas of Jefferson County. The 65 fourth-, fifth-, and sixth-class cities would be given the option to join the enlarged city, but would not be forced to do so. Several city and county functions would be merged, but county constitutional officers would continue to perform functions such as health and welfare. As authorized by a constitutional amendment ratified by voters in November 1969, the city would be empowered to establish separate tax rates for each area based upon services provided. Under the task force's proposal, the plan would become effective upon approval by a simple majority of all voters in Louisville and the unincorporated areas of the county.

An attempt was made in 1955 to reorganize the government system in the area when a six-member Local Government Improvement Committee, appointed by the mayor, recommended that the city annex 46 square miles of urbanized land containing approximately 68,000 residents and 31 suburban cities. The proposal was approved by city voters, but rejected by suburban voters by more than a two-to-one margin.

At the request of the Salt Lake City and Salt Lake County Commissions, the University of Utah undertook a local government modernization study. In January 1970 a report was released recommending city-county consolidation, exemption of smaller municipalities from the consolidation, and the use of service and tax districts by the consolidated government.

CONSOLIDATION IN THE SOUTH

With the exception of the Indianapolis-Marion County merger, all 20th-century city-county consolidations and a major semiconsolidation, Dade County, have occurred in the South. Furthermore, a three-judge annexation court in Virginia in 1969 allowed Richmond to annex 23 square miles of territory and 44,000 residents; the largest annexation in terms of population and area in the state's history.[12] The city had sought to annex 51 square miles of territory and 72,000 residents. And indications, as reflected by the creation of charter commissions, are that most consolidations in the next few years will occur in the South.

What factors, other than general geographical location, are common to each area or to each reorganization plan where consolidation has occurred or current interest in consolidation is strong? Even a superficial analysis of the areas indicate that they possess a number of similarities with each other and dissimilarities with metropolitan areas in other sections of the United States.

Number of Units

There were relatively few units of local government in each metropolitan area prior to consolidation, and each unit had a small population with the exception of the central city.

The partial consolidation in the Baton Rouge area involved only four units, and the partial consolidation in the Nashville area involved only seven municipalities, six of which are small and were exempted from the consolidation. In Duval County there were only five municipalities and six special districts; only four of the special districts had property-taxing powers. Aside from Jacksonville, the largest municipality had a population of 16,000. And the four small municipalities were given the option of remaining out of the consolidation.

In the Charlotte area there are only six municipalities and one special district with property-taxing powers. Other than Charlotte, the largest municipality has a population under 5,000. We find a somewhat similar situation in the Savannah area where there are six small municipalities, four of which have a population under 5,000. In the Chattanooga area, three of the six municipalities have a population under 5,000, and in the Charleston area six of the eight municipalities have a population under 5,000.

Dade County with 27 municipalities is the exception, and the fact that there were such a large number of municipalities may account at least partially for the fact the two-tier approach was adopted. Proposals were made in 1945, 1947, and 1953 to consolidate the county and the City of Miami, but were defeated.

Partial Consolidations

The Nashville and Jacksonville reorganizations were partial consolidations in that the few existing small municipalities were given the option, by referendum, to remain out of the consolidation, and all chose to do so.

The Baton Rouge consolidation retained the city, the parish, and two small municipalities. The Dade County reorganization provided only for functional consolidation and not for the merger of governments. And most of the proposed consolidations in the South offer the smaller municipalities the option of continuing their separate corporate existence.

Use of the County

An established government, the county, was utilized as the base to build the new metropolitan government. This strategy improves the prospects of creating an areawide government with sufficient power since it usually is easier, under state enabling legislation, to restructure the county government than to create a new regional unit. In the South, the county traditionally has been a stronger unit of government than in the Northeast. In North Carolina, for example, the county can perform nearly all urban-type functions.

Irving G. McNayr, the second manager of Dade County, in a 1964 speech, stated:

Realizing that the county's inadequate tax structure and lack of long-range plans for operating special districts held little hope for expansion of urban services throughout the county, the citizens of the unincorporated area began supporting the new concept for an areawide government with broad powers.[13]

Incremental Consolidation

City-county consolidation is not entirely new in most southern areas, as partial consolidation has occurred incrementally over the years and citizens, consequently, were accustomed to look to the county for solutions to areawide problems.

In the 1940s the Dade County school system was created by the consolidation of 10 school districts, a county health department was created by the consolidation of all municipal health departments, and a county port authority was created to operate all airports and terminals. In 1948 Miami turned its hospital over to the county.

In the Jacksonville area health, tax assessing, tax collecting, voter registration, and planning and zoning had been consolidated prior to 1967.

Charlotte-Mecklenburg County currently have consolidated school, public health, and public welfare systems, and jointly finance a single agency responsible for elections, a second agency responsible for planning, and a third agency responsible for property tax administration. According to a recent report, "only thirty per cent of combined city and county expenditures are in areas where further consolidation or joint financing arrangements would appear to deserve consideration."[14]

Special Service Zones

The consolidations, starting with the Baton Rouge one in 1947, rely upon special service and taxing zones. A separate tax rate is established for each zone based upon the number and level of services provided. The use of service zones has made consolidation more appealing to residents of unincorporated territory, and proposed southern consolidations provide for the use of service zones.

Dade County is not allowed by the Florida constitution to utilize tax and service zones. This means that residents of unincorporated territory receive urban services from the county and pay *ad valorem* property taxes to the county at the same rate as residents of the 27 municipalities who do not receive these services from the county.

Lack of a Competitive Political System

The political system in southern metropolitan areas is, in general, not highly competitive. In 1957 Edward C. Banfield wrote, "it will be difficult or impossible to integrate local governments where the two-party system operates. . . . In effect, advocates of consolidation schemes are asking the Democrats to give up their control of the central cities or, at least, to place it in jeopardy."[15]

The term "No-party system" has been used by Edward Sofen to describe the absence of powerful political parties in Dade County.[16] In Charlotte, elections are nonpartisan, but all councilmen are Democrats. Partisan elections are used in Mecklenburg County, and two of the five county board members currently are Republicans; the system, however, is not highly competitive.

Scandals

Scandals in Nashville and Jacksonville worked in favor of the consolidationists. In Nashville prior to the referendum there were charges of police scandals. Jacksonville was plagued by a high crime rate and insurance and police scandals. In November 1966 the grand jury indicted two city commissioners, four councilmen, the recreation director, and the city auditor. In addition, the tax assessor resigned and the city's 15 senior high schools were disaccredited shortly before the referendum.

Racial Overtones

There were racial overtones attached to the Nashville and Jacksonville referenda campaigns, as it was charged in each case that consolidation was designed to dilute the growing black voting strength in the central city. It has been suggested that Richmond's 1969 annexation of 44,000 persons, most of whom are white, would help to offset black political strength in the city. Prior to annexation, an estimated 55 per cent of the population was black. It must be pointed out, however, that City Manager Alan F. Kiepper testified at the annexation trial the city's need was for land for new industry and housing. Only 6.4 per cent of the city's land prior to annexation was vacant, whereas 27.7 per cent is now vacant. The city maintains that the annexation will strengthen the economy of the metropolitan area by providing a more realistic economic base for the central city.

State Senator LeRoy Johnson of Atlanta has charged that the 1969 bill providing for the consolidation of Atlanta and Fulton County was designed not as "an effort of extending the tax base of the City but from an effort of curtailing and limiting the Negro voting strength."[17] Mr. Johnson pointed out that nearly 50 per cent of Atlanta's population is black and that a black vice-mayor, five black aldermen, and two black school board members were elected in the fall of 1969. Nevertheless, a black has never been elected to a county office.

Motivations for consolidation are many and varied. Although the growing political power of blacks in central cities may predispose a number of whites to favor consolidation, it must not be overlooked that the deep and growing fiscal crisis of many central cities is a major reason why certain groups favor consolidation. If conditions in the central city, which increasingly is becoming black, are to be improved, new financial resources must be found. A metropolitan government would be in a position to mobilize considerably larger resources than a central city to solve the most pressing problems in the area.

The Nashville consolidation was endorsed by a number of prominent blacks, even though black voting strength would be decreased from approximately 40 per cent in the city to 25 per cent countywide. According to 1960 census data, 37.9 per cent of Nashville's population was black and 19.2 per cent of the county's population was black. Currently, approximately 19.3 per cent of the population of the consolidated government is black.

Professor Brett W. Hawkins analyzed the 1962 Nashville referendum and pointed out that "both whites and nonwhites in the old city voted against Metro, and by very similar percentages."[18] He concluded that the racial factor was relatively unimportant and that blacks and whites may have voted in the same manner for different reasons.

Prior to consolidation there were two blacks serving on the 31-member Nashville City Council and none on the 55-member county court or in any other local office. Currently, five members of the metropolitan council are black; 35 of the 40 members are elected by districts. All other elective offices are held by whites. There is a black attorney in the Metropolitan Department of Law, a second black attorney in the Office of Public Defender, and one black has been appointed a judge of the Court of General Sessions.

Jacksonville had a population which was 42 per cent black in 1967, yet black areas voted in favor of the consolidation which was endorsed by civil rights groups and resulted in black population dropping to approximately 23 per cent of the total population. Fourteen members of the 19-member Jacksonville City Council are elected by districts, and blacks felt that this system would guarantee them increased representation. L. A. Hester, former executive director of the Local Government Study Commission of Duval County, has testified that the most popular aspect of the proposed consolidation was district elections.[19] The proposed electoral system was designed to guarantee blacks three seats immediately, with prospects of two or more additional seats in the future. Whites favored district elections because they felt that blacks had been exercising the balance of power in the at-large city elections. There is some evidence that suburban whites favored consolidation to prevent the blacks from capturing control of the core city.

Two blacks were elected to the nine-member city council shortly before the referendum creating the consolidated government was held; the first time a black had been elected to local office. Currently, there are four blacks on the 19-member council, three elected by districts and one at-large. Furthermore, a black has been elected to the school board and another black has been elected to the Civil Service Board. A black has been appointed head of the Motor Pool Division, a second black has been appointed a legislative aide to the mayor, and several blacks have been appointed to the Community Relations Commission and other advisory boards.

The black population in Dade County in 1957 was approximately 15 per cent, but no black had ever been elected to the Board of County Commissioners or any other elective county office. The nine-member county board presently has one black member, and the black population has increased to 18 per cent of the total population. Blacks have been appointed to a number of top offices, including the director and assistant director of the Housing and Urban Development Department, director and assistant director of the Welfare Department, director and assistant director of the Community Relations Board, executive director of the Fair Housing and Employment Commission, head of the Waste Division of the Public Works Department, and head of the Children's Home in the Youth Services Department.

Other Factors

The fact there is less industry in southern metropolitan areas compared to northern areas is of some significance, as it may indicate a lesser role played by manufacturing interest groups in the areas' politics. Table 1 clearly indicates that white-collar employment is of much greater impor-

TABLE 1

Manufacturing and White-Collar Employment
in Selected Metropolitan Areas, 1960

Area	Per Cent of Employed in Manufacturing Occupations	Per Cent of Employed in White-Collar Occupations
East Baton Rouge Parish, La.	24.4	41.0
Davidson County, Tenn.	23.1	45.9
Dade County, Fla.	11.6	46.3
Duval County, Fla.	13.2	45.4
Mecklenburg County, N. C.	22.8	45.7
Hamilton County, Tenn.	31.1	40.0
Charleston County, S. C.	23.2	39.0
Charlottesville, Va.	15.1	49.1
Fulton County, Ga.	19.3	44.3
Cook County, Ill.	34.1	45.3
Erie County, N. Y.	36.9	43.3
Genesee County, Mich.	50.7	33.4
Lehigh County, Penn.	45.1	38.9
Mahoning County, O.	41.9	37.4
Monroe County, N. Y.	42.8	45.8
Summit County, O.	44.7	42.1

Source: United States Bureau of the Census, *U. S. Census Population: 1960*, Vol. I, "Characteristics of the Population," Tables 33 and 36 (Washington, D. C.: U. S. Government Printing Office, 1963).

tance than manufacturing. Although no hard evidence has been produced, it is possible that northern industrial firms which have found a haven in suburbia from central-city woes may be opposed to consolidation or the creation of a federation if it appears that their taxes will be increased substantially to help solve central-city problems. Conversely, central-city industry may favor creation of a metropolitan government because of the tax relief it would afford.

Finally, Nashville annexed 49.46 square miles of territory and 82,000 citizens subsequent to the defeat of the proposed consolidation charter in 1958, and the threat of further annexations helped to persuade outlying areas to vote in favor of consolidation. Voter rejection of two proposed Virginia mergers — Winchester and Frederick County in December 1969 and Charlottesville and Albemarle County in March 1970 — have led to the initiation of annexation proceedings. The threat of continued annexation in time may make county voters more receptive to a merger.

THE SEMICONSOLIDATIONISTS

The semiconsolidationists advocate a two-tier system of local government in metropolitan areas, the upper tier to handle areawide functions and the lower tier of municipalities to handle local functions. The metropolitan county, federation, and metropolitan special district are three varieties of two-tier systems which have been employed. Each may be viewed as a type of semiconsolidation in that certain functions are consolidated at the upper-tier level. A new unit of local government, the upper tier, is formed by a decision to create a federation or a special district, whereas an existing unit is utilized in the case of the metropolitan county. Under federation, of course, a number of lower-tier governments could be consolidated as they were in the Toronto area in 1966.

A metropolitan county may be developed either by the incremental approach or the revolutionary approach. Los Angeles County, which developed as a major provider of urban services since the turn of the century, represents the first, and Dade County, Florida, which adopted a home rule charter in 1957, represents the second. It must be pointed out that Metropolitan Dade County simultaneously is a two-tier and a single-tier system. There is a two-tier system in the 27 areas of the county where there are municipalities, but there is only one local government in unincorporated areas — the county.

Opponents of metropolitan Dade County challenged its constitutionality and entered a total of 155 suits affecting aspects of the new government during its first three years; the courts ruled in favor of the county.

Attempts were made to emasculate the government by charter amendment in 1958 and 1961, but each was defeated. However, two amendments weakening the power of the county manager were approved in 1962; his administrative orders creating or combining departments and his appointments of department heads were made subject to the approval of the county commissioners.

In 1963 voters approved amendments providing for the at-large election of one commissioner from each of eight districts. More recently, voters in November 1968 defeated a proposed amendment consolidating all police and fire-fighting functions on the county level.

In spite of the fact the Dade County League of Municipalities has led a strong fight against metro, city-county cooperation has been common and the county provides services to a number of cities on a contract basis. In addition, cities gradually have turned functions over to the county under the charter provision authorizing a city council, by a two-thirds vote, to turn over functions. To cite two recent examples, Florida City and North Miami turned their fire departments over to the county in 1968 and 1969 respectively.

Pressure for the creation of a regional government for the San Francisco area has been growing for a number of years. In March 1969 the legislature's Joint Committee on Bay Area Regional Organization (BARO) introduced a bill creating a 36-member board to be in charge of a nine-county regional government which, in terms of functions, would be limited to reviewing applications for state and federal grants, signing joint agreements with local governments, and preparing and adopting a regional general plan.

The Association of Bay Area Governments (ABAG) has recommended since 1966 that it be converted into a regional government, and a bill was introduced in the 1969 legislature creating a 14-member Bay Area Transportation Authority to prepare a plan for highways and mass transportation facilities. However, no action was taken by the legislature prior to its adjournment.

Addressing a meeting of the Council on Regional Issues in Concord, Massachusetts, on November 25, 1969, Mayor Kevin H. White of Boston proposed the creation of the Eastern Massachusetts Council of Governments consisting of a general council of 200 representatives — two from each of the 100 cities and towns in the region — and an executive committee of 18 members chosen by nine districts of approximately equal population.

Mayor White did not propose the creation of a traditional council of governments, a voluntary association of elected officials, but rather an upper-tier metropolitan government which would be the governing body of the Metropolitan Area Planning Council, Massachusetts Bay Transportation Authority, Massachusetts Port Authority, Metropolitan District Commission, and Metropolitan Boston Air Pollution Control District, all of which are state-controlled agencies.[20] The Task Force on Regional Legislation of the Council on Regional Issues in January 1970 prepared a draft enabling bill for introduction in the General Court.

On March 26, 1970, the Volusia County Charter and Study Commission presented the legislative delegation a proposed charter providing for the consolidation with the county government of 38 boards, districts, authorities, and agencies; Daytona Beach and other municipalities would not be consolidated with the county.

Under provisions of the charter, a seven-member county council would be chosen in nonpartisan elections. The five members elected by districts would serve two-year terms and be limited to three consecutive terms. The two at-large members would serve four-year terms and be limited to two consecutive terms. By a two-thirds vote, the council would be authorized to hire and fire a county manager. Ten departments would be created to receive the powers of former constitutional officers.

The new county would "have all powers and duties prescribed by the Constitution, laws of Florida, and this charter," and may establish service and tax districts. Furthermore, municipalities and special districts are authorized to transfer functions to the county.

The charter stipulates that a:

county ordinance in conflict with a municipal ordinance shall not be effective within the municipality to the extent of such conflict . . . provided that county ordinances shall prevail over municipal ordinances whenever the county shall set minimum standards protecting the environment by prohibiting or regulating air or water pollution or the destruction of the resources of the county belonging to the general public.

THE STATISTS

The creation of state authorities has been a third major organizational response to metropolitan exigencies. Massachusetts in the late 19th century created three state agencies, a metropolitan water district, a metropolitan sewer district, and metropolitan parks district in the Boston area; they later were merged to form the Metropolitan District Commission. In more recent years, other state authorities were created in eastern Massachusetts.

New York State, under Governor Nelson A. Rockefeller, decided in the 1960s to use its plenary authority to directly solve areawide problems and adopted the authority approach. Both statewide and regional authorities have been created for special purposes: Urban Development Corporation (UDC), Environmental Facilities Corporation, Job Development Authority, Metropolitan Transportation Authority, Niagara Frontier Transportation Authority, Capital District Transportation Authority, Central New York Regional Transportation Authority and Rochester-Genesee Transportation Authority. UDC, for example, may override local codes and laws by a two-thirds vote of its nine-member board of directors.

The rationale for the creation of state authorities is a simple one: only the state has the authority and resources to solve critical metropolitan problems. Other reasons for the use of authorities in New York State include a desire to avoid the constitutional debt limit and civil service, and to remove items from the state budget and annual appropriation processes.

A different state approach has been adopted by Minnesota whose legislature created in 1967 a 15-member Metropolitan Council for the seven-county Twin Cities area. Fourteen members are selected from equal population districts by the governor who also appoints the chairman at-large.

The Council assumed the functions of the abolished Metropolitan Planning Commission, and was granted authority to review and suspend plans of special districts in conflict with the Council's development guidelines. The Council initially also was authorized to appoint a nonvoting member to the board of each special district, conduct research, operate a data center, and intervene before the Minnesota Municipal Commission in annexation and incorporation proceedings. Contracts subsequently signed with the Metropolitan Transit Commission and the Minnesota Highway Department provide that the Council is responsible for metropolitan transportation planning. And the Governor's Crime Commission designated the Council as the criminal justice planning agency.

The Council's principal function is the establishment of policy and not its execution. In December 1968 the Council proposed that the legislature create three, seven-member service boards; one to operate a metropolitan zoo, one to operate a sewage collection and treatment system, and one to operate an open space system. The legislature responded by creating a sewer service board and a metropolitan park board and authorizing the Council to appoint their members. The Council is responsible for determining policies and priorities in these two functional areas and each board is responsible for carrying out the Council's policies relative to the service.

Debate in the legislature on the creation of the Council centered on the question of whether it should be popularly elected. An amendment providing for the popular election of members in 1970 failed to pass by three votes in the House of Representatives and by a tie vote in the Senate. This issue is not dead and it is possible that legislation will be enacted in the foreseeable future transforming the Council from a state agency to a popularly elected metropolitan government.

THE ECUMENICISTS

Coming into prominence during the 1960s primarily as the result of conditional federal grants-in-aid, the ecumenicists hold that metropolitan exigencies can be solved by inter-local cooperation within the existing governmental framework. In particular, ecumenicists maintain that conjoint action will be stimulated by the development of areawide plans identifying problems and mechanisms for their solution.

Comprehensive metropolitan planning is a form of intergovernmental cooperation which may be traced in origin to the Regional Plan for New York and Its Environs completed in 1929 under the sponsorship of the Russell Sage Foundation. By 1961 it was generally concluded that areawide planning had been ineffective because of a schism between the planners and the decision makers. In that year, the Advisory Commission on Intergovernmental Relations suggested that planning should be the responsibility of an organization composed of local elected officials and private citizens, and indicated its opposition to the creation of commissions "comprised solely of part-time commissioners, and dominated by professional planning staff."[21]

The sharp increase in the number of metropolitan planning agencies since 1963 resulted from a conclusion reached by the federal government that areawide planning is the most feasible method of guaranteeing coordinated development of metropolitan areas. A decision was made by Congress in 1965 to involve local elected officials in the planning process, and was implemented by the Housing and Urban Development Act of 1965, which made organizations of local elected officials – councils of governments (COG's) – eligible for the receipt of grants for the preparation of comprehensive metropolitan plans.[22] The following year Congress provided an additional stimulus for the formation of commissions by enacting a requirement that all local government applications for federal grants and loans for 30 specified projects must be submitted for review to an organization responsible for areawide planning "which is, to the greatest practicable extent, composed of or responsible to the elected officials of a unit of areawide government or of the units of general local government."[23] This requirement promoted the formation of a COG or planning commission in each of the 233 standard metropolitan statistical areas.

Until 1965 most commissions were composed of nonelected officials and COG's generally were composed only of elected officials.[24] The 18 COG's active in the spring of 1966 were strictly voluntary associations of governments seeking to identify problems and develop a consensus for coordinated remedial action.[25] The 1966 act led a number of planning commissions to convert themselves into COG's while retaining their original names and others to change their membership and names. Furthermore, several COG's assumed responsibility for planning. As a consequence, it no longer is possible to make a clear distinction between the two types of organizations.

Several early appraisals of the COG movement were relatively optimistic regarding its future potential. One study concluded that ABAG "is a quasi-governmental agency. It is an agency of government which administers governmental programs and functions at a regional level. It is no longer a narrowly oriented discussion group."[26] A similar conclusion was reached by another organization which concluded ABAG was "transforming itself from one of the myriad discussion forums into a vigorous and potent governmental force."[27] And the executive secretary of the Metropolitan Washington Council of Governments wrote that COG's "may show the way toward finding a new and better means of coordinating the governing of the metropolis."[28]

During the past three years, however, there has been a growing consensus that the potential of COG's, a form of voluntarism, is limited in view of the increasing magnitude of metropolitan exigencies.[29] Any organization built upon cooperation between local governments with widely differing socioeconomic makeups and aspirations is predestined to experience serious difficulty in attempting to develop a program, based upon conjoint action, to solve major problems. The fact that a COG member from a given community ratifies a proposed plan of action does not necessarily mean that his community will take steps to initiate the plan. COG's have developed and helped to implement programs to solve minor problems, but no COG has successfully implemented a program to solve a highly controversial problem such as housing in the metropolis.

Furthermore, COG officials are beginning to question whether regional organizations are becoming "arms of the federal government."[30] Board Chairman Joseph L. Fisher of the Metropolitan Washington COG maintains that most federal grants-in-aid received by his COG are dedicated to specific purposes and "virtually all of the one-quarter of our total funds that come from the contributions of local jurisdictions is used in matching and otherwise accommodating the specific activities that federal and state agencies would like us to undertake."[31]

CONCLUSIONS

The continued existence of a fractionated local government system is attributable to political inertia, strong opposition to reorganization, and the failure of the federal and state governments to promote a rationalization of the government of metropolitan areas. The constitution and statutes in most states inhibit or prevent a reorganization of the local government system, and federal and state grants-in-aid have strengthened the ability of smaller units of government to survive. Should the ecumenical approach succeed in solving major areawide problems, the pressure for a major overhaul of the governmental system will be reduced.

Barring a dramatic reversal of federal policy, it is unlikely that the 1970s will be a decade of metropolitan reform. The current interest in consolidation in the South may prove to be transitory, and it is unlikely that interest in consolidation will become widespread elsewhere without federal or state encouragement.

If either the federal or state government decides to promote a rationalization of the local government system, it is probable that the prescription will call for the use of revenue sharing and grants-in-aid to encourage the creation of a two-tier system, as it is less disruptive to the existing system, allows for uniformity in certain functional areas and diversity in other areas, and would not be as susceptible as consolidation to promoting alienation between citizens and their governments. If a federation is not formed, a number of urban states probably will follow New York State's lead and create authorities to solve problems transcending local political boundaries.

The formation of a megalopolis as metropolitan areas grow and amalgamate with each other has effectively limited the use of the ecumenical, single- and two-tier approaches to smaller areas. The only governments able to cope with the major problems of an interstate megalopolis are the state and federal governments, and this means that greater reliance will be placed upon direct federal and state action, interstate compacts, and federal-state compacts.

Notes

* The author acknowledges a special debt of gratitude to the following for providing detailed information in response to his requests: William F. Hampton, budget director of Dade County; W. M. Carr, Jr., metropolitan clerk of Nashville and Davidson County; and Richard A. Martin, chief of the Public Relations Division of the City of Jacksonville. Professor John C. Bollens of the University of California (Los Angeles); Colleagues Ronald M. Stout and Lewis C. Welch; and Carl Stenberg and David B. Walker of the Advisory Commission on Intergovernmental Relations read the manuscript and offered helpful comments. Special thanks are due to P. David Billett, graduate assistant, for assembling census data.

1. *Metropolitan Surveys: A Digest* (Chicago: Public Administration Service, 1958), p. vii.

2. Daniel R. Grant, "General Metropolitan Surveys: A Summary," in *Metropolitan Surveys: A Digest, op cit.*, p. 3.

3. See *Metropolitan Surveys* (Albany: Graduate School of Public Affairs, State University of New York, published annually).

4. John C. Bollens and Henry J. Schmandt, *The Metropolis* (New York: Harper and Row, Publishers, 1965), p. 438.

5. *Modernizing Local Government* (New York: Committee for Economic Development, July, 1966).

6. *Reshaping Government in Metropolitan Areas* (New York: Committee for Economic Development, February, 1970), p. 19.

7. National Commission on Urban Problems, *Building the American City* (Washington, D.C.: U.S. Government Printing Office, 1968), pp. 376-382.

8. *Indiana Acts of 1969*, chapter 173.

9. *Charter for the Consolidated City* (Charlottesville, Va.: City of Charlottesville and Albemarle County, 1969).

10. *North Carolina Acts of 1969*, chapter 67.

11. *Partnership for Progress* (New York: Institute of Public Administration, November, 1969).

12. "Virginia Capital Wins Big Annexation," *National Civic Review* (October, 1969), p. 436.

13. Irving G. McNayr, "The Promise of Metropolitan Government," paper delivered at a Boston College Conference, May 26, 1964 (mimeographed), p. 2.

14. *Single Government* (Charlotte, N.C.: Charlotte Chamber of Commerce, 1968), p. 12.

15. Edward C. Banfield, "The Politics of Metropolitan Area Organization," *Midwest Journal of Political Science* (May, 1957), p. 86.

16. Edward Sofen, *The Miami Metropolitan Experiment* (Bloomington: Indiana University Press, 1963), pp. 74, 86, and 212.

17. "Abolish Atlanta Gains in Georgia," *The New York Times*, November 9, 1969, p. 65.

18. Brett W. Hawkins, *Nashville Metro* (Nashville: Vanderbilt University Press, 1966), p. 133.

19. "Statement by L. A. Hester," *Hearings Before the National Commission on Urban Problems*, Vol. 3 (Washington, D.C.: U.S. Government Printing Office, February, 1968), p. 272.

20. Joseph F. Zimmerman, "An Areawide Federation," *National Civic Review* (June, 1969), pp. 248-252.

21. *Governmental Structure, Organization, and Planning in Metropolitan Areas* (Washington, D.C.: Advisory Commission on Intergovernmental Relations, 1961), p. 34.

22. Housing and Urban Development Act of 1965, 75 STAT. 502, 20 U.S.C. Sec. 461 (g) (1965).

23. Demonstration Cities and Metropolitan Development Act of 1966, 80 STAT. 1255, 42 U.S.C. Sec. 3301-14 (1966).

24. Royce Hanson, *Metropolitan Councils of Governments* (Washington, D.C.: Advisory Commission on Intergovernmental Relations, August, 1966).

25. Joseph F. Zimmerman (ed.), *1966 Metropolitan Area Annual* (Albany: Graduate School of Public Affairs, State University of New York, 1966), pp. 5-6.

26. *ABAG Appraised* (Berkeley, Calif.: Institute for Local Self Government, December, 1965), p. 19.

27. "The Association of Bay Area Government – A Gathering Force," *Bulletin* (San Francisco Bureau of Governmental Research, April 1, 1965), pp. 1-2.

28. Samuel Humes, "Organization for Metropolitan Cooperation," *Public Management* (May, 1962), p. 107.

29. Joseph F. Zimmerman, "Metropolitan Ecumenicism: The Road to the Promised Land?" *Journal of Urban Law* (Spring, 1967), pp. 433-457.

30. "Chairman Urges Assessment of COG's Future Status," *National Civic Review* (March, 1970), p. 158.

31. *Ibid.*

ALAN EDWARD BENT

HOME RULE vs. REGIONALISM:
THE EXPERIENCE OF A TRI-STATE C. O. G.

A growing phenomenon since the latter 1960s has been the encouragement of the regionalization of local government. This movement has been fostered principally by the federal government in order to realize area-wide planning and policy-making, and federal program coordination. Directions toward regionalization have been provided by congressional legislation and Office of Management and Budget circulars requiring areawide governmental agencies as a condition for the receipt of grants.[1]

The injection of federal authority into local government development has resulted from the rapid growth of metropolitanization and the inability — or, reluctance — of local jurisdictions to adjust to this reality. Governmental parochialism is still prevalent despite the economic, social, and physical interdependence of localities within a metropolitan region. The anarchy of metropolitan governments has allowed haphazard sprawl, despoliation of the environment, blight to the cities, and vital services to be unmet or apportioned unequally and subsidized inequitably.

The history of voluntary metropolitan governmental reforms is one of multiple frustration and scant fulfillment. Five city-county consolidations have occurred in this century: Baton Rouge and East Baton Rouge Parish (1949); Nashville and Davidson County (1962); Jacksonville and Duval County (1967); Carson City and Ormsby County (1969); and, Indianapolis-Marion County (1970). Metro Dade County, Florida, is the sole exemplar of a comprehensive urban county, and Los Angeles County serves as the model of an urban county providing services to constituent

Reprinted with permission of the National Municipal League, *National Civic Review* (June, 1973), pp. 320–322. This article has been revised and enlarged.

units on a contractual basis.

The paucity of formal governmental reconstitutions and the difficulties encountered with their realization has prompted a new metropolitan reform emphasis. This has taken the form of a "guided voluntarism" toward inter-local cooperation for the solution of areawide problems. In particular, areawide planning has been identified as the key mechanism for metropolitan government coordination.

The optimism about areawide planning concerns its latent capability to arouse conjoint action by discovering common problems and their possible solutions. However, the rationale pursues that for planning to be an effective stimulus for conjoint action it must be tied to the decision-making foci in metropolitan communities. This has been understood because of an earlier lack of success of areawide planning suffering from the traditional bifurcation of planners and decision-makers.

The "guidance" toward metropolitan regionalism has been provided by federal legislation compelling the creation of areawide institutions capable of involving local elected officials in the planning process. This resolve was instituted in the characteristic federal "carrot and stick" approach utilized in the subvention of grants-in-aid.

The carrot was first proffered by the Housing and Urban Development Act of 1965 which made organizations of local elected officials — Councils of Government (COG's) — eligible to receive grants for the preparation of comprehensive metropolitan plans. This provided the initial guidance toward metropolitan regionalism by stimulating the creation of COG's legitimized as appropriate areawide institutions. The following year Congress added the stick to the carrot when the Demonstration Cities and Metropolitan Development Act of 1966 specified that the continued eligibility of a local government for the receipt of federal grants for 30 projects necessitated the submission of grant applications to an organization charged with areawide planning. The development of COG's was further aided by the Act's requirement that organizations responsible for areawide planning be "to the greatest practicable extent, composed of or responsible to the elected officials of a unit of areawide government or of the units of general local government."

Federal inducements have influenced the growth of COG's from the 18 voluntarily created prior to 1966 to the 352 in existence today.[2] This development is indicative of the federal government's regard for COG's as vehicles for the coordination of federal policy at the local level, and as potential catalysts to metropolitan integration. Just as important, the proliferation of councils in response to federal requirements singularly underscores the leverage afforded the national government over local government development.

COG'S: PARADIGM

The emergence of COG's was greeted with optimism regarding their potential impact on government actions in metropolitan areas. Early hopes about councils envisioned them as being more than "one of the myriad discussion forums" and capable of transforming into a "vigorous and potent governmental force."[3]

The description of COG's by the National Service to Regional Councils (now known as the National Association of Regional Councils) provided a realistic functional model:

Councils of Governments (Councils of Elected Officials) are associations of local governments in a given geographical area . . . covering a single or several counties. Major purposes are: to provide a forum for discussion of issues and challenges commonly shared by the member governments; to determine policies and priorities on these issues; to implement decisions through the member governments; and to coordinate federal, state, and local programs with regional impact.[4]

The National Service to Regional Councils, in a Draft Goals Statement, subsequently went beyond this definition to propose directions for the regional movement in the future.[5] These considerations visualize a more active role for COG's in order to "make local government more effective" in dealing with metropolitan exigencies. This creates the suspicion that there is uncertainty about the role and capability of COG's in the current regional political environment.

The essential thrust of the Draft Goals Statement of 1972 is that COG's must strengthen local government by serving as "umbrella agencies" for coordinating independent jurisdictional planning and policy decisions to enable their collective implementation consistent with adopted goals. In order to fulfill this requirement regional councils "should develop an umbrella policy planning-coordinative management system to resolve regional issues."[6] Not having this ability to rationalize local government treatment of regional problems, the statement warns, would invite the intervention of federal or state actions, or their created authorities, in metropolitan affairs.

The recommended direction for COG's adheres to the self-analysis that "regional councils are extensions of local government and their efforts to deal with challenges which cross local government boundary lines."[7] The functional energizing of COG's is sought on behalf of the preservation and strengthening of local government. There is a sense of urgency in the Draft Goals Statement suggesting the potential diminution of local government at the expense of higher levels of authority if local jurisdictions fail to respond to regional issues. COG's provide the means for a concerted intergovernmental resolution of common problems. The challenge is to the local governments to support regional councils as vehicles for joint action in dealing with challenges that transcend jurisdictional boundaries and require an areawide geographic perspective.

The national government's concern about metropolitan problems and the need for regional and program coordination triggered legislation influencing the development of COG's as mechanisms for metropolitan cooperation and coordination. This was the initial stimulus for intergovernmental interaction for local units that are joined economically, socially, and geographically. But, federal legislation cannot induce success in regional cooperation and activity unless there is a willingness among local governments to innovate in order to effectively challenge boundary-crossing problems. The efficiency of regional institutions − COG's − is dependent upon the commitment of local governments to conjoint action on behalf of areawide exigencies. The viability of COG's is linked to the support granted them by their local government constituents.

MATCOG

The Memphis metropolitan region has growth and development problems common to other urban areas. In addition, the region is characterized by an overspill of urbanization across three state boundaries. This phenomenon of an interstate urban area appears to be a developing pattern for the nation thus making the Memphis metropolitan council of government experience an especially relevant model of "guided voluntarism."

The land area and population of the city of Memphis have grown rapidly in recent decades as a result of annexations and an influx of immigrants from surrounding rural communities. At the same time, the city's urban growth has been spilling over into Arkansas and Mississippi. Urged by the Demonstration Cities and Metropolitan Development Act's requirement for an areawide review agency for federal grants eligibility, the three-county Memphis region formed a council of government in July, 1967. Writing about this event, Robert McArthur stated that "it seems highly unlikely that a council of governments would have been formed had it not been for the federal legislation requiring a regional review agency for clearance of applications for federal funds."[8]

The regional organization is named the Mississippi-Arkansas-Tennessee Council of Governments (MATCOG) and consists of Shelby County, Tennessee, Crittenden County, Arkansas, and DeSoto County, Mississippi, along with eleven municipalities including Memphis.[9] The tri-county region had a population of approximately 800,000 in 1970 and is the largest urban center in the area bounded by St. Louis, Houston, New Orleans, and Atlanta. "From 1960 to 1967, Memphis grew at a rate twice that of the United States average, and projections indicate a three-county population of over 1,200,000 by 1990. Memphis is the major distribution, trade and financial center for more than 50 counties in Tennessee, Mississippi, Arkansas, and Missouri, and functions as a regional hub in the national transportation and communication system."[10]

The council is represented by the chief elected official of each constituent unit, or a designated alternate who is also an elected official. Each constituent member is entitled to one vote in the council. The council meets quarterly and the total membership elects an executive committee consisting of five officers. The executive committee holds periodic meetings for the consideration of policies which are offered as recommendations to the full council. The executive committee is also charged with the discharge of contracts and other routine duties.

Except for Memphis, the full council had been represented by the chief elected officials of the member governments. Prior to this year, during Mayor Henry Loeb's term of office, the city of Memphis was represented by an alternate designated by the Mayor, Councilman Robert James. Although MATCOG is authorized six staff positions it had been manned by an Executive Director, an Administrative Manager, and a Secretary. On April 1, 1972, MATCOG gained an additional staff member with the hiring of a new executive director and the demotion of the previous officeholder to the newly-created position of deputy executive director. The staff is located in MATCOG's one-room office housed in Memphis City Hall.

MATCOG receives its funding from federal grants and membership dues. Dues provide the council with the matching funds requisite for the obtaining of its principal source of revenue — federal grants. Currently, the council's dues per member are a $200 basic fee plus five cents per capita. According to this formula Memphis contributes 72% of the local funds. The 1972-1973 approved budget increased the per capita fee to $.06. Units contributing the most revenue are generally represented on the executive committee. Accordingly, the executive committee normally includes representation from Memphis and Shelby County.

MATCOG, in similarity with other councils, receives financial support from the federal government through the department of Housing and Urban Development (HUD). The HUD administration of the 701 (g) program of the 1965 Housing and Urban Development Act furnishes MATCOG with a yearly revenue grant. In 1970-71 the amount of the grant was $88,670[11] and in 1971-72 it totaled $85,000.[12]

MATCOG was established to provide "coordination of planning and program activities among the member governments, and among the various Federal programs in the area."[13] To fulfill a part of the prescribed functions the Council has been designated as:

1. Federal Program Review Agency under Section 204 of the Demonstration Cities and Metropolitan Development Act of 1966.

2. Metropolitan Clearinghouse for project notification and review as authorized in Title IV of the Intergovernmental Cooperation Act of 1968 and U. S. Bureau of the Budget Circular A-95.

3. Metropolitan Reception Center Agency for receiving all federal program information for the tri-county area under the provisions of the Budget Circular A-95.[14]

TABLE 1

Membership Dues, MATCOG, Fiscal 1973

Unit	Dues	Unit	Dues
Memphis	$37,610	Earle	$400
Shelby County	4,265	Marion	300
DeSoto County	2,115	Olive Branch	290
West Memphis	1,750	Arlington	280
Millington	1,465	Bartlett[a]	270
Crittenden County	1,150	Crawfordsville	250
Collierville	415	Turrell	245
Germantown	410		

Total: $51,215 based on $200 plus $.06 per capita.

[a]Bartlett became a MATCOG member effective July 1, 1972.
Source: *Minutes,* MATCOG, January 19, 1972.

The review and comment activity is integral to MATCOG as regional conduit of federal funds. In 1972, MATCOG's processed grant applications included the following projects: (1) Memphis Delta Law Enforcement Region; (2) Neighborhood Development Program for West Memphis; (3) Federal Aviation Administration Grant for taxiway construction in the West Memphis Municipal Airport; and (4) Kansas Street Urban Renewal Project as part of the Neighborhood Development Program in Memphis.[15] Table 2 shows the increasing amounts of federal funds requested by local grant applicants in the region. Grant eligibility requirements have made MATCOG indispensable to local jurisdictions, for without its existence this federal money could not be obtained.

In order for it to be able to perform its appointed function as co-ordinator of local plans and programs dealing with areawide issues, MATCOG had established the following goals:

1. To foster locally conceived programs which may achieve maximum benefits for each member government in perspective with the total metropolitan area.

2. To provide local government unity in securing maximum assistance from outside sources so that the local jurisdictions may be more adequately equipped to meet problems of urban growth.[16]

TABLE 2

Grant Requests Processed by MATCOG
for Review and Comment, 1969–1970

Year	Number of Grants Processed	Total of Federal Funds
1969[a]	27	14.5 million
1970[b]	60	49.0 million

Sources: a. *1969 Annual Report* (Memphis: MATCOG, 1970), p. 5.
          b. *Memphis Press Scimitar,* July 27, 1971.

In 1970 MATCOG hired a group of consultants to evaluate the council's impact on regional programs and policy and to recommend spheres of responsibility for the organization's development. The consultants' report established that region-wide needs and programs in the tri-county area are beyond the scope of individual local or single county organizations or agencies, and necessitate a strong and active regional organization. However, the consultants concluded that "as presently constituted ... MATCOG has not made the impact of which it is potentially capable. This is primarily due to inadequate programming, staffing, and financing, and a set of responsibilities which are too little understood throughout the region."[17]

COG, HUD AND THE CITY

In December 1971 approximately 50 million dollars in federal grants to the Memphis metropolitan area were threatened when the Department of Housing and Urban Development announced in a letter that it was considering suspending the existing comprehensive planning assistance program and withdrawing areawide planning organization certification from MATCOG. The letter addressed to Robert James, Memphis City Councilman and MATCOG chairman, from C. G. Oakes, HUD area director, served notice that MATCOG needed "to serve the entire three-state area, to have more minority representation, to operate on a more regular basis, and to improve planning . . . "[18]

The HUD letter listed seven deficiencies in the council's operation:

. . . The major emphasis and focus is on the City of Memphis and not on the entire council area.

MATCOG is neglecting establishment of goals and policies for the entire area and serving only as a coordinating body.

The agency is inadequately staffed and relies too heavily on outside consultants.

There is only one minority race representative on the 14-member MATCOG board.[19]

Executive committee meetings are not held regularly and attendance is low 'which indicates a lack of interest and support in the total program.'

Office facilities are located in the Memphis City Hall.

Major contracts for the fiscal year program which began in July have not been executed.[20]

The letter concluded: "The council should be aware of the consequences of [possible fund withdrawal] . . . since virtually every community in the MATCOG area will be affected. It is evident that MATCOG's area wide planning program is nil."[21]

Faced with this criticism, the then executive director of MATCOG, Neil Smith, pointed to the attitude of the City of Memphis as the source of most of the council's problems. Memphis dominates the region with approximately 77 per cent of the area's population and without the active support of its largest member the council's functional capability to effect an areawide governmental direction is trivial. Statements and actions by Memphis public officials underscore the city's trivialization of MATCOG's role. *The Commercial Appeal* captured this attitude in a recent article entitled "MATCOG is Seen as Joke to Council":

The City Council, sitting in its normal Tuesday morning semiserious state, turns to the topic of MATCOG. Immediately, a flurry of jibes, satirical cuts and broken laughter erupts. The reaction to any reference to the tri-county coordination agency is predictable. 'It has become established as a joke,' said Councilman Robert B. James, who also serves as MATCOG Chairman.[22]

Since the inception of the council in 1967, Memphis has hampered MATCOG by regarding it as redundant. Memphis officials have felt that the council posed a threat to the city's governmental prerogatives and was an imposition of "another layer of bureaucracy" to "slow down progress."[23] City officials have been especially critical of MATCOG's areawide planning aspirations preferring to retain this function with the existing Memphis-Shelby County Planning Commission. Former Mayor Henry Loeb showed his disinterest in the council by never attending any of its meetings.

The official sentiment of Memphis can be seen by this statement made by a key city official in 1971:

It appears we must have this kind of agency to get certain federal funds. We're not talking of doing away with it. Why don't we just hold it to the very minimum to put the stamp [of approval] we need?[24]

Holding MATCOG to a minimum has meant restricting MATCOG's operations to reviewing federal grant applications.

Memphis has also been critical of the council because the city bears much of the local financial support and claims to have received scant gains from the agency. Finally, city officials attribute management problems in MATCOG as the cause for the council's ineffectiveness. In this regard, Neil Smith, who served as executive director of MATCOG, was singled out. "He's inadequate," was the comment of one city councilman.[25]

In general, the smaller member units have deplored the poor relations between Memphis and MATCOG because this has impaired the stability of the council which threatens federal funding. However, the functional performance of MATCOG has not pleased representatives from its smaller member units either. "No one outside of the MATCOG staff is exactly sure what the agency does, but members agree that, outside of reviewing the funding applications, it has produced nothing of benefit to them."[26] Tom Hall, the Mayor of Millington — a member of MATCOG — was quoted by the press to have said, "The studies [MATCOG has] made, we haven't needed them. They may have been beneficial to somebody."[27] Another MATCOG member, Mayor Tilden Rodgers of West Memphis, added, "[if MATCOG wasn't] the clearinghouse, I guarantee you we wouldn't belong. Funding is the primary interest we have got. We can get the services we need out of Jonesboro [the economic development district office]."[28]

It would seem that the staff of the agency had been remiss in informing the membership about MATCOG's functions. The region has maintained its political atomization, paying little regard to areawide exigencies. Interestingly, local jurisdictions are not particularly impressed with assertions about their interdependence necessitating a common front *via-a-vis* regional considerations. The Memphis *Commercial Appeal* spoke for the metropolitan community when it challenged MATCOG to prove its relevance:

> Although the three-county area is considered to be interdependent, there is very little information to back up this assumption. For example, there is no information concerning growth patterns, no catalog of regional problems, and few projections of what the region will be like 15 or 20 years from now.[29]

In an interview for this article,[30] Neil Smith offered that the council was handicapped by insufficient financial contributions and by inadequate working space for his staff. Furthermore, he attributed these conditions specifically to the negative attitude of Memphis toward MATCOG.

Memphis prevented the adoption of a recommended fiscal '70–'71 local dues rate of a $200 basic fee plus seven cents per capita. The new budget never materialized when the Memphis City Council adhered to the previous year's dues as a line item in their budget and this provided the cue for MATCOG's smaller unit members to do the same.

Despite repeated requests for more office space in Memphis City Hall, MATCOG continued to operate in an office measuring 560 square feet. Smith maintained that the cramped working quarters prevented him from hiring a full staff complement and the lack of adequate personnel constrained MATCOG's operational capability. Additionally, he was prevented from filling the position of planner for MATCOG, although a vacancy existed, because Memphis officials expressed that this would be "an unfriendly act." Memphis did not want MATCOG to assume an area-wide planning role, thereby potentially obviating the function performed by the joint city-county planning commission. Consequently, this caused Smith to rely heavily on outside consultants for the performance of council functions which brought on the wrath of HUD.

In response to the emergency of the threatened loss of certification of MATCOG and the subsequent denial of expected federal grants for the localities, the council members rallied to conjointly address themselves to HUD's criticisms. In particular, HUD was assured of the following improvements: (1) expansion of MATCOG's staff; (2) hiring of a full-time planner; (3) an increase in members' dues; and, (4) removing MATCOG from the cramped quarters at Memphis City Hall. The question of expanding minority representation on the council was left unresolved. The new mayor of Memphis, Wyeth Chandler, who, unlike his predecessor, has personally represented the City in MATCOG since taking office this year, "[objects] to suggestions that membership requirements should be relaxed in order to assure black membership in MATCOG . . ."[31]

Apparently pleased by MATCOG's positive response the Department of Housing and Urban Development announced in March, 1972, that it will recertify the council, thus releasing the held-up federal grants to the localities. C. G. Oakes, the regional HUD director, was also pleased to inform MATCOG that, for the first time, it had obtained the comprehensive planning certification.[32]

Finally, MATCOG had also decided to replace its executive director with someone who would provide "more vigorous leadership."[33] On April 1, 1972, William Fondren, a retired Army general and federal programs coordinator for the City of Memphis, became the new executive director of MATCOG. Fondren's candidacy for the position was backed by Shelby County Commission Chairman Jack Ramsay and Mayor Wyeth Chandler of Memphis, representatives of the two largest units in MATCOG. Neil Smith, the previous executive director, agreed to remain with the agency as deputy executive director. Shortly thereafter, MATCOG obtained a larger one-room office in Memphis City Hall.

In an aftermath, the Memphis *Commercial Appeal* hailed a new era of rapprochement between MATCOG and the city. The paper described the extent of Memphis's new interest in the agency:

The mayor [Wyeth Chandler] has indicated . . . that while he will add his support to the agency, his concept of it has not changed. It should do only what is necessary to keep federal funds flowing into the tri-county region and as little else as possible. Mr. Fondren [MATCOG's newly appointed executive director] apparently supports that approach.[34]

CONCLUSION

The MATCOG experience demonstrates the control exercised by its largest member — Memphis — in the region. The City's negativism toward the council has forestalled MATCOG's potential as an areawide planning and policy coordinating body. Therefore, MATCOG has not contributed toward a collective resolution of metropolitan considerations. The Memphis metropolitan region is as indifferent to areawide issues today as it was prior to MATCOG's formation.

The inability of MATCOG to be observed as an extension of local government in the resolution of boundary-crossing problems has obscured its potential as an "umbrella policy planning-coordinative management system to resolve regional issues." Instead, the council's utility has solely been comprehended in terms of its ability to attract federal grants for its member units. This dramatizes the impression of the agency as an imposed arm of the federal government with controls over the flow of federal funds. Hence, the council is "tolerated" in the region and lip service is paid to its prescribed functions, in order for the local jurisdictions to retain their eligibility for federal revenues.

On its part, MATCOG has been a timid vehicle for the resolution of areawide issues. "Buried" in a "closet" in Memphis City Hall, MATCOG's existence was unappreciated until member units were threatened with the loss of federal funds because of the council's possible loss of certification. MATCOG's sensitivity to the City's political jealousy had caused an expedient concession of many of its vital functions and a minimization of the exposition of regional exigencies. As a result, "low profile," in this case, almost led to "no profile."

The attitude of Memphis toward the agency is of concern. Without the active support of its largest member MATCOG's utility in the ordering of rational areawide directions is, at best, marginal. Memphis has not been persuaded that an areawide umbrella agency could do much toward solving metropolitan problems. Instead, recent history has shown that Memphis would rather "go it alone" in planning for its development.

Clifford Tuck, executive director of the Shelby County Development Coordination Department and a MATCOG partisan, observed that, if only for defensive purposes, Memphis should support an active regional organization. He explained the defensive rationale in a recent conversation:

> One of the big problems that Memphis and Shelby County have always had has been the in-migration from rural areas. As rural communities die, the people come to Memphis. They come and, black or white, they wind up in ghettos stuck with a welfare rope around their necks. I'm saying that these problems, the big people problems, are not confronting the small communities; they're confronting the large communities, the communities where the action is. Once the big towns realize that their destiny is tied to what's happening in their region, they'll go out there and help develop some of these small towns to keep them alive, to keep their residents employed. The only way that the big cities can stay healthy is if the region is healthy, and the big city will have to play a part in this.

At present, COG's are creatures of federal legislation and dependent on federal grants for their existence. Yet these measures were undertaken by Congress as a way to stimulate local units of government to act conjointly on behalf of their region; it is the national level's stimuli of local governmental responsibility for a rational metropolitan development.

This has been necessitated by the virtual absence of locally induced areawide devices.

The MATCOG example would indicate a cynical observance of local government voluntarism. The principal utilization of the areawide agency in the Memphis metropolitan area has been as a means of obtaining federal grants. Federal "guidance" of metropolitan ecumenism has not produced a voluntary embracing of the COG as an extension of local government for areawide considerations. This would suggest that if COG's are indeed arms of the federal government, as described by some critics, they may be so by default.

The regional challenge of this decade may be the last opportunity for local effort and action. Regionalism is "home rule" because metropolitan regions are the localities of a modern urban society. Should the local units fail to respond to this challenge then they will have endangered their ability to govern as urban problems become insuperable for atomized jurisdictions. The direction of urban governance will depend on whether local citizens and officials develop a "regional awareness." The alternative is the intervention of higher levels of government, and this likelihood is especially increased with the proliferation of interstate urban sprawls. The question is whether local intergovernmental voluntarism or added "guidance" will prevail in the future governance of the metropolis. Ultimately, the choice lies with the local units of government.

Notes

1. Housing and Urban Development Act of 1965; Demonstration Cities and Metropolitan Development Act of 1966, Intergovernmental Cooperation Act of 1968; U.S. Bureau of the Budget Circular A-95.
2. *1972 Regional Council Directory* (Washington, D.C.: National Association of Regional Councils, 1972), p. i.
3. "The Association of Bay Area Government – A Gathering Force," *Bulletin* (San Francisco Bureau of Governmental Research, April, 1965), pp. 1–2.
4. *1971 Regional Council Directory* (Washington, D. C.: National Service to Regional Councils, 1971), pp. 4–5.
5. *Regional Review Quarterly* (Washington, D. C.:: National Service to Regional Councils), January, 1972.
6. *Ibid.,* p. 3.
7. *Ibid.,* p. 1.
8. Robert E. McArthur, "Three Mississippi Councils of Government," *Public Administration Survey* (Bureau of Governmental Research, University of Mississippi, Vol. 19, No. 1, Sept., 1971), p. 3.
9. Crittenden County, Arkansas, is represented by the county and five municipal-

ities; Shelby County, Tennessee, is a member together with five of its municipalities; the membership from DeSoto County, Mississippi, is limited to the county and one municipality, Olive Branch.
10. McArthur, *op. cit.*
11. *Minutes,* MATCOG, July 30, 1969.
12. *Minutes,* MATCOG, July 29, 1970.
13. Five-Year Program for Operation for the Mississippi-Arkansas-Tennessee Council of Governments, Memphis, Tennessee. Prepared by Carl Feiss and Associated Consultants, January, 1970, p. 1.
14. *Ibid.*
15. *Minutes of Executive Committee Meeting,* MATCOG, February 23, 1972.
16. *1969 Annual Report* (Memphis: MATCOG, 1970), p. 2.
17. Five-Year Program of Operation, *op. cit.,* p. 1.
18. *The Commercial Appeal,* Memphis, Tennessee, "HUD Threatens MATCOG Fund Cutoff," December 23, 1971.
19. A Chinese-American mayor of a rural community in Arkansas.
20. "HUD Threatens MATCOG Fund Cutoff," *op. cit.*
21. *Ibid.*
22. James Denley, "MATCOG is Seen as Joke to Council," Memphis: *The Commercial Appeal,* Memphis, Tennessee, December 17, 1971.
23. *Ibid.*
24. *The Commercial Appeal,* Memphis Tennessee, April 22, 1971.
25. Denley, *op. cit.*
26. Dale Enoch, "MATCOG Wins Memphis Support, To Get New Director – Era of Drift May End," *The Commercial Appeal,* Memphis, Tennessee, March 9, 1972, p. 27.
27. *Ibid.*
28. *Ibid.*
29. *Ibid.*
30. Interview with Neil Smith, former executive director of MATCOG, Memphis, February 10, 1972.
31. "MATCOG Opens Door for New Executive," *Memphis Press Scimitar,* March 16, 1972; "The rural communities of Sunset and Edmison in Crittenden County have black mayors but have not elected to join the organization and pay the basic $200 fee," *Ibid.*
32. "HUD Gives Agency OK," *The Commercial Appeal,* Memphis, Tennessee, March 3, 1972.
33. "MATCOG Gets a Partner," *The Commercial Appeal,* Memphis, Tennessee, February 27, 1972.
34. Enoch, *op. cit.,* p. 27.

7

URBAN ADMINISTRATION
AND CITIZEN SATISFACTION

"Quis custodiet ipsos custodes?" This question — who guards the guardians? who regulates the regulators? — constitutes one of the fundamental problems for urban administration as it does for politics generally. As the introductory essay to this volume has emphasized, urban administration is typically preoccupied with amassing political power through mobilizing support, demonstrating expertise, and limiting those who participate in the actual decision-making process. It is frequently more concerned with preserving and extending its influence and hegemony than it is with implementing the substantive programs before it. How is this administrative apparatus to be regulated? How is it to be kept responsible, and to whom? These questions and the answers urban America has given to them provide the focus for this chapter.

For the greater part of America's urban development, these questions were ignored; the only social control recognized as legitimate was competition. Market competition or capitalism provided an automatic, mechanistic, self-regulating control. Adam Smith's "invisible hand" was trusted to regulate the society and to do so in such a manner as to provide maximum freedom and benefit to all. The need for rational social control or administration was denied. Yet, as Theodore J. Lowi has noted, "Capitalism is third only to the Church and warfare in its contribution to the rational approach to control, administration."[1] Market competition has encouraged at least four forms of differentiation: (1) a multiplication of individual roles; (2) a multiplication and specialization of the units of production and distribution; (3) a multiplication of the units of social control; and (4) spatial differentiation, or a multiplication and specialization of land uses. These differentiations have intensified the need for rational administrative control.

With administration acknowledged as inevitable, *Quis custodiet ipsos custodes?* could no longer be ignored. For the most part, the contemporary answer to this question has been a reliance on an expression of group politics which Lowi calls "interest group liberalism." This "New Public Philosophy" is "an amalgam of capitalism, statism, and pluralism."[2] It is an attempt to preserve the attractiveness of capitalism's automatic self-regulation by adapting it to group competition for control over positive and expanding government. Administration can be properly regulated, interest group liberals argue, only if all interested groups have access to or representation in the administrative apparatus so that they can bargain or compete with each other and the administrative unit itself over what policy is to be formulated and executed. Thus, decentralization and broad delegation of power are encouraged; decentralization allows access to all groups and delegation of power assures that decisions reached by the administrative agency are the result of pluralistic bargaining. Formalism and procedure, on the other hand, are depreciated; they tend to restrict access and preclude certain bargains. Interest group liberalism wants nothing to interfere with the automatic self-regulating control which group competition provides. Thus, who regulates the regulators?: the clear answer of interest group liberalism is the regulated themselves.

As this movement for greater governmental responsiveness and more direct forms of citizen involvement in local public affairs has proceeded, it has precipitated numerous conflicts between local administrators and neighborhood groups. It has highlighted the importance of making urban political systems and their service-providing bureaucracies more accommodating to resident participation and more sensitive to constituency wants and feelings. Henry J. Schmandt, in "Municipal Decentralization: An Overview," promotes such accommodation and sensitivity by exploring: (1) the conceptual and theoretical perspectives, such as federalism and the neighborhood, which support delegation of power and functions to subcity units; (2) the claims advanced in support of such decentralization; (3) the various forms that decentralization may take; (4) the organizational and political factors such as size, boundaries, powers, and finance, which are associated with each type; and (5) the consequences and prospects of each approach. Schmandt sees definite utility in devolving certain powers to municipal subunits in large cities so that urban residents can exercise some control over the day-to-day administration of public functions and programs. However, he also acknowledges the limitations of decentralization: "the major social problems plaguing American cities cannot be solved primarily from a neighborhood base, whether the solution is offered through control over the delivery of services or through political organization."

Assuring greater accommodation to citizen participation and greater sensitivity to citizen needs requires more than an elaboration of the arguments on behalf of decentralization. It also requires action consistent with these arguments. Thus, Adam W. Herbert contends that citizen participation in the administrative aspects of public affairs must be encouraged "to offset the feelings of helplessness, frustration, powerlessness, and bitterness" which have become increasingly evident in the United States.[3] He asserts that traditional management values and beliefs regarding efficiency and the need for hierarchy must be challenged and, if necessary, redefined in such a way as to incorporate more fully citizen perceptions of program effectiveness. This may create personal and professional discomfort for administrators, but Herbert believes that this is the only way to insure that citizen needs and demands will be adequately identified and balanced against the potentially conflicting demands and socio-emotional needs of public employees, elected officials, and administrative superiors.

Michael Lipsky in "Street-Level Bureaucracy and the Analysis of Urban Reform" agrees. He contends that street-level bureaucrats such as policemen, teachers, and welfare workers are subject to three kinds of relatively severe stress: lack of sufficient organizational resources to accomplish their jobs; distinct physical and psychological threats and challenges to their authority; and contradictions and ambiguities concerning expectations of job performance. They have responded to these stresses by developing psychological and behavioral reactions which have widened the already existing differences between them and their nonvoluntary clientele. Thus, they have developed simplifications which allow them to make decisions quickly and expeditiously. Likewise, they have developed defense mechanisms, which provide an accommodation and resolution of stress tendencies but which also result in a distortion of the perceived reality. Finally, they have developed the tendency to employ self-fulfilling prophecies to create the very reality which they either fear or want to overcome. Lipsky gives as an example of this last development the teacher who, by categorizing students as low or high achievers, predicts their capacities to achieve and thereby creates validity for the very simplifications concerning their potential in which he engages. To reduce these differences between street-level bureaucrats and the public, Lipsky supports radical decentralization and neighborhood control. He believes that they can provide increased citizen participation in and loyalty to the political system, and, thereby, heighten the administrative efficiency and political responsibility and accountability of bureaucracies currently remote from popular influence.

This practice of attempting to regulate the regulators through the politics of decentralization and interest group liberalism is open to serious criticisms, however, As Grant McConnell has observed in *Private Power and American Democracy:*

A politics of interest groups and small-constituent units is unlikely to develop its own checks. Government offers the best means of limiting both the conflicts between such groups and the agreements by which conflicts are ended or avoided. To give this service, however, government must be formal and distinct. It cannot be either if it is broken into units corresponding to the interests which have developed power.[4]

Yet, this is precisely what decentralization and interest group liberalism have accomplished. They have fragmented the government into units dominated by particular interests and have thereby deprived the government of the ability to check these interests. In so doing, they have provided "carte blanche for the vested interests."[5]

Anxious to allow local neighborhood groups to determine the problems that are to be addressed and how, interest group liberals have been reluctant to formulate laws or define programs with much detail or specificity. They have preferred delegation of power to definition by law. But, in so doing, they have parceled out the sovereignty or policy-making power of the state to those agencies and interest groups close to and most affected by the problem. Lowi has indicated five consequences of this practice.[6] To begin with, it has atrophied institutions of popular control. "Parceling out policy-making power to the most interested parties destroys political responsibility."[7] Second, it has maintained old and created new structures of privilege. The clearer and more legitimized the representation of a group or its leaders in policy-making, the less voluntary is membership in that group and the more important is loyalty to its leadership. As Robert Michels is famous for noting: "Who says organization, says oligarchy."[8] Those who respond to the question, *Quis custodiet ipsos custodes?* by answering, the regulated themselves through group competition, must also be prepared to answer who regulates the leadership of the groups? Third, and directly related to the above, this reliance on decentralization and interest group liberalism has proved to be conservative in almost every sense of the term. As Robert Paul Wolff has observed, this practice

systematically favors the interests of the stronger against the weaker party in interest-group conflicts and tends to solidify the power of those who already hold it. The government, therefore, plays a conservative, rather than a neutral, role in the society. . . . It is as though an umpire were to come upon a baseball game in progress between big boys and little boys in which the big boys cheated, broke the rules, claimed hits that were outs, and made the little boys accept the injustice by brute force. If the umpire undertakes to "regulate" the game by simply enforcing the "rules" actually being practiced, he does not thereby make the game a fair one.⁹

Fourth, it has for all practical purposes made conflict of interest a principle of government rather than a criminal act. Interest group liberalism has wrapped the government in shrouds of illegitimacy. Its operative principle appears to be: "Destroy privilege by universalizing it. Reduce conflict by yielding to it. Redistribute power by the maxim of each according to his claim."¹⁰ Finally and perhaps most importantly, this practice has failed to accomplish its ultimate purpose: all of the good intentions of the interest group liberals to the contrary notwithstanding, it has failed to provide adequate solutions to the problems that beset urban areas. Through its broad delegation of authority, it has declared to administrative agencies and their clientele groups: "We don't know what the problems are; find them and deal with them." But this had led to what Lowi calls "sincere humanitarianism gone cockeyed."¹¹ Policies that result from broad delegation of power typically come "to ends profoundly different from those intended by their most humanitarian and libertarian framers."¹² Thus, for example, urban renewal has not so much provided decent and adequate housing for all as it has promoted "Negro removal" and apartheid.

The only way to avoid these tragic consequences, Lowi argues, is to return to the rule of law. Thus, he would require legislation possessed of detailed standards of procedure, implementation, delegation, and enforcement. James Q. Wilson concurs; the only way to cope with the problem of administration is by deciding "what it is we are trying to accomplish."¹³ So does Julia Vitullo-Martin; she blames the failure of urban renewal to provide adequate housing for the poor, redistribute resources, and integrate urban centers racially and economically on the lack of specificity in housing legislation.¹⁴ This "conspicuous lack of both standards and coercion" has allowed urban administrative agencies to exercise extensive delegated powers in conjunction with private and local interest groups. The result has been an overwhelming disparity between intention and execution. Again, the good intentions of the interest group liberals have not been sufficient to insure social reform. Neither have they proved competent to regulate the regulators. Such regulation, critics of interest group liberalism maintain, can be achieved only through the rule of law. Yet, *"Quis custodiet ipsos custodes?"* Who regulates the law? This problem of urban administration has now become the problem of urban politics, tying even tighter the knot of politics and administration.

Notes

1. Theodore J. Lowi, *The End of Liberalism* (New York: W. W. Norton & Company, Inc., 1969), p. 28.

2. *Ibid.,* p. 29.

3. Adam W. Herbert, "Management Under Conditions of Decentralization and Citizen Participation," *Public Administration Review,* XXXII (October 1972), pp. 622–637.

4. Grant McConnell, *Private Power and American Democracy* (New York: Alfred A. Knopf, 1967), p. 363.

5. Lowi, p. 268.

6. *Ibid.,* pp. 85–93, 287–293.

7. *Ibid.,* p. 86.

8. Robert Michels, *Political Parties* (New York: Dover Publications, Inc., 1959), p. 401.

9. Robert Paul Wolff, "Beyond Tolerance," in Robert Paul Wolff, Barrington Moore, and Herbert Marcuse, *A Critique of Pure Tolerance* (Boston: Beacon Press, 1969), pp. 46–48.

10. Lowi, p. 292.

11. *Ibid.,* p. 248.

12. *Ibid.,* p. 263.

13. James Q. Wilson, "The Bureaucracy Problem," *The Public Interest* No. 6 (Winter, 1967), p. 8.

14. Julia Vitullo-Martin, "Liberals and the Myths of Urban Renewal," *Public Policy,* XIX, No. 2 (Spring, 1971), pp. 355–371.

HENRY SCHMANDT

MUNICIPAL DECENTRALIZATION: AN OVERVIEW

The contemporary movement for greater governmental responsiveness and more direct forms of citizen involvement in local public affairs has left no major American community untouched. In challenging the capability of existing institutional structures and mechanisms to serve human needs, the decentralization movement has precipitated numerous conflicts between local functionaries and neighborhood groups. The widespread attention generated by these activities has highlighted the necessity of making urban political systems and their service-providing bureaucracies more accommodative to resident participation and less insensitive to constituency wants and feelings. It has also forced both theorists and practitioners to address themselves to the issues raised by these developments.

The ideology of the new reformist thrust is traditional in content, although the accompanying rhetoric is at times radical in tone. Its call for political decentralization, community control, or neighborhood government — the terms are used almost indistinguishably — is compatible with the deep-seated historical preference of Americans for small-scale government and grassroots rule.[1] What is new in the current setting is that the notion of urban decentralization has taken on added meaning, becoming part of the vocabulary of social change. As one writer aptly notes, the term has become an attractive ideal because it "symbolizes attempts to find formulas for social justice, democratization, and liberal, redistributive politics," and because it exhibits a "kind of sociointellectual empathy with the disadvantaged".[2]

Reprinted from the *Public Administration Review*, journal of the American Society for Public Administration, XXXII, Special Issue (October 1972), pp. 571-588.

Although it is easy to exaggerate the significance and viability of the present decentralization movement, local policy makers and administrators are likely to find themselves increasingly in situations that call for expanded community participation and greater devolution of authority. The demands of the new urban programs along with the activism of recent years have already had impact on administrative thought and practice, witness the growing emphasis on client involvement in the service delivery process.[3] This concern for an enlarged consumer role is reflected not only in the more scholarly and technical journals, but more significantly in such association periodicals as *Nation's Cities,* the official publication of the National League of Cities, and *Public Management,* the house organ of the International City Management Association.[4] The movement receives its most vigorous support from minority group leaders and sympathetic liberals, but the concept it embodies has also proved appealing to conservatives and white working-class residents of the large central cities.

The decentralization literature clearly indicates that the priorities assigned to administrative values are undergoing change. Instead of the traditional stress on economy, efficiency, and centralization as guides for institutional reform, consumer control and client-oriented services have assumed a far more important place in the discourse. Two reports on local government reorganization by the Committee on Economic Development (CED) are noteworthy in this regard because they illustrate this shift in perspective. The first, issued in 1966, is predominantly centralist in tone, emphasizing efficiency and the consolidation of local units.[5] The second, published in 1970, while still pointing to the desirability of centralizing certain responsibilities and functions at a metropolitan or regional level, stresses the need for accountability and responsiveness on the part of local officials and suggests the creation of neighborhood councils as a means of furthering these values.[6] Similar concern for bringing government "closer to the urban dweller" has been expressed in recent years by several prestigious national bodies, among them the Advisory Commission on Intergovernmental Relations, the National Advisory Commission on Civil Disorders, and the National Commission on Urban Problems. It has also been emphasized by at least two municipal charter commissions, one in Los Angeles, the other in Boston. Each of these groups has made recommendations calling for some measure of submunicipal decentralization.

It is against this backdrop that the present essay is framed as an aid to curriculum development in the general area of municipal decentralization. As such, it is devoted to an examination of the literature and other material relevant to: (a) the conceptual or theoretical basis for transferring power and functions to subcity units or instrumentalities; (b) the claims advanced in support of such delegation; (c) the various forms that decentralization may take; (d) the organizational and political factors associated with each type; and (e) the consequences and potential of the approach.

THEORETICAL PERSPECTIVES

Decentralization in the modern context represents the convergence of two major strands in American urban theory and practice. The first, the historical emphasis on federalism, has long provided normative and political justification for the grass-roots or local autonomy doctrine. The second, the concept of the neighborhood as a basic unit for planning and administration, is of later origin, but it has contributed importantly to the theoretical base of community control. Since colonial days the notion of government "close to the people" has been an established article of democratic faith, even though more honored in the breach than in the practice. Today, with the increasing concern over the protection of life styles and neighborhood values, interest in locality control has grown. For those municipal administrators and policy makers who are attempting to respond constructively to new participatory demands, the historical antecedents of the current movement are of more than academic interest.

Federalism

The debate over governmental decentralization began in Philadelphia almost 200 years ago; it continues unabated today although the setting and issues have assumed new forms. Initially concerned with the territorial distribution of functional authority between the national and state governments (state rights), the focus of attention shifted during the early decades of this century to disputes over the degree of power and autonomy that states should grant to their cities (municipal home rule). In the 1930's the emphasis changed once again, this time to the sharing of power between areawide agencies and municipal governments (local federalism). During most of this period, despite the nation's long-standing ideological commitment to local autonomy, the vast bulk of writings on city and school government was strongly influenced by centralist perspectives. By the middle 1970's, however, new forces had begun to emerge which saw in decentralization the basis for a restored sense of legitimacy in the institutions of government.[7] As a consequence, the concept took on added dimensions, with its meaning extended to include the delegation of public power to submunicipal units and organizations, such as community development corporations, outside the normally constituted governmental structure.

The term "urban decentralization" encompasses a remarkably broad array of variations, as the looseness with which it is employed in much of the current literature indicates. At times it is used to refer to the delegation of authority to lower territorially based echelons of municipal government or other local agencies; on other occasions it is equated with community control and even with citizen participation. These latter linkages are misleading because it is possible to decentralize without providing for any resident input at the service area level. To avoid this confusion, some writers suggest that the term's meaning be restricted to the delegation of power from superior to lesser officials within a given hierarchical chain, and that "devolution" be used in cases where authority is transferred to geographic units outside the formal command structure of the central government or bureaucracy.[8] Others, following British practice, advocate the employment of decentralization as the generic term to describe all types of power distribution, with the adjective "administrative" tacked on to identify instances of internal allocation and "political" to cover the transfer of authority to officials who are responsible to a subjurisdictional electorate or clientele.[9]

The latter usage (which will be followed here) is helpful for purposes of clarity, but preciseness is still impeded by the wide assortment of forms that both administrative and political decentralization can take and by the many gradations of authority possible within each category. Moving part of a municipal department's workload to field offices, for example, may involve anything from a slight to a substantial delegation of discretion to personnel at the territorial or "street level." Similarly, endowing powers on groups outside the governmental structure, such as resident councils, may range from the merely nominal to actual autonomy over certain types of decisions.

When public officials speak of decentralization, they usually have in mind administrative delegation, or the internal allocation of authority to lower echelons within the governmental system[10] When neighborhood activists, on the other hand, employ the term they invariably refer to the transfer of power to locality residents. Whatever sympathy exists at the top for the latter form is shaped by the frustration of policy makers and administrators, many of whom are beginning to feel that large bureaucracies are incapable of managing social action programs effectively. Whatever active support there is for it comes from consumers at the bottom, bred from frustration at their seeming helplessness to influence the structures that so intimately affect their lives.[11]

The literature on federalism explicitly recognizes that (a) urban areas differ in their orientations toward public policy issues; and (b) this variation is a reflection of their different social and economic institutions.

One of the more intriguing attempts to develop a theory of local federalism which takes these factors into account is contained in *Area and Power,* a volume edited by Arthur Maass in 1959.[12] Seeking to identify the values that a territorial division of power is presumed to further, the authors analyze how the organizational location of authority in a governmental system affects not only the kind and quality of public decisions but also the will or desire of the citizenry for political participation. An earlier, but still pertinent, work in this regard is James Fesler's classic essay, *Area and Administration.*[13] Its treatment of the circumstances under which the national government should appropriately administer a function through a field office (administrative decentralization) instead of through state or local governments (political decentralization) is relevant to the current question of submunicipal delegation.

The long and continuous debate over the structuring of governmental authority has been accompanied by attitudinal changes on the part of those who believe in broad public commitments to social action. Initially opposed to the accretion of power at higher echelons of government, social reformers and liberals had come by the time of the New Deal to regard political centralization as the most effective means for achieving human goals. In their eyes, the grass-roots and local self-determination doctrines were largely myths that served only to avoid or deter meaningful social change. By the late 1960's, however, many of them had become disillusioned with centralist trends and were looking more sympathetically at various forms of devolving authority. Minority group leaders, in particular, began to give serious consideration to schemes for transferring power to the neighborhood level. Unable to secure a meaningful voice in the existing structure, a significant number of them turned to political decentralization as a means of gaining some control over the institutions that impinge upon the daily lives of deprived urbanites. While generally accepted by minority activists, this approach has failed to win universal approbation among leaders for the disadvantaged; in fact, it has drawn severe criticism from some black intellectuals and strategists.[14]

The Neighborhood

The mounting concern for making the larger cities more manageable and livable has been paralleled by an increasing interest in the neighborhood as a focus for program and service administration. This emphasis, as Howard Hallman and others point out, is not new.[15] Neighborhoods have been the concern of one movement or another since the mid-1800's when American municipalities began to grow rapidly. Settlement houses, for example, which made their appearance in the late years of the 19th century, were specifically oriented to locality needs. So were the citizen organizations formed around school centers in efforts to promote integrated neighborhood life. Sidney Dillick's study, *Community Organization for Neighborhood Development: Past and Present,* provides valuable background data on these historical antecedents of the present movement.[16]

Despite these earlier experiences, the first clear formulation of the neighborhood as a physically and socially defined entity for planning and administrative purposes did not emerge until the post-World War I period. What became known as the neighborhood unit plan initially appeared in the influential report of the *Regional Survey of New York and Its Environs,* published in 1929.[17] The work of Clarence Arthur Perry, a sociologist and community center worker, the plan was advanced as a guiding concept and set of principles for designing the residential urban environment.[18] Perry defined his basic unit as a self-contained area embracing "all the public facilities and conditions required by the average family for its comfort and proper development within the vicinity of the dwelling." The underlying assumption was that such an area, of sufficient size to support an elementary school, would enable people to know their neighbors, take part in civic affairs, and contribute to their self-fulfillment as human beings.

The concept of the neighborhood unit was not entirely new. It had its roots in utopian thinking, in the "city beautiful" movement, and in previous sociological writings, such as those by Charles Horton Cooley.[19] It was particularly inspired by Ebenezer Howard, the English planner, whose "garden city" was first presented to the public in 1892 as an alternative to growing congestion in the large cities.[20] Unlike its predecessors, Perry's plan proved to have unusually broad appeal, a fact noted by Suzanne Keller in her excellent study of the urban neighborhood.[21] Among the diverse groups and individuals attracted to it were social workers stationed in slums and immigrant districts, real estate developers seeking to protect their investments, architects and planners impressed with its aesthetic and design potentialities, and social critics who saw in it a possible antidote to the dysfunctional effects of large urban aggregations on human beings.

Despite its immediate popularity, Perry's ideal construct did not go unchallenged. Countervailing trends in both the private welfare and public sectors were already at work at the time of its formulation. These forces were reflected in the move toward federated fund-raising activities and the establishment of citywide social agency councils, and in the "good government" reform movement that was seeking the concentration of power in the hands of a professional city bureaucracy as the answer to municipal corruption and inefficiency. By World War II, opposition within the planning guild itself had also arisen. The dissenters criticized the neighborhood unit as an invitation to economic, social, and cultural parochialism;[22] as sentimental in conception, ignoring the trends in modern society;[23] as a nostalgic attempt to imitate suburban living;[24] and as an instrument of racial and ethnic segregation.[25] Sociologists similarly voiced their disagreement, pointing out that the behavior of the modern city dweller is highly mobile and no longer rooted in local territory but diffused throughout the metropolis.[26]

Although planners have remained divided on the question, the neighborhood unit idea has continued to influence planning practices to the present day. As late as 1960, a report of the American Society of Planning Officials concluded, with a touch of hyperbole: "From Atlanta to the Pacific and from Canada to Mexico, the basic Perry neighborhood unit with only minor modifications has served as the development model".[27] Meetings of the American Institute of Planners in 1966 and 1967 to consider the future environment were also mindful of the enthusiasm with which the profession had endorsed the concept in prior years.[28] The currently heightened interest in the neighborhood as an organizing principle was stimulated by the events of the 1960's: the stepped-up pace of the civil rights movement, the demonstrations and riots, the crime-in-the-streets issue, and the demands for greater citizen participation and control. New federal urban programs also contributed to the renewed attention by explicitly accepting and relying upon the neighborhood concept as an important project component. Model Cities has been particularly influential in this respect because of its emphasis on creating intimate urban environments in which people can participate together in improving the quality of their surroundings. These developments are described by Anatole Solow and his associates in a recent analysis of issues and findings pertaining to the neighborhood unit.[29]

As we have seen in the case of decentralization generally, the neighborhood idea is plagued by conceptual ambiguity.[30] The big question is one of definition. Is the neighborhood simply a spatial area having certain physical properties or is it essentially a social grouping, the members of which meet on a common ground within the vicinity of their homes for primary social contacts? The definition of neighborhood, as one sociologist observes, has been an intractable problem in the discipline since the 1920's. The difficulty is that its essence cannot be captured whole within the net of a single concept. If the social scientist "isolates it as a piece of territory, he often finds little or no correspondence with human behavior; if he concentrates instead on social relationships, he finds that these do not synchronize with geography.[31]

The Chicago sociologists of the 1920's spoke of neighborhoods as "natural areas" marked off by differences in social class and ethnicity and by physical barriers.[32] More recent studies, however, have cast doubt on this theory by documenting the wide variance that exists among individuals in the way they perceive and identify their neighborhood.[33] Current sociological writings also reflect the belief that urban neighborhoods no longer represent meaningful social systems. From this perspective it serves little purpose to attempt to define the boundaries of such units, since social and physical groupings do not often coincide in an urban society.[34] In the words of one sociologist, it is more useful to "consider the social relationships themselves than to worry about where neighborhoods begin and end".[35] This conclusion, however, is questioned by others who point to studies showing that a substantial portion of an individual's behavior and activity is still locality-oriented.[36]

The difficulty in demonstrating that the spatial and social aspects of the neighborhood construct are part of a single phenomenon has prompted some social scientists to separate the two conceptually and make their relationship problematic. As Scott Greer has noted, people are concentrated in space for various reasons and, given a whole, one may divide it in any manner that suits his purpose.[37] Partitioning space in some ways may result in a rough congruence with the boundaries of certain social groupings, but in other instances this correspondence may not be possible to achieve. The objective an analyst has in mind will, in short, determine the limits he fixes. That the neighborhood concept has long been utilized in this way is evident from even a cursory examination of the literature. Sociologists, for example, have employed it to delineate significant social subunits within the urban mosaic, while physical planners have used it to mark out the boundaries of residential enclaves for developmental purposes.

Much of the rationale for utilizing the neighborhood as the basic unit in urban decentralization schemes rests on the premise that it comprises the geographical area in which social relationships and community participation can be optimized. Viewed from this standpoint, its role in modern society and the criteria for defining its boundaries are of major importance. These are matters that have received little attention from decentralization advocates. Milton Kotler is one of the few writers to deal with them conceptually, but his treatment leaves much to be desired.[38] He conveniently bypasses the spatial-social dilemma by defining the neighborhood in almost exclusively political terms. As his argument runs, many central city neighborhoods originated as autonomous political units (village and town settlements) and later deteriorated to mere geographical expressions after they were annexed by stronger governments in the region. They were never to be considered as social entities since they were not sufficient for friendship and social intercourse. However, because their territorial identity has survived, they constitute the logical physical areas for the organization of the new political subdivisions.

Although Kotler fails to show what relevance these settlements of the past have to the organization of present-day communities, the concept of the neighborhood as a political unit is not without merit. Political scientist Peter Eisinger goes so far as to maintain that those who advocate the idea of territory as the basis of decentralized organization need not assume the prior existence of integral, self-conscious communities based on common demographic characteristics. "By the very act of defining the geographical boundaries of a subdivision, a decentralized system actually serves to form a political community." Each such unit "becomes the locus of an integrated political life, which revolves initially around the administration and control of the service in question".[39] Whether an effective or cohesive political unit can be established in this way without some underlying social commonalities is open to question. Whatever the case in this respect, the criteria to be utilized in defining the territorial units will depend largely on the objectives sought to be accomplished by decentralization. The standards employed, for example, to designate boundaries for purposes of political mobilization may well differ from those drawn on to demarcate subdistricts for administrative reasons.

THE DECENTRALIZATION RATIONALE

The literature supporting municipal decentralization in one or another of its forms is extensive, although a substantial portion of it is normative and prescriptive in nature. While the latter serves a useful purpose in challenging the assumptions on which present structures and policies are based, it leaves many questions unanswered. In the main, the justifications for a decentralized political and administrative system at the municipal level parallel those set forth for increased citizen participation and involvement in the local political process. Summaries of these various arguments are found in monographs by John Bebout,[40] Donna Shalala,[41] and Joseph Zimmerman.[42] A more detailed treatment of factors underlying the current debate is contained in *Urban Confrontation: City versus Neighborhood in the Model Cities Planning Process,* a study by Stephen Mittenthal and Hans Spiegel.[43] Discussion of the issues from a strong pro-neighborhood perspective is found in Alan Altshuler's *Community Control,*[44] while a negative viewpoint is represented by Irving Kristol in his article "Decentralization for What?"[45]

The arguments supportive of municipal decentralization tend to fall into four broad categories: administrative, psychological, sociological, and political. The first regards the device as a means of improving the delivery of services; the second stresses the psychic benefits which flow to the clients or consumers from its use; the third emphasizes its value in adapting policies and practices to locality differences in life styles, preferences, and priorities; and the last views it as a mechanism for mobilizing power.

The administrative arguments focus on the alleged unresponsiveness of large bureaucratic structures and their predominant orientation to the values of efficiency and economics of scale. As the recent Los Angeles charter commission complained: "Current trends in municipal administration have had the effect of reducing the responsive capacity of local government to needs. The pursuit of administrative efficiency and cost cutting have brought about the withdrawal of many operations of city government from direct contact with the neighborhood and citizen".[46] Unlike private industry, local government — or government in general for that matter — seldom pursues actively the question of consumer satisfaction with public goods and services; instead it reacts to sporadic complaints and gross indicators of citizen dissatisfaction such as revealed by referenda and elections. Reducing bureaucratic scale through decentralization would presumably ameliorate this situation by enabling providers to concentrate on smaller territorial areas and more circumscribed ranges of demands. In this way, they would be in a better position to pay close attention to the concerns of their constituencies and to react responsively to them. More significantly, such a restructuring would give residents of large-city neighborhoods what Herbert Kaufman refers to as "representativeness" or client influence over the manner in which needs are defined and met.[47] The result, it is claimed, would be more satisfactory relations between providers and consumers, leading to not only better services but also more effectively administered programs in terms of positive impact.

The psychological claims for decentralization are based on the belief that the alienation and distance which many urbanites now feel toward a remote city government can be overcome by reducing the scale of the service delivery system and giving the consumer a direct input to it. Studies indicate that without such input, the needs of neighborhood residents are seldom correctly defined or properly met.[48] The ordinary person is psychologically overwhelmed by huge, impersonal bureaucracies that characteristically are indifferent to the uniqueness of individuals. The neighborhood, on the other hand, can play an important role in the social and mental adjustment of urban residents through reconstructing a small-town atmosphere within the larger societal complex. At the least, it can provide them with an institutional structure with which they can identify and over which they can enjoy a sense of control.[49]

These are important considerations for racial minorities and the poor. The demand for community control emanating from their ranks reflects the feeling that the schools, hospitals, welfare agencies, and police departments are colonial institutions run by hostile or self-serving members of another culture. In this context decentralization is looked upon as a means of protecting lower-income and disadvantaged citizens from the indignities that often attend centrally determined administrative practices. It is argued that such an approach would bridge the cultural-and bureaucratic gaps between providers and consumers by enabling the latter to be served by personnel who share their life experiences and perspectives and are attuned to their feelings and values.[50]

The sociological justification emphasizes the marked differences among neighborhoods both in physical and socioeconomic characteristics and the incidence and type of social problems peculiar to them.[51] Empirical studies show that subdistricts within the same city exhibit patterns of consumption of public services noticeably distinct from each other.[52] They also reveal that such areas differ appreciably in their attitudes toward public agencies and activities. James Q. Wilson's study, *Varieties of Police Behavior,* for example, finds that blanket citywide policies of law enforcement frequently prove inadequate or ineffective because socially and ethnically differentiated neighborhoods vary in their conception of proper police behavior.[53] Decentralization addresses itself to this problem of discongruity by enabling services to be shaped more closely to the tastes of the residents. Some proponents even assert that its adoption on an extensive scale could make possible a truly pluralistic society in which economic and ethnic groups are free to act out their own life styles without foreclosing access or opportunities for others. The point they seek to emphasize is that decentralization can be treated as a mechanism for reordering the local political structure so as to make it more clearly reflect the full range of societal values.[54]

From an administrative standpoint, the argument is sometimes made that cost-effectiveness considerations in the performance of social tasks call for a greater degree of decentralization than presently exists.[55] However, the extent to which this economic model is applicable to the local public sector is questionable. Middle-class urbanites tend to leave local government to experts and technicians so long as the latter operate within certain parameters compatible with dominant community norms. Suburban school districts provide a good example of this practice. They hire a professional educator whose basic philosophy accords with theirs and then leave the day-to-day administration of the system to him. Such a practice requires decentralization, not for reasons of efficiency or economy but for purposes of accommodating the diversity among subpopulations in large urban areas. This diversity, it is suggested, is likely to increase as personal income rises and people want to consume more elaborate and highly differentiated governmental goods.[56]

The final category of arguments, the political, relates to the transfer of power to neighborhood residents. Under the existing centralized arrangements, minorities and the poor generally lack access to and a means of intervening in the administrative process. They consequently are unable to make effective demands on the service delivery and reward allocating structures. Disaggregation of authority to submunicipal levels is viewed as a way of making the system more amenable to citizen influence and control. For some who argue from a political perspective, improvement of the local service delivery structure is secondary to the broader objective of mobilizing power. They look upon the devolution of control to the neighborhoods as a mechanism or strategy for enabling deprived groups to build a viable power base capable of pressuring the larger society for major institutional change.[57] The political arguments, whether they stress the promotion of effective and responsive services or laying the groundwork for a social movement, are cognizant that crisis-oriented organizations or locality groups seldom have lasting impact, since the established centers of control possess sufficient resources to fend off any attack which is likely to play itself out in a matter of months. Neighborhood government assumedly offers a way out of this difficulty by creating a more permanent organizational structure, one that is capable of gaining the adherence and loyalty of the residents and getting them to think of themselves as a political force.

THE CRITICAL VIEW

The literature reflecting opposition to urban decentralization is sparse compared to the body of supportive writings. No comprehensive presentation of the opposition case equivalent to Altshuler's defense of community control has as yet appeared. This state of the literature, however, is not so much an indication of the degree of political and intellectual support for municipal decentralism as it is of default on the part of potential critics. Perhaps the most important reason for the relative dearth of critical analysis is that most Americans, liberal and conservative, are ideologically sympathetic to the concept of decentralization. And because its applicability to municipal government has thus far received only minimal translation into concrete forms, few have seen necessary to question it.

In fact, the major portion of nonsupportive writings to emerge thus far deals with community control of the schools, the one area that has precipitated the most active change efforts. This batch of literature, much of which is pertinent to the subject of municipal decentralization, is treated elsewhere in the present collection of essays.

What unfavorable commentary can be found is directed almost exclusively at the more extreme forms of decentralization; little of it is relevant to the question of administrative delegation of authority. This orientation is apparent from the nature of the objections most commonly advanced. Principally, the critics charge that neighborhood control would promote racial separatism;[58] intensify social friction;[59] weaken the capacity of local government for vigorous and effective action;[60] ignore the technical and social forces that demand centralized control and treatment;[61] and result in oligarchical patterns of rule by locality cliques and interest groups.[62] These objections obviously echo much of the opposition earlier manifested toward the neighborhood concept by planners and sociologists. They emanate not only from those who regard decentralization as a threat to their individual interests but also from social activists and theorists who question its relevance to the problems of contemporary urban communities.

OPERATIONALIZING THE CONCEPT

Municipal decentralization is more prominent in the literature than in practice. Despite all that has been said about it, only its lesser forms have achieved a measure of limited acceptance. No multifunctional neighborhood government has been established nor any significant delegation of authority made to locality subunits within any American city. This situation is reflected in the sparseness of empirical studies relating to specific applications of the concept. Little is known about what types and degrees of urban decentralization will work and under what circumstances, who will benefit from them, and what possible trade-offs or actions will be necessary to promote their adoption. The experiences of Model Cities and the CAP agencies provide helpful material, but even in this area the literature is largely descriptive and impressionistic. The same may be said of the operations of new communities, such as Columbia and Reston, both of which have governments that combine public services from the county level with municipal-type functions performed by private homeowners associations.[63] Experiments of this kind may well prove to be test tubes for the idea of decentralization, but as yet little is available in the way of systematic analysis or evaluation.

Both administrative and political decentralization have been prominent in reorganization proposals offered in recent years. The first type is
represented by the recommendations of the National Commission on
Urban Problems to the effect that city governments provide certain aspects
of municipal services through neighborhood offices.[64] This notion is not
new, since the physical decentralization of various local government activities is a well-established practice. Facilities, such as police precincts and
fire stations, and branch offices of various departments (e.g., city hall
annexes in Kansas City for tax collection and license issuance purposes),
have long been located in outlying sections of the large municipalities.
The motivating factor in such cases has been administrative convenience
and efficiency, a concern that contrasts with the more recent emphasis
on communication, responsiveness, and citizen involvement.[65]

Municipal multiservice centers, an extension of the neighborhood
city hall or outreach concept, are largely a product of the last decade.
Area offices administering several functions had existed earlier in some
cities, such as San Antonio, but these were concerned primarily with
public works and physical maintenance operations. Service subcenters
devoted to people-oriented functions began to emerge only with the
Community Action and Model Cities Programs. These units help to identify locality needs, offer various social welfare programs, and engage in
ombudsman-type activities. In the manner of the traditional social service
agency, they respond to the immediate problems of their clientele, but
make little or no effort to pressure for societal and institutional changes
that would attack the root causes of the difficulties.[66] The extent to
which governmentally operated centers of this nature have been adopted
is documented by a 1970 mail survey of the largest cities and urban
counties in the United States. Of the 437 communities responding, 50
municipalities had organized multiservice centers and 21 had established
little city halls.[67] (There are over 2,000 other multiservice centers operated
by social agencies and voluntary associations.) The experiences of city
government with this form of neighborhood facility are analyzed in a
detailed and informative survey conducted by the Center for Governmental Studies in 1970 and reported in two published volumes.[68]

An intermediate set of proposals combines features of citizen input
or representativeness with administrative decentralization. Typically
they call for the use of neighborhood boards or councils in advisory,
monitoring, and advocacy capacities. Recommendations along these
lines have been made by the Citizens League of Minneapolis,[69] Mayor
John Lindsay,[70] and the Los Angeles Charter Commission, among others.
The Los Angeles report proposes the creation of neighborhood organizations "with an elected board and an appointed neighborhoodman as an

institutional mechanism for communicating neighborhood needs and goals, involving citizens in city affairs, and reducing feelings of alienation".[71] Several communities have already moved to establish instrumentalities of this nature. Independence, Missouri, for example, is in the process of setting up 40 neighborhood councils to serve as links between the individual localities and city hall. Those who support efforts in this direction argue that the neighborhood concept can provide an administrative framework within which a meaningful participation component can be realistically developed.[72]

Proposals for political decentralization move beyond administrative delegation to forms of community control. The Advisory Commission on Intergovernmental Relations takes this approach in urging state legislation to permit the creation of municipal subunits of government in metropolitan areas.[73] Under the commission's recommendation, these new entities would possess limited powers of taxation and perform whatever functions were transferred to them by the city. Proposals of a similar character involving some delegation of authority to the locality level have also been made by the Committee on Economic Development,[74] the Boston Home Rule Commission,[75] and the Association of the Bar of the City of New York.[76] All the recommendations in this category recognize the futility of ignoring the issue of control and trying to consider decentralization on purely administrative terms.

Another type of decentralization that takes on certain features of locality government is the community corporation. An outgrowth of the war on poverty, the first of these agencies were organized as private nonprofit corporations by neighborhood residents seeking a greater voice in the administration of Community Action Programs. In New York City they gained authority to plan and coordinate antipoverty activities in the deprived neighborhoods; in other municipalities they became service-providing or project-administering organizations under contract with CAP agencies. Model Cities further generated the formation and utilization of these bodies. In both Oakland and Dayton, for example, corporations were formed as a means of bargaining for resident control over program planning and execution. These various developments are described by Howard Hallman in *Neighborhood Control of Public Programs: Case Studies of Community Corporations and Neighborhood Boards.*[77]

In contrast to the earlier political thrust, the more recent emphasis of the community corporations is on economic objectives. Now commonly referred to as CDCs (community development corporations), these indigenous and locality-controlled organizations represent an attempt to use business methods and activities to generate revenue and social benefits for the neighborhoods they serve.[78] A sympathetic overview of them is given by Geoffrey Faux in a background monograph, *CDCs: New Hope for the Inner City*, prepared for a Twentieth Century Fund task force. Faux defines CDCs as "organizations created and controlled by people living in impoverished areas for the purpose of planning, stimulating, financing and, when necessary, owning and operating businesses that will provide employment, income, and a better life for the residents".[79] This definition contrasts with Kotler's politically oriented description of a neighborhood corporation as a "legal organization of neighborhood territories of the city for the purpose of local self-government".[80] Implicit in many of the discussions, however, is the notion of CDCs as mechanisms for developing power bases.[81] Like Kotler, some supporters see the experience with them as a point of departure for neighborhood government.

If community corporations of all varieties are taken into account, their number probably exceeds 1,000; if only those which fit the more restricted definition of CDCs are included, the total is less than 100. The latter encompass such well-known organizations as the Hough Area Development Corporation in Cleveland and the Bedford-Stuyvesant Corporation in Brooklyn. The large majority represent predominantly black constituencies, although Chicanos and other minority groups have begun to make greater use of the device. Among the activities commonly engaged in by these bodies are job training, owning and managing businesses, providing technical assistance to locality entrepreneurs, and stimulating investments in their individual neighborhoods. Most of the existing CDCs depend heavily on OEO grants, Model Cities funds, and Small Business Administration loans to sustain their operations.[82] The tenuous nature of this financing has severely impeded their effectiveness and militated against any serious effort on their part to become, as Kotler envisaged, neighborhood governments. In actuality, no decentralization of municipal authority or functions of any significance has occurred as a consequence of their existence.[83]

DECENTRALIZATION ABROAD

Interest in forms of urban decentralization has not been confined to the United States.[84] As a recent issue of *Studies in Comparative Local Government* shows, there is scarcely any country where proposals cannot be found reflecting concern for greater citizen involvement in local public affairs.[85] Even in Canada where restricted participation and deference to political leadership are traditional traits, neighborhood organizations have begun to seek a greater voice in the municipal decision-making process.[86] The same is true in England where the Association for Neighborhood Councils is vigorously pushing for the establishment of submunicipal councils in urban areas as part of the local government reform package now before Parliament. The main functions of such bodies would be to represent neighborhood opinion in the governmental process and assume responsibility for providing certain amenities and making various local improvements. In support of the proposal, the Association cites a national survey showing that three-fourths of the electorate in large communities define their "home area" as no larger in size than the equivalent of a ward.[87]

Socialist countries have likewise evidenced strong interest in urban decentralization. Planning in many of them, as Jack Fisher notes, is aimed at dividing the large cities into self-contained neighborhood units with uniform social mixtures.[88] As an integral part of this approach, socialist policy also tends to view the neighborhood as the basic unit in the total administrative system. Yugoslavia represents the most advanced steps in this direction in its efforts to place the day-to-day decision-making power over selected locality matters in elected bodies at the sub-municipal level. Zagreb, to cite one instance, is divided into nine communes which, in turn, delegate the administration of certain services, such as the operation of day nurseries or the maintenance of local parks, to neighborhood associations. The expressed purpose is to create a system of administrative pluralism in which bureaucracy is minimized.[89] These brief observations of experiences abroad serve to underscore the widespread pervasiveness of the urban decentralization concept, a fact that would seem to suggest its viability and potential.

ORGANIZATIONAL ISSUES

The issue of whether to establish neighborhood subgovernments is, as Altshuler observes, controversial but simple to understand. The hard questions relate to such organizational concerns as size, boundaries, powers, and financing, and to the meaning of such terms as accountability and representativeness. Widely diverse opinions have been expressed on these matters, with little consensus evident among advocates of community control or lesser forms of urban decentralization. Most of the analysis and commentary concerning them appears in the various proposals that have been advanced for operationalizing the concept.

Size and Boundaries

Population size and territorial boundaries are closely related questions, although the factors associated with each are not always easily reconcilable. If, for example, the establishment of a viable political entity is the major objective, the critical mass essential for this purpose may run counter to historic neighborhood lines encompassing much smaller populations. Or if natural boundaries or clusters of culturally homogeneous residents are employed as the determining guides in setting the limits of the subdistricts, the resulting pattern may be one of individual units of widely varying size. Some governmental or administrative areas established on the basis of these criteria may, in fact, contain an insufficient number of residents to warrant the operation of functions or facilities deemed important to locality home rule. Contracting with larger agencies may provide a solution to this dilemma in some cases but prove unworkable in others.

The size specifications proposed for municipal subunits range so broadly that few meaningful generalizations can be drawn from them. This variation is not surprising given the little empirical evidence available as to the optimum size of communities or as to the linkages between size and the objectives sought through decentralization. Some proponents favor areas as large as 200,000 to assure economies of scale and specialization; others advocate neighborhoods as small as 2,500 to maximize social relationships and foster a sense of community. Kotler argues that the best practical unit lies somewhere between these extremes: large enough so it can have political viability and small enough so residents can identify with it.[90] One writer suggests that this balance can be achieved by utilizing junior high school attendance areas as the basic unit.[91] Altshuler, in proposing neighborhoods of 50,000 to 100,000 — the range most frequently mentioned — maintains that they need not be of such size as to possess the capability of exploiting all potential benefits of scale.[92]

More revealing than the statistics relating to population size are the proposals for marking out the geographical limits of the neighborhood units. These suggestions fall essentially into three categories determined by whether the task is left to popular petition, governmental action, or private initiative. The first places the choice of areal boundaries in the hands of the affected residents. Recommendations of both the Advisory Commission on Intergovernmental Relations and the Los Angeles City Charter Commission follow this approach. Under the ACIR proposal, city and county governing bodies in SMSA's would be authorized by state law to establish, at their option, neighborhood service districts on the petition of residents.[93] The Los Angeles provisions are similar; only in this case the unit would not come into being unless approved by referendum in the affected area.[94]

The second method of boundary determination entrusts the task to the city government or other official body. Both the Boston Home Rule Commission and the Citizens League of Minneapolis suggest this means. According to the former, the city administration would divide Boston into 14 districts;[95] under the latter's proposal, a boundary commission of Minneapolis officials would draw the lines.[96] Neither set of recommendations designates specific guidelines for performing this task. One simply calls for "logical and contiguous" districts; the other states that recognition should be given to subcommunities previously marked out for city planning purposes. Altshuler, who also favors this type of approach, would avoid the problem of social criteria by making scale (fixing the population size) the key issue and then shaping the neighborhoods geographically in the same manner that legislative or councilmanic districts are drawn up.

The third category is represented by Kotler's neighborhood corporation and the CDC movement in general. This approach is activated by resident initiative in organizing a private nonprofit corporation to undertake developmental-type activities within a given geographical area of the city. Through this process, the sponsors of the new agency in effect determine the limits of its spatial jurisdiction. Once established, the corporation is theoretically in a position to negotiate with municipal authorities or other governmental bodies to perform designated public functions within its prescribed turf. Little, however, is said about the guidelines to be employed in fixing the boundaries of such areas. Kotler would have the spatial limits coincide with the "historic neighborhood" which, he says, can be identified by such factors as physical boundaries, ward lines, centers of local association, and people's perceptions.[97] He does not make clear how these often conflicting criteria can be reconciled or what priority should be given to each.

Powers and Functions

The powers and functions suggested as appropriate for municipal decentralization cover a wide spectrum, ranging from information and referral activities to a complete array of local public services.[98] Discussions about the division of responsibilities suffer from the same conceptual ambiguities that plagued the earlier debates over federalism. Because of the complexities inherent in the allocational process, few proposals examine in any detail the question of what powers or functions should be assigned to submunicipal levels. Where efforts have been made to formulate guidelines for making this determination, the resulting criteria have been couched in highly generalized terms. Those suggested by the Association of the Bar of New York are typical in this respect: (1) what gains in service quality are likely to result from decentralization of a particular function; (2) what administrative and political costs might be imposed on the city as a whole by such action; and (3) what functions are sufficiently complementary to become either completely decentralized or retained in full as responsibilities of the city. A more analytical treatment of the allocational problem as it applies to administrative decentralization is contained in a monograph by Guy Black, entitled *The Decentralization of Urban Government: A Systems Approach.*[99] A list of general standards to be considered in judging the appropriateness of a proposed division of authority is suggested by Jeptha Carrell in a *Midwest Review of Public Administration* article.[100]

For the most part, the decentralization literature accepts the CED statement — long recognized by students of federalism — that the emphasis should be on the sharing of power and responsibilities and not on the assignment of entire functions to any particular level.[101] In view of the mutual dependence of governments on one another and the close interrelationships among public activities, neither policy making nor fiscal and administrative responsibilities for most urban functions can be regarded as indivisible.[102] Zoning is a case in point. It can be used as a tool for shaping the kind of neighborhood environment the residents want; yet it can also be employed to the detriment of the larger community by legitimizing unreasonable exclusionary practices. The interests of both levels can best be protected by permitting the more inclusive tier of government to establish overall standards and designate broad areas for various land usages, with the details and execution left to the neighborhoods. Law enforcement activities lend themselves to similar treatment. Routine patrolling, which is of special concern to locality residents, might be placed under submunicipal control, while criminal investigation, communications, and other specialized activities that require a broader geographical jurisdiction and greater technology would be assigned to a higher level.

Virtually all decentralization proponents, no matter how limited or far-reaching their plan, recognize the necessity of viewing the issue within the larger context of total community needs and problem-solving capabilities. Few would contend that neighborhood government can go it alone or deny that certain urban-type functions properly belong to a more inclusive unit. An increasing number maintain that we must look simultaneously in two directions: toward the centralization of certain powers at the metropolitan or regional level and toward the decentralization of others to the neighborhood.[103] The first, they note, is essential to permit equitable financing and the handling of critical systems-maintenance functions such as transportation, environmental protection, waste disposal, and general land-use regulation. Conversely, the latter is necessary to allow greater involvement and more control by urban residents over governmental actions that intimately affect their neighborhoods.

Decentralization of municipal powers is, of course, closely related to the question of governmental structure. As we have already seen, administrative decentralization involves no major change in the existing pattern but simply the assignment of operational responsibilities to field personnel of the city bureaucracy. Political decentralization, on the other hand, entails the establishment of a two-level system of government, within either the central city itself or the metropolitan area as a whole. In the latter case, the central city would be abolished as a political entity and two levels of local government created: one consisting of neighborhood units and existing suburban municipalities; the other of a metropolitan government encompassing the entire area.[104] Intermediate between the pure forms of administrative and political decentralization are various arrangements that combine features of both. Among those most frequently advanced is the use of elected resident councils with a limited policy-making role, such as the right to take part in budgetary decisions pertaining to the neighborhood and veto personnel assignments to the area by city departments. Each approach has differential implications for the institutional structure and procedures of urban governmental systems.

Finance

Questions relating to the financing of neighborhood units have not been considered in detail. The bulk of the proposals, while varying in their provisions, agree that the economic base on which the localities would draw their revenue should not be decentralized. Almost without exception they seek to tap the resources of the wider community, with each subdivision enjoying discretion over the specific allocation of its share. The Association of the Bar of New York plan provides that the city itself be the basic unit for taxation and that the funds be distributed to the individual localities on a formula basis reflecting population and relative need.[105] Most of the recommendations follow this approach in calling for some form of block grants from the city or metropolitan government. Although a number would also give the subunits limited power of taxation for specialized purposes, none envisions these minigovernments as self-supporting, recognizing the gross inequalities that would result if they were left to their own funding devices. Neither do any of the plans consider decentralization as a substitute for the basic fiscal changes now badly needed by local governments.[106] Kotler provides perhaps the single exception in his more recent arguments for the self-sufficiency of the neighborhood, convinced, as he says, that the larger society will do little to correct the existing inequities.[107]

The financing proposals in the main rest on the assumption that policy control and tax- or revenue-raising capacity can be divorced. The difficulty, as some observers point out, is that intracity or even intrametropolitan budget sharing based on this principle is likely to run into serious complications.[108] Because the suggested arrangement involves income redistribution (the transfer of funds from the wealthier to the poorer subunits), the prospect of negotiating a meaningful allocational formula within the internal arena of urban government is extremely problematic. Such a process would generate considerable conflict, since it would make the extent of resource redistribution — now hidden in the overall city budget — highly visible. With the political strength of the "haves" far greater than that of the "have-nots" in most urban areas, the latter would undoubtedly suffer from this procedure. The problem could be alleviated only by shifting a larger share of the fiscal responsibility to state or national levels where officials are removed from the immediate arena of conflict and in a better position politically to balance resources with needs.

A complementary question, the economic costs involved in implementing and operating a system of neighborhood governments, has likewise received little attention. Lack of a definitive model for costing out subcommunity control plans as well as the nonexistence of programs of sufficient scale to provide experiential data render efforts to place a price tag on the various proposals speculative. One of the few attempts to explore the issue of costs is made by Donald Haider in his essay "Political Economy of Decentralization".[109] His conclusions, which apply principally to the more extreme types of municipal decentralization, are not encouraging. On the basis of the scant evidence available he finds that such measures would probably: (1) impose added administrative and operating costs in the provision of many services; (2) cause higher governmental levels to incur additional expenditures in dealing with multiple subcity governments rather than a single unit; and (3) enable municipal unions to gain bargaining advantages over the locality governments. The question of economic costs would undoubtedly assume a more important place in the discussions once decentralization plans began to be considered seriously at the political level.

Most decentralization proposals, whether of the administrative or political type, call for a representative council of neighborhood residents. No consensus, however, exists on the selection or composition of this body. The recommendations vary from appointment by city officials, as in the Lindsay plan, to at-large elections, as in the ACIR report. Some argue for elections by proportional representation; others would have the council composed of members designated by established neighborhood organizations; and still others support various combinations of these alternatives.[110]

The manner of structuring representation constitutes a key issue, since municipal decentralization rests on the rationale that big-city government is too remote from the residents and not sufficiently responsive to their needs. Congruence between the actions of local functionaries and the wishes of their constituents is not, however, automatically assured by reducing the size of the political jurisdiction. Democracy, as its history indicates, does not necessarily function best in small governments; nor, as Madison argued many years ago, are such units immune from oligarchical control and domination by some elements to the exclusion of others. There is no reason to believe that neighborhood area governments would be free of factions or internal competition for whatever rewards the system may offer — the experiences of Model Cities and the Poverty Programs demonstrate otherwise — but there is the prospect that they will be more representative of and more accessible to the people they serve than are present structures.

FUTURE PROSPECTS

The prospects of the urban decentralization movement are difficult to assess. Lacking an organizational base, unified leadership, and a clearly defined set of goals and strategies, its current manifestations have been fragmented and sporadic. Some observers feel it has reached the peak of its popularity and is now on the ebb. Others are of the opinion that we have seen only the tip of the iceberg; that beneath the surface manifestations widespread latent sympathy for the concept exists. The reality probably lies somewhere between these two views. It would be naive to believe that the demand for the neighborhood control has broad grassroots support; the pressure for it, as the evidence indicates, is not intense or extensive, even among blacks.[111] At the same time, it would be equally erroneous to assume that the movement is a passing fancy, soon to be forgotten. The antipathy which many deprived (and not-so-deprived) citizens feel toward large urban bureaucracies is too real to be dismissed lightly.

Even though the demise of OEO may be imminent and the absorption of Model Cities into the regular structure of local government a strong possibility, the participatory practices engendered by these and other urban programs of the past decade are too well established to be ignored. The chances appear slight that the more extreme forms of community control, such as neighborhood government, or large-scale decentralization and development schemes, such as new-towns-in town and the paired community concept proposed for the Detroit area, will be experimented with on a broad basis in the immediate future.[112] There are indications, nevertheless, that municipal decentralization of less extensive proportions will increase in favor with the passage of time. The trends noted in the report by the Center for Governmental Studies — greater use of field office operations, multi-center subcenters, and mini-city halls — point in this direction even though they embody changes of only modest scope.[113] Most importantly, they reflect the growing sensitivity of large-city bureaucracies to the criticism and pressures to which they are being subjected by both political leaders at the top and organized community groups at the bottom.

Given existing trends, it seems reasonable to assume that whatever decentralization of municipal functions takes place over the next decade will be largely administrative rather than political in character. Where this is the case, however, such action will be accompanied by mechanisms (resident councils, ombudsmen, advocacy planning, and similar devices) to assure greater neighborhood input into the service delivery and program development processes. These changes will fall far short of those advocated by the more ardent neighborhood partisans who argue that if decentralization is to be taken seriously, the exercise of certain powers cannot be merely dispersed to submunicipal units but must be altogether forsworn by government on any other level.[114] Yet if incrementalism in reorganizing local governmental institutions is to continue to prevail in the immediate years ahead as it has for the last half-century or more — there are no strong indications to the contrary — the most we can expect are structural modifications to help mitigate the size of public service delivery systems and make them more available and responsive to the citizens they serve. Even the more modest forms of decentralization at least move in this direction.

What is important to understand, verbal overkill to the contrary, is that the major social problems plaguing American cities cannot be solved primarily from a neighborhood base, whether the solution is offered through control over the delivery of services or through political organization.[115] The forces that maintain deprivation and alienation — among them institutional racism, low income, unavailability of jobs, and underemployment — are largely beyond the pale of neighborhood action. Disaggregating certain powers to municipal subunits in the large cities can give urbanites some control over the day-to-day administration of public functions and programs that are locality oriented. To expect more of municipal decentralization in a society of increasing scale and complexity would be unrealistic.

Notes

1. Martin Diamond, "On the Relationship of Federalism and Decentralization," in Daniel J. Elazar, et al., eds., *Cooperation and Conflict: Readings in American Federalism* (Itasca, Ill.: Peacock, 1969), pp. 72-81.

2. Suzanne Farkas, "The Federal Role in Urban Decentralization," *American Behavioral Scientist*, Vol. 15 (September/October, 1971), pp. 15-35.

3. H. George Frederickson, *Recovery of Structure in Public Administration* (Washington, D.C.: Center for Governmental Studies, November, 1970).

4. Robert A. Aleshire, "Organizing for Neighborhood Management," *Public Management*, Vol 53 (January, 1971), pp. 7-9; John E. Arnold, "People Involvement: Participation to Restore Confidence," *Public Management*, Vol. 53 (September, 1971), p. 11; Kenneth D. Wilson, "Neighborhood Proposals Aimed at Citizen Participation," *Public Management*, Vol. 53 (January 1971), pp. 12-13; and Joseph Zimmerman, "Heading Off City Hall-Neighborhood Wars," *Nation's Cities*, Vol. 8 (November, 1970), pp. 18-21, 31.

5. Committee on Economic Development, *Modernizing Local Government* (New York: Committee on Economic Development, July, 1966).

6. Committee on Economic Development, *Reshaping Government in Metropolitan Areas* (New York: Committee on Economic Development, February, 1970).

7. Bruce L. R. Smith, "Introduction to Decentralization," *American Behavioral Scientist*, Vol. 15 (September/October, 1971), pp. 3-14.

8. Frank P. Sherwood, "Devolution as a Problem of Organization Strategy," in Robert T. Daland, ed., *Comparative Urban Research: The Administration and Politics of Cities* (Beverly Hills: Sage Publication, 1969), pp. 60-87.

9. James W. Fesler, "Centralization and Decentralization," *International Encyclopedia of the Social Sciences*, Vol. 2 (New York: Macmillan, 1968), pp. 370-377.

10. Dwight Ink and Alan Dean, "A Concept of Decentralization," *Public Administration Review*, Vol. 30, No. 1 (January/February, 1970), pp. 60-63.

11. Alice M. Rivlin, *Systematic Thinking for Social Action* (Washington, D.C.: The Brookings Institution, 1971), pp. 122-133.

12. Arthur Maass, ed., *Area and Power: A Theory of Local Government* (New York: Free Press, 1959).

13. James W. Fesler, *Area and Administration* University, Ala.: University of Alabama Press, 1949).

14. Bayard Rustin, "The Failure of Black Separatism," *Harpers*, Vol. 24 (January, 1970), pp. 25-34.

15. Howard W. Hallman, "The Neighborhood as an Organizational Unit: An Historical Perspective," in H. George Frederickson, ed., *Politics, Public Administration and Neighborhood Control* (San Francisco: Chandler, 1972).

16. Sidney Dillick, *Community Organization for Neighborhood Development: Past and Present* (New York: William Morrow, 1953).

17. Clarence A. Perry, "The Neighborhood Unit: A Scheme of Arrangement for the Family Life Community," in *Regional Survey of New York and Its Environs*, Vol. 7 (New York Committee on the Regional Plan of New York, 1929), pp. 22-140.

18. Clarence A. Perry, *The Neighborhood Unit and Housing for the Machine Age* (New York: Russell Sage Foundation, 1939). See also Perry, "The Neighborhood Unit Formula," in William C. Wheaton, et al., eds., *Urban Housing* (New York: Free Press, 1966), pp. 73-81.

19. Charles H. Cooley, *Social Organization* (New York: Schocken, 1962), pp. 23-31.

20. Ebenezer Howard, *Garden Cities of Tomorrow* (London: Faber and Faber, 1951).

21. Suzanne Keller, *The Urban Neighborhood: A Sociological Perspective* (New York: Random House, 1968).

22. Richard Dewey, "The Neighborhood, Urban Ecology, and City Planners," in Paul K. Hatt and Albert Reiss, eds., *Cities and Society* (New York: Free Press 1957),

pp. 730-790; and Svend Riemer, "The Neighborhood Conception in Theory and Application," *Land Economics*, Vol. 25 (February, 1949), pp. 67-88.

23. Reginald Isaacs, "The Neighborhood Theory: An Analysis of Its Adequacy," *Journal of the American Institute of Planners*, Vol. 14 (Spring, 1948), pp. 15-23.

24. Jane Jacobs, *The Death of the Life of Great American Cities* (New York: Random House, 1961).

25. Reginald Isaacs, "The Neighborhood Unit as an Instrument for Segregation," *Journal of Housing*, Vol. 5 (August, 1948), pp. 215-219.

26. Bessie A. McClenahan, "The Communality: The Urban Substitute for the Traditional Community," *Sociology and Social Research*, Vol. 30 (March/April, 1946), pp. 264-274; and Judith Tannenbaum, "The Neighborhood: A Socio-Psychological Analysis," *Land Economics*, Vol. 24 (November, 1948), pp. 358-369.

27. American Society of Planning Officials, *Neighborhood Boundaries* (Chicago: American Society of Planning Officials, 1960).

28. Williams R. Ewald, *Environment for Man* (Bloomington: Indiana University Press, 1967).

29. Anatole A. Solow, C. Ham, and E. Donnelly, *The Concept of the Neighborhood Units: Its Emergence and Influence on Residential Environmental Planning and Development* (Pittsburgh: Graduate School of Public and International Affairs, University of Pittsburgh, October, 1969).

30. Norman Dennis, "The Popularity of the Neighborhood Community Ideas," in Raymond E. Pahl, ed., *Readings in Urban Sociology* (Oxford: Pergamon Press, 1968), pp. 74-84.

31. Terence Lee, "Urban Neighborhood as a Socio-Spatial Scheme," *Human Relations*, Vol. 21 (June, 1968), pp. 241-267.

32. Robert E. Park, *Human Communities* (New York: Free Press, 1952).

33. Keller, *The Urban Neighborhood;* see also Terence Lee, "Urban Neighborhood as a Socio-Spatial Schema," pp. 241-267.

34. Raymond Morris and John Mogey, *The Sociology of Housing* (London: Routledge and Kegan Paul, 1965).

35. Peter H. Mann, "The Socially Balanced Neighborhood Unit," *Town Planning Review*, Vol. 28 (July, 1958), pp. 91-98.

36. Herbert J. Gans, *The Urban Villagers* (New York: Free Press, 1962); and *The Levittowners: Ways of Life and Politics in a New Suburban Community* (New York: Pantheon Books, 1967); and Peter Willmott and Michael Young, *Family and Class in a London Suburb* (London: Routledge and Kegan Paul, 1960).

37. Scott Greer, "Neighborhood," *International Encyclopedia of the Social Sciences*, Vol. 11 (New York: Macmillan, 1968), pp. 121-125.

38. Milton Kotler, "Two Essays on the Neighborhood Corporation," in Joint Economic Committee, U. S. Congress, *Urban America: Goals and Problems* (Washington, D.C.: U.S. Government Printing Office, August, 1967), pp. 170-191; and *Neighborhood Government: The Local Foundations of Political Life* (Indianapolis: Bobbs-Merrill, 1969).

39. Peter K. Eisinger, "Control-Sharing in the City: Some Thoughts on Decentralization and Client Representation," *American Behavioral Scientist*, Vol 15 (September/October, 1971), p. 40.

40. John Bebout, *Decentralization and the City Charter* (Detroit: Citizens Research Council of Michigan, August, 1971).

41. Donna E. Shalala, *Neighborhood Governance: Issues and Proposals* (New York: American Jewish Committee, 1971).

42. Joseph Zimmerman, "Neighborhoods and Citizen Involvement," paper presented at National Conference on Public Administration, Denver, April 20, 1971.

43. Stephen D. Mittenthal and Hans B. C. Spiegel, *Urban Confrontation: City versus Neighborhood in the Model Cities Planning Process* (New York: Institute of Urban Environment, School of Architecture, Columbia University, 1970).

44. Alan A. Altshuler, *Community Control: The Black Demand for Participation in Large American Cities* (New York: Pegasus, 1970).
45. Irvin Kristol, "Decentralization for What?" *Public Interest,* Vol. 11 (Spring, 1968), pp. 17–25.
46. Los Angeles City Charter Commission, *City Government for the Future* (Los Angeles: City Charter Commission, July, 1969); National Advisory Commission on Civil Disorders, *Report of National Advisory Commission on Civil Disorders* (New York: Bantam Books, 1968), p. 285.
47. Herbert Kaufman, "Administrative Decentralization and Political Power," *Public Administration Review,* Vol. 29, No. 2 (January/February, 1969), pp. 3–15.
48. Mania L. Seferi, "Resident Participation in Relocation Planning: The Case of the Denver Neighborhood of Auraia," (unpublished Ph.D. dissertation, University of Colorado, 1970).
49. Tannenbaum, "The Neighborhood: A Socio-Psychological Analysis," pp. 358–369.
50. Phyllis Southwick and Milton Thackeray, "The Concept of Culture in the Neighborhood Center," *Social Casework,* Vol. 50 (July, 1969), pp. 385–388.
51. Albert J. Reiss, "Servers and Served in Service," in John P. Crecine, ed., *Financing the Metropolis* (Beverly Hills: Sage Publications, 1970), pp. 561–576.
52. Charles S. Benson and Peter B. Lund, *Neighborhood Distribution of Local Public Services* (Berkeley: Institute of Governmental Studies, University of California, 1969).
53. James Q. Wilson, *Varieties of Police Behavior* (Cambridge: Harvard University Press, 1968).
54. Richard L. Featherstone and Fred Hill, "Urban School Decentralization," *American School and University,* Vol. 41 (April, 1968), pp. 46–48; and Vol. 42 (September, 1969), pp. 62–66.
55. Manfred Kochen and Karl W. Deutsch, "Toward a Rational Theory of Decentralization: Some Implications of a Mathematical Approach," *American Political Science Review,* Vol. 63 (September, 1969), pp. 734–749.
56. Frank Levy and Edwin Truman, "Toward a Rational Theory of Decentralization: Another View," *American Political Science Review,* Vol. 65 (March, 1971), pp. 172–179.
57. Frances Piven, "Participation of Residents in Neighborhood Community Action Programs," *Social Work,* Vol. 2 (January, 1966), pp. 73–81.
58. Rustin, "The Failure of Black Separatism," pp. 25–34.
59. Lyle E. Schaller, "The Challenge to Representative Democracy," *Mayor and Manager* (March/April, 1969), pp. 10–16.
60. Kristol, "Decentralization for What?", pp. 17–25.
61. Langley Keyes, *The Rehabilitation Planning Game: A Study in the Diversity of Neighborhood* (Cambridge, Mass.: The M.I.T. Press, 1969).
62. Theodore J. Lowi, *Politics of Disorder* (New York: Basic Books, 1971).
63. University of Chicago Law School, "Democracy in the New Towns: The Limits of Private Government," *University of Chicago Law Review,* Vol. 36 (Winter, 1969), pp. 379–412.
64. National Commission on Urban Problems, *Building the American City* (Washington, D.C.: U.S. Government Printing Office, 1969).
65. George J. Washnis, *Little City Halls* (Washington, D.C.: Center for Governmental Studies, 1971).
66. Edward J. O'Donnell and Otto M. Reid, "The Multiservice Neighborhood Center: Preliminary Findings from a National Survey," *Welfare in Review,* Vol. 9 (May-June, 1971), pp. 1–8.
67. Judith E. Grollman, "The Decentralization of Municipal Services," *Urban Data Service,* Vol. 3 (March, 1971) (Washington, D.C.: International City Management Association).

68. George J. Washnis, *Neighborhood Facilities and Municipal Decentralization*, 2 vols. (Washington, D.C.: Center for Governmental Studies, 1971).

69. Citizens League of Minneapolis, *Sub-Urbs in the City* (Minneapolis: Citizens League, 1970).

70. John V. Lindsay, *A Plan for Neighborhood Government for New York City* (New York: Office of the Mayor, June, 1970).

71. Los Angeles City Charter Commission, *City Government for the Future*, p. 19.

72. Bert W. Johnson, "Governance of the Municipality: Fracture and Divorce," *Public Administration Review*, Vol. 31, No. 2 (March/April, 1971), pp. 187-191.

73. Advisory Commission on Intergovernmental Relations, *State Legislative Program, 1970* (Washington, D.C.: U.S. Government Printing Office, 1970).

74. Committee on Economic Development, *Reshaping Government in Metropolitan Areas*.

75. Washnis, *Neighborhood Facilities and Municipal Decentralization*, Vol. 2, pp. 211-214.

76. Association of the Bar of the City of New York, *A Discussion Draft for a Symposium on Decentralizing New York City Government* (New York: Association of the Bar of the City of New York, 1970).

77. Howard W. Hallman, *Neighborhood Control of Public Programs: Case Studies of Community Corporations and Neighborhood Boards* (New York: Praeger, 1970).

78. Harvard Law School, "Community Development Corporations: A New Approach to the Poverty Program," *Harvard Law Review*, Vol. 82 (January, 1969), pp. 644-667.

79. Geoffrey Faux, *CDCs: New Hope for the Inner City* (New York: Twentieth Century Fund, 1971), p. 29.

80. Kotler, "Two Essays on the Neighborhood Corporation," p. 183.

81. Frederick D. Sturdivant, "Community Development Corporation: The Problem of Mixed Objectives," *Law and Contemporary Problems*, Vol. 36 (Winter, 1971), pp. 35-50.

82. Harvard Law School, "Community Development Corporations: Operations and Financing," *Harvard Law Review*, Vol. 83 (May, 1970), pp. 1559-1671.

83. Georgetown University Law School, "From Private Enterprise to Public Entity: The Role of the Community Development Corporation," *Georgetown Law Journal*, Vol. 57 (May, 1969), pp. 956-991.

84. William Hampton and Jeffrey Chapman, "Toward Neighborhood Councils," *Political Quarterly*, Vol. 42 (July-September, 1971), pp. 247-255; and Vol. 42 (October-December, 1971), pp. 414-422.

85. International Union of Local Authorities, "Participation," *Studies in Comparative Local Government*, Vol. 5 (Winter, 1971).

86. Bureau of Municipal Research, *Neighborhood Participation in Local Government: A Study of the City of Toronto* (Toronto: Bureau of Municipal Research, January, 1970).

87. John Baker and Michael Young, *The Hornsey Plan* (London: Association of Neighborhood Councils, April, 1971).

88. Jack C. Fisher, "Urban Planning in the Soviet Union and Eastern Europe," in H. Wentworth Eldredge, ed., *Taming Megalopolis*, Vol. 2 (Garden City: Doubleday, 1967), pp. 1069-1099.

89. Eugene Pusic and Annmarie Walsh, *Urban Government for Zagreb, Yugoslavia* (New York: Praeger, 1968).

90. Kotler, *Neighborhood Government*, pp. 40-41.

91. Johnson, "Governance of the Municipality," pp. 187-191.

92. Altshuler, *Community Control*.

93. Advisory Commission on Intergovernmental Relations, *State Legislative Program, 1970*.

94. Los Angeles City Charter Commission, *City Government for the Future*.

95. Washnis, *Neighborhood Facilities and Municipal Decentralization.*

96. Citizens League of Minneapolis, *Sub-Urbs in the City.*

97. Kotler, *Neighborhood Government,* pp. 63-68.

98. Henry J. Schmandt, "Decentralization: A Structural Imperative," in H. George Frederickson, ed., *Politics, Public Administration and Neighborhood Control* (San Francisco: Chandler, 1972).

99. Guy Black, *The Decentralization of Urban Government: A Systems Approach* (Washington, D.C.: Program of Policy Studies in Science and Technology, George Washington University, August, 1968).

100. Jeptha Carrell, "Citizen Participation and Decentralization," *Midwest Review of Public Administration,* Vol. 3 (February, 1969), pp. 3-12.

101. Committee on Economic Development, *Reshaping Government in Metropolitan Areas,* p. 56.

102. Daniel Elazar, *The American Partnership: Intergovernmental Cooperation in the 19th Century United States* (Chicago: University of Chicago Press, 1962); and Morton Grodzins, "Centralization and Decentralization in the American Federal System," in Robert A. Goldwin, ed., *A Nation of States* (Chicago: Rand McNally, 1963), pp. 1-23.

103. Richard F. Babcock and Fred P. Bosselman, "Citizen Participation: A Suburban Suggestion for the Central City," *Law and Contemporary Problems,* Vol. 32 (Spring, 1967), pp. 220-231; Committee on Economic Development, *Reshaping Government in Metropolitan Areas;* and Henry J. Schmandt, "Solutions for the City as a Social Crisis," in John Palen and Karl Flaming, eds., *Urban America: Conflict and Change* (New York: Holt, Rinehart and Winston, 1972), pp. 356-358.

104. Robert A. Dahl, "The City in the Future of Democracy," *American Political Science Review,* Vol. 61 (December, 1967), pp. 953-970, and Schmandt, "Solutions for the City as a Social Crisis."

105. Association of the Bar of the City of New York, *A Discussion Draft for a Symposium on Decentralizing New York City Government.*

106. John Callahan and Donna Shalala, "Some Fiscal Dimensions of Three Hypothetical Decentralization Plans," *Education and Urban Society,* Vol. 2 (November, 1969), pp. 40-53.

107. Milton Kotler, "The Politics of Community Economic Development," *Law and Contemporary Problems,* Vol. 36 (Winter, 1971), pp. 3-12.

108. Farkas, "The Federal Role in Urban Decentralization," pp. 15-35.

109. Donald Haider, "The Political Economy of Decentralization," *American Behavioral Scientist,* Vol. 15 (September/October, 1971), pp. 108-129.

110. Hallman, *Neighborhood Control of Public Programs.*

111. Joel D. Aberbach and Jack Walker, "The Attitudes of Blacks and Whites Toward City Services," in John P. Crecine, ed., *Financing the Metropolis* (Beverly Hills; Sage Publications, 1970), pp. 519-538; and Peter L. Goldman, *Report from Black America* (New York: Simon and Schuster, 1970).

112. Metropolitan Fund, Inc., *Regional New-Town Design: A Paired Community for Southeast Michigan* (Detroit: Metropolitan Fund, Inc., February, 1971); and Harvey S. Perloff and Royce Hanson, "The Inner City and a New Urban Politics," in Joint Economic Committee, U.S. Congress, *Urban America: Goals and Problems* (Washington, D.C.: U.S. Government Printing Office, August, 1967), pp. 162-169.

113. Washnis, *Neighborhood Facilities and Municipal Decentralization.*

114. Philip Green, "Decentralization, Community Control, and Revolution," *Massachusetts Review,* Vol. 11 (Summer, 1970), pp. 415-441.

115. Frances Piven, "Community Control: Beyond the Rhetoric," *New Generation,* Vol. 50 (Fall, 1968), pp. 7-10.

MICHAEL LIPSKY

STREET-LEVEL BUREAUCRACY AND THE ANALYSIS OF URBAN REFORM

In American cities today, policemen, teachers, and welfare workers are under siege. Their critics variously charge them with being insensitive, unprepared to work with ghetto residents, incompetent, resistant to change, and racist. These accusations, directed toward individuals, are transferred to the bureaucracies in which they work.[1]

STREET-LEVEL BUREAUCRACY

Men and women in these bureaucratic roles deny the validity of these criticisms. They insist that they are free of racism, and that they perform with professional competence under very difficult conditions. They argue that current procedures are well designed and that it is only the lack of resources and of public support and understanding which prevents successful performance of their jobs. Hence bureaucrats stress the need for higher budgets, better equipment, and higher salaries to help them do even better what they are now doing well, under the circumstances.

How are these diametrically opposed views to be reconciled? Do both sides project positions for advantage alone, or is it possible that both views may be valid from the perspective of the policy contestants? Paradoxically, is it possible that critics of urban bureaucracy may correctly allege bias and ineffectiveness of service, at the same time that urban

"Street Level Bureaucracy and the Analysis of Urban Reform," by Michael Lipsky is reprinted from *Urban Affairs Quarterly*, Vol. 6, No. 4 (June, 1971), pp. 391–409 by permission of the publisher, Sage Publications, Inc.

bureaucrats may correctly defend themselves as unbiased in motivation and objectively responsible to bureaucratic necessities?

What is particularly ominous about this confrontation is that these "street-level bureaucrats," as I call them, "represent" American government to its citizens. They are the people citizens encounter when they seek help from, or are controlled by, the American political system. While, in a sense, the Federal Reserve Board has a greater impact on the lives of the poor than, say, individual welfare workers (because of the Board's influence on inflation and employment trends), it nonetheless remains that citizens *perceive* these public employees as most influential in shaping their lives. As ambassadors of government to the American people, and as ambassadors with particularly significant impacts upon the lives of the poor and of relatively powerless minorities, how capable are these urban bureaucrats in providing high levels of service and responding objectively to individual grievances and needs?

It is one conclusion of this paper that both perspectives have some validity. Their simultaneous validity, reflecting differences in perspective and resulting from the responses of street-level bureaucrats to problems encountered in their jobs, focuses attention on one aspect of the institutional racism with which the Kerner Commission charged American society.

In analyzing the contemporary crisis in bureaucracy, and the conflicting claims of urban bureaucrats and their nonvoluntary clients, I will focus on those urban bureaucrats whose impact on citizens' lives is both frequent and significant. Hence the concentration on street-level bureaucrats — those government workers who directly interact with citizens in the regular course of their jobs; whose work within the bureaucratic structure permits them wide latitude in job performance; and whose impact on the lives of citizens is extensive. Thus, the analysis would include the patrolman on the beat, the classroom teacher, and the welfare investigator. It would be less relevant to the public school principal, who deals primarily with subordinates rather than with pupils, or to the traffic cop, whose latitude in job performance is relatively restricted.

Further I want to concentrate on ways in which street-level bureaucrats respond to conditions of stress imposed by their work environment, where such stress is relatively severe. Analytically, three kinds of stress may be readily observed in urban bureaucracies today.

Inadequate resources

Street-level bureaucracies are widely thought to lack sufficient organizational resources to accomplish their jobs. Classrooms are overcrowded.

Large welfare caseloads prevent investigators from providing all but cursory service. The lower courts are so overburdened that judges may spend their days adjourning but never trying cases. Police forces are perpetually understaffed, particularly as perceptions of crime and demands for civic order increase.[2]

Insufficiency of organizational resources increases the pressures on street-level bureaucrats to make quick decisions about clients and process cases with inadequate information and too little time to dispose of problems on their merits. While this may be said about bureaucratic decision-making in general, it is particularly salient to problems of street-level bureaucracy because of the importance of individual bureaucratic outcomes to citizens subject to the influence of urban institutions. The stakes are often high – both to citizen and to bureaucrat.

Threat and challenge to authority

The conditions under which street-level bureaucrats work often include distinct physical and psychological threats. Policemen are constantly alert to danger, as are other street-level bureaucrats who function in neighborhoods which are alien to them, are generally considered dangerous, or are characterized by high crime rates. Curiously, it may make little difference whether or not the probabilities of encountering harm are actually high, so long as people think that their jobs are risky.

Even if actual physical harm is somewhat remote, street-level bureaucrats experience threat by their inability to control the work-related encounter. Teachers especially fear the results of loss of classroom discipline or their ability to manage a classroom. Policemen have been widely observed to ensure the deference of a suspect by anticipatory invocation of authority.

Contradictory or ambiguous job expectations

Confronted with resource inadequacies and threats which increase the salience of work-related results, street-level bureaucrats often find their difficulties exacerbated by uncertainties concerning expectations of performance. Briefly, role expectations may be framed by peers, by bureaucratic reference groups, or by public expectations in general.[3] Consider the rookie patrolman who, in addition to responding to his own conceptions of the police role, must accommodate the demands placed upon him by '
1. fellow officers in the station house, who teach him how to get along and try to "correct" the teachings of his police academy instructors;

2. his immediate superiors, who may strive for efficiency at the expense of current practices;
3. police executives, who communicate expectations contradictory to station-house mores; and
4. the general public, which in American cities today is likely to be divided along both class and racial lines in its expectations of police practices and behavior.

One way street-level bureaucrats may resolve job-related problems without internal conflict is to drift to a position consistent with dominant role expectations. This resolution is denied bureaucrats working under conflicting role expectations.

Controversy over schools, police behavior, or welfare practices exacerbate these stress conditions, since they place in the spotlight of public scrutiny behavior which might otherwise remain in the shadows. These stresses result in the development of psychological and behavioral reactions which seem to widen the already existing differences between street-level bureaucrats and spokesmen for the nonvoluntary clienteles. Three such developments may be mentioned here.

First, it is a common feature of organizational behavior that individuals in organizations need to develop simplifications, or some kind of "shorthand," by which they can make decisions quickly and expeditiously. A policeman develops simplifications which suggest to him that crimes are in the process of being committed. Teachers develop simplifications to allow them to determine which pupils are "good" students and which are "troublemakers."

This is a cliche of organizational behavior.[4] But it is portentous, and not trivial, when we recognize the conditions under which these simplifications tend to be developed in stereotypic ways with racist orientations. When a black man driving through a white neighborhood is stopped by a policeman merely because he is black and therefore (according to the policeman's mode of simplification) suspiciously out of place, he has been stopped for good reason by the policeman, but for racist reasons, according to this aggrieved citizen. Teachers may select students for special attention or criticism because of their manners of speech, modes of dress, behavior in class, parental backgrounds, or other characteristics unrelated to their ability. Policemen, judges, and welfare investigators may be significantly influenced by symbols of deference or defiance to themselves or their authority. These signs may be related to general and generational responses to the enforced passivity of the past, and unrelated to the bureaucracies or bureaucrats themselves.

Race-oriented simplifications are particularly explosive even if only a few street-level bureaucrats engage in racist name calling. The objects of bureaucratic abuse understandably engage in the same kind of simplifying of the world that bureaucrats do. Thus, it takes only a few racist incidents to develop and sustain the impression that overall police behavior toward blacks is discriminatory. We are truly in a crisis because greater black community solidarity and greater willingness to object to police behavior create the very conditions under which race-oriented simplifications are increasingly invoked, leading to an escalation of tension and hostility. The greater the tensions and the images of conflict in the minds of street-level bureaucrats, the more likely they will be to invoke the simplifications they think provide them with a measure of protection in their work. This increase in discrimination under tensions occurs above and beyond the more overtly discriminatory attitudes that are sanctioned by the larger community and society.

The second development heightening the existing bureaucratic crises is the tendency on the part of street-level bureaucrats to develop defense mechanisms, in order to reach accommodation and resolution of stress tendencies, that result in a distortion of the perceived reality.[5]

One such reaction is the tendency to segment psychologically, or fragment conceptually, the population which the bureaucrat considers his clientele. Some police bureaucracies have regularly dealt with Negro crime through this technique.[6] If one can think of black people as "outside" the community, then one can perform according to "community standards" without experiencing the stresses exerted by diverse community elements. The police riots during the 1968 Chicago Democratic Convention, and more recently in various university communities, can only be understood by assuming that long-haired, white college students, some of whom are verbally abusive, are thought by the police to be "outside" the community which can expect to be protected by norms of due process.[7]

Similarly, teachers reduce their own sense of stress by defining some students as uneducable or marginally educable. Early selection of some students for higher education, based upon such characteristics as the ability to speak English and class background, permits the educators to perform in their expected roles according to a more limited definition of the population to be served. As Nathan Glazer[8] has suggested, tensions in city schools and over police practices in ghetto neighborhoods are not only a function of the apparent "foreignness" of teachers and policemen to blacks. The process of determining "foreignness" did not begin yesterday with black people. If nothing else, black labeling of whites as "foreigners" has been reinforced, if not inspired, by bureaucratic processes of categorizing nonvoluntary clients.

The development of tracking systems in public schools illustrates

the development of *institutional* mechanisms for segmenting the population to be served so as to better ensure teacher success through population
redefinition.[9] This is the latent function of tracking systems. It should be
noted that population redefinition, as I have described it, must find
support in general community attitudes, or else cross-pressures would
emerge to inhibit this development. The growing cleavage in American
cities between whites and blacks may never result in actual apartheid,
as threatened by the Kerner Commission. But the subtle psychological
apartheid resulting from redefinitions of the populations served by
public programs and institutions is equally ominous and may be already
accomplished.

A third development in the bureaucratic crisis is the way in which
the kind of behavior described here may work to create the very reality
which people either fear or want to overcome. For example, in categorizing students as low or high achievers — in a sense predicting their capacities
to achieve — teachers may create validity for the very simplifications
concerning student potential in which they engage. Recently evidence has
been presented to demonstrate that on the whole, students will perform
better in school if teachers think they are bright, regardless of whether
or not they are.[10] Similarly the propensity to arrest black youngsters for
petty crimes, the increasing professionalization of police forces (resulting
in the recording of more minor offenses), and society's concern for clean
arrest records as criteria for employment may create a population inclined
toward further illegal activity per force if not by choice. The society's
penal institutions have been characterized as schools for criminal behavior
rather than for rehabilitation. Thus we create a class of criminal types
by providing them with informal vocational training.

Not only individual teachers, but schools themselves communicate
expectations to students. Increasingly, educators of disadvantaged minorities are convinced that student high school achievement is directly related
to the extent to which schools communicate expectations of high potential to their students. Various street academies which have grown up in
New York, Newark, and other cities, the Upward Bound program, and
other experimental programs for poor and ghettoized youth, are premised
on the assumption that if educators behave as if they think college — and
hence upward mobility — is a realistic possibility for their students, high
school dropouts and potential dropouts will respond by developing motivation currently unsuspected by high school personnel.

In their need to routinize and simplify in order to process work
assignments, teachers, policemen, and welfare workers may be viewed
as bureaucrats. Significantly, however, the workload of street-level bureaucrats consists of *people*, who in turn are reactive to the bureaucratic

process. Street-level bureaucrats, confronted with inadequate resources, threats, challenges to authority, and contradictory or ambiguous role expectations, must develop mechanisms for reducing job-related stresses. It is suggested here that these mechanisms, with their considerable impact on clients' futures, deserve increasing attention from students of urban affairs.

PUBLIC POLICY REFORM IN STREET-LEVEL BUREAUCRACIES

Although much more could be said about the stresses placed on street-level bureaucrats, the remainder of this paper will focus on the implications for public policy and for public perceptions of urban bureaucracy, of an analysis of the ways street-level bureaucrats react to problems related to specified work conditions. Where does this kind of analysis lead?

First, it may help bridge the gap between, on the one hand, allegations that street-level bureaucrats are racist and, on the other hand, insistence by individuals working in these bureaucracies that they are free from racism. Development of perceptual simplifications and subtle redefinitions of the population to be served — both group psychological phenomena — may be undetected by bureaucracies and clientele groups. These phenomena will significantly affect both the perception of the bureaucrats and the reactions of clienteles to the bureaucracies. Perceptual modes which assist bureaucrats in processing work and which, though not developed to achieve discriminatory goals, result in discriminatory bias may be considered a manifestation of institutional as opposed to individual racism. So there must be a distinction between institutional routinized procedures which result in bias and personal prejudice.

Second, we may see the development of human relations councils, citizen review boards, special equal opportunity units, and other "community relations" bureaus for what they are. They may provide citizens with increased marginal access to the system, but, equally important, they inhibit institutional change by permitting street-level bureaucrats to persist in behavioral patterns because special units to handle "human relations problems" have been created. These institutional developments do not fundamentally affect general bureaucratic performance. Instead, they insulate bureaucracies from having to confront behavioral factors affecting what appears to be racist work performance. These observations particularly obtain when, as is often the case, these units lack the power to impose on the bureaucracy decisions favorable to aggrieved citizens.

Third, tracking systems, vocational schools with basically custodial functions, and other institutionalized mechanisms for predicting capacities should be recognized as also serving to ease the bureaucratic burden at the expense of equal treatment and opportunity.

Fourth, the inherent limitation of "human relations" (sensitivity training, T-group training) training for street-level bureaucrats should be recognized as inadequate to the fundamental behavioral needs of street-level bureaucrats. Basic bureaucratic attitudes toward clients appear to be a function of workers' background and of socialization on the job. Training designed to improve relationships with black communities must be directed toward helping bureaucrats improve performance, not toward classroom lessons on equality which are soon forgotten.[11] The psychological forces which lead to the kinds of biased simplifications and discriminatory behavior mentioned earlier, appear sufficiently powerful to suggest skepticism over the potential for changing behavior patterns through human relations training efforts.

Fifth, just as training should be encouraged which relates to job performance needs, incentives should be developed which reward successful performance-utilizing indicators of clientele assistance. While performance standards can be trivialized, avoided, or distorted through selective use of statistics, their potential utility has hardly been explored. For example, it would be entirely appropriate to develop indices for teacher success and to develop appropriate merit rewards, based upon adequately assessed performance indicators. For teachers, pay raises and promotions might be based upon average reading score improvements in relation to the school or citywide average for that grade level. In some ghetto schools, this index might initially reward those teachers who minimize the extent to which their students fall behind citywide averages. Public employee unions, of course, would oppose such proposals vigorously. There is every reason to think such proposals would be strongly endorsed in experimental educational units.

To improve public bureaucracies, the American political system has moved from public service as patronage to public service recruitment through merit examination. But in American cities today, administrators are frustrated because of the great difficulty in bringing talented individuals into government at high levels and introducing innovation at lower levels. Mobility in the civil service is based too little on merit. "Dead wood" is built into the systems, where the least talented public employees remain in public service.

These conditions have prevailed for some time. What is new to the discussion is that black educators and critics of police forces now argue that (a) merit examinations do not test abilities for certain kinds of tasks that must be performed in ghetto teaching and ghetto police surveillance; and (b) on the basis of the records of ghetto schools and ghetto law enforcement practices, in many cases, civil service protection cannot be justified. The society cannot afford to continue to protect civil servants, or the natural allies of the bureaucracies, at the expense of their clienteles.[12] The criticism and reevaluation of bureaucratic standards that have accompanied demands for community control are supportive of these proposals.

Sixth, this analysis is more generally supportive of proposals for radical decentralization and neighborhood control. Advocacy of neighborhood control has recently revolved around five kinds of possible rewards resulting from a change in present organizational arrangements. It has been variously held that neighborhood control would

1. increase loyalty to the political system by providing relatively powerless groups with access to governmental influence;
2. increase citizens' sense of well-being as a result of greater participation;
3. provide greater administrative efficiency for overly extended administrative systems;
4. increase the political responsibility and accountability of bureaucracy currently remote from popular influence; and
5. improve bureaucratic performance by altering the assumptions under which services are dispensed.[13]

The analysis of street-level bureaucracy presented here has been supportive of that strand of neighborhood control advocacy which focuses on the creation of standards by which to judge improved bureaucratic performance. Specifically, it has been proposed, among other things, that the performance of policemen, teachers, and other street-level bureaucrats is significantly affected by the availability of personal resources in the job situation, the sense of threat which is experienced, the ambiguity of role expectations, and the diversity of potential clientele groups. Most community control proposals are addressed to these considerations.

Recommendations for decentralization of police forces provide an opportunity to demonstrate the applicability of these ideas. For example, it has been proposed that the police function be divided into order maintenance (such as traffic control, breaking up domestic quarrels, parade duty, and so on), and crime fighting. The first is said to be a function that could easily be performed at the neighborhood level, whereas the crime fighting function, requiring both weaponry and greater technical training, might continue to be a citywide function. This kind of task redefinition would restore the cop to the beat, would replace city policemen with neighborhood residents more sensitive to community mores, and would relieve the city police of some of the duties they regard as least rewarding and most aggravating.[14] Such reorganization might reduce the stresses resulting from the variety of duties policemen are currently asked to perform, as well as increase the resources available to individuals in police duties.

Radical decentralization is also commended by this analysis because the increased homogeneity of district populations would permit greater uniformity and responsiveness in designing policies directed toward neighborhood clienteles. The range represented by the new clientele would be narrower and could be planned for with greater confidence. The system would not be so constrained by competing definitions of appropriate bureaucratic methods or by competing demands on the conceptualization of service. Citywide performance standards and appropriate regulations concerning nondiscriminatory behavior could be maintained with the expectation that they would be no *less* honored than currently.

This analysis is further supportive of proposals for radical decentralization to the extent that minority group employment under community control would be increased through changes in recruitment methods and greater attraction (for some) of civic employment. Increasing minority group employment in these street-level bureaucratic roles is not suggested here for the symbolism of minority group inclusion or for the sake of increasing minority group opportunities (although these reasons are entirely justified). Rather, this analysis suggests that such people will be less likely to structure task performance simplifications in stereotypic ways.

Potential clients might also have greater confidence and trust in individuals with whom they can relate, and who they can assume have greater understanding of their needs. However, it is not clear to what extent such predictions are reliable. Black recruits to police bureaucracies as currently designed would undoubtedly continue to be governed by the incentive systems and job perceptions of the current force. Black patrolmen today may even be the objects of increased community hostility. But in systems encouraging increased community sensitivity, black patrolmen might thrive. The benefits of community control, perhaps like most political arrangements, may ultimately depend upon the development of political consciousness and arousal. Voter turnout is low when community participation is introduced through elections in which people have previously developed little stake or involvement (such as elections for Community Action Agency boards and the recent school elections in New York City).[15] Similarly, the potential for greater rapport between street-level bureaucrats and clients may ultimately depend upon the extent to which community involvement in the issues of community control precedes transfer of power. Without such prior arousal, community control may only provide unrealized structural *opportunities* for increased community participation and greater bureaucracy-client rapport should community groups seek to influence public policy in the future.

These comments are made in full recognition that they are supportive of structural and institutional changes of considerable magnitude. If the analysis developed here is at all persuasive, then it may be said that the bureaucratic crises I have described are built into the very structure of organizational bureaucratic life. Only structural alterations, made in response to a comprehensive analysis of the bureaucratic crisis, may be expected to be effective.

CONCLUSION

Let me conclude and summarize by indicating why the current situation, and this analysis, point to a continuing crisis in city politics. It is not only that bureaucracy-client antagonisms will continue to deepen or that black separatism will continue to place stress on street-level bureaucracies which they are poorly equipped to accommodate. In addition to these factors, we face a continuing crisis because certain modes of bureaucratic behavior effectively act to shield the bureaucracies from the nature of their own shortcomings.

Street-level bureaucrats, perceiving their clients as fully responsible for their actions — as do some policemen, mental hospital workers, and welfare workers — may thereby absolve themselves from contributing to the perpetuation of problems. Police attribution of riots to the riff-raff of the ghetto provides just one illustration of this tendency.[16]

On the other hand, attributing clients' performance to cultural or societal factors beyond the scope of human intervention also works to absolve bureaucrats from responsibility for clients' futures.[17] While there may be some validity to both modes of perception, the truth (as it often does) lies somewhere in between. Meanwhile both modes of perception function to trivialize the bureaucrat-client interaction, at the expense of responsibility.

Changing role expectations provides another mechanism which may shield street-level bureaucrats from recognizing the impact of their actions. This may take at least two forms. Bureaucrats may try to influence public expectations of their jobs, so as to convince the public of their good intentions under difficult conditions. Or they may seek role redefinition in such a way as to permit job performance according to role expectations *in some limited way*. The teacher who explains that "I can't teach them all, so I will try to teach the bright ones," is attempting to foster an image of fulfilling role expectations in a limited way. While this may be one way to utilize scarce resources and deserves some sympathy, it should be recognized that such tendencies deflect pressures *away* from providing for more adequate *routine* treatment of clients.

But perhaps most significantly, it is difficult for street-level bureaucrats to acknowledge the impact of their behavior toward clients because their very ability to function in bureaucratic roles depends upon routines, simplifications, and other psychological mechanisms to reduce stress. Under such circumstances, attacks upon the substance or content of these reactions to job stress may be interpreted as criticisms of the basic requirements of job performance. As such, the criticisms are interpreted as ignorant or inaccurate.

Even if street-level bureaucrats are prepared to accept the substance of criticisms, they are likely to view them as utopian in view of the difficulties of the job. They may respond by affirming the justice of criticism in theory, but reject the criticism as inapplicable in the real world. Because they (and we) cannot imagine a world in which bureaucratic simplifications do not take place, they reject the criticism entirely.

This inability to recognize or deal with substantive criticism is reinforced by the fact that street-level bureaucrats find the validity of their simplifications and routines confirmed by selective perception of the evidence. Not only do the self-fulfilling prophecies mentioned earlier confirm these operations, but street-level bureaucrats also affirm their judgments because they depend upon the routines that offer a measure of security and because they are unfamiliar with alternative procedures which might free them to act differently. That street-level bureaucrats are in some sense shielded from awareness of the impact to their job-related behavior ensures that the crisis between street-level bureaucrats and their clients will continue; even while administrators in these bureaucracies loudly proclaim the initiation of various programs to improve community relations, reduce tensions among clientele groups and provide token measures of representation for clientele groups on lower-level policy-making boards.

The shelter from criticism may contribute to conservative tendencies in street-level bureaucracies, widely commented upon in studies of bureaucracy generally. For our purposes they may help to explain the recourse of community groups to proposals for radical change, and the recognition that only relatively radical alternatives are likely to break the circle of on-the-job socialization, job stress, and reaction formation.

An illustration of relatively drastic changes may be available in the recent recruitment of idealistic college students into the police and teaching professions.[18] These individuals are not only better educated, but are presumed to approach their new jobs with attitudes toward ghetto clients quite different from those of other recruits. What higher salaries, better working conditions, and professionalization were unable to accomplish is being achieved on a modest level by the selective service system, the war in Vietnam, and the unavailability of alternative outlets for constructive participation in reforming American society. Higher salaries (which go mostly to the kinds of people who would have become policemen and teachers anyway) have not previously resulted in recruitment of significantly more sensitive or skillful people in these bureaucracies, although this has been the (somewhat self-serving) recommendation for bureaucratic improvement for many years. On the contrary, the recruitment of college students whose career expectations in the past did not include this kind of public service orientation may accomplish the task of introducing people with the desired backgrounds to street-level bureaucratic work independent (or even in spite) of increased salaries, professionalization, seniority benefits, and the like.

It is obviously too early to evaluate these developments. The new breed of street-level bureaucrat has yet to be tested in on-the-job effectiveness, ability to withstand peer group pressures and resentments, or staying power. But their example does illustrate the importance of changing basic aspects of the bureaucratic systems fundamentally, instead of at the margin. If the arguments made here are at all persuasive, then those who would analyze the service performance of street-level bureaucracies should concentrate attention on components of the work profile. Those components discussed here — resource inadequacy, physical and psychological threat, ambiguity of role expectations, and the ways in which policemen, teachers, and other street-level bureaucrats react to problems stemming from these job-related difficulties — appear to deserve particular attention.

Notes

1. This paper draws heavily upon and extends two recent papers (M. Lipsky, "Is a Hard Rain Gonna Fall: Issues of Planning and Administration in the Urban World of the 1970's." Prepared for delivery at the Annual Meeting of the American Society of Public Administration, Miami Beach, May 21, 1969, and "Toward a Theory of Street-Level Bureaucracy." Prepared for delivery at the Annual Meeting of the American Political Science Association, New York, September 20, 1969). For a more detailed analysis of street-level bureaucrats and the factors affecting their performance, see the latter.

The reader will recognize the tentative nature of some of the conclusions and analyses which follow. The analysis of street-level bureaucracy thus far has consisted of trying to discover characteristics common to a certain set of urban bureaucrats which obtain beyond the narrow contexts of individual bureaucracies such as the police or teachers. The latter half of this paper is similarly a tentative attempt to relate the analysis to issues of current public policy.

2. A. Silver, "The Demand for Order in a Civil Society," in D. Bordua, ed., *The Police: Six Sociologist Essays* (New York: John Wiley, 1967).

3. T. Sarbin and V. Allen, "Role Theory," in G. Lindzey and E. Aronson, eds., *The Handbook of Social Psychology* (Reading, Mass.: Addison-Wesley, 1968).

4. A. Downs, *Inside Bureaucracy* (Boston: Little, Brown, 1967), pp. 2–3. and 75–78.

5. For a general discussion of psychological reaction to stress, see R. Lazarus, *Psychological Stress and the Coping Process* (New York: McGraw-Hill, 1966), esp. ch. 1, pp. 266–318. This work is particularly useful in providing conceptual distinctions for various phenomena related to the coping process.

6. J.Q. Wilson, *Varieties of Police Behavior* (Cambridge, Mass.: Harvard Univ. Press, 1968), p. 157.

7. D. Walker, *Rights in Conflict* (New York: Bantam, 1968).

8. N. Glazer, "For White and Black Community Control Is the Issue," *New York Times Magazine,* April 27, 1969, p. 46.

9. See the decision of Judge Skelly Wright in *Hobson* v. *Hanson,* June 19, 1967, 269 F. Supp. 401 (1967); see also K. Clark, *Dark Ghetto* (New York: Harper & Row, 1965); see also R. Rosenthal and L. Jacobson, *Pygmalion in the Classroom* (New York: Holt, Rinehart & Winston, 1968), pp. 116–118.

10. R. Rosenthal and L. Jacobson, *op. cit.*

11. J. McNamara, "Uncertainties in Police Work: the Relevance of Police Recruits' Background and Training," in D. Bordua, ed., *op. cit.*

12. For example, the requirements for becoming a building department inspector in New York City have virtually assured the building trade unions of public employment for their members.

13. A. Altshuler, *Community Control: The Black Demand for Participation in American Cities* (New York: Western, 1970). Also M. Kotler, *Neighborhood Government* (Indianapolis: Bobbs-Merrill, 1969).

14. A. Waskow, "Community Control of the Police," *Transaction* (December, 1969). Also, J. Q. Wilson, *op. cit.*

15. A number of writers have commented on the low turnout for elections to CAP and Model Cities boards. See, e.g., A. Altshuler, *op. cit.,* pp. 138–139. On decentralized school board elections, see the issues of the *New York Times* dated from February 19 to March 22, 1970.

16. P. Rossi, *et al.,* "Between White and Black, the Faces of American Institutions in the Ghetto," in *Supplemental Studies for the National Advisory Commission on Civil Disorders* (Washington, D.C.: 1968), pp. 110–113.

17. *Ibid.,* p. 136.

18. See, for example, the *New York Times* of February 13, 1970.

8

ADMINISTRATION OF
THE URBAN NATION

This volume has explored the various managerial, functional, structural, and political problems of urban administration. It has repeatedly underscored what John Rehfuss has observed: ". . . there is no area of administration where nonpolitical issues can be found."[1] But, what are the future prospects for urban administration? Will this blend of politics and administration be able to meet these many problems and challenges? What steps, if any, can be taken to insure its success?

Frederick C. Mosher, for one, has addressed these questions.[2] He has explored the problems urban administrators can expect to face in the future and the way in which they can be prepared to meet these probable future demands through our systems of public service management and higher education. He anticipates an emerging public administration forced to deal with society's increasingly anomalous demands for both greater rationality and irrationality, formality and flexibility, professionalism and participation, and centralization and decentralization. To prepare urban administrators to manage these "social directions and dilemmas," Mosher places a great deal of emphasis on education at the universities. "[T]he universities and colleges do and should have a broad responsibility for preparing public leaders for their occupational roles."[3] But, he continues, universities have failed in four respects to meet this responsibility.[4] First, they have provided a narrow vocational preparation with little exposure "to the society and culture in which they will live and practice their trade." Second, they have encouraged increasing depth and specialization of disciplines and subdisciplines at the cost of interdisciplinary and interprofessional study. Third, they have systematically ignored the "possibilities of social invention, experimentation, innovation, and direction to resolve and correct public problems." Fourth, they have failed to promote continuing education capable of broadening the administrator's knowledge of social problems and developments relevant to agency programs and significant to the continuing understanding of a dynamic society.

Mosher regards these educational shortcomings as becoming increasingly critical; consequently, he calls on universitites and educational planners to redouble their efforts to overcome them. However, as Graham W. Watt, John K. Parker, and Robert R. Cantine point out in "Roles of the Urban Administrator in the 1970s and the Knowledges and Skills Required to Perform These Roles:"

[T]he educator planning a program works largely without the information about the urban administrator's real work world that would help him design a better education program. This information gap is being closed somewhat through continuing education activities of professional associations and training institutes, and through a limited exchange of persons between the academic and practitioner environment; yet, as a general rule the educational planner is not well situated to secure original information. And what is available through secondary source materials is in scarce supply, of questionable quality, and fragmentary in character, with the possible exception of a few case studies.

To develop information about the urban administrator and to contribute thereby to greater knowledge of the changing character and requirements of the public service as a whole, they have conducted, and reported the findings of a series of surveys and workshops designed to obtain "the practitioner's view of the roles of urban administrators and the knowledge and skill requirements they [feel] important to their performance."

Watt, Parker, and Cantine find that urban administrators see themselves as "sitting in the middle of the proverbial kitchen with the stove going full blast." They feel the heat of "the disadvantaged, the disenfranchised, the disenchanted, the establishment, the average taxpayer, [their] superiors, and [their] own organization." In the midst of these conflicting interests, they are expected to respond to new pressures concerning how the community is to be governed procedurally, what the appropriate dimensions of governmental responsibility and response are to be, and how public resources are to be managed to get the job done. Clearly, these conflicts and pressures have expanded the "area of uncertainty" for urban administrators. They have led practitioners to seek particular knowledges and skills to deal with these uncertainties. As Watt, Parker, and Cantine report, they have led urban administrators to seek greater knowledge of human relations, the values motivating people in our urban population, and the causes underlying major urban problems; and greater skills in bargaining and related consensus building techniques, interpersonal relations, situation analysis, analytical thinking, assessing community needs, and delegating authority.

As the co-authors stress, urban administrators seek an education which will prepare them to meet "the challenge of dealing with people and their problems and seeking to achieve agreement from among different points of view." Yet, such an education is very likely impossible. As it is increasingly realized that no area of administration is free from political issues, so, too, it is increasingly recognized that there is no subject matter that can form the basis for principles of administration. In other words, it is increasingly acknowledged that administration is and will remain an art, not a science. As John Rehfuss points out: "At present, training administrators for the public service is still much like coaching artists rather than training scientists."[5] Basically, the urban administrator must be "an expert in human relationships, intelligent, aware of political and social reality, able to tolerate ambiguity, and . . . [committed] to his problem area. Unfortunately, these qualities cannot be extracted from his personality and environment as a whole; there is no way, for example, to teach tolerance for ambiguity."[6] James Q. Wilson is in fundamental agreement:

All the fellowships, internships, and "mid-career training programs" in the world aren't likely to increase . . . [the supply of able experienced executives] very much, simply because the essential qualities for an executive — judgment about men and events, a facility for making good guesses, a sensitivity to political realities, and an ability to motivate others — are things which, if they can be taught at all, cannot be taught systematically or to more than a handful of apprentices at one time.[7]

Education, it appears, is by itself inadequate to assure urban administration success in meeting the problems and challenges of the future. As a consequence, other proposals have also been advanced. One far-reaching proposal has been advanced by Alan Edward Bent in "Administration of the Urban Nation." Bent argues that urban development is "not a self-balancing mechanism." There is a desperate need for increased communication and coordination among the various political subsystems in the United States in order to reverse the "mounting urban chaos, destruction of the physical environment, and the atrophy of the values and mores of civilization." To provide this communication and coordination, he proposes a five-tier federalist framework, consisting of (1) the federal government; (2) the federal regions; (3) the states; (4) the metropolitan councils of government or regional planning institutions; and (5) the local jurisdictions.

Bent's proposal is innovative in that Bent applies a version of the principle of management by objectives to the federal framework and its governance. The concept of management by objectives, emphasizing the integration of external control (by management) and self-control (by subordinates), is urged on our system of intergovernmental relations. Just as in an enterprise, superior and subordinate levels — in this case, levels of government — jointly identify goals, determine each unit's area of responsibility and the expected results, and employ these measures as a means for governing urban America and assessing the contribution of each governmental component. Moreover, it is not a static model; it is prepared to review performance and objectives, and to discard inappropriate goals, and to adjust to a dynamic environment. However, three obstacles block likely adoption of this scheme. First, it departs appreciably from the traditional federal-state-local arrangement with which Americans are accustomed and familiar. Second, it focuses all planning and management responsibility in the political system in the Office of the President, thereby imparting even greater power to America's increasingly "Imperial Presidency," a consequence not likely to win much popular support today. Third, and perhaps most seriously, it is questionable whether this entire five-tier system — with its reliance on efficiency rather than effectiveness — can ever attain the citizen support necessary for it to function properly. The issues of alienation and technology raised in Chapter Five of this volume simply must be confronted. Despite these obstacles, however, Bent's proposed application of management principles and planning to the administration of the urban nation represents an innovative and provocative approach which merits close scrutiny.

Even if Bent's five-tier federalist scheme were to be implemented, the future success of urban administration would still not be assured. As James Q. Wilson has reminded all who take up these issues, there are inherent limits to what can be accomplished by administrative agencies.[8] This is especially true when, as Edward C. Banfield has pointed out in his recent "A Critical View of the Urban Crisis," the major cause of the urban crisis is changes in the states of the public mind.[9] Banfield argues that the causes commonly given to account for the urban crisis are not satisfactory. Thus, congestion has decreased, not increased; the flight of the middle class to the suburbs has not left the central cities on the verge of bankruptcy; housing for the most part has improved; "white racism" has long been on the decline, with blacks making rapid income and other gains; and the fragmentation of local governments does not seem to account for its ineffectiveness. Rather, the urban crisis is the result of "changes in the way things are perceived, judged, and valued, and in the expectations that are formed accordingly."[10] Presently, the state of the public mind stresses

(1) a decline in all forms of authority; (2) a preoccupation with the self and its fulfillment; (3) a rational egotism which justifies any act expected to benefit the individual involved; (4) a "hedonism which takes plenitude rather than scarcity to be the fundamental fact;" (5) an equality of condition which "asserts not that equals should be treated equally, but that all should be treated as if they were the same;" and (6) a consumerism whose moral fervor is directed not against the sins of individuals but rather against those of institutions such as business firms or government.[11] In Banfield's estimation, as long as this state of the public mind prevails, the urban crisis will continue. It will not be "solved or alleviated by governmental programs, however massive,"[12] nor by administrative efforts, however much assisted by educational schemes or five-tier federalism. As this volume has continuously emphasized, politics and administration are intimately intertwined. This relationship bears repeating once again. Even when administrative resolution of the problems that beset urban America becomes possible, the urban crisis may still remain, awaiting the union of a politics willing to work a change in the state of the public mind and an administration dedicated to its success.

Notes

1. John Rehfuss, *Public Administration as Political Process* (New York: Charles Scribner's Sons, 1973), p. 221.

2. Frederick C. Mosher, "The Public Service in the Temporary Society," *Public Administration Review,* XXXII (January, 1971), pp. 47–62.

3. *Ibid.,* p. 59.

4. *Ibid.,* pp. 60–61.

5. Rehfuss, op. cit., p. 221.

6. *Ibid.*

7. James Q. Wilson, "The Bureaucracy Problem," *The Public Interest,* No. 6 (Winter, 1967), p. 7. See also Edward C. Banfield, "The Training of the Executive," *Public Policy,* Vol. X (1960), pp. 16–43. "Possession of such knowledge, indispensable as it is to good judgment, is no guarantee of it. The executive must have also a mysterious faculty – there is no other way of describing it – which enables him to draw correct conclusions more often than does the 'average' person. To the extent that this skill can be learned or developed, it must be learned or developed as other skills are – by doing, and especially by imitation." p. 35.

8. Wilson, *op. cit.,* p. 6.

9. Edward C. Banfield, "A Critical View of the Urban Crisis," *The Annals of the American Academy of Political and Social Sciences,* CDV (January, 1973), p. 13.

10. *Ibid.*

11. *Ibid.*

12. *Ibid.,* p. 14.

GRAHAM W. WATT, JOHN K. PARKER, and ROBERT R. CANTINE

ROLES OF THE URBAN ADMINISTRATOR IN THE 1970s: THE KNOWLEDGE AND SKILLS REQUIRED TO PERFORM THESE ROLES

WHAT ARE WE EDUCATING FOR?

Twenty, ten, five, even one year ago this writer would have answered this query with a great deal more confidence than he possesses in the Spring of 1971 as we plunge deeper into what Peter Drucker has aptly termed the Age of Discontinuity. . . . Alas, much of what I learned at the collegiate and graduate levels and during a quarter century of public service (at various levels of municipal government) is as naught when facing the problems and issues of today — to say nothing of the near future.

The foregoing quotation is from one of forty-seven papers written by urban administrators participating in the assessment of changing requirements for graduate education for future urban administrators.

What has happened that would cause a top flight urban administrator to feel this uncertainty? What changes in role have occurred? What new situations is he facing? What knowledges and skills are essential to what his job is becoming? Should more time be spent in enlarging his knowledge of services delivered by government, or in enlarging his knowledge of individual and group behavior? Is his understanding of the political, social, and economic philosophies that have shaped our urban institutions as important as his knowledge of techniques in governmental planning?

Those responsible for the design of educational programs for urban administrators must come to grips foursquare with these questions as they

Reprinted by permission of the American Academy of Political and Social Science, from Frederic N. Cleaveland (ed.), *Education for Urban Administration* (1973), pp. 50-79.

make choices of program content and emphasis. The results of these choices, reflected in curriculums and instructional methods, may have an important effect on the career effectiveness of urban administrators, current and future.

Choices made by the educational planner involve assumptions, explicit or not, concerning the roles of urban administrators, the balance among these roles, the relative importance of various program and managerial aspects of those roles, and the relevance of various knowledges and skills to the effectiveness of the urban administrator's performance.

But the educator planning a program works largely without the information about the urban administrator's real work world that would help him design a better education program. This information gap is being closed somewhat through continuing education activities of professional associations and training institutes, and through a limited exchange of persons between the academic and practitioner environment; yet, as a general rule the educational planner is not well situated to secure original information. And what is available through secondary source materials is in scarce supply, of questionable quality, and fragmentary in character, with the possible exception of a few case studies.

One of the early efforts addressing this information need of the educator was published in 1957, entitled *Education for Administrative Careers in Public Service.* In addition, the efforts of the former Council on Graduate Education for Public Administration helped to narrow the information gap. But the years that have passed have been characterized by momentous change. The subject is in urgent need of reassessment, for the sake of the educational planner and thus for the sake of the future generation of those seeking careers in the public service.

This particular effort, with its focus on the urban administrator portion of the public service, is intended to contribute toward such a reassessment. Other endeavors with a similar objective, particularly the National Academy for Public Administration's broad study of the needs for education and training in the public service, extend beyond the urban administrator and his needs. We have thus conducted our efforts in developing information about the urban administrator and his world so as to contribute also to greater knowledge of the changing character and requirements of the public service as a whole.

GAINING THE PRACTITIONER'S VIEWS

During the spring and summer of 1971, a series of surveys and workshops was conducted to gain the practitioner's view of the roles of urban administrators and the knowledges and skill requirements they felt important to their performance.

The American Academy of Political and Social Science provided overall sponsorship of these activities to provide a foundation for a symposium, "Educating Urban Administrators." The International City Management Association, National Academy of Public Administration, and Fels Institute Graduate Associates, out of their concern for improving the professional quality of urban administrators, served as general cosponsors and provided staff support for the project. The Lyndon Baines Johnson School of Public Affairs at the University of Texas and the University of Texas Coordinating Board hosted and funded one of the workshops held in Austin, Texas. The Von KleinSmid Center of Public Affairs, University of Southern California, and the Graduate School of Public Administration, University of Kansas, also joined in supporting the Austin, Texas workshop. The main participants were, of course, the more than 130 practitioners who took significant time from their busy schedules either to fill out lengthy questionnaires, prepare written statements, or attend one of the workshops.

It was recognized from the beginning that coverage would be extended only to a selected group of urban administrators and that this sample, limited as it would be, would form the basis for the assessment. Consequently, the sample included as many different job situations as possible, practitioners of various career spans and patterns, various geographic areas of the country, and differing sizes of organization.

Included in the survey were city and county administrators and their assistants; department heads; planning, finance, and personnel directors; professional leaders of regional councils and other regional organizations; senior members of urban research and service organizations; executive officials of civic and community action agencies; principal staff members of professional associations; and key officials in state and federal programs directed at urban areas.

Participants initially were asked to complete an extensive questionnaire focusing on their participation in various service program and managerial activities, the assumed importance of these activities in the future, and the importance of various knowledges and skills for the effective performance of urban administrators.

A smaller number of participants, approximately fifty, prepared short papers, expressing their own ideas, in their own language, on the roles of urban administrators — now and in the future — and the knowledges and skills they felt were important to those roles.

Finally, two workshop sessions were held to bring approximately seventy-five participants together for a face-to-face, in depth discussion of the topic,"Educating Urban Administrators." These discussions were taped and transcribed.

We think the information is of considerable value to educators. We will use extensively in this paper the questionnaire responses, prepared papers, and workshop discussions to provide the content and tone of what practitioners see the job of urban administrator becoming, how the urban administrator participates in the various aspects of community governance, and what knowledges and skills he sees necessary for effective performance. In doing so we have necessarily provided a framework for this information derived from our own experience as urban administrators.

WHAT IS THE JOB BECOMING?

Yet this very fact — that of coping with accelerating change — is what has made urban administration so challenging, interesting, and dynamic. Truly it is the job where the action is, where there is never a dull moment, and where no two days on the job are ever alike.

This statement is from a paper prepared by the manager of a suburban township. It emphasizes the environment of change within which the urban administrator continuously seeks to find his various roles. These roles are forged from the urban administrator's own expectations concerning his behavior and from the expectations that others have of him.

The context within which these roles can be assessed centers on the critical choices made by the body politic concerning community governance. As we see these choices in broad perspective there are at least three:

1. determining the procedural aspects of how the community should be governed, that is, who does what, when and how;
2. determining the appropriate dimensions of governmental responsibility and response for the safety, health, and welfare of the community;
3. determining how best to manage public resources to get the job done.

The urban administrator continuously searches for his appropriate role in making these determinations, and based upon his findings exercises the future responsibilities which follow. Each of these three critical choice situations bears further exploration. Here are some of the conclusions that emerged from our inquiry.

Determining the procedural aspects of community governance

Of fundamental significance to the urban administrator is the matter of his participation in the task of developing and applying the procedures manual for how the community will be governed. The central problem is one of determining how issues will be processed. Who will participate and when? How will issues be presented? This aspect of community governance involves not only internal rules within his agency or community but also relating each of these to their environment, including other agencies and levels of government.

The urban administrator brings to his task two perspectives, not necessarily separate: (1) his own role in making program and managerial policy as it is affected by the rules; and (2) the public interest as it is similarly affected. To what extent, and in what way, the urban administrator participates, or has an opportunity to affect the process, is determined partly through formal instruments such as the city charter and position controls. However, the English language is often ambiguous. Moreover, there continuously arise situations for which there are no established precedents to govern the urban administrator's behavior. Under these conditions there exists considerable flexibility for the urban administrator's participation.

In their own essays, practitioners described in a variety of ways their changing role in determining procedural aspects of community governance:

1. The urban administrator will increasingly be expected to assist in the process of allocating responsibility to various governmental units — that is, defining what are local, state, and federal affairs.

2. Administrators should push for the inclusion of the disadvantaged and speak for those who do not sit at the decision-making table.

3. The emerging formality of citizen participation is placing new demands on the urban administrator. He is being called up . . . to decentralize services and increase opportunities for citizen involvement in the decision-making process. . . . He must strive to increase the visibility and accessibility of municipal agencies by using such approaches as ombudsmen, community advocates, and neighborhood city halls and service centers. New mechanisms need to be developed for obtaining citizen input before decisions are made and for monitoring feedback regarding ongoing programs.

These three practitioners point to the urban administrator's increasing obligation to be aware of whom the system serves, whose voices are heard in the formation of policy, and where responsibility rests for the resolution of various issues. His actions in the future will call for the application of values that are fundamental to determining how the community will govern itself.

Many of the tough issues reported by practitioners in the survey reveal more pointedly the nature of the urban administrator's participation in determining how issues will be processed. Consider these examples:

1. whether to develop a Citizen's Advisory Committee for preparing a Comprehensive Plan and select its composition;
2. whether to recommend appointment of a Citizen's Advisory Committee for housing;
3. whether and how to establish a system of ward-based town meetings;
4. whether the city should divest itself of health functions and organize an area-wide agency for the same service at lower cost;
5. whether to bargain for employees before city council or let employees unionize and bargain with city council directly;
6. how to get the city council to listen to the administrator's advice before taking public positions;
7. whether to continue executive briefing sessions for the council;
8. how to determine the most effective methods to inform the public on city activities and problems;
9. how to communicate with thirty-six community groups;
10. how to deal with private interest groups and individuals who wanted to strengthen the roles of advisory boards;
11. how to keep the council out of purely administrative matters.

This list easily can be expanded to illustrate other aspects of the urban administrator's involvement in determining how the system is to function. What items should be placed on the meeting agenda? When should they appear? Should the departmental budget be submitted to the community?

These specific choice situations go on almost ad infinitum, some more critical than others, some with longer-term effect than others, some initiated by the urban administrator, while others are thrust upon him. But each reflects his participation in determining which issues are processed through the governmental system, how they are to be processed, and who participates at various stages in the process.

In a slow-moving situation these choices may occur less frequently and permit the luxury of intense analysis. In other cases, the urban administrator may be bombarded with several crises simultaneously, severely straining his ability to do more than note the events as they fly by. But by and large, simply by virtue of his position, he is an active participant in this procedural aspect of community governance. In these times of criticism of the system, the task is becoming ever more delicate and sensitive. It goes almost without saying that what happens in this area of policy reflects directly upon the urban administrator's roles in other policy areas.

Determining the dimensions of governmental responsibility and response

In addition to choices about functioning of the system, the body politic makes choices concerning governmental responsibility for community life. Several determinations are encountered. First, in what areas of community life is it desirable for government to assume responsibility? Second, what should be the nature of this responsibility, for example, regulator, operator, enforcer? Third, to what level of service should the government commit itself? Fourth, what is the appropriate response to bring about the desired effect?

These questions call for the application not only of values, but also of analytical ability, legal judgments, political acumen, salesmanship, and a host of other skills and tools that may be essential to the resolution of the issues.

However, in these times of questioning, habit and tradition are challenged for their consequences. Furthermore, there is widespread recognition that the public sector can have a critical impact on the community's standard of living, even in well-to-do communities. In addition, the rapid pace of change in knowledge, values, and technology has contributed to experimentation with new living styles and a feeling that very few things are impossible if commitment and resources are available. In this environment the political system faces a real challenge in responding to questions of responsibility, scope, type, and level of service.

What is the role of the urban administrator? What is expected of him and what does he expect of himself? Excerpts from the short essays written by practitioners help us understand what they see their role becoming:

Thus, the generalist administrator might spend his time . . . faithfully advocating the consumer while drawing elected officials into a common camp with the oppressed and disenchanted; and developing a sense of community whereby neighborhoods not only have clean streets and fire protection but neighborliness, life, jobs, opportunity, hope, and dignity. Not a small order but not unreachable.

Administrators now and in the future must seek to achieve a more equitable way of allocating benefits and resources to groups that have been omitted from participating in our society.

He must acquire political acumen that will cause him not to be labeled as purely a nuts and bolts paper-shuffling, accounting, internal management administrator but rather a politically responsible, effective policy executive who can marshal total community and regional resources to solve community problems and meet community opportunities.

The most significant role of the urban administrator today is his influence on policy formulation. He has the facts about existing conditions. He has the data on the unmet needs and unsolved problems. He has access to the literature and his peers to learn of possible solutions. Hopefully, he has some creativity to develop new solutions.

The urban administrator has to be a developer of new programs. Once he has demonstrated the competence to find new solutions or encourage his subordinates to do so, he must help persuade their acceptance by the legislative body or the public.

Managers should throw themselves into the role of political leader of the community if this is necessary to fill a vacuum that often exists. . . . If this is not done the urban community may not get the leadership it so desperately requires to bring itself back together as a viable entity.

The urban administrator must be a social engineer responsive to the community's social needs as well as its physical needs. He must be able to respond effectively to needs of the disadvantaged who are increasingly becoming a very vocal element within the urban area.

It is my contention that the major role of the urban administrator is to act as a catalyst for the reallocation of resources to people-oriented programs.

Advocacy role: here, the job is to plead the case of the disadvantaged — the poor, the minorities, the young — before his own agency.

The role of administrators as consensus seekers of conflicting interests and the conversion of those interests into policy recommendations and programs is a growing and vital role.

The urban administrator seems to function best as a broker, in the old sense of the word; as one who is paid a fee for acting as an agent in the making of an agreement. The urban administrator never fully understands the process he goes through, or does he need to. The manager, as broker, must know what the demands for change are and what is possible within the system. In most cases the manager serves as the one who searches for the possible. The manager's influence and authority rests on his ability to seek and find the possible. This is what his expertise is built upon.

This image of the manager (as broker) seems to work smoothly as long as there are no absolutes for managers. The manager, however, always seems to have to face the moment when there is no possible way, only the just way. That moment varies with every manager, and so does the response. It can only be said that every manager must leave his (broker's) role when his own conscience dictates. Every manager is a man, and his moral problems are no less complex than those of Hamlet.

One of the most vital roles of the urban administrator is as a planner. This role involves policy formulation and a determination of what is in the public interest in a given situation.

For these practitioners the role of the urban administrator is more and more one of continuous and intensive involvement in all aspects of determining the dimensions of governmental responsibility and response. He becomes both philosopher king and high-powered analyst. He becomes sensor of the human situation, pleader for the cause, and searcher for the possible. He becomes a needs identifier for all segments of the community; special advocate for the disadvantaged; broker of differences, seeking the possible; moral human being who must live with his conscience; developer of solutions to bring about the desired effect; salesman for his ideas; action clock for the community with a sense of timing for action; and protector of, and promoter of, change in community values.

Yet not all urban administrators agree with these role concepts. The disagreements are illustrated in the following terms by two urban administrators, one a city manager and the other a Model Cities Program executive:

With all these new roles added on to the importance of preserving the essential administrative role, the question becomes, can the urban administrator be all things to all people? This is a very real question for which I have no answer than to observe that many urban positions are being created which are essentially man killers. . . . The only area of remedy I can suggest is . . . the role of facilitator of change. I would suggest that with everything else, the urban administrator should not take it upon himself to become a forcer of change. The role of primary policy leadership should be left to others. This permits him to play a more appropriate staff role to the policy changers and does not draw as greatly upon the energy which is required for him to play his other roles.

It is my opinion that the structure of local government will materially change during the 1970s. . . . I foresee an emphasis on placing more responsibility and authority upon the elected offices of mayor and councilmen. . . . Such a change in the environment within which urban administrators operate will result in the administrator acting more as a technician and less as an outward initiator of policy and political spokesman for the city.

For different reasons both statements argue that the urban administrator's role as outward advocate of various social, economic, or political policies will be limited. Both arguments are strong — job survival, and the possible advent of structural change affecting leadership roles. However, the projection of a stronger advocacy role prevailed among the majority of these urban administrators.

Evidences of what these roles mean in operational terms are illustrated by the types of tough issues encountered by urban administrators as reported in their questionnaires, including:

1. seeking to strengthen citizen planning board responsibility even though its members were not supported by the council;

2. providing personnel and equipment to black citizens groups to help them clean the neighborhood;

3. deciding whether to assert the administrator's own recommendations in a highly volatile citizen participation setting;

4. seeking legal action by federal authorities to halt local discriminatory practices;

5. pushing for equalization of refuse collection in all neighborhoods;

6. obtaining consensus on a major new administrative position to deal with youth needs of the community;

7. seeking modification of civil service rules to open jobs to the disadvantaged;

8. recommending against using the city housing agency for suburban, low-income housing;

9. deciding whether to recommend funding new neighborhood grants to build neighborhood action if it meant cutting other services;

10. choosing whether to recommend the enactment of local open housing regulations in light of federal action;

11. facing a split council over the building of public housing;

12. determining how stringently to enforce the new housing code;

13. selling realtors and developers on a public housing program;

14. deciding whether to play the leading role in achieving local consensus on expressway routes;

15. choosing among economy, environment, the travelling public, and the neighborhood in aligning major streets;

16. developing and proposing very strict controls on commercial uses along major arterials;

17. determining whether to assume public operation of a hospital;

18. undertaking conversion of private mental health operations to public funding and control;

19. recommending increases in the welfare department budget that were opposed by a large segment of the community.

A far greater number of tough issues/problems were actually cited by the urban administrators, illustrating the nature and extent to which they have been, and are now, involved in determining the dimensions of governmental responsibility and response. This role is intensive, continuous, and full of hazards. What these practitioners have said to the educational planner about the future is to expect a further extension of their participation in raising and seeking resolution to the people problems of urban areas, with all the consequences this portends for their need to perform as brokers, salesmen, analysts, and so forth.

The urban administrator, like the educational planner, is faced with choices in terms of where he concentrates his energies among various program areas. How he allocates his involvement is partly a reflection of his community's needs, but also is partly a result of his personal choice among competing needs. For those surveyed, Tables 1 and 2 illustrate career-to-date involvement in various service programs and how the importance of these services is expected to change in the future.

If an educator had to choose the five service categories for which greatest substantive knowledge should be imparted through continuing or pre-entry professional education, responses of this group of practitioners concerning career-to-date involvement might turn the educator's attention towards ecology/environment, public order, land use, transportation, and employment. Least attention would be given to welfare, public health and education.

TABLE 1

Extent of Career-to-Date Involvement by Service Category (n = 133)

Category	No Answer*	Limited	Moderate	Extensive	Weighted Score**
Ecology	7	25	51	50	2.20
Public Order	5	32	42	54	2.17
Land Use	10	30	44	48	2.13
Transportation	15	32	42	44	2.10
Employment	15	36	38	44	2.07
Economic Development	15	35	47	36	2.01
Housing	12	38	47	36	1.98
Race Relations	12	50	38	33	1.86
Education	27	48	39	19	1.73
Public Health	15	66	29	23	1.64
Welfare	30	73	16	14	1.43

*Includes "no involvement" and unusable responses.
**Weighted score is formed by weighting responses as follows:
    Limited = 1, Moderate = 2, Extensive = 3, and then dividing the sum of these products by the number of respondents.

Such a conclusion, however, would be too simplistic. Broad differences of involvement exist within several of the categories, particularly public order, housing, transportation, employment, economic development, and race relations. In several of these service categories significant proportions of these practitioners have experienced limited, moderate, or extensive involvement, reflecting perhaps their unique local situations.

Secondly, if their assessments of the relative future importance of these categories prove correct and bear any relationship to future involvement, then such service areas as ecology, housing and race relations will take on increasing importance. These assessments, it should be noted, are highly consistent with the practitioner's role descriptions quoted earlier, in which they stressed their growing responsibilities as advocates and pleaders for the disadvantaged and minority groups, and as active participants in the formulation of policies affecting the human situation in urban areas.

TABLE 2
Future Importance by Service Category

Category	No Opinion	Less Important	No Change	More Important	% More Important
Ecology	12	1	14	106	88%
Housing	21	1	16	95	85
Race Relations	22	3	26	82	74
Public Health	27	4	28	72	68
Employment	20	4	34	75	66
Public Order	14	4	36	79	66
Transportation	20	5	38	70	62
Welfare	44	14	22	53	60
Education	37	3	39	54	56
Land Use	19	2	48	64	56
Economic Development	21	5	59	48	43

How best to manage public resources

Whatever decisions are made concerning the procedural aspects of community governance and dimensions of governmental responsibility and response, there remains the conventional task of managing the public enterprise to get the job done. Despite the image of management as the urban administrator's traditional role, there are many cases of promise outstripping performance — of severe breakdowns in effective, efficient, and sensitive delivery of service. For the disadvantaged this failure has often meant further suffering. For the average taxpayer it has often added to frustration and anger, leading to the not-so-pleasant taxpayers' revolt. How do urban administrators view their management role? Consider these excerpts from their own statements:

To me the vital part of the urban administrator is his administrative sense. This intangible commodity is that knowledge and ability needed to get a job done, including the division of work into subordinate tasks, the identification of the sequential logic between tasks, and the ability to assign limited and specialized resources to the accomplishment of the various subtasks in a reasonably efficient manner.

He must be an organizational leader employing concepts of team management and management by objectives. He must seek out and cultivate the talents of his staff and integrate them with a coordinated management team.

The manager provides the leadership for change within the organization. He creates the atmosphere for innovation.

In managing his organization the urban administrator sets goals, shapes strategies for their fulfillment, marshals resources, sets them into motion, monitors progress, and takes corrective action when necessary. . . . He has to be constantly aware of and sensitive to what is going on both inside and outside his organization and what the implications are for the organization.

There are at least two important facets to the role of any urban administrator — (a) conducting the ongoing affairs of the organization for which he is responsible, and (b) reshaping the organization as necessary to better meet the responsibilities set upon it.

The urban administrator is or can be a leader of the administrative organization. He can provide direction, energy, and moral tone for the staff. He can encourage career development through further education, training, and increased responsibility.

The urban administrator must be an evaluator, not only of the new programs he has developed as they move into fruition but also of those which he has inherited. . . . The conclusions [of his evaluation] must be put into effect to modify the activity when it is needed.

While highlighting the general nature of their managerial role, several practitioners viewed the managerial function from a different perspective:

The urban administrator will delegate to functional specialists the management of, and decision-making involving the traditional local departments. In so doing, his role in departmental matters will become more passive except for major items or interdepartmental disputes.

Secondly, the administrator will be further removed from operational line and staff matters which have consumed much of his time and energy and these matters will be increasingly handled by better trained technicians.

Basically, these practitioners see their managerial role becoming one of using the organization creatively, adapting it to new circumstances, and orchestrating the responses of its various components. While not contradictory, the emphasis on delegation of authority does stress a fairly commonly held viewpoint among these practitioners that, for reasons of developing and retaining an effective management team as well as to achieving more effective allocation of his time, the urban administrator will delegate whatever tasks he can. As one practitioner put it:

Managers tend to delegate anything and everything they can. They end up with a repository of things they haven't figured out how to delegate and those are the things they spend their time on.

From the standpoint of fulfilling managerial responsibilities, the most interesting part of this statement is the repository of things they haven't figured out how to delegate. For along with some of the more routine managerial tasks the urban administrator ends up performing, his managerial role has come to involve some very unconventional challenges. The nuts and bolts of management have taken on new dimensions.

The old concept of budgeting as a control mechanism is made secondary to its critical importance in policy formulation. Skyrocketing costs, slow revenue growth, and citizen outrage at growing tax bills have forced the urban administrator to squeeze more performance out of his organization. The old concept of the executive budget, open to citizen scrutiny on sort of a referendum basis, is giving way to the notion of early community input. The remolding of the budget document and process to focus on results and performance has introduced a new complexity into the program planning and budgeting process, requiring new analytical and communication skills.

In the medium- and larger-size cities and counties the pressure continues to mount for neighborhood or area management, requiring development and experimentation with new organizational structures oftentimes involving large overhead costs. If the movement to pattern decentralized management after the Model Cities concept succeeds, many of the old forms of organization and the principles upon which they were based are in for a real wrenching.

The systems approach has also taken its toll on organizational arrangements as the conflict is exposed between old organizational boundaries and the need to coordinate a complex network of resources necessary to accomplish specific results.

For the urban administrator, internal organizational and management problems are also compounded by changing patterns of intergovernmental relations. While there is movement toward decentralization at the local level, at the same time there is pressure for allocation of certain responsibilities on a regional scale, generated in part by urban administrators working at the regional level. Moreover, with the increasing entanglement of local, regional, state, and federal governments, it becomes more essential for the urban administrator to gain knowledge of, and access to, these centers of influence. In addition, the management burdens of high overhead costs, inflexible use of manpower, excessive paper pushing, and intricate grants procedures associated with state and federal assistance programs have further complicated the management task.

At the community level the community organization movement has added to the unconventional challenges facing the urban administrator. In particular, the maze of quasi-public enterprises, such as non-profit housing corporations, have added to the expanding range of management requirements associated with coordination of service delivery.

These unconventional management challenges emphasize perhaps most heavily the task of communication — upwards, downwards, and outwards. The intensity of exchanges, complexity of the information to be exchanged, and the points to which communication is directed have all multiplied. The characteristics of those for whom the message is intended are also varied and must be considered in the communication.

The types of tough issues or problems urban administrators mention in describing their managerial roles reflect some of the conventional and unconventional challenges that make up their real world, including:

1. handling a walk-out by sanitation employees;
2. averting strikes with four employee unions;
3. taking action when council refuses to accept a negotiating agreement with employees;
4. modifying civil service rules to open jobs to disadvantaged;
5. seeking to persuade cities, counties, and other special districts to join a regional sewerage program;
6. recommending only a two percent raise for all city employees;
7. cutting personnel drastically while maintaining essential services;
8. hiring social workers to do police work related to narcotics abuse;
9. determining when to break up an existing organization and remold and restructure activities;
10. directing municipal activities during student demonstrations;
11. coping with complexities introduced by the use of new management approaches such as Program, Planning, Budgeting (PPB), management by objectives, and so on;
12. administering the personnel system equitably in the face of a need to reduce staff;
13. helping to shape up subordinates for job responsibilities; firing incompetents;

14. changing organizational structure to handle urban development problems;

15. achieving an equalization of refuse collection;

16. granting a request from the Human Relations Commissioner for a community relations program over objections of public safety employees;

17. determining the level of police service;

18. developing an adequate executive reporting system for managerial decisions — without entailing extreme overhead costs;

19. determining an appropriate allocation and means of coordination of central and departmental planning;

20. achieving increased employee productivity;

21. achieving coordination of housing and human resource programs within the organization and with outside agencies and community organizations.

Some feeling for how these practitioners extend themselves in various managerial activities, and the importance they see these activities taking on in the future, is shown from their questionnaire responses set forth in Tables 3 and 4.

In terms of current personal involvement, the educator would find that determining the budget and related financial strategies, maintaining effective relations with superiors, and determining appropriate organizational structures stand out as demanding the most extensive involvement of urban administrators.

Responses to the survey also suggest that urban administrators are extensively involved in planning and designing governmental programs, determining policy and program priorities, directing program operations under emergency or politically sensitive situations, determining operating systems and procedures, administering personnel management, and seeking the cooperation of other jurisdictions or levels of government.

Finally, their responses suggest the urban administrator is least personally involved in establishing communication systems for sending or receiving information about his organization or community, and for involving citizens, particularly minority groups, in the decision-making process.

However, the educator would want to look further at the extent of variation in these responses for additional clues to guide his educational planning. If he did, he would find several very different patterns.

On the one hand, there exist cases of near unanimity on the extent of the urban administrator's involvement. This is particularly true with respect to their extensive involvement in determining the budget and related financial strategies. On the other hand, the educational planner would find a second pattern that reflected broad differences in the involvement of urban administrators within a particular managerial activity, for

TABLE 3
Extent of Current Personal Involvement by Managerial Category (n = 133)

Category	No Answer*	Limited	Moderate	Extensive	Weighted Score**
Determine budget and other financial strategies	14	12	27	80	2.57
Develop and maintain relationship with governing body or other superiors	16	13	33	71	2.50
Determine organizational structure	24	13	35	61	2.44
Plan and design govermental programs	33	13	42	45	2.32
Determine policy and program priorities	29	21	31	52	2.30
Direct and administer program operations, particularly under emergency conditions or in politically sensitive situations	34	28	32	45	2.29
Determine operating systems and procedures	19	19	45	50	2.27
Administer personnel systems and procedures including recruitment, selection and discipline of key employees	16	24	40	53	2.25
Seek the cooperation of other governmental levels and neighboring jurisdictions whose cooperation is critical to success of a program	13	23	44	53	2.25
Develop and maintain a communication system both for sending directives and for keeping informed about community and organizational development	29	26	44	34	2.08
Negotiate with employee unions and other employee groups	15	53	30	43	2.07
Involve citizens, particularly minorities and disadvantaged persons, effectively in the decision-making process	16	33	52	32	1.99

*Includes "no involvement" and unusable responses.

**Weighted score is formed by weighting responses as follows: Limited = 1, Moderate = 2, Extensive = 3, and then dividing the sum of these products by the number of respondents.

TABLE 4
Future Importance by Managerial Category (n = 133)

Category	No Opinion	Less Important	No Change	More Important	% More Important
Involve citizens, particularly minorities and disadvantaged persons effectively in the decision-making process	22	1	23	87	78
Seek the cooperation of other governmental levels and neighboring jurisdictions whose cooperation is critical to success of a program	14	1	28	90	76
Negotiate with employee unions and other employee groups	25	19	27	62	57
Determine organizational structure	31	2	44	56	55
Determine budget and other financial strategies	16	7	53	57	49
Develop and maintain a communication system both for sending directives and for keeping informed about community and organizational developments	38	1	49	45	47
Direct and administer program operations, particularly under emergency conditions or in politically sensitive situations	36	5	46	46	47
Plan and design governmental programs	41	1	40	41	45
Develop and maintain relationships with governing body or other superiors	24	2	60	47	43
Determine operating systems and procedures	26	14	59	34	32
Administer personnel systems and procedures including recruitment, selection and discipline of key employees	24	8	67	34	31
Determine organizational structure	35	12	58	28	29

example, involving citizens in the decision-making process. Here there is almost an equal likelihood that an urban administrator will have limited, substantial, or extensive involvement.

Finally, the educator would find at least one case of very sharp differences reflecting a situation in which the urban administrator is either involved extensively or almost not at all in a particular managerial activity, for example, negotiations with labor unions.

When the educator looks at how urban administrators assessed the future importance of these managerial activities, he might draw the following inferences. First, few, if any, categories of managerial activity will be less important to the effective performance of an urban administrator in the immediate future.

Second, urban administrators indicated strongly that intergovernmental relations and citizen involvement will take on increasing importance to the effective performance of urban administrators.

Third, such aspects of managerial responsibility as personnel management, an appropriate organizational structure, and established operating systems and procedures will remain nearly constant in their importance.

Finally, for several managerial activities, including budgeting, program planning, developing and maintaining a communication system, and directing program operations under emergency or politically sensitive situations, there is an absence of agreement about their changing importance in the future.

THE URBAN ADMINISTRATOR'S NEED FOR KNOWLEDGE AND SKILLS

Although it is tempting to recommend that a modern urban administrator needs the skill and knowledge of a Renaissance man, the administrator must always be learning. (Excerpted from an urban administrator's comments on graduate programs.)

The educator, in order to market his program or to fit it within a fixed time frame, must make choices among what skills and knowledges he will try to impart. What should the content of his program be? What knowledges and skills are important to the effective performance of urban administrators?

This was no easy question for the practitioners themselves, despite their continuous experience with situations calling for the application of particular knowledges or skills. With their enlarged domain of activities has come a sense of need for new knowledges and skills. Tables 5 and 6, taken from their questionnaire responses, reveal what they sensed as most or

TABLE 5

Importance of Various Categories of Knowledge (n = 133)

Category	No Answer*↑	Least Important	Moderately Important	Most Important	Weighted Score**
Knowledge of human relations i.e., theories of individual and group behavior relevant to managing organizations	6	9	34	84	2.59
Knowledge of values motivating the behavior of people in urban areas	6	16	44	67	2.40
Knowledge of causes underlying major urban problems	6	9	57	61	2.39
Knowledge of various political institutions and processes	6	19	59	49	2.24
Knowledge of social characteristics, institutions and processes of urban areas	11	18	63	41	2.19
Knowledge of concepts in personnel administration, including labor relations	6	15	84	28	2.10
Knowledge of urban economic development including both public and private sector	7	27	56	41	2.08
Knowledge of the history and aspiration of minority and disadvantaged groups and how these characteristics are reflected in contemporary behavior	7	25	78	23	1.98
Knowledge of organization principles and practices	6	37	59	31	1.95
Knowledge of principles and practices of governmental planning	6	49	60	19	1.78
Knowledge of specific services government provides its citizens: health care, welfare, model cities, etc.	6	62	44	21	1.68
Knowledge of various techniques such as data processing, information systems, etc.	6	65	43	19	1.64
Knowledge of engineering principles	6	110	12	5	1.09

*Includes "no response" and unusable responses.
**Weighted score is formed by weighting responses as follows: Limited = 1, Moderate = 2, Extensive = 3, and then dividing the sum of these products by the number of respondents.

TABLE 6

Importance of Various Categories of Skills (n = 133)

Category	No Answer*	Least Important	Moderately Important	Most Important	Weighted Score**
Skill in situation analysis i.e., "sizing-up" the community political milieu, organization, and staff	6	16	39	72	2.57
Skill in bargaining, negotiation and other consensus-seeking techniques	6	13	32	82	2.54
Skill in handling interpersonal relations	7	13	47	66	2.42
Skill in analytical thinking, problem solving and associated techniques of analysis including those employed in program evaluation	6	18	42	67	2.39
Skill in assessing community needs	7	23	49	54	2.25
Skill in the process of delegating authority and responsibility to subordinates	7	20	55	51	2.25
Skill in relating to and understanding minority, disadvantaged, and other culturally distinctive groups	8	23	69	33	2.08
Skill in audience-oriented communication, i.e., speaking effectively	8	31	55	39	2.06
Skill in financial analysis	7	59	49	18	1.67
Skill in organizing and writing policy statements, reports, etc.	7	74	37	15	1.53
Skill in system design and operations analysis	8	94	25	7	1.32
Skill in job analysis, i.e., assessing the requirements and responsibilities of positions	7	106	14	6	1.21

*Includes "no response" and unusable responses.
**Weighted score is formed by weighting responses as follows: Limited = 1, Moderate = 2, Extensive = 3, and then dividing the sum of these products by the number of respondents.

least important for the future in terms of knowledge and skills.

In terms of knowledge areas, the practitioners assigned greatest importance to knowledge of human relations, knowledge of values motivating people in our urban population, and knowledge of causes underlying major urban problems. During later workshop sessions and in their essays, knowledge of one's self and knowledge of various social, economic, and political philosophies also stood out prominently. They would have the educator place least importance on knowledge relating to technological innovation, engineering principles, the specific services rendered by government, and the principles of governmental planning.

These emphases are consistent with the urban administrator's role perceptions requiring sensing of the human situation in urban communities, dealing directly with individual people and their values, and achieving improvement in the quality of community life. These responsibilities are not accomplished by the urban administrator in solo — but by working with people — individual citizens, community groups, elected officials, employees in his own organization, and so forth. Success must also be achieved in the context of political institutions and processes — existing or new — set up to handle the processing of community issues and management of the public enterprise. And to deal with the challenges, frustrations, disappointments, and successes of his job, the urban administrator must understand not only others, but himself as well.

Although he may be possessor of considerable knowledge relevant to his roles, achieving their fulfillment demands the acquisition of particular skills which facilitate the application of knowledge to the situations he encounters. Here the urban administrator would have the educator turn most of his attention toward skill in bargaining and related consensus building techniques, skill in handling interpersonal relations, skill in situation analysis, skill in analytical thinking and processes, skill in assessing community needs, and skill in the process of delegating authority.

The practitioner's emphasis again focuses on the challenge of dealing with people and their problems and seeking to achieve agreement from among different points of view. This applies not only to people in the community but also to those in his administrative organization. In the case of the latter, there is a clear implication that if the urban administrator is to devote such a substantial part of his energies to outside roles — developing effective relations with superiors, developing effective community participation, and seeking the cooperation of other jurisdictions and levels of government — the orderly functioning of the public enterprise will require that he be capable of, and skilled in, the process of delegating authority and responsibility. Reflected in his assessment of what skills are least important is his rejection of the role of technical expert and his view of the changing nature of the nuts and bolts of his managerial role.

SUMMARY

Our analysis and review of the practitioner's responses, prepared statements, and workshop discussion have been outlined in the foregoing sections.

It has been clear throughout their responses that these urban administrators feel new pressures on their jobs, and upon the public enterprise as a whole. These new pressures stem partly from society's enlarged expectations concerning the appropriate dimensions of governmental responsibility. The pressures are also partly a product of the complex and quickly changing environment in which public issues get raised, debated, and acted upon.

These practitioners see the urban administrator sitting in the middle of the proverbial kitchen with the stove going full blast. He is feeling the heat of the disadvantaged, the discriminated-against, the disenchanted, the establishment, the average taxpayer, his superiors, and his own organization.

Among the many conflicting interests he will have to find the possible, or when conscience dictates, stand as an advocate of what he sees as the just way. While he will necessarily be an active participant in determining how issues will be processed through the public system, he will have to have a keen sensitivity for the consequences of these determinations on the participation of all segments of the community. His sensitivity must extend equally to determinations of the appropriate dimensions of governmental responsibility and response.

He will identify community needs, plead actively for various causes, serve his superiors and the community as high-powered analyst, serve as salesman for his ideas, serve as strategy developer, and act to protect, or promote change in community values.

Along with these roles he remains the leader of his organization and responsible for effective, efficient, and sensitive delivery of service. For most of the decisions in this policy area, the buck stops here. Although often considered the conventional role of the urban administrator, management is, and will be, full of unconventional challenges.

In all of this, the urban administrator will be enlarging his areas of uncertainty. The areas where events and responses are more or less under his control will be diminishing correspondingly. He will face an open system with changing actors and centers of influence.

From this perspective of their roles, these practitioners expressed an

urgent need for knowledges and skills that will help them cope more effectively with growing uncertainty. In particular, they attach increasing
importance to knowledge of individual and group behavior, political institutions and processes, causes underlying major urban problems — not
merely a description of the problems — values motivating people in our
urban population, a thorough understanding of themselves, and a deeper
appreciation of social, economic, and political philosophies which have
shaped and are shaping our institutions.

To act effectively in his changing world, the urban administrator will
require skills that will help him bargain and build consensus, cope with
sensitive people relationships, size up his organizational and community
situation, perform his analytical tasks in a complex environment, assess
community needs, and effectively delegate authority to other members
of the team. Enhanced skills in these areas will contribute to his ability
to cope with the ambiguities and uncertainties of his changing job.

STEPS TOWARD IMPROVED EDUCATION
FOR URBAN ADMINISTRATORS

For many practitioners it would probably be a real awakening to
return to the campus and observe the skills and knowledges being taught
to the new generation of urban administrators. Some parts would be hailed
as significant advances, other parts would be judged irrelevant.

But if there is to be a reasonable degree of correspondence between
the career being prepared for and what is imparted through the formal and
continuing education process, then many curriculums and approaches to
instruction will have to be revamped. Educators will have to be concerned
with the development of the whole individual and the situations he will
face, not just with certifying that he or she has made passing grades.

Access to knowledge and skills must not be dependent upon whether
a person is pursuing a master's or doctorate, but rather geared to meeting
the end product objectives of an educational program which corresponds
to the dimensions of the real world toward which the student is oriented.
Too often, other criteria prevail in determining program content.

Underlying all of this is the necessity and desirability of increased
collaboration between educational planners and the practitioners. This
collaboration can take a variety of forms, including consultation between
professional associations and educational planners, participation of practitioners in the development and conduct of the educational program, and
participation of educational planners in the world of the practitioners.

For the practitioner who sits back and complains about the quality

of education for urban administrators, he should be reminded that there is
a two-way street to improvement. Only an active partnership between
educators and practitioners can enable higher levels of achievement for
each and it is incumbent on both groups to take initiative to bring about
this partnership.

ALAN EDWARD BENT

ADMINISTRATION OF THE URBAN NATION

Modern systems analysis suggests that a socio-cultural system with high adaptive potential, or integration as we might call it, requires some optimum level of both stability and flexibility: a relative stability of the social-psychological foundations of interpersonal relations and of the cultural meanings and value hierarchies that hold group members together in the same universe of discourse and, at the same time, a flexibility of structural relations characterized by the lack of strong barriers to change, along with a certain propensity for reorganizing the current institutional structure should environmental challenges or emerging internal conditions suggest the need. A central feature of the complex, adaptive system is its capacity to persist or develop by changing its own structure, sometimes in fundamental ways.[1]

The linkage between the system and the environment are boundary-crossing transactions by way of inputs-outputs. These transactional processes of exchange are dependent upon reliable communication networks and information flows. Information is the regulator of the feedback loop and keys the political system to necessary behavior modifications and structural changes for coping with changes in the environment. Feedback enlightens the self-steering system about its proximity to objectives, thus enabling behavior modification, if required, for purposive goal-seeking. Management is the critical system component for the achievement of communication and control. Management is the information-processing function which converts data about system objectives, environment, components, and resources into action outputs.

Reprinted from Alan Edward Bent, *Escape from Anarchy*, (1972), pp. 155–183, by permission of Memphis State University Press.

Management is the "steersman" of the political system. It generates plans for the system's execution, and insures their implementation. Management is the control center of the system's "cybernetic loop" with the environment. It institutes appropriate information systems in order to best evaluate the system's performance *vis à vis* its goals, and, through the feedback cycle, is able to correct goal-deviating execution. Hence, management is the fact-finding and action component indispensable to systemic transformation for persistence. However, systems management cannot provide its essential contributions to system persistence unless it is tied to the power foci of the political system. Fact-finding is often divorced from the action processes in the political system, thereby negating the potential attributes of efficacious control centers. Cybernetics feedback and action must be integrated; Kurt Lewin suggests that for fact-finding to be effective, it

. . . has to be linked with the action organization itself: it has to be part of a feedback system which links a reconnaissance branch of the organization with the branches which do the action. The feedback has to be done so that a discrepancy between the desired and the actual direction leads "automatically" to a correction of actions or to a change of planning.[2]

Contemporary systems analysis intends the consideration of the overall system. The "meaning of a system" can be explicated in the context of its objectives, constraints, components, resources, and management. These are the crucial variables participating in system execution, and are causally linked to the morphogenic process of system adaptiveness to change. The interacting variables of the political system's "parts" offer an insight into its processes and capabilities for adaptiveness to the dynamic and unstable urban system.

PERFORMANCE OF THE POLITICAL SYSTEM THROUGH ITS "PARTS"

System Objectives

The actual performance of the political system has been less than paradigmatic of an adaptive, goal-seeking system. There has been appreciable concern articulated by political actors about the conditions of the urban system, and the past two decades have witnessed a proliferation of policy outputs and resources addressed to urban conditions. However, there has been a singular lack of coordination of outputs or purposive resource allocation. If anything, the multiplicity and fragmentation of outputs, albeit well-intentioned, have created a confusion within the political system without efficiently attending to the stresses in the urban system.

These outputs have usually been in the form of fiscal aid from the federal government to the states and local communities, to stimulate action on urban problems. The fiscal subvention has been engendered by a variety of legislation and programs. Unfortunately, each of these outputs had been enacted piecemeal — and oftentimes totally unrelated — to be administered by multifarious agencies, each requiring a bewildering assortment of compliance procedures.

The intensified activity at the national level of government has served to transform the character of the American federal system.

The total volume of federal aid to state and local governments more than tripled; between 1961 and 1966 alone, the Congress authorized federal assistance in 39 new fields of state and local activity. And this massive federal intervention in community affairs came in some of the most sacrosanct of all the traditional preserves of state and local authority, such as education and, in 1968, local law enforcement.[3]

But, despite the rhetoric of national objectives, which peaked in recent times during the "New Frontier" and the "Great Society," the actual implementation of these goals has had to be executed by the officials in the country's myriad communities, "whom the federal government could influence — but not control."[4] The task of achieving goals promulgated by the central government through the operation of legally independent state and local governments, then, is a matter of coordination. Yet, it is not only a matter of coordination of the administration of national programs, but also a question of "bringing order to the maze of coordinating structures that federal agencies were independently propagating."[5]

The federal government has responded to the exercise of coordination at the local level by providing influences toward changing the structures and the distribution of influence in local government, in order to pursue nationally established goals. Parenthetically, the diseconomies of large-scale national bureaucracies and local demand for participation in public decisions have urged the movement toward the decentralization of federally defined and funded programs to subnational levels.[6] A meaningful development among the federal government's contributions to local structural innovation for purposes of coordination in behalf of national goals has been the prompting of a growth of regional institutions.

Along with the federal government's concern with structures appropriate for coordinated administrative management at the local level, has been the vexing problem of efficacious national level management of the overall system. The consideration of Executive-centered coordination and control evidences possibly the most noteworthy development in American public administration since World War II. The Nixon Administration's Reorganization Plan Number 2, creating the Domestic Council, and transforming the Bureau of the Budget into the Office of Management and Budget, with added responsibilities, is a significant attempt to provide integrated and systematic management. At the same time, the Administration has opted for a decentralized procedure of operational program coordination, by establishing the "federal region" concept for purposes of integrating administrative agencies' policies under the supervisory auspices of the newly-founded Office of Management and Budget.

It is premature to assess the possible effects of Reorganization Plan Number 2 and the federal region device, but meanwhile, the political system's cybernetic adaptiveness to its environment continues to be impeded by normative and practical constraints.

A simple, cybernetic feedback model of explicit group goal-seeking does not fit most societies of the past and present because of a lack in those societies of informed, centralized direction and widespread, promotively interdependent goal behaviors of individuals and subgroups.[7]

System Constraints

The decentralized nature of the American political system, and a normative preference for the persistence of this phenomenon, posits dysfunctional attributes. The political system is characterized by a diffusion of decision centers which occasions the existence of several feedback loops, possibly contradictory, operating in the same system simultaneously. The multiplicity of unsynchronized and incompatible feedback cycles makes cohesive goal-seeking management, under existing conditions, unrealistic.

The unwieldiness of the diffused and expansive political structure insures goal slippage during the course of implementation throughout the system. Goal-realization is impeded by the distance and quantity of linkages from the originating source. Practically, "goal decisions are translated by an administrative apparatus into concrete activities and rules of action to be applied by still another set of groups and individuals."[8] This would allow for deviations from original goal intentions, without explicit discernment of administrative failure or selective attention in output execution. The faulty cybernetic processes of multiple and differentiated linkages produces haphazard gathering and feeding back of information.

Consequently, there exists an inevitable slack between action outputs and concrete manifestations of desired results.

The conditions involved in frustrating systemic goal-seeking through the cybernetic loop are also causal in blocking purposive structural changes. A rational delineation of state and local structures and functions, designed for mission-orientation, are subject to philosophic, legal, and political impediments throughout the system. The rigidity occurring in governmental units, fixed by normative and legal designations, encourages an irrelevance of present political structures to environmental problem-solving.

Finally, the political culture of the system has formalized parochialism in policy making and policy implementation. Fractionalization and compartmentalization of federal programs are the result of alliances between singular bureaucratic agencies and their congressional oversight committees. This relationship has led to an institutionalization of functional fiefdoms, each jealously guarded by an involved administrative agency and its congressional partners.[9] The phenomenon of functional fiefdoms has been particularly occlusive to the system's adaptive performance by its denial of an integrated treatment of programs.

System Components and Resources

In a systems analysis context, "missions" or "activities" are the components whose standard of performance truly narrates the performance of the overall system. The measure of a component's contribution to system performance is that if the standard of a component's performance increases, so should the standard of performance of the total system. In the political system, as constituted, there is no serviceable systems analysis of the whole system in terms of genuine mission-oriented components. This is particularly true at the state and local level where historical dictates have assigned governmental units with scant relationship to the true components of the system. Hence, because

. . . the decision-making that governs different missions is not centralized, the real missions of the state, e.g., in terms of health, education, recreation, sanitation, and so on, cannot be carried out because there is no management of these missions.[10]

The components of the political system, albeit non-rationally defined, are made up of the myriad political, administrative, and judicial functional subsystems in the federal structure. And it is the specific actions taken by these subsystems in behalf of systemic goals which contribute to the measure of the total system's goal-seeking performance.

Despite the essential characterization of the American political system as non-centralized, the supremacy of the national government has been assured by constitutional and environmental circumstances. Stresses in the environment leading to demands for effective public policy have been the centripetal influences compelling a political functional nationalization. The irresistible urge toward centralization of public policy has been occasioned by the national level's financial predominance and the states and local governments' oftentimes functional incapacity or indifference.

The resources of the system are the general reservoir out of which the specific actions of the components can be formed. Hence, resources apply to finances, manpower, equipment, and information about the system and the environment. The 16th Amendment to the Constitution has given the national government a distinct financial advantage over the other levels, thereby instigating the focality of public policy. The national government's fiscal potency has also served to shape its preemption of professional talent and equipment. The states and localities, on their part, have either been legally restrained from expanding their resources, or have been remiss in developing new sources or in redefining their revenue-obtaining parameters.

Information about the system and the environment, a crucial variable for rational action by the system's components, has been randomly obtained because of the lack of coordination and control over the political system's many linkages. Despite the growth of centripetal tendencies in policy-making, the dearth of adequate systems management has dispelled the latent advantages of centralized mission direction. While several municipalities and other governmental institutions utilize some form of computerized information systems, there has been little attempt made to integrate information systems, or to prepare for a fully integrated information systems network by the ordering of standards for data congruity across department lines and between echelons of government. Ultimately, rational subsystem action through a feedback loop, for goal-seeking outputs adjustment, is dependent on coherent information systems.

Systems Management

The management of a system is the most important part of the system, for management engenders the plans fixing the component goals, allocating and utilizing the resources, and controlling the system's performance. Without appropriate planning and management the system operates in a random manner, much like a ship at sea without a steersman. The essence of systems management is administrative coordination, and logic dictates that the single point of leadership and coordination is in the national government, specifically in the Executive Office of the President. Administrative coordination posits a process which integrates management and planning. Planning is a constituent phase of management for "it is not easy to separate the determination of objectives and the preparation of a course of action from consideration of the means of execution."[11] Yet, the function of government planning, particularly central government planning, has met with more hostility than any other government activity. To many people planning can only be defined as government direction of industrial production and distribution. But, in actuality, the

... purpose of central planning in the federal government is comparable to the goal of comprehensive urban planning: a mutually consistent set of plans for many different government activities. The problem in central planning is not to produce plans; it is to bring all plans together at a central point where detailed proposals for action can be made to fit each other and at the same time to promote the realization of general national objectives. The job of central planning is to make sure that plans are prepared by operating agencies; that these plans are reviewed; and that the plans of any one agency do not come into conflict with the plans of another agency.[12]

The federal government's experience with centralized coordination and control was especially prolific during the New Deal and the subsequent war years. During World War II there occurred scant controversy about government planning. It was the national consensus, and basic national policy, that it was necessary to mobilize all national productive resources under the direction of the federal government in order to defeat the enemy. The War Production Board, established to this end, was granted control over raw materials, productive plants, prices, transportation, and labor.

During this period of severe environmental stress, there were two additional coordinating arms at the Executive level, the National Resources Planning Board, and the Bureau of the Budget, created in 1939. However, in 1943, Congress signalled the demise of the NRPB by refusing any additional appropriations for the Board, and the House Committee on Appropriations stipulated a prohibition in the Independent Offices Appropriation Act, preventing the President from transferring any funds to the Board. The House's justification for its action was that the NRPB iterated the activities of other agencies. Hence, after August 31, 1943, the Bureau of the Budget was left as the sole coordinating arm of the Office of the President, for the purpose of "insuring mutually harmonious plans."[13]

President Roosevelt, earlier in 1943, created the Office of War Mobilization by executive Order. This agency was designed to

. . . develop unified programs and to establish policies for the maximum use of the nation's resources in the war effort. It was directed to "unify" the activities of various agencies concerned with the production, procurement, distribution, and transportation of military and civilian supplies.[14]

After the obliteration of the NRPB, the President prescribed to the Office of War Mobilization the additional function of coping with war and postwar adjustment problems. In 1944 Congress added "and Reconversion" to the title of the Office of War Mobilization, and provided a statutory basis for the OWM's formulation of plans for the transition from war to peace.

The directors of the OWMR were more than planners assisting the President; they were essentially coordinators of wartime and immediate postwar government activities, who gave much of their attention to the policy and planning phases of these activities.[15]

Its task of postwar reconversion completed, the agency ceased to function in December, 1946.

The Employment Act of 1946 created the Council of Economic Advisers. The Council's economic report to the President and the Bureau of the Budget's preparation of appropriation estimates were designed to provide the President with administrative efficiency controls. The Council of Economic Advisers, made up of three experts designated by the President, with the advice and consent of the Senate, were "'to formulate and recommend national economic policy to promote employment, production, and purchasing power under free competitive enterprise.'"[16] The attention of the Council was to be primarily focused on the economic effects of government programs. The Bureau of the Budget was to be concerned primarily with the preparation of detailed appropriation estimates and with general administrative efficiency. But the Bureau went beyond its charter specifying it as the fiscal and management arm of the Presidency, and participated in the shaping of public policy because its Directors were convinced that resource management equated with influencing policy.[17]

On March 12, 1970, President Nixon released his Reorganization Plan No. 2 of 1970, calling for the creation of a Cabinet-level Domestic Council, and the transformation of the Bureau of the Budget into the Office of Management and Budget. The Plan was subsequently approved by Congress. The President's plan for organization changes was devised to "make the Executive Branch a more vigorous and more effective instrument for creating and carrying out the programs that are needed today."[18] The Plan is the Nixon Administration's rationale for improving the management processes of the Executive Branch, by the careful coordination of programs, and an adequately informative information system.

The Plan differentiates between the

". . . closely connected but basically separate functions" centered in the President's Office; "policy determination and executive management. This involves (1) what Government should do, and (2) how it goes about doing it."[19]

With this perceived dichotomy spelled out, the reorganization thus

. . . creates a new entity to deal with each of these functions:
—It establishes a Domestic Council, to coordinate policy formulation in the domestic area. This cabinet group would be provided with an institutional staff, and to a considerable degree would be a domestic counterpart to the National Security Council.
—It establishes an Office of Management and Budget, which would be the President's principal arm for the exercise of his managerial functions.
    The Domestic Council will be primarily concerned with *what* we do; the Office of Management and Budget will be primarily concerned with *how* we do it, and *how well* we do it.[20]

The Domestic Council will be chaired by the President, and its membership will consist of the Vice President, and the Secretaries of Housing and Urban Development, Health, Education, and Welfare, Treasury, Interior, Agriculture, Commerce, Labor, Transportation, and the Attorney General, and the Director of the Office of Economic Opportunity. Although the Council will operate with a staff under an Executive Director, designated to be a Presidential assistant in addition, the Plan contemplates having most of the substantive work done by *ad hoc* project committees — task forces, planning groups, and advisory bodies — with the support of the departmental staff. The intended functions of the Council are as follows:

—Assessing national needs, collecting information and developing forecasts, for the purpose of defining national goals and objectives.
—Identifying alternative ways of achieving these objectives, and recommending consistent, integrated sets of policy choices.
—Providing rapid response to Presidential needs for policy advice on pressing domestic issues.
—Coordinating the establishment of national priorities for the allocation of available resources.

—Maintaining a continuous review of the conduct of ongoing programs from a policy standpoint, and proposing reforms as needed.[21]

The Office of Management and Budget will still perform its predecessor's key function of preparing the annual federal budget and overseeing its execution, drawing on the transplanted career staff of the Bureau of the Budget, but this task will no longer be its dominant interest. The Plan emphasizes that the creation of the Office of Management and Budget is more than a mere change of name, but is basic to the broader management needs of the Office of the President. Hence, the new Office will apply greater stress on fiscal analysis, together with program evaluation and coordination, information and management systems, organizational improvement, and executive development, while maintaining its legislative reference service. To enable it to fulfill its increased responsibilities, the staff resources of the OMB will be augmented.

An additional emphasis of the OMB will be to respond to the need of developing and overseeing administrative coordinating mechanisms throughout the nation. The new federal region concept, inaugurated by the Nixon administration, provides for interagency coordination to be centralized in ten regional "capitals" and stimulated through Washington-based OMB "deskmen." Each federal region "capital" will house an interagency council coordinating administrative programs throughout its geographic jurisdiction which normally will encompass several designated states. The regional coordination system will involve three departments — HUD, HEW, and Labor — and two agencies — the Office of Economic Opportunity and the Small Business Administration.

Already a regional council, made up of the ranking field officers of each of the agencies, is in operation in every one of the regional headquarters. It selects its own chairman, and meets as often as necessary to thrash out mutual problems. . . .

So far there is no resident representative of the President at regional headquarters, to knock heads together when necessary and make sure that White House policy is consistently carried out. But the Office of Management and Budget does have a "deskman" for each region, who pays frequent visits to the field. He is expected to mediate bureaucratic hassles on the spot, whenever possible, and to report back to Washington on the way each agency is doing its job.[22]

The administrative reorganization in the Executive Branch, coupled with the promulgation of the federal regions, posit major advances in the structural efficiency of the Presidency, and in intergovernmental coordination. It would be difficult for anyone concerned with Executive control and coordination to take issue with either the proposed functions of the Domestic Council, or with the new emphasis on management, program coordination, and fiscal and evaluative functions. However, there are logical inconsistencies and glaring omissions in Reorganization Plan No. 2, which require attention.

It is unfortunate that the Plan was conceived from a *Weltanschauung* of divided management functions, specifically: (1) what Government should do, and (2) how it goes about doing it. This criterion was applied in clearly defining the schism between the Domestic Council, which "will be primarily concerned with *what* we do," and the OMB, "with *how* we do it, and *how well* we do it." The reasoning of this simplification is a casuistry; all evidence points to the unreality of an organic separation of planning and policy shaping from resource management. Finally, for organizational *desideratum*, the non-inclusion of the Director of the Office of Management and Budget, the Chairman of the Council on Environmental Quality, and the Chairman of the Council of Economic Advisers, on the membership of the Domestic Council is unconscionable.

The structural and functional innovations of Plan No. 2 and the federal regions signal a comprehension of the magnification of Executive managerial dimensions, and a need for strategic applications. The attraction of this development is not only in expectation of a departure from a prolonged bureaucratic inertia, but also in its germinal potential for fully-integrated communication and control throughout the federal system. The stresses in the urban system now require nothing less than the problem-solving facility of an adaptive, goal-seeking political system. This intends a political system which can regulate outputs from each succeeding subsystem in order to fashion an integrated flow.

Once before, under the compelling environmental conditions of World War II, American government was able to respond in a concerted goal-seeking attitude. This enabled us to defeat the enemy abroad. Now anew, compelling conditions in the environment require a dynamic, adaptive political system. We defeated the enemy then. Again we face a dangerous enemy, and he has been identified; in the immortal words of Pogo, "We have met the enemy, and he is us."

The task of integrating the political and urban systems for effective responsiveness to urban stresses and demands necessitates an adaptive political system. This intends action outputs within the context of integrated goal-seeking, goal-setting, communication, and control. Goals are then challenged under an uninterrupted cybernetic feedback loop. The experience of the real political system evidences an unfulfillment of the paradigm. Utilizing the structural-functional reordering of Reorganization Plan No. 2 and the federal region device as the launching points for organizational evolution, the study is resolved with a systems model of an adaptive political system through the goal-directed execution of its governmental subsystems. The model is a heuristic scheme for the development of a self-steering, adaptive political system which provides conjunctive linkages with the urban system.

A MODEL OF AN ADAPTIVE POLITICAL SYSTEM

The inefficiencies caused by the multiplicity of power centers and linkages in the political system, and the spotty performances of these diffused subsystems, tempts the expediency of a one-tier centralized, national government. This posits the eradication of the states as autonomous political units, and their replacement by Washington-appointed administrative components, strategically placed for organizational control efficacy.

The justification often placed for the abolition of the federal form of government is that the states have become a political *non-sequitur*. Although, it is correct that too many states have been remiss in the exercise of leadership and governmental perspicacity in numerous policy areas, this can also be said of the federal government, and no one has seriously advocated its dissolution. Furthermore, a careful examination of the political culture should immediately dispel any notions of a drastic structural metamorphosis.

The viability of government is based on the criterion of how well government serves the needs, and provides for the well-being of its constituents. If the political system fulfills these requisites it is assured of persistence; and, persistence is the *sine qua non* of the political system. But, in order for it to persist in the face of dynamic processes of environmental change, the political system must demonstrate a dynamic flexibility of its own, by an adaptiveness through structural and functional innovations, in search of new equilibria. The American political system is historically, legally, and culturally rooted in the framework of federalism. Persistence for the American political phenomenon is to adapt creatively to its environment, while retaining its essential federalism. It is within this context that the system persistence objectives operate.

The total system goal would be to provide control and communication for integrated inputs-outputs to serve desired contemplations of urban physical and activity patterns. This posits a strategic consideration of public policy influencing human activities, economic locational, activity, and investment alternatives, and social development. At the same time, the objective is to bifurcate the actual implementory components from the control focalities along a national-subnational, system-subsystem continuum. However, while the system-subsystem structures would offer functional differentiation, they would also be organically cohesive and integrated by mission linkages and cybernetic controls.

The total political system would retain its denationalized nature, but each subsystem would be organically linked to an ascending subnational control and communication center, up to a focality of strategic coordination located in the Executive Branch of the national government. This intends the "regionalization" of federalism, conceptualized as a five-tier federalist framework. The five tiers would be (1) the federal government; (2) the federal regions; (3) the states; (4) the metropolitan councils of government or regional planning institutions; and (5) the local jurisdictions.

Operationally, the system would operate in this manner: National agencies, at the Executive branch, would fulfill all of the intended activities described in President Nixon's Plan No. 2. The federal regions would retain their function of interagency coordination, but in addition, would be the subnational control and communication focalities for intergovernmental collaboration and coordination, as applied to inter-state and state-national government intercourse. In view of the increased responsibilities, the interagency council would be presided by a high-ranking resident executive responsible to a specified national management control agency. The national agency would provide the federal region councils with an operating staff, to include state "deskmen." The states would be the first-level "action" centers for the execution of urban strategies. The states, in effect, thus become the tactical arm of the federal regions. Their performance would be evaluated in terms of the quantity and quality of mission-outputs in response to total system goal objectives, and especially, in their stimulation of goal-seeking subsystem action agencies. The metropolitan councils of government and regional planning agencies are those action subsystems which would be responsible for the effectuation of authoritative outputs regarding urban area-wide considerations. The local communities would be expected to adhere to area-wide and state-wide goal formulations.

Goal formulation and attainment, and resources and components management are indissolubly linked, consequently it is germane to depict the management process in the explication of system objectives. The realization of systemic self-steering is keyed to management as the steersman of the system. And management is the control and communication mechanism which strives for an integrated pattern of system-subsystem outputs to a desired terminal point. The focus of the management responsibility in the political system is in the Presidency. Thus, it is essential that the management process in the Office of the President be provided with the requisite tools for mission effectiveness.

The Domestic Council and the Office of Management and Budget are the structures designed for efficacious management. However, this model necessitates some fundamental changes in the functional parameters defined in Plan No. 2. Specifically, the dialectic of bifurcating planning and action would be eschewed. Instead, what would occur is that the Domestic Council would retain all of its prescribed functions, but the OMB would be designated as the collaborating agency responsible for the preparation of strategic plans for the Council. The guidelines for the planning of objectives would originate with the Council, and the OMB would design them accordingly. The OMB would be closely associated with the Council's operating staff for the planning of strategic national urban objectives, which subsequently would serve as policy options for the President and Congress. Of course, the Council, through its staff, would, in association with other involved agencies in the Office of the President, maintain a close liaison with Congress and provide all necessary assistance toward the fulfillment of requisite legislation and financing. Conversely, the legislative process, as well as the judicial, would serve as a check on imprudent behavior by these components and their agents. Finally, the Council membership would include the Director of the OMB, and the Chairmen of the Councils of Economic Advisers, and on Environmental Quality.

The federal region is the ideal geographic locale for the working-out of individualized patterns of relationships between the national government and particular states, and between states within the region. The formation of federal regions as federal government surrogates is an essential step toward the de-centralization of the national government. The regions embrace a large enough geographic area to provide a measure of comprehensive overview and control, while, at the same time, are sufficiently intimate to afford an appreciation for regional and local idiosyncracies.

Washington's representative at the federal region level would be a resident top-echelon executive of the OMB, assisted by a locally recruited staff. His duties would entail chairing interagency councils, and he would be charged with the authority and responsibility to speak for the national government in matters of intergovernmental relations and revenue-sharing. His office would be the recipient of block grants for subsequent subvention to the states or to lesser jurisdictions, according to strategic "missions" criteria. However, like the parent office in Washington, the federal region OMB would administer no substantive programs; it would be the communication and control center for the states in its jurisdiction, and the coordinating agency of intergovernmental programs in the region.

The states would be encouraged, by financial inducement, to establish agencies of state-wide program coordination, comprehensive planning, and urban development. The substantive mission-goals with which the states would be charged would include development of "new towns," transportation — specifically, rapid transit — environmental quality control, recreation, and open space and wildlife preservation. This would intend the creation of pertinent authoritative goal-action agencies; and their vigorous support at gubernatorial and legislative levels.

To encourage the importance and viability of metropolitan-region governmental and planning units, all revenue-sharing with the localities would be channeled through these agencies. They, in turn would allocate funds in accordance with missions related to area-wide comprehensive plans. The localities, however, would continue to receive grants-in-aid directly for territorially discrete missions. The local jurisdictions would be expected to provide inputs in the development of area-wide plans to be screened by a state comprehensive planning agency to insure compatibility with state-wide objectives.

Basic to management is communication. The hierarchy of management is connected by a communications network. It is the communication flow about the environment and about itself which enables systems management to effect control over its constituent parts, and to re-direct its processes according to goal feedback mismatch information. In effect, management is communications, and the quality of management is a product of the quality of its communications. Hence, the integration of the control centers at each level of the five-tiered federal system is dependent on a connecting chain of communications. Communication, in this sense, entails various forms: face-to-face contact, telephone, telegraph, letters, and so on. However, a cybernetic feedback loop requires a far more elaborate process of information flow. The enormous volume of data about the environment necessitates the utilization of the most up-to-date computer facilities. Therefore, a crucial element in the communication and control ability of the political system is its integration through a congruent management information system. This posits the utilization of extensive, computerized information systems.

The environmental constraints, as depicted in this study, range from the mundane to the monumental. However, the ground-work for an incipient five-tier federal framework has already been set in Plan No. 2, and there has not been, as yet, serious opposition to its development. This is not to suggest that President Nixon has in mind the gradual evolution to the proffered model; it is only to put forth that adaptive processes stand a better chance of ultimate goal-fruition if cultivated incrementally. In the case of our model, procedural steps may be taken sequentially; for instance, the implementation of the information systems network, under auspices of federal government financing, would precede the expanded role of the OMB at the federal region, and so on. However, to foreclose the possibility of inchoate inertia, the five-tier federal framework should become operational within five years after the establishment of an integrated information systems network.

A legitimate criticism of the model is that it follows the form of federalism, but not its substance; that the OMB's role in the federal region is tantamount to that of the historic Roman proconsols; and, that the federal region is prototypical of a European provincial government. And too, that the model anticipates the withering away of the federalist framework as bureaucratic surrogates of the national government preempt the legitimacy of state governments. In fairness to this kind of an observation it must be admitted that the model poses a latent opportunity for an unrestrained evolutionary structural transformation of the total political system, its subtler intentions notwithstanding. In effect, the model poses a challenge to the components of the political system, a challenge which may be met by dynamic adaptive behavior along the system-subsystem continuum. The challenge of the state governments is especially compelling: whether we remain a federal republic may ultimately depend on their creative capacity for dynamism.

SYSTEM-SUBSYSTEM RESOURCES AND COMPONENTS MANAGEMENT

The most potent leverage possessed by the national government, on behalf of goal implementation, is its vast fiscal resources. It is through the proffering or withholding of grants that the federal government is able to induce its subsystems toward desired objectives. President Nixon, in his State of the Union Message of 1971, proposed that Congress legislate an unconditional revenue-sharing program with the states. While this concept poses benefits in terms of energizing state governments to unilateral action-programs, it is unfortunate from the standpoint of encouraging a disregard for strategically-defined considerations. By unconditionally relinquishing its major power resource, the federal government can expect to minimize its control effect on goal-seeking processes.

Instead, while committed to the concept of revenue-sharing, this model opts for a form of conditional disbursing. This would require the allocating of sizeable block-grants per federal region according to a per-capita and performance formula. The resident-director of the region's OMB would be charged with the authority and responsibility for allocating the fiscal resources to the separate states in his jurisdiction.

For a state to qualify for its share of the revenue it would need to meet several conditions, as defined by national strategic goals and OMB-defined state missions. If a state failed to meet these goals, then the OMB's federal-region "deskman" charged with "servicing" the affected state, would be assigned as OMB resident-coordinator within the state. He would establish an office in the state and deal directly with urban-region governments or planning regions located therein. Revenues earmarked for the state would come from the federal region, through the state's resident OMB coordinator, expressly for the urban-region institutions. The state government, however, although now ineligible for any portion of the block grant, could still qualify for its share of traditional grants-in-aid. But, of course, its chances for this revenue could possibly be lessened by the stigma of its ostracism from substantive programs by the federal region.

Generally, it is expected that most, if not all, states would fulfill their eligibility requirements and receive their block grant from the federal region. Some portion of the funds would be retained by the state government, for utilization in state-operated activities; the rest would be allocated, again in block-form, to the urban-region institutions. These, in turn, would retain a portion for their use, the rest to be parcelled out to the local jurisdictions. The eligibility for the state-meted out funds, in the case of the urban-regions, would be determined by an appropriate coordinating agency; the urban localities, last in line, would receive their disbursement according to the urban-region agency's prescription of mission requirements.

Fiscal resources are the means by which the linkage-centers effect control over the actions and performance of their charges. The development of an adequate feedback loop information system is the requisite for management communication. It is the coupling of these two aspects of management which enables goal-setting and goal-seeking to become realities. The exercise of management communication and control in contribution to integrated system outputs is basic to a cybernetic, adaptive system.

The establishment of management control-centers throughout the political system, by the strategic allocation of fiscal resources, would still fall short of system-subsystem integration, for until the control-centers are linked by an effective information network, they do not form a part of the cybernetic process. In the development of a fact retrieval computer-based information system, conducive to systemic management control integration, feasibility and hardware design should be important considerations. But, primarily, standards must be established immediately for data congruity throughout the information system's network. The design of the overall information system network should utilize the most current techniques, tempered by the "matrix" of anticipated information trans-actions within the system.

Because of the myriad system and subsystem components of the political system which would be interconnected in the information system network, and the huge volumes of data expected from these sources, the system could easily become very cumbersome and thereby, ineffectual. Therefore, it would behoove the political system to operate with as "streamlined" a network as possible, preferably within a real time, on-line retrieval context. The information system recommended to the state of California, in a study commissioned by Governor Brown in the early 1960's, is seductive by its simplicity. It would involve having components maintaining repositories of information files in various agencies with a central information component providing the basic information about where the data is stored.

The remaining components consist of the linkages and terminals that connect the information requester to the central information system and thence to the files in which he is interested, as well as computer programmers located at each "data bank."[23]

The user of the system would have to specify the information requested by the use of a symbolic device, such as a code number, relayed to the central system, which would then direct him to where the information is located, or transmit his requisition to the appropriate agency.

Transformed to our model, this would involve the urban-region institutions as dynamic data acquiring, maintaining, and transmitting centers — or "data bases" — for the areas of their jurisdiction. The state governments would be the central information systems — keyed to infor-mation retrieval — linked to the larger information system at the federal regions. The federal regions would duplicate all the information retained by the linking states' central information systems. The national govern-ment would also be linked to the ten federal-region information centers. By the linking of all management control centers, and all those centers to other components, the system becomes amenable to a feedback loop relating to data about the urban system and about itself. However, the acquisition of non-quantifiable data, such as "happiness" data emanating from the members of the political system, undoubtedly, would still remain a matter of subjective assessment of environmental demand inputs.

The efficacy of the total system's goal-directed behavior is predi-cated upon the performance of its various components. A component's performance is measured by its sum contribution to mission accomplish-ment, through specific actions in behalf of system goals. This requires the designation of performance guidelines and evaluative criteria by the management control centers of the political system. In effect, this posits a management quality control requirement in a social-political system. In the model, system quality control is to be exercised at the subnational level of the federal regions. Subsystem quality control would be fashioned at the state level, and this activity would be performed down the line, potentially insofar as the subsystem components in the localities.

Component quality control is to be the device used by management control centers in the determination of block-grant subvention eligibility. In order to receive these funds each succeeding component will have to fulfill minimum performance criteria. Operationally, the federal regions would, first of all, expect a comprehensive plan drawn up by an appropriate state agency addressing itself to an ordered spatial and activity development in the state. The plan would also include substantive recommendations regarding environmental quality control, open space, "new towns," transportation, and other vital missions.

Next, the state government would show that it had created or elaborated fitting structures for the execution of the missions outlined in the plan. This is to say, the state government would have to demonstrate satisfactory progress toward the implementation of the comprehensive plan, by citing activities of state-wide agencies and other components. An example of an appropriate goal-seeking state-wide agency would be the New York State Urban Development Corporation; another representative component suitable for metropolitan area-wide coordination is the Metropolitan Council of the Twin Cities.

Finally, the state would have to evidence an energized expenditure of its own funds on plan-related missions, and a competence in enlarging its own resources. The latter manifestation could be demonstrated by an imaginative tax structure, to include one or more devices such as a state graduated-income tax, a state operated lottery, legitimized off-track betting, among several others. Once the state had obtained its share of the national financial resources it would then make its own allocations according to a discretionary quality control formula. The same procedure is to be repeated by succeeding block-grant distributors.

In effect, the five-tier federalism concept is based on the conceptualization of a supra-urban space defined in terms of delineated regions. The region is generally the spatial expression of linked physical and activity patterns. Hence, governmental control centers are defined in terms of appropriately sized regions for efficient servicing of these phenomena. The metropolitan region is the first unit of regional governmental endeavor; next, the state may not be a proper expression of interrelated activities and settlements, but it is scaled compatibly with a government-service region, and crucial to the scheme of systems management persistence because of its status of normative political legitimacy; and finally, the federal-region is the super-region designed for administrative expediency and the delivery of national government authority in a particularized, coherent fashion. The goal of their integration awaits an unravelling of the complexities of systems management through strategic goal-planning and an ensuing process of cybernetic communication and control.

NATIONAL STRATEGIC GOAL-PLANNING

The urban region is a complex of linked centers of activity interacting through space. The basis for regional strategies is founded on the need for resolution of economic efficiencies, social satisfactions, space shortages, and urban design.[24] The maximization of economic efficiency intends a general development strategy which will equalize the distribution of resources, and provide for services at minimum cost; social satisfactions are obtained by ordering an environment with suitable compatibilities of the scale and spacing of communications, the location of facilities and workplaces, and the means of transportation; regional strategies must consider the shortage of space for an appropriate arrangement of activities and settlements, and anticipate the growth of population and activity; and, urban design must be ordered so as to provide for the best possible scheme for patterns of settlement to allow its inhabitants to optimize their human experience and potential for personal development. Hence, regional planning contemplates the integration of economic, social, and aesthetic factors and the devising of effective controls for their coordination.

The achievement of a balanced integration can only be fulfilled at the national level through appropriate policy and design in the elaboration of a strategy responsive to the holistic pattern of activity and interaction. Regions are the spatial expressions of these patterns indissolubly linked in super-space. Consequently, for a plan to be truly comprehensive, it must attach itself to a national spatial dimension which comprehends the regions as subsystems having internal balances and external flows. After all,

. . . every regional definition is, of necessity, bound to a purpose derived from a national delineation of problems and goals, the definition is generally more mindful of what is socially valuable and politically significant than of scientific accuracy. Planning regions are best defined to be congruent in space with the socioeconomic functions to be carried out.[25]

The method by which to integrate the myriad activity flows and interdependencies is the formulation of a national urban policy. This is the process which affords a comprehensive respect for the wholeness of spatial structure of development, in terms of both physical and activity patterns. A national urban policy focuses upon broader regional considerations, but planning on a national scale is founded on the prior attention given to regional needs. The basic allocation decisions are made with an awareness that problems and methods of development differ within each region despite the interdependence to a great extent of these allocations across all regional categories. Consequently, the very closest coordination of city and regional planning is essential for a definition of the urban problem, for "regional space is structured primarily through a hierarchy of urban places, and through the fields of interaction which relate them."[26]

From the aggregate inputs of coordinated city and regional plans, the national goals, standards, and priorities can be structured and the national interest rendered specific.

[Decisions] must be made where, in what manner, and with what resources the national government is to support such urban activities as public housing, mass transit, sanitary works, and metropolitan highways.[27]

Finally, the national government can effect a strategic program for controls over the inter-spatial flows of resources and activities to coincide with regional tactics, in order to rationally manage the urban systems for the realization of a desired pattern of development.

The full utilization of the hierarchy of planning levels is indispensable to the coordination of activities. The hierarchy is essential to the feedback loop, initially as input devices articulating the urban condition to the national level, where these inputs are converted into policies of strategic controls which flow as outputs down through the succeeding echelons serving as conduits for their coordination and implementation. Thus, national strategic planning requires the mobilization of the many structures of administrative and political processes for the organization of supra-urban space to desired criteria.

The rationale for national controls over urban development is based on the Keynesian view of the economy as not a self-balancing mechanism, and applying it to the non-self-balancing urban realm. The urban realm is an organically interrelated system of people, economic activities, social institutions, and communications flows. Governmental intervention in the management of these activities is the injection of a countervailing force to frustrate the interplay of individual egoisms and their unwanted consequences. To do otherwise is to retain a governmental inertia in the face of mounting urban chaos, destruction of the physical environment, and the atrophy of the values and mores of civilization.

Notes

1. Walter Buckley, *Sociology and Modern Systems Theory* (Englewood Cliffs, N.J.: Prentice-Hall, Inc., 1967), p. 206.

2. *Ibid.*, p. 173.

3. James L. Sundquist with the collaboration of David W. Davis, "Organizing U.S. Social and Economic Development" *Public Administration Review*, No. 6 (November /December, 1970), p. 625.

4. *Ibid.*

5. *Ibid.*, p. 626.

6. Robert Warren, "Federal-Local Development Planning: Scale Effects in Representation and Policy Making" *Public Administration Review*, No. 6 (November/December, 1970), p. 584.

7. Buckley, *op. cit.*, p. 206.

8. *Ibid.*, p. 175.

9. Harold Seidman, *Politics, Position, and Power: the Dynamics of Federal Organization* (New York: Oxford University Press, 1970).

10. C. West Churchman, *The Systems Approach* (New York: A Delta Book, Dell Publishing Co., Inc., 1968), p. 42.

11. John D. Millett, *The Process and Organization of Government Planning* (New York: Columbia University Press, 1951), p. 87.

12. *Ibid.*, p. 91.

13. *Ibid.*, p. 97.

14. *Ibid.*, p. 152.

15. *Ibid.*, pp. 156–157.

16. *Ibid.*, p. 160.

17. "Reorganization Plan No. 2: Remarks by William D. Carey," *Public Administration Review*, No. 6 (November/December, 1970), p. 631.

18. The White House, "Reorganization Plan No. 2 of 1970," *Ibid.*, p. 611.

19. *Ibid.*, p. 612.

20. *Ibid.*

21. *Ibid.*, p. 613.

22. John Fischer, "The Easy Chair: Can the Nixon Administration Be Doing Something Right?" *Harper's Magazine*, November, 1970, p. 35.

23. Churchman, *op. cit.*, p. 130.

24. Derek Senior, ed., *The Regional City, An Anglo-American Discussion of Metropolitan Planning* (Chicago: Aldine Publishing Co., 1966), pp. 39–40.

25. John Friedmann and William Alonso, "National Policy and Regional Development," *Regional Development and Planning, A Reader,* Friedman and Alonso, eds., (Cambridge, Mass.: The M.I.T. Press, 1964), p. 489.

26. *Ibid.*, pp. 65–66.

27. *Ibid.*

LIST OF CONTRIBUTORS

EDWARD C. BANFIELD is William R. Kenan, Jr., Professor of Public Policy Analysis and Political Science at the University of Pennsylvania. Formerly, he was Henry Lee Shattuck Professor of Urban Government at Harvard University.

ALAN EDWARD BENT is Associate Professor and Chairman, Department of Public Administration at California State College, Dominguez Hills, California.

ROBERT R. CANTINE is County Manager of Burke County, North Carolina.

A. LEE FRITSCHLER is Professor and Dean of the School of Government and Public Administration, American University.

HERBERT J. GANS is Professor of Sociology at Columbia University.

MICHAEL LIPSKY is Associate Professor of Political Science at the Massachusetts Institute of Technology.

GLENN W. MILLER is Professor of Labor Economics at Wichita State University and Emeritus Professor of Economics at Ohio State University.

FELIX A. NIGRO is Professor of Political Science at the University of Georgia.

GEORGE W. NOBLIT is Assistant Professor of Sociology and Coordinator of Urban Studies, Memphis State University.

JOHN K. PARKER is Deputy Director of the Office of Revenue Sharing in the Federal Government.

RALPH A. ROSSUM is Assistant Professor of Political Science at Memphis State University.

HENRY J. SCHMANDT is Professor of Urban Affairs and Political Science at the University of Wisconsin-Milwaukee.

MORLEY SEGAL is Professor of Political Science at American University.

DAVID NEIL SILK is Assistant Professor of Education at Indiana University at Kokomo.

MICHAEL P. SMITH is Associate Professor of Political Science at Tulane University.

GARY L. WAMSLEY is Associate Professor of Political Science at the University of Kansas.

GRAHAM W. WATT is Deputy Mayor of Washington, D. C.

JAMES Q. WILSON is Henry Lee Shattuck Professor of Government at Harvard University.

MAYER N. ZALD is Professor and Chairman of the Department of Sociology and Anthropology at Vanderbilt University.

JOSEPH F. ZIMMERMAN is Professor and Chairman of the Department of Political Science at the Graduate School of Public Affairs, State University of New York at Albany.

LIST OF AUTHORS

Advisory Commission on Intergovernmental Relations   81
Edward C. Banfield   88
Alan Edward Bent   3, 46, 267, 360
Robert R. Cantine   19, 335
A. Lee Fritschler   217
Herbert J. Gans   152
Michael Lipsky   316
Glenn W. Miller   31
Felix A. Nigro   62
George W. Noblit   46
John K. Parker   335
Ralph A. Rossum   3, 121
Henry Schmandt   287
Morley Segal   217
David Silk   141
Michael P. Smith   201
Gary L. Wamsley   181
Graham W. Watt   335
James Q. Wilson   105
Mayer N. Zald   181

LIST OF TITLES

Administration of the Urban Nation	330, 360
Alienation and Bureaucracy: The Role of Participatory Administration	201
Beginnings of a Balanced Fiscal System	81
Challenges to Urban Administration	3
Collective Bargaining in Local Government: Effects of Urban Political Culture on Public Labor-Management Relations	40
Dilemmas of Police Administration	105
Education and Liberal Reform: An Interpretation	141
Financing Urban Government	73
Home Rule vs. Regionalism: The Experience of a Tri-State C. O. G.	267
How Practicing Urban Administrators View Themselves	19
Implications for Public Administration, The	62
Intergovernmental Relations and Contemporary Political Science: Developing an Integrative Typology	217
Manpower in the Public Sector	31
Metropolitan Reform in the U. S.: An Overview	245
Municipal Decentralization: An Overview	287
Planning for People, Not Buildings	152
Political Economy of Public Organizations, The	181
Problems of Judicial Administration: The Effect of Supreme Court Decisions on Courts of Limited Jurisdiction	121
Revenue Sharing in Theory and Practice	88
Roles of the Urban Administrator in the 1970s: The Knowledge and Skills Required to Perform These Roles	335
Service Delivery and Urban Administration	100
Street-Level Bureaucracy and the Analysis of Urban Reform	316
Urban Administration and Citizen Satisfaction	281
Urban Administration and Collective Bargaining	40
Urban Administration: Structures for Efficiency	212
Urban Administration: The State-of-the-Art	175
Urban Administrator, The	16